A STUDY ON GLOBALIZING CITIES

Theoretical Frameworks and China's Modes

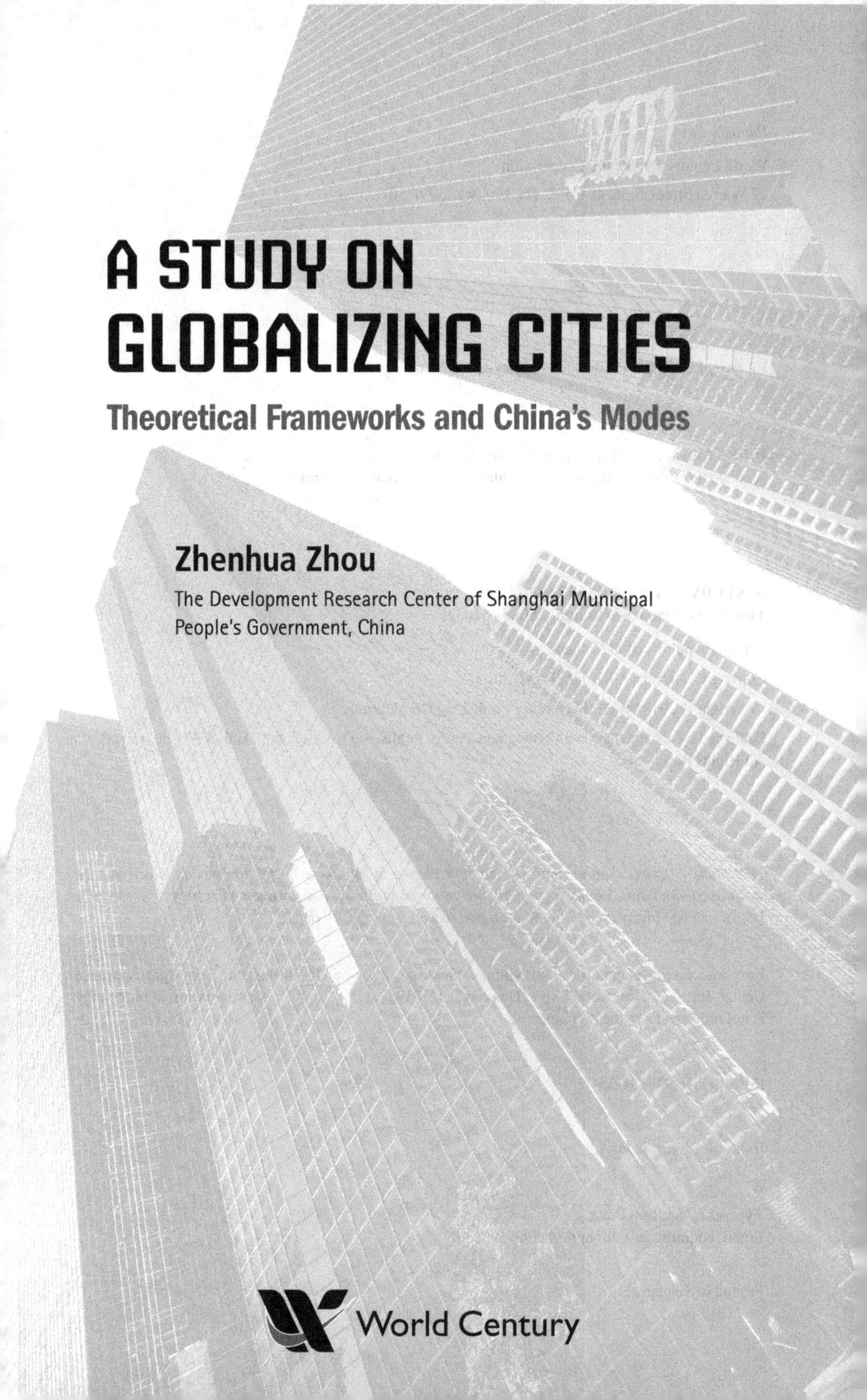

A STUDY ON GLOBALIZING CITIES

Theoretical Frameworks and China's Modes

Zhenhua Zhou

The Development Research Center of Shanghai Municipal People's Government, China

World Century

Published by

World Century Publishing Corporation
27 Warren Street, Suite 401-402, Hackensack, NJ 07601

Library of Congress Control Number: **2013957736**

British Library Cataloguing-in-Publication Data
A catalogue record for this book is available from the British Library.

A STUDY ON GLOBALIZING CITIES
Theoretical Frameworks and China's Modes

Originally published in Chinese

ISBN 978-1-938134-35-7

In-house Editor: Dong Lixi

Typeset by Stallion Press
Email: enquiries@stallionpress.com

Printed in Singapore

Abstract

In the background of interaction of globalization and informatization, the increase of economic resources flow on the globe has transgressed national boundaries, and what dominates the global economic lifeline is the global city networks, in which some global cities beyond nations in the space power have emerged. With the world urbanization speeding up, the continuous expansion and enrichment of the global city network will lead to the emergence of more global cities.

Since the reform and opening-up, China has maintained a sustainable rapid economic growth and increasing economic strength, which is recognized as "a rising great power" by the international community. But what is more important is that China's economy has been increasingly involved in the historical process of the economic globalization and holds an increasingly prominent position in the world economy. With the transfer of world's economic center and the rapidly increasing flow of China's inside and outside economy connections, the presence of globalizing cities has increasingly become China's urgent requirement to speed up economic development and hold an important position in global economic network.

In the course of global city development, the object pursuits or positioning of global cities are likely to become the same, but global city development tend to take a variety of forms because of the different backgrounds, foundations, location factors, and historical processes and their specific path dependence. In comparison with the global cities in developed countries, China's global cities are quite different with respect to background, reality basis, and control conditions. So, while China may refer to the global cities in developed countries with regard to the object pursuits and positioning of China's global cities, it must not simply imitate their development models and path options but have an in-depth study and active exploration.

The globalizing cities should have been an important component of the theoretical study of global cities, but the traditional global city theory only pays much attention to those established global cities, having an isolating or empirical analysis, or making a static comparative study, and ignoring their formation process, which have actually excluded those cities that may possibly become global cities in the future. This is not a problem of simple neglect or inadequate attention: the innermost reason is that the theoretical framework of the traditional global city study cannot accommodate the study of the "evolving process" or globalizing cites. Since the mainstream study of global city theory directly derives the simple logic of global city formation from the background of globalization and informatization, their scope and perspective of study has been greatly limited, thereby becoming a major theoretical defect.

However, the fact that major cities in the developing countries are changing rapidly into regional centers and important nodes in the global economic system has already caught attention. Since the mid-1990s, scholars of the global city study began to study the possibility of globalizing cities in the developing countries and transitional economy systems. In recent years, many research documents of the international metropolis in the Mainland focus their topics on the "globalizing cities". But generally speaking, for the issues of globalizing cites in developing countries, there are no in-depth and systematic researches but only mostly countermeasures study, which lack the corresponding theoretical frameworks and analytical tools. Therefore, the study of globalizing cities will not only fill a blank in the global city research but also enrich and improve the existing global city theory.

Yeung and Olds first put forward the concept of globalizing concept and incorporated it into the global city system study. According to the meaning of the word, globalizing cities are those cities that already possess corresponding infrastructure and are moving toward becoming global cities. To understand the concept, what is done first is not to make a simple definition (in fact, no single complete definition is given) but to acquire directly a number of related concepts such as globalization city and global city to understand the conceptual meaning of globalizing cities from their relations with each other. Here the study put special emphasis on the "globalization city" concept, which refers to many cities that have direct participation in the global economy and act as a node of the world city network. That is, it is the general name given to all cites incorporated into global city network, including the global cities, globalizing cities, and ordinary cities involved in the globalization process. A globalization city is not only an essential explanatory variable used by us to describe logic relations between the process of globalization and global city but is also used to form a direct theoretical basis of globalizing cities. A globalizing city must first be a globalization city and be interconnected with other cities based on the global city network.

Since the framework of a traditional global city theoretical cannot accommodate the globalizing cities, based on the theoretical framework of the mainstream global city theory and its limitations, this study introduces globalization city as a new intermediate explanatory variable, re-interpreting the world city system reform in the background of globalization and informatization; explaining the relations and variation among global cities, globalizing cities, and ordinary globalization cities from the perspective of global city network; and discovering the basic functions of global cities and the functional evolution trends of globalizing cities. In response to some control conditions such as background, development basis, and path dependency of globalizing cities in the developing countries, this study introduces new theoretical elements into the theory like global production chains, industrial clusters, and global city regions in order to form a new theoretical integration of analysis framework.

Applying the newly integrated framework of theoretical analysis, the main focus of this study is the positioning of globalizing cites' strategic goal and its development path under the corresponding binding conditions, providing answers to the key questions regarding the development model and path selection of globalizing cities in the developing countries, for example, what means of participation should China, as a developing country, take in the globalization and informatization; what are its characteristics; and what kind of impact will it have on China's globalizing cities? What kind of favorable and unfavorable conditions will China's present stage of economic development and economic growth form to support China's globalizing cities? How should we select the development model and path of globalizing cites according to China's actual situation on the basis of following the general rule, basic spirit and principles of global city development? The explanation and analysis of this series of questions is also one of main contents of the study.

In conclusion, this study is problem-oriented, trying to probe a development mode and path selection of globalizing cities through a more creative angle of observation and analytical methods and tools, in hoping to achieve a certain results in academic value and practical value. Its main creative aspects are:

(1) To re-examine the inner logic between global cities and the interaction of globalization and informatization. By criticizing that the traditional global city theory directly derives the logic relations of global cities from globalization city, and the concept of a globalization city has been put forward. The global city network based on globalization city has been used as intermediate variables, thereby expanding and improving the logic relationship between the global city and the interaction of globalization and informatization, with globalizing cities incorporated into this logic. This lays a theoretical foundation for us to study globalizing cities in the background of globalization and informatization.

(2) This study focuses on the analysis of the internal drive mechanism or functional mechanisms of globalizing cities, which does not answer such issues as the general necessity and inevitability of globalizing cities but on how to promote globalizing cities from structure and function, and to explore the route of globalizing cities in line with the world trends and China's national situation. This will help perfect the comprehensive and systematical study of global cities, deepen the study of the global city theory, and result in a more realistic guidance to the promotion of China's globalizing cities.

(3) This study emphasizes that the globalizing cities are reflected not only in the distribution of urban space and urban economic development but also in comprehensive construction of multiple structure and function of cities. Moreover, we explore how the comprehensive construction and development can come into being in the interaction with outside or in the flow of globalization from a new perspective, which will not only help us to deepen the study of globalizing cities but also help us grasp its path and process more clearly.

Contents

Chapter 1

Literature Review

The study on "globalizing cities" is indeed a new research topic, however, the phenomenon of a globalizing city is not a completely isolated one. Especially, it is closely linked to the concept of a "global city". Theoretically, it refers to a further expansion and explication of the global city studies. Therefore, the theoretical source of studies on this issue is the global city theory, even urbanology. After the 1980s, several hypotheses, such as "world city", "global city", "global city-system", and "global city-region" came into being in succession, and a series of empirical researches exploring the world city network relationships and countermeasures constructing modern international metropolises both provide the necessary theoretical preparation and analysis tools for research on the concept of a "globalizing city".

1.1. Formation and Development of the Global City Theory

Studies assuming the city as a separate object has a long history, resulting in the formation of the offshoot research area of urbanology, with an independent system. After the 1980s, an increasing number of scholars began to pay attention to and focus on some special types of cities (e.g., global city), and started carrying out in-depth studies, forming various hypotheses that differed from that of traditional urbanology. At present, the study of the global city remains deep, continuously producing new theoretical results.

1.1.1. *Traditional urban studies*

In traditional urban theory, there exists a deep-rooted idea that cities are service centers of rural areas whose influences on urban theory are fundamental and very strong. Based on this concept, the traditional urbanologists commit themselves to the understanding and description of the urban spatial distribution. Among them are some representative theories such as Christaller (1996) and Lösch's (1954) urban theory of "central location", based on traditional agricultural areas; Burgess' (1923) concentric pattern theory; Hoyt's (1939) fan pattern theory; and Harris and Ullman's (1945) multicore pattern theory. The core contents of these so-called classical urban development models are as follows: in the broader scale, between cities or regions, there is a relatively self-sufficient agricultural economic region, with the urban centers and its rural hinterlands exchanging goods and services; in the narrower scale of the inner city, there is a centralized urban area in which the Central Business District (CBD), as the dominant node, is connected with the suburbs by traditional radial public transport routes, with the suburbs relying on its services and providing labor force requirements (Hall, 1997).

Of course, there are different opinions about the understanding and interpretation of the system nature of spatial distribution of urban centers. For example, from the perspective of social organization, Chicago sociologists put forward very simplistic, superficial urban development patterns, that is, it is deemed that social organization comes from spatial competition, which leads to an "ecological classification" pattern associated with a bid-rent model (bid-rent). Since then, the traditional theoretical framework describing layouts of urban land use and land values centers on the concept of "the highest value and best use" and the methodology of bid–rent curve. The urban land use layout model develops simultaneously with a population distribution model. Among the different types of analysis, the most typical is to reveal that there exists "a crater-like density distribution area" around the CBD, the intersection of whose highest land value are probably those areas with most concentrated pedestrians and heaviest traffic.

Later, some studies try to adapt this standard "single center" model to the multicenter structures of many modern cities, which mushroom as a result of their suburbanizing activities. Hamilton assumes the "centrifugation-decentralization" model produced by the "mechanized transport and electricity distribution", competing with the "centripetence-centralization" model explicated by economies of scale and economic integration. For example, factories moved to the suburbs, and urban areas that spread outward in both radial and frontal directions as a result of population diffusion mutually inosculated, often swallowing up previously existing centers of neighboring areas. Although these remote centers are swallowed into the cluster, they usually function as commercial sub-centers. In 1963, Berry also amended the "single nucleus" model in his paper on the US urban retail structure to distinguish between the ribbon development areas and sub-centers. Although these researches break through the limitations of the "single nucleus" model, their theoretical models are still built on a field with towns and their hinterlands relatively self-enclosed, tending to describe the layouts of urban space as an integrated economy and with a physical boundary, almost not paying attention to more complex and wider relations.

Therefore, in the traditional urban studies, there is an obvious feature, namely, that the analysis of urban problems, including the inter-city relations, is mostly limited within a country. The commonly used approach is to analyze the "national urban system". In this analysis, the typical method is to select the unrelated data in the national census and classify cities by the size of the urban population, with such models as "law of the primacy city" and "city size class rule" often used to describe this "city hierarchy". Of course, a few scholars are dedicated to the study of "port city", investigating how goods flow toward cities around the world through these ports. However, this study is of little effect in the academic community and is enlisted by only a small number of scholars.

With increasing accretion of the impacts of economic globalization, some researchers began to notice its effect on urban development but did not cast off the shackles of the traditional framework of urban theory, so that it is deemed that all cities attach themselves to the single center location system (Chase-Dunn, 1985). In this case, at best, the connection between a city and its hinterland should be developed in a larger scale. Perhaps, the classical city center location system model can still reasonably explain regional, but not global, urbanization patterns very well. The theoretic framework of traditional urbanology is unable to contain the kind of broader, more complex relationships or contacts of the global range when cities exceeds their own hinterlands, so that those studies on the global city based on worldwide connections and inner-city relationships of the global range are excluded.

1.1.2. *Early research and theoretical hypothesis formation of global city*

As early as 1889, the German scholar Goethe used the term "world city" to describe Rome and Paris. In 1915, the British master of urban and regional planning, Geddes (1915) clearly put forward the concept of world cities in his book *Cities in Evolution*, where he defined them as cities that occupy a disproportionate scale in the business world and used, as examples, the commanding roles of national capitals (such as Paris, Berlin) and industrial centers (such as Düsseldorf, Chicago) in the business and transportation network to illustrate his theory. Hall (1966) used the two concepts of size and intensity to measure the function of cities and conducted a comprehensive study of seven cities: London, Paris, Randstad, Rhine-Ruhr, Moscow, New York, and Tokyo from the polity, trade and communication facilities, finance, culture, technology, higher education, and other aspects, assuming that the world city is basically the product of the single European system of industrial capitalist economy, which ranks at the top of the world city system.

After the 1960s, multinational companies increasingly became the main carriers of globalization, playing an important role in driving capital, technology, labor, and goods to flow among countries, and thereby attracting global researchers' attention. Hymer (1972) introduced the multinational companies into the study of global cities with pioneering spirits. In his view, in the global economy with increasingly close contacts, the importance of corporate decision-making mechanism impels multinational companies to locate their headquarters in the world's major cities such as New York, London, Paris, Bonn, and Tokyo. Therefore, the importance and status of these cities can be confirmed, and they can thereby be ranked by measuring the number of multinational headquarters hosted by them.

However, it was not until the early 1980s that the direct combining of urban studies with the world economy change began, along with large-scale studies of the global city. With the new international division of labor coming into being, the world urban distribution has undergone major changes. Many Western researchers find it increasingly complicated to observe changes, and it has become difficult to explain urban development and its changing function with respect to the traditional urban theory. When turning their attention to the deepening international economic exchanges, they found that economic globalization has led to the redivision of regional economic activity, further contributing to the new formation of urban form and function. Conhen (1981) is one of the scholars who earlier thought of the world city system in connection with the economic activities of transnational corporations, believing that the new international division of labor is an important bridge between the two, and the global city is seen as the coordination and control center of new international division of labor. Therefore, the main criteria to judge the countries of the world lie in their position and impact in the global economy. It is the study directly combining this process of urbanization with the world economic power that provides a theoretical framework for studying global cities, whose basic hypothesis is completed by Friedmann and Sassen.

Inspired by the new international division of labor studied by Frobel, Scott, and other researchers, Friedmann advanced the famous "world city hypothesis". In 1981, he and Wolff published the paper "Notes on the World Urban Future", beginning to show concern for the study of the world city. In 1982, he and Wolff published the paper in collaboration World City Formation: an Agenda for Research and Action, further exploring the formation of the world city. In 1986, he published the paper "World City Hypothesis", presenting seven famous judgments, and further improving the study of the world city. This hypothesis attempts to provide the theoretical basis of spatial organization for the new areal division of international labor, emphatically revealing the structure of world city hierarchy and classifying the world cities. Friedmann's world city hypothesis comes from non-empirical observations, but owns considerable rationality. His unique views of spatial structure and layout of world cities are generally accepted by the academic sector and recognized as the pioneering contents of the world city literature (Knox and Taylor, 1995). Although great progress in this research field has been made, his original theory in this field is still dominant and is the basic theory that explores the inner-city mutual relationships in the world (Hamnett, 1994).

Sassen (1991), a University of Chicago professor, studies the degree of internationalization and concentration and the intensity of major producer services of cities from the perspectives of the world economic system and explains global cities through the world's leading producer services, thus making him a representative having a significant impact on the research field.

Different from Friedmann's initial idea of seeing the world cities as general "command centers", Sassen defines the global city as the financial and business services center, whose essence is to provide services for the global capital rather than specific local management, avoiding the kind of "centralized command" as something naturally possessed by the global city.

Sassen visualizes the global city as the birthplace of producer service industries of the times, which is considered as the key difference from Friedmann's definition of the world city. With comparison to Friedmann studying the global city development from a macro point of view, Sassen more emphatically studies the global city from the micro perspective (enterprise location choice). With regard to the research method, Sassen's study is based on empirical research, with a lot of empirical analysis being conducted on New York, London, Tokyo and other cities. Therefore, in fact, Sassen's global city hypothesis is a kind of global city paradigm developed on the basis of empirical evidence of the USA (or New York/London/Tokyo). Because of her establishing theory and testing methods of the global city, the particular global city Sassen describes becomes the global city in a general sense.

There exist large differences but also considerable complementarities between the results of studies of Friedmann and Sassen on "world/global city". Friedmann's research has a global scope of vision but lacks adequate empirical experience; on the contrary, Sassen's research is considered to have an overview on the evidence, but because it limits its studies to London, New York, and Tokyo, it is seen as lacking global inclusiveness (Taylor and Walker, 2001). Although there are various criticisms of the current "world/global city" assumptions, these theories boldly place the city under the perspective of the global hierarchy, in combination with globalization, and conduct a comprehensive re-examination of the city's function, grade, society, and space, which, no doubt, provides the study a new perspective of seeing about the globalizing city as well as the global city.

1.1.3. *Development of the global city theory*

Friedmann and Sassen's "world/global city" hypothesis caught scholars' widespread attention but also brought in a variety of criticism. First, Friedmann's hypothesis is mainly speculative and declarative, lacking information and database (Korff, 1987), and this defect has been widely mentioned (Short *et al.*, 1996; Taylor, 1997, 1999). Of course, there are also objective reasons, e.g., only those data collected according to countries are available and there is a lack of multinational data. Second, this hypothesis pays more attention to high-level cities of the world city system. Friedmann (1995) put forward only 12 core and 18 semi-peripheral world cities, without more important cities included in the world city hierarchy. Of course, this also largely owes to the lack of adequate data. Furthermore, Friedmann first, as a whole, constructs the hierarchy of world cites with pioneering spirits, which is related to the construction of a domestic city hierarchy in the study of "national urban system".[1] However, according to observations,

---

[1] "National urban system" is a paradigm for the research of a country's internal major cities prior to the study of global cities.

even in a country, a mechanical simple hierarchical pattern does not exist (Pred, 1977). From the transnational point of view, a simple hierarchical pattern looks even more unreasonable (Taylor, 1997). Typically, the division of the city level is in accordance with the city's "importance" or size, but no matter what standards are maintained, they do not suggest the formation of the hierarchy of world cites. Moreover, the definition of an urban hierarchy depends on not only the "importance" or the size and other factors but also "a series of factors" (Lukermann, 1966). Especially, with the rapid worldwide development of communication, simultaneously, there exist two trends: the centralized and decentralized in economic functions, which lead to the uncertainty of the world city hierarchy. It is in this academic criticism and debate that "the world/global city" hypothesis can be further developed, and the various theories and schools of the global city come into being, the relatively typical examples among which are as follows:

(1) Post-modernism Global City Research as Represented by Los Angeles School

According to this school of thought, the core of Friedmann and Sassen's "world/global city" hypothesis is that economic globalization has the impact of these cities going beyond the nation-state, bringing their control functions into play at the global level, but, recent years' research on global cities based on different politics, economy, cultures, and governance shows that the influences of state administration, culture, and history on these global cities are not necessarily similar to the hypothesis. Therefore, they argue that the Friedmann and Sassen's "the world/global city" hypothesis is too dependent on the US urban context and the special nature of a few cities and therefore is not able to reflect the influences of different political backgrounds. There are also some critical scholars who think that Friedmann's point of view is economic determinism. In their view, the internationalization of some cities is influenced by their identity as a country's capital, for example, Washington, D.C., Beijing, Seoul, and Tokyo (Hill and Kim, 2000).

The Los Angeles School takes the ideas of post-modernism, bringing the understanding of the world city back to the earlier broader definition by Hall. For example, Soja (1996) takes the political, historical, cultural, and social criticism, holding the view that the contemporary urbanization is a fully social process of globalization, with urbanization and global social changes concomitant and globalization-based, and that post-Fordist urbanization creates global cities such as Los Angeles. Scott and other researchers think Los Angeles is an important node of the world's economic, social, cultural, and ecological systems, possessing both the generality and individuality of world cities. In addition to economic factors, culture and ideology play an unusual role in Los Angeles' development, being widely spread all around the globe (Scott and Soja, 1986). Knox's (2002) belief is also that today's global city has become both the cause and consequence of economic, political, and cultural globalization.

(2) Researches into the Relationship between Information Technology Revolution and the Global City Development

The development of information technology has resulted in a profound impact on linkages among cities. Scholars such as Castells, Batten, Warf, Hepworth, and Lanvin, from the angles of the information network, study the global cities and global city network, which has become a mainstream direction of the global city research after the 1990s. In particular, Castells (1996) first proposed the theory of information city. He holds the view that information is raw materials of all social processes and social organization. The social structures that economic production, cultural mainstream, politics, and military depend on will be based on collection, storage, processing, and production of information and knowledge. The most important result of the new technological revolution is service change, and our world will be transformed into a new social structure — information society, with the information city serving as its embodiment. On this basis, he brings Sassen's point of view into his theoretical framework, and global cities, as the mesosphere of "space of flow", are regarded as "the most direct interpretation of the world's most direct influential nodes and network centers" (Castells, 1996). Despite their different starting points, Castells also sums up the dual spatial structure model similar to that of Friedmann, providing strong support for the latter's world city theory from the side.

(3) The Global City Network Research

Globalization and World Cities Study Group and Network (GaWc), formed by scholars of Department of Geography, Loughborough University, UK, has made the most systematic probe into the quantitative division of the global city network (Taylor, 1995). The research team believes that the traditional study of "world/global city" places emphasis on the characteristics they have, thereby at best being a kind of static study. If scholars want an understanding of the "world/global city" nature, they should pay more attention to the analysis of "relationships" among global cities. In particular, Taylor studies the globalization of business activities of New York, Washington, Miami, Boston, San Francisco, Los Angeles, and other large US cities, realizing that, with regard to theoretical or empirical research on the "world/global city", the static view in the past should be abandoned and be replaced by a dynamic angle. At the same time, the trend of globalization means that the global city should be placed in the skeleton of political economics for observation. Therefore, in constructing the "world/global city" hierarchy, Taylor and his colleagues advocate launching a special joint research around the world, to bring together "global/world city" materials. Taylor and other researchers have constructed a large number of case studies by using the company case study method, determining the size of the global city network force, and putting forward key factors that aid in forming the global city network. The results of these studies have drawn sharp attention in the international academic field.

In addition, many researchers perform theoretical analysis and empirical research of the global city from different perspectives (mainly including three aspects: characteristics, assessment, and governance of global cities). For example, Hall (1996) studies the nature of the global city, believing that the advent of new international division of labor and globalization promotes the global expansion of production and innovation, which lays material foundations for the emergence of the new global hierarchy network structure, and stresses the historical influences on reality and future of the city and the differences in various regions. Lefevre (1991) sees changes in the urban space as a kind of reflection of social, political, and economic changes, emphasizing that it is necessary that spatial changes should be associated with capital circulation and economic and social change of different spatial scales, even global scale. Abu-Lughod (1999) makes comparative studies on global cities such as New York, Chicago, and Los Angeles in the background of the US, with Hamnett (1994, 1996) debating the issue of social polarization of the global city. Some scholars study the structure and mechanism of the global cities from multinational organizations, governmental action, space structures, sustainable development, and suitability for living.

1.2. Main Viewpoints of the Global City Theory and Relevant Research

The global city theory and its relevant researches are comprehensive and interdisciplinary, with most based on certain perspectives such as globalization, information technology, and internetization, involving economic, social, organizational, spatial, and other fields. The existing literatures pays main attention to the connotation and descriptive concept of the global city, developing the mechanism, function, and role of the global city; classification and its system of the global city; the global city internetization characteristics; the global city-regions, etc.

1.2.1. *The meaning and its interpretation of the global city*

Although researchers have not arrived at a mutually acceptable definition of the global city, they are not affected to make a probe into the basic content of the global city. The existing literature gives a variety of explanations on the connotation of the global city, which are based on different perspectives and emphases, but emphasizes that the basic property of the global city mainly lie in fact that the global city is "whether as a capital accumulation and the accumulation of land and whether as an organization to control the distribution of production, circulation of the role" (Mollenkopf, 1993).

Hall (1966) saw the global city as a world-class metropolis that has economic, political, and cultural influences worldwide, which means that a global city: is a major center of political power, is the location of the country's trade centers and major banks, hosts the country's financial center and all kinds of professionals centers; is the place for information collection and dissemination; contains large population centers (with a considerable proportion of the wealth population); and also has entertainment industries and important industrial sectors.

Friedmann (1986) points out that a world city, in the modern sense, is the hub or organizational node of the global economic system; the base where global capitalists organize and coordinate their production and market; the main place where international capital pool; and the destination of a large number of domestic and international migrants. It has a variety of strategic functions which control and command the world economy, and the global control functions are directly reflected in its production and employment structure and vitality. In 1995, based on the absorption of other relevant researches, Friedmann summed up five main features of the world city:

(1) The world city is the connection point of the global economic system, where the economy of all regions is connected to become an organic whole.
(2) The world city is the hub of global capital, but because of different political systems, economic scale, city size, and the impact of international politics, the capital scale that is converged in the world city is much smaller than the size of global capital.
(3) The world city has wider range of urban areas, and the degree of economic and social interaction of the world city is very high.
(4) The world city can be ranked according to its economic scale and controlled economic strength, such as regional world city, state-class world city, or world-class world city. The ability to control

global capital is the final decision of grades of the world city, and the ability to digest technological innovation, political changes, and other external shocks also has influences on its ranking in the world city hierarchy.

(5) The world city development is basically dependent on multinational capitalists.

Sassen (1991) holds the view that the transformation of the global economic restructuring to services and financial industries results in new importance being placed on major cities as centers of production, service, marketing, and innovation. Global cities are not only nodes of coordination process but also the places where particular works are undertaken. They serve as the supply bases of professional services, which are required when the headquarters of multinational companies manage their geographically dispersed factories, offices, and sales representatives in services and other networks. They are also the production bases of financial innovative products and market factors, which are essential to the internationalization and expansion of financial industries. Sassen stressed the following four basic features of global cities in that:

(1) they serve as a highly centralized control centers of the world economy;
(2) they are the main locations of financial and professional service sectors;
(3) they are the seat of leading industries, including the innovation industry;
(4) they act as the markets of products and innovation. She also pointed out that the global city has a special space, internal dynamics, and social structure.Global cities are full of vitality and create more job opportunities for the low-income groups, also simultaneously making the senior personnel in income distribution more affluent. However, the new economic growth in global cities provides greater contribution to the income gap.

Castells (1996) thinks that the information is not of spatial characteristics, and information technology also renders the geographic friction almost nonexistent. Therefore, the world economy will transfer from "space of place" to "space of flows", with the flow of information economy (moving) also characterized by a special network structure. In this sense, the global city is not a place but a process, that is, a process in which the production centers, consumption centers, service centers, and their societies of location are integrated into a whole network. As major nodes in global networks, global cities are "those places where production and consumption centers of high-level service and their subsidiary societies are linked up in the global network". He also stressed that "that the city gets and accumulates wealth, control and power is not relying on what it has but by what flows through it". Thus, moving away from the past interpretation of the basic connotation of a global city, Castells entrusted dynamic, linked contents to the concept.

1.2.2. *The basic motivation of formation of the global city*

In connection with discussing the basic content of the global city, the kind of forces that promotes its formation is also one of important issues the global city theory seeks to study. In this issue, there are different theoretical explanations and instructions.

Friedmann (1986) thinks that the extent of integration of cities with the world economy and their status in the new international division of labor will determine the function and structural reorganization of the cities. The world's major cities will become the beginning and the ending points and the commanders and coordinators who integrate the global production and market through a complex system of global cities. Therefore, the basic motivation of the global city formation comes from the new international division of labor. In 1995, Friedmann further points out that the world cities are the spatial expression of the world economic system, which is made up of regional economic systems with different levels of economic development. The more solid a region's economic strength, the higher is the number of the world cities in that region, and vice versa.

Sassen (1991) thinks that the changes in geographical distribution and composition of the global economy may result in economic activities of spatial decentralization and global integration, entrusting major cities with new strategic roles. The basic driving force of its existence is: the more globalized economy, the higher the degree of concentration of central functions in a few cities (i.e., global cities). The increase in capital flows not only brings about the changes in geographical location of the production organization and financial market network but also calls for new forms of production to ensure that the new production and financial organization be managed and controlled and related services provided. In this process, a number of cities become the transnational economic space where domestic and foreign enterprises operate. Sassen further notes that an important basis for the formation of global cities is investment internationalization and finance securitization, which have their roots in those changes of technology and space and give a special role to the global city in the world economy at this stage. That is, the internationalization of industrial production resulting from trade and foreign direct investment call for the appropriate support services in trade, finance, accounting and law fields. Especially, since the 1980s, nonbank financial institutions dominate the international financial markets, which are complex, competitive, innovative, and risky, and thereby determine their needs of financial centers with highly specialized services as their important basis. But Sassen (1995) also notes that the global city is an analytical framework by which its generality can be grasped, and only depending on a strong local institutional environment and legal and administrative framework, to a considerable extent, can every function of the global city work. From the perspective of the global space of flows, Castells reanalyzes the dynamic base of the global city formation. He believed that making use of the global network with "instant" accessibility can eliminate barriers to national territories. This fully reflects in the communication links based on the world capital market transactions. In this case, gaining access to the information spaces and having control over their main nodes is the key to win the final victory in the race to accumulate international capital and complete the transformation into global cities. Therefore, the "world city results from the relationship among company network activities and inner-city contacts based on the knowledge complex and economic reflection". Moss (1987) also points out that intelligent buildings, telecommunications port, fiber, and other key technologies have become a part of the emerging information city's infrastructure. The construction and expansion of telecommunications facilities will play a decisive role in a city's future economic growth and the status of the global city system. Lanvin (1993) expresses the same meaning with his belief that information has become strategic resources of the new world economy, with telecommunications systems becoming the key infrastructure of cities, and concentration of advanced telecommunications facilities in a few cities around the world guaranteeing their further prosperity. Leyshon and Thift's (1997) research findings also show that the development and function of global cities are increasingly dependent on advanced telecommunications networks and services. The telecommunications network has accelerated the accumulation of social and economic factors, thus promoting the formation and development of global cities. In order to emphasize the important role of telecommunications facilities in the formation of global cities, some scholars also study global or regional network structure, such as Warf's (1989) study on distribution of fiber chains and telecommunications ports ringing the Pacific Ocean, and on the accessibility of US BITNET NSFNET and Internet (1995); Hepworth's (1990) study on the IP Sharp network and the network of the London Stock Exchange; and Langdale's (1989) research on international leased networks and the like, which have proved that the global city is a hub in the global telecommunications network. Although it has been recognized that the information network is crucial to global cities, the lack of relevant data make its impact beyond measurement.

1.2.3. *The functions and status of the global city*

That the global city has become a special object of study is largely due to its specific functions and status. In this issue, most of the researchers study its particular functions and status based on the global perspective, and therefore their opinions are easier to unify, but specific perspectives are chosen differently.

Friedmann and Wolff (1982) hold the view that the world city economy's rapid transfer from manufacturing industries to service and financial sectors is the special express of the process of global changes, and many local issues in the world cities, especially those cross-border fast and irregular capital flows, can always be understood as the results of those ultranational influences. So, Friedmann (1986) points out that the basic characteristic of a world city is to have control over the global economy, which results from clustering of major multinational company headquarters in the city. World cities are the seats of multinational company's headquarters, with their growth supported by a few fast-growing industries, such as international finance, international trade, and various business services. Another important role of world cities is its "example effect", namely, world cities are not only the production and consumption centers but also production and dissemination centers of formation, entertainment, and other cultural products. Meanwhile, the world cities are the main venues of international and domestic workers and immigrants. Because of their developed economy, prosperous markets, and diversified and relatively high-level employment opportunities, the world cities can attract large numbers of workers and professionals.

Sassen has studied the "producer services complex" of global cities systematically, assuming that the highly specialized producer service is the major component of the global city development. First, the specialization and agglomeration economies make the city a favorable location of producer service, which is the most strategic and most complex service. Second, the emerging information technology plays an increasingly important role in the production and distribution of such services, not only helping to spread but also to re-collect the service technology. Organizational complexity enables enterprises to obtain the maximum benefits from these new technologies; while the city may provide this complexity through dense business and market networks and close social relations. Furthermore, providing services for globally operating enterprises means that the leading global producer service firms are continuously expanding and operating in global city networks. Producer services are characterized by their high concentration in urban centers and greater degree of specialization in major cities, which, to some extent, is linked to the major cities as a suitable producing bases and markets for these services. Sassen (1995) also points out that, because of the rapid growth of global investment and trade and, as its results, strong demands for financial and professional service sectors, the global city service functions are further strengthened. As international trade becomes the main body of the world economy, the government's management and service functions in the world's economic affairs will be gradually replaced by the world cities. Acting as an international financial center is one of the most important economic functions of the world's cities, in particular, the main function of the highest level global cities. Therefore, the study on international financial centers is a special branch of the world city's study. Reed (1981) has conducted pioneering work, collecting from 76 US cities, more than 50 indicators in the financial, economic, cultural, geographical, political aspects in the period 1900–1980, constructing a multivariate analysis using these data, and outlining the hierarchy of financial centers in the US and their evolution. Later, Reed (1989) performed a study of the global financial centers system, assuming that New York and London comprise the first level of the global financial centers; Amsterdam, Frankfurt, Paris, Tokyo, Zurich form the second level of the international financial centers; Brussels, Chicago, Toronto, Sydney, Sao Paulo, Singapore, and Hong Kong are the third level of regional financial centers. In addition, Budd and Whimster (1992), Lee and Schmidt-Marwede (1993), Drennan (1996), Meyer (1998), and other researchers have also studied the function and role of international financial centers of the global city. In these studies, it is more accepted that New York, London, and Tokyo comprise the first level of global financial centers; while there are differences about the classifications of the second- and third-level financial centers.

Some scholars study the functions and roles of global cities as global major communications network nodes from the background of global informatization. Castells (1996) points out that, as a historical trend, dominant functions and processes of the global information age is organized by networks. New communications technologies promote inner-city international connections, which act as major nodes of the global city in the global information network, and control the Internet's global geographic structure. Graham and Marvin (1996) also believe that the global city has a key influence in shaping the emerging development patterns of the global geography and telecommunications infrastructure; in particular, the global city's CBDs play the leading role in the world's rapidly changing communications landscape. Drennan's (1991) study suggests that information-intensive US corporate headquarters tend to be located in a global city. Malecki (2001), using the data such as the number of backbone broadband service providers and networks in the world cities, discovers the global network information tends to locate in the global city spatially.

There are some scholars who have also revealed the functions of global cities as political and cultural centers through research, such as Hall (1966), taking political factors as an important basis of the global city to differentiate it from other types of cities. In his view, the global city should be "a major center of political rights, the location of global organizations such as the world most powerful governments and international trade organizations".

1.2.4. *Classification and system of the global city*

Friedmann proposes seven standards measuring world cities: major financial centers, seats of headquarters of multinational corporations, venues of international institutions, high growth of tertiary industry, main manufacturing centers (processing industry of international significance, etc.), important hubs of world transportation (especially port and international airport), and urban population with a certain scale. According to these standards, Friedmann, using the "core–periphery" approach, and based on the World Bank classification into core countries (19 industrialized countries with the market economy system) and semi-peripheral countries (including those economies with high industrialization and the market economy system among middle-income economies), divides cities into the major and secondary in order to build the hierarchy of world cities (see Table 1.1). Thereafter, Friedmann (1995) adds the indicator "migration destination" to original measures, and changes the dividing standards of core and periphery economies, redividing the world city in accordance to the size of economic regions connected by the city. Among them, world cities of the first level are: New York, Tokyo, and London; the second level are: Miami, Los Angeles, Frankfurt, Amsterdam, Singapore, Paris, Zurich, Madrid, Mexico City, Sao Paulo, Seoul and Sydney; and the third level are: Osaka, Kobe, San Francisco, Seattle, Houston, Chicago, Boston, Vancouver, Toronto, Montreal, Hong Kong, Milan, Lyon, Barcelona, Munich, and Rhine-Ruhr.

Table 1.1. John Friedmann's "World Cities Hierarchy".

Core Countries		Semi-peripheral Countries	
Major cities	Secondary Cities	Major Cities	Secondary Cities
London*I	Brussels*III		
Paris*II	Milan III		
Rotterdam III	Vienna*III		
Frankfurt III	Madrid*III		
Zurich III			Johannesburg III
New York I	Toronto III	Sao Paulo I	Buenos Aires*I
Chicago II	Miami III		Rio de Janeiro I
Los Angeles I	Houston III		Caracas*III
	SF III		Mexico City I
Tokyo*I	Sydney III	Singapore*III	Hong Kong II
			Taipei*III
			Manila*II
			Bangkok*II
			Seoul*II

*National capital.

Note: I, cities with a population of 10–20 million; II, cities with a population of 5–10 million; III, cities with a population of 1–5 million.

Thrift (1989), on the basis of Friedmann's world cities classification, stresses the importance of services, and selects the two indicators of number of corporate headquarters and the Bank's headquarters to divide global cities into: global centers (New York, London, Tokyo), intercontinental centers (Paris, Singapore, Hong Kong, Los Angeles), and regional centers (Sydney, Chicago, Dallas, Miami, Honolulu, San Francisco). Knox (1995) puts forward the three criteria of global cities from the functional point of view of:

(1) transnational business activities, measured by the number of Fortune 500 companies settling there;
(2) international affairs, measured by the number of non-governmental organizations and international organizations locating there; and

(3) cultural concentration ratio, reflected in the city's primacy ratio in the country. Simon (1995) sees the global city as the spatial basic points of global economic and social activities, having the following criteria: first, there being complete financial and other service systems facing customers such as international institutions, multinational corporations, and government and non-governmental organizations; second, the city serving as the global capital flow, information flow, and communication flow distribution center; third, there being high-quality living environment attracting international migration, professional and technical personnel, government officials, and diplomats.

The London Planning Advisory Committee (1991) compares and classifies global cities based on four areas: infrastructure, wealth-creating capability, increase in employment and income, and improving quality of life. Of the cities studied, London, Paris, New York, and Tokyo are placed in the first level and Zurich, Amsterdam, Hong Kong, Frankfurt, Milan, Chicago, Bonn, Copenhagen, Berlin, Rome, Madrid, Lisbon, and Brussels are classified in the second level.

Beaverstock *et al.* (1989) analyze the distribution of four producer services, including accounting, advertising, financial, and legal service industries, in major cities in the world, and determine their values in accordance with the number of their headquarters and branch offices. The greater the number of their distribution, the higher the score, with a maximum of 12. The cities with 3 points or less means that they have not yet satisfied compulsory conditions of becoming "world/global cities", and are thereby classified as D class. Based on whether they satisfy the requirements or have the potential of becoming the world's cities, these cities may be further divided into three categories, namely, cities with relatively strong evidence of becoming "world/global cities" (3 points); cities with some evidence of becoming "world/global cities" (2 points); cities with minimal evidence of becoming "world/global cities" (1 point). Taylor and Walker (2001) distinguish three main levels of "world/global cities" from the cities with a score of 12–4 (see Table 1.2).

Table 1.2. Taylor and Walker's "World Cities By Strata" (with a Maximum Value of 12).

Points		Cities
Alpha world cities	12	London, Paris, New York, Tokyo
	10	Chicago, Frankfurt, Hong Kong, Los Angeles, Milan, Singapore
Beta world cities	9	San Francisco, Sydney, Toronto, Zurich
	8	Brussels, Madrid, Mexico City, Sao Paulo
	7	Moscow, Seoul
Gamma world cities	6	Amsterdam, Boston, Caracas, Dallas, Düsseldorf, Geneva, Houston, Jakarta, Johannesburg, Melbourne, Osaka, Prague, Santiago, Taipei, Washington
	5	Bangkok, Beijing, Rome, Stockholm, Warsaw
	4	Atlanta, Barcelona, Berlin, Buenos Aires, Budapest, Copenhagen, Hamburg, Istanbul, Toronto, Manila, Miami, Minneapolis glass Aires, Montreal, Munich, Shanghai

Source: Taylor and Walker (2001).

After this classification, a number of scholars in Britain, Germany such as Taylor, Doel, Hoyler, Walker and Beaverstock, according to a three-level "world/global city" system, conducted a principal component factor analysis of 28 cities and 46 global services in the Asian regions situated in the Pacific Rim and summarized five main factors to interpret 74.2% of variance, finally, determining the world/global city-level system in the region (see Table 1.3). But generally speaking, these scholars believe that the Asia-Pacific region, repeatedly mentioned and stressed by academicians, does not seem to exist because the objects of most cities' economic transactions are not located in the Atlantic Ocean, that is, the Pacific Ocean of North America, and the inner-city economic interactions in the Asia-Pacific region seem fully unestablished.

1.2.5. *Network-based global city research*

With deepening of globalization and informatization and the strengthening of the global city contacts, the world city hierarchy,

Table 1.3. Pacific Rim cities.

Alpha world cities	Tokyo, Los Angeles, Singapore, Hong Kong
Beta world cities	San Francisco, Sydney, Seoul
Gamma world cities	Jakarta, Melbourne, Osaka, San Diego, Taipei, Bangkok, Beijing, Colombo, Manila, Shanghai
Cities with evidence of world city formation	Auckland, Brisbane, Ho Chi Minh City, Lima, Seattle, Vancouver, Adelaide, Guangzhou, Hanoi, Tijuana, Wellington

Source: Taylor *et al.* (2000).

proposed by Friedmann and further developed by descendants, has become increasingly difficult measure to describe changing global cities. Short *et al.* (1996) first points out that academic studies on the core issues of globalization and global cities neglect the data testing of inner-city flows. Knox (1998) more clearly points out that there almost no data available to reveal communication and interdependence among the world cities, which are the basic viewpoints of the transnational capitalist world city. Hannerz (1996) also observes that understanding of the world city should be based on the combination of its inherent characteristics and external links. Therefore, some scholars are transitioning from the comparative study of its inherent similarities and differences to the study of inner-city relationships, with the ideas and methods of networking being gradually adopted.

Amin *et al.* (2000) define a city as a process of interactions, and thus the city is seen as interacting social arena, not just a conglomeration of buildings. As the "city where there are interactions", its social relationships and activities in the geographical sense are intensive. Massey *et al.* (1999) also holds a similar view that the city is a social relations-intensive place. Thus, Massey (2000) sees the global city as a way to build human networks. For example, New York and London are regarded as the centers with highly intensive social relations and activities, and then the relationship between the two cities can be conceptualized and described as the level of intensity. Of course, its purpose is not to determine to what extent social relations of a place are, where how close are, as the city, because it may limit great increase in the numbers of city, a city may not see different people the different groups may be involved in international contacts in different ways.

More scholars study the global city networks empirically, such as Taylor (1997), who analyzes the geographical distribution of the global city newspaper industries; Short *et al.* (1996), who discuss the global city networks from telecommunications capacity; and Tee and Chen (1994) and Smith and Timberlake (1995), who use international flight passenger data to study the links among the global city networks. Beaverstock *et al.* (2001) also carry out a new empirical study, describing Castells's "space of flows" through the new data and to seize the relationships among cities which constitute the global city networks.

In 1999, three professors, Beaverstock, Taylor, and Smith, began research on urban network "nodes" (i.e., global cities) and their relationship, communication, and contacts. As for research methods, they believe that at least the following three data collection methods are helpful for the analysis of global cities: (1) making use of the analysis of commercial news of major newspapers to understand the business agent relations among cities; (2) making use of in-depth interviews to grasp the status of a city's main producer services, such as banks, accounting firms, law firms, advertising and immigration services, and then position the global city; (3) depending on distributing status of a city's main producer service to explore relationships among global cities organizationally. Accordingly, Taylor *et al.* (2002) determine the force of the global city networks from three major aspects: "accommodation, domination and channel", and seven different profiles (global city connections, international financial center connection, control centers, global command centers, regional command centers, high-connection channels, and emerging market channels).

1.2.6. *Research on the global city-region*

One of the problems that exist in the analysis of the global city network is the lack of the research of general cities' role in today's globalization, which has led to a bias in that the study tends to focus on higher-level cities but neglect the lower-level cities. However, it is very obvious that globalization is not supported by a few major cities but entails the involvement of many cities in the world. Assuming the existence of a global city means local, regional, and national economies have integrated into the world economy, therefore, as a logical extrapolation, extensive contacts among global cities clearly has been extended to other dimensions. Parnreiter (2003) points out that the world city network as a whole is based on the netting partition that contains all levels, that is, most are channels operating in the macro-regional, national, subnational, and regional levels. Brown *et al.* (2002), Derudder *et al.* (2003), and Rossi and Taylor (2004) and other scholars have attempted to study urban networks in the larger range so that its understanding is not only confined to a few of the major cities. However, this analysis, which is only equal to some kind of logical thinking of global nodes, does not explain the link among cities of other level, making it difficult to reveal the connection way between city networks of national and regional level and the wider world city networks.

In the late 1990s, some scholars began to pay attention to a gradually formed, new regional phenomenon, namely the global city-region. Scott, in his book *The Global City-region*, points out that the world in the global city-region is different compared to that of the city region in the ordinary sense and also from megalopolis formed by local linkages, but under the premise of highly developed globalization and economic ties, the product of expansion and unification of the global cities and secondary big or medium-sized cities with relatively strong economic strength in their hinterlands, which is a unique spatial phenomenon. In view of some scholars, the global city-region, which is the theoretical and practical extension of the global city concept, increasingly becomes a unique space in the international political and economic arena. In fact, urban areas have become the main space of modern life, and globalization is main driving force behind the appearance of this phenomenon. Under the premise of globalization, the development of the city's industries, whether manufacturing or service industries, high-tech industries or low-tech industries, depends on unprecedented contacts among them, while the degree of the contacts may even determine the market competitiveness of an industry. Therefore, a study only from the perspective of the city cannot fully explain the phenomenon of industrial competition and development in the era of globalization. The city-region not only is an expansion of the city in space but also a geographical phenomenon which forms in the process of city function upgrading, industry spread, and increasingly close contacts of economic space, so as to provide reasonable interpretation for regional economic development in the era of globalization.

1.3. Current State of Domestic Research

Since the 1990s, with the deepening of China's opening up and rapid economic development, some cities have proposed the strategic objectives of developing a modern international metropolis, or an international city. Correspondingly, the domestic academic research on global cities has come into vogue, obtaining a number of research results in succession.

At present, domestic research results are characterized by the following two aspects: First is the introduction of foreign global city theory and its literature, whose masterpieces include Zhou *et al.*'s (2004) Chinese translations of Sassen's *Global City: New York, London, Tokyo, World City — International Experience and the Development of Shanghai*; Ning's (1991) paper entitled "New International Division of Labor, the World City and Center of the City's Development in China", Tang's (1993) paper titled "The Basic Characteristics Of the International City and Forming Conditions", Li's (1994) paper "City of Internationalization and International Cities", Yao's (1995) paper "International City to Establish the Background and Opportunities", Yu and Wei's (2003) paper "International City, City of Regional and International City", and Zhang's (1996) paper "Talk About an International Metropolis". Second is about the analysis of the necessity and possibility to build global cities in China, the submission of strategic thinking of building global cities, especially empirical research on Shanghai, Beijing, Guangzhou, and some coastal cities, of which relatively systematic studies include Cai *et al.*'s (1995) "The Growing up of Cities as

International Economic Centers", and Gu's (1999) "Economic Globalization and China's Urban Development — A Study on Trans-Century City Development Strategy".

The specific contents of related research mainly focus on the following areas:

(1) The economic causes of the global city: Cai *et al.* (1995) fully explore the basic contents, compulsory conditions, and development trends of cities and especially analyze the relationship between transferring of international economic growth centers and development of international cities. Yao (2003), through the analysis of the internal and external economic environment of New York, London, and Tokyo's paths toward their transformation as global cities, explores the conditions that aid the growth of international cities, trying to prove that transferring from the present industrial structure to a service economy forms the basis of an international metropolis, and service trade is the driving force of the growing up of a metropolis, in order to grasp the organic links between economic development and the urban system evolution. Shen (2003) separately examines Tokyo's road to establishing itself as a world city, revealing that, with the increase in Japan's foreign direct investment and formation of her transnational economic system, how Tokyo, which was originally acting as Japan's economic center, became the key management center of Asian and the world economic systems. Transnational flows of financial capital further promote the development of central management functions of Tokyo, consolidating and strengthening the control status of Tokyo as the world economy center. Cai (2002) designs a six-dimensional model to comprehensively define the formation of world cities, which involves political and economic environment, population and technical personnel, economic vitality/control, initiative infrastructure, quality of the living environment, and city's comprehensive image, thinking that the gathering of advanced manufacturing industries and financial sectors are more conducive to reflect the city's global control. Guo (1995) summarizes the basic conditions of building a modern international city.

(2) New trends of development of international metropolis: Liu *et al.* (2003) investigates the specific mode and driving force of Tokyo's industrial structure evolution, Yu (1999) makes a detailed analysis of the post-war social and economic structure evolution and its effects on New York, London, and Tokyo. Zhou (2000) prospects China's international city development in the new century from the global urban development trend; Hong and Wen (2000) analyze the international metropolitan development trends in their paper "Urbanization Patterns of the New Development"; Shen (2001), observing the international city's comprehensive competitiveness as a research subject and focusing on the development trend of international metropolises in the 21st century, makes an empirical analysis of the practical approaches and planning ideas of a number of international cities in terms of improving competitiveness, and thereby gains some inspiration and reference. Also, Shen and Zhou (2003) believes that, the more globalized economy, the more concentrated in a few international cities is its central control, and the shift of global economic centers lead to significant changes of the world city hierarchy and setups, and that there is a possibility that a number of world cities may mushroom in the develop countries (especially in East Asian countries). Gu *et al.* (1999) systematically studies development of China's urban system in the background of globalization and informatization, based on the global city system framework.

(3) With the existing global city as frame of reference, a number of researchers have focused on proposing the standards and metrics of the growth of global cities and conducting comparative studies. Bai (1996) reveals the general properties and basic characteristics of global cities as an example of New York, Yang *et al.* (1996) make a comparative study on economy, society and environment of Shanghai and international metropolises, Shen *et al.* (2001) compare Shanghai city's comprehensive competitiveness with that of the other international metropolises, proposing suggestions of improving the Shanghai city's comprehensive competitiveness and new advantages in building an international

metropolis. In addition, there are some scholars who study and learn from the layouts and its implementation mechanisms of an international city, such as Sun (1998), who discusses planning and implementation mechanisms to construct a modern international metropolis and so on.

(4) Studies have also focused on countermeasures to transform Beijing, Shanghai, Guangzhou and other cities into international metropolises, according to the specific national conditions, such as Ning's (1994) analysis of Shanghai's efforts toward becoming a modern international metropolis; Li and Xu's (1994) initial thoughts on the construction of Guangzhou into an international city; Zhen's (2001) analysis of Shanghai's international metropolis; Wang's (2002) study on the basic foundation of Beijing's modern international metropolis; and Gu *et al.*'s (2000) detailed analysis of the opportunities and challenges Shanghai faces in its transformation into an international economic center.

These studies successfully use ideas and methods of foreign research as a source of reference, better understanding the special nature of the construction of modern international metropolis in China, which give them practical pertinence. But the domestic research on the global city began late, focusing more on empirical analysis, comparative study between individual cities, and study of corresponding countermeasures, with the theoretical framework not established, resulting in relatively weak theoretical guidance.

Chapter 2

Globalization, Informatization, and the Change of the World City System

In the framework of the mainstream global city theory, globalization and informatization are indispensable theoretic backgrounds and its main variables. Various theoretical analyses and empirical experience show that the tide of globalization shapes the spatial relationship at the center of the city, and the wave of informatization has brought the building of the city "space of flows", with the interaction of these two waves being one of the main driving forces of formation and development of global cities. No doubt, the study on the global city should be placed in the context of globalization and informatization in order to reveal the endogenous nature and their logic of growing up of global cities. But the mainstream theory of the global city, which only investigates a small number of cities at the top (i.e., global cities) in the background of globalization and informatization, reveals a simple logic between globalization, informatization, and global cities as "command centers", excluding the globalizing city as well as general cities integrating into the globalization process. So, when investigating globalizing cities in the background of globalization and informatization, studies are necessary to amend the logic, add new explanatory variables, and expand the theoretical framework, in order to be able to include broader objects and contents, especially in the context of globalizing cities.

2.1. Relations Between the Wave of Globalization and the Cities Centered by Space

The springing up of globalization and its continuous progress have produced multiple, integrated impacts, one important aspect of which is the changes in the international division of labor, bringing profound changes of both economy and space to the world economy, thereby reshaping the city-centered spatial relationships.

2.1.1. *The changes in the international division of labor in the process of globalization*

While there are still some differences in academia's understanding of the exact meaning of globalization and its full extension, most scholars believe that globalization is driven by regional economic expansion, which prompts the new international division of labor and leads to cultural, political, and even environmental interactions all over the globe, a process of the reconfiguration of global resources in terms of space.

In terms of economic geographic expansion in a general sense, globalization is not a new phenomenon and can be dated back to the 16th century. Since then, a series of global events have occurred, including many countries and regions being brought into the fold of the British Empire, implementation of economic colonization, and signing of a variety of world trade treaties. The mid-1800s witnessed the mushrooming of basic conditions satisfying globalization, such as the emergence of a number of international agencies and strategic cooperation between national governments and its institutionalization, establishment of way of world communication and standard time system, formation of the universal rules of international market competition, and motivation and basic consensus on civil and human rights. But it was not until 1980s that, for the first time, globalization, which was till then marked by colonialism and progressed in a slow pace, gained traction. Globalization was based on the traditional international division of labor, mainly reflected in the global division between industrialized countries and non-industrialized countries, with the industrialized countries being mainly engaged in production of industrial products, the non-industrialized countries being involved in the production of non-industrial products and industrial non-manufactured products, and exchanging their goods through trade.

As the ideological reflections and theoretical explanation of the traditional international division of labor, the centripetal spatial organization theory comes into being, which was originated in the 19th century and prevailed in the 20th century, namely, the so-called "core and periphery" space structure.

The core region consists of advanced, industrialized, and white-race-dominated countries, while the outlying region comprises backward, non-industrialized, and colored-race-dominated states. This theory divides the world into different functional areas, namely the central industrial areas of the North Atlantic and peripheral areas (rest of the world), providing mineral resources, industrial raw materials, and agricultural products. At the same time, the highly popular, traditional international trade theory also came into being, which views international trade as a diversified geo-spatial phenomenon reflecting import and export activities between the countries.

The state, as a single economic unit (or economic actors) at the level of the world economy, plays a very important role in this traditional pattern of international division of labor and international trade. In contrast, the city's importance in the world economy is not significant. The world city system formed in this process of globalization is also a kind of the "center" hierarchy-dominated basic framework. So the study thinks that, although the first colonialism-marked globalization laid the foundation for acceleration of today's globalization, the historic direct logic between globalization and the characteristics of globalized cities (especially global cities) still remains unestablished. In that sense, it does not constitute the city's historical background of the globalized cities that the study wants to observe.

Since the 1980s, accelerating globalization brought about a series of new changes in the global economy. Especially in the traditional "core and periphery" spatial structure, industrialization in some non-core countries began to rise, forming so-called "newly industrialized countries", such as "Four East Asian Tigers" and so on. This challenges the traditional division of the world into non-industrialized countries and industrialized countries. Frobel *et al.* (1980) and Arrighi and Drangel (1986) have pointed out that the rise of "newly industrialized countries" indicates that the pattern of trade can no longer be simply viewed as a concept based on the geographical separation of manufactured goods and raw materials, which is proved true by the reality of accelerating globalization, too. For example, since the 1980s, the intra-industry trade has assumed increasing importance. In many OECD countries, the share of manufacturing intra-industry trade has increased by two-thirds or more. From 1996 to 2000, the intra-industry trade in total trade of the manufacturing industry accounted for 68.5% in the US, 72% in Germany and 73.7% in UK, and in France, it is as high as 77.5%. Similarly, the middle-income countries also have witnessed growth in the share of intra-industry trade, such as Mexico (73.4%), Hungary (72.1%), and South Korea (57.5%) (OECD, 2002).

In the 1990s, the development of transnational corporations in developed countries led to a speeding increase in their cross-border economic activities, the proportion of which in all economic activities experienced a decisive change (Sassen, 1997). In today's world economy and international division of labor, multinational corporations play a pivotal role. There have been 62,000 multinational corporations in the world, which not only have one-third of the world's production and 70% of technology transfer, but also hold two-thirds of the world's international trade and 90% of foreign direct investment (FDI). Today's most important industries (such as automotive, electronics, aerospace, petrochemical, etc.) and important services (such as finance, insurance, telecommunications, etc.) have been brought into multinational corporations' global manufacturing and service network system. Moreover, the nature and organization of such large-scale, cross-border economic activities has also undergone a fundamental change. The traditional trade of rare materials and manufactured goods among countries trade are replaced by goods, capital, and information flow within multinational companies (Castells, 1996), resulting in a great increase in the share of internal trade of multinational companies in global trade. In the late 1990s, it is estimated that one-third of global trade was constituted by the intra-firm trade, and the other one-third of the trade volume is completed by product network controlled by TNCs (UNTCAD, 1995). For example, in the US, intra-firm trade of goods and services rose from 30.9% in 1982 to 34.5% in 2001. In Japan's exports-concentrated growth during the 1990s, intra-firm trade rose from 16.6% to 30.8% (USDC, 2000). In some specific industrial sectors and countries, the weight of intra-firm trade seems higher. For example, two-thirds of US imports of computers and electronic products are derived from the American subsidiary companies abroad. In 1999, 56% of trade between the US and Mexico is composed of intra-firm trade (OECD, 2002).

In the 21st century, this wave of globalization continues to drive development and prosperity of the world economy and continues to influence the world economy and political structure. In this process, two major new changes have also taken place, i.e., the transformation of transnational corporations into global corporations and the rise of multinational or global companies in developing countries.

While economic globalization promotes a wider global market expansion, it also greatly changes the business environment and competition rules. Facing the rapidly developing global market, a group of multinational corporations began to adjust their development strategy, management structure, and management philosophy, tranforming their past multinational business to global businesses, in order to absorb and integrate global resources to create the global industrial chain. Compared with the general multinational companies,[1] the degree of globalization of such companies is higher, and the internationalization index (ratio of foreign assets, foreign sales and foreign employees and total assets, total sales and total employees) is more than 50%. According to statistics of the United Nations Conference on Trade and Development, in 1995, the overseas assets

[1] In accordance with the definition of the relevant agencies of United Nations, a multinational company refers to an economic entity that establishes branches in two or more countries and is coordinated and controlled by the parent company, engaging in cross-border production and business activities.

of the world's largest 100 multinationals was 41% of its total assets, and by 2004, this proportion rose to 53%; its overseas assets rose from US $900 billion in 1994 to US $4,728 billion in 2004, increasing by 4 times in 10 years.

During the same period, the proportion of the top 100 multinational corporations' overseas sales in their total sales increased from 46% to 56%. According to UNCTAD data, in 1994, among the largest 100 transnational corporations, internationalization index of only 43 is more than 50%; and only 16 is more than 70%; by 2004, 61 is more than 50% and 27 is more than 70%. The purpose of strategic transformation from multinational companies to global companies is to attract and integrate global resources, including finance, market, raw materials, technology, and human resources, using global resources in competition with the global markets (Wang, 2007). Thus, the global companies often dedicate a lot of resources into a global business network, especially those important taches and nodes, such as locating purchasing centers, manufacturing and assembly centers, research and development centers, financial settlement centers, and marketing service centers in the most appropriate worldwide places, and setting up regional headquarters in a number of key areas and countries in the global market, to centralize management and coordinate company business units in the local business activities, which is a multicenter, multinode network management model. As a developer and operator of the global market, the global company has become one of major strengths actively promoting economic exchanges and cooperation among countries.

At the same time, globalization prompts large enterprises in developing countries to go abroad, extensively involve in global business, make efforts to improve their position in overseas markets, actively participate in cross-border M&A activity, carefully build a global brand, and increasingly become emerging multinationals expanding in the world (including developed countries). According to Statistics of *World Investment Report 1997*, from 1979 to 1981, the flow of average annual FDI of developing countries was only US $13 billion, accounting for 2.3% of the world's total FDI flow. However, since the mid-1980s, FDI of developing countries has rapidly grown. In 1986–1990, the average annual FDI flow reached US $11.7 billion, with its proportion increasing to 6.7%. In 1995–1996, the average annual FDI flow of developing countries increased rapidly to US $49.2 billion, with its proportion reaching 14.3%, mainly driven by the Asian newly industrialized countries and regions from the regional distribution. In 1996, FDI of South, East, and Southeast Asia increased by 10%, namely, US $40 billion, accounting for 89% flow and 80% stock of FDI of developing countries. Among them, India and China's FDI and multinational business development of developing countries grew more rapidly. For example, overseas investment of Indian companies is only US $15 billion in 2004, increasing to US $45 billion in 2005, and more than US $100 billion in 2006. Before 2004, only one company in India (Ranbaxy Medicine) undertakes transnational business, the number rose to about 18 in 2005–2006. According to Grant Thornton's research, the average size of each foreign acquisition of Indian companies has ranged from US $10 million 3 years ago to US $42 million. In 2006, the number of overseas acquisitions by Indian companies stood at 266, amounting to US $15.3 billion, coming fifth among the world's overseas acquisitions, second only to Spain, the US, Germany, and Australia. Although the total funds of M&A action initiated by the emerging countries comprise only 15% of the total global M&A, multinational corporations of developing countries are rapidly growing and beginnning to venture into the global markets, thereby signaling that globalization has entered an unprecedented new stage. In this new phase, masters of the initiative of global economy not just the West.

Therefore, since the 1980s, the wave of globalization is not only of greater breadth and intensity but also its content and nature have experienced a completely different change. In particular, the organization of global economic activity and its spatial structure gradually are experiencing a deep restructuring, forming a new international division of labor with important changes in its patterns, transforming from an inter-industry into an intra-industry enterprise. During this period, globalization became a process in which product, exchange, and consumption are integrated all over the globe, and coordination and related services are integrated in the world (Sykora, 1995). So, globalization of this period is characterized by creation of global markets, rapid flow of capital, transfer of global manufacturing sectors, global extension of complex production chain, and internal relations of global consumer market. Associated with this, globalization is also contributed to the combination the new world view of and cultural awareness. It is of particular note that globalization is the ecological concerns of global resources and environment, and the state of non-class-oriented, decentralized world system in post-modern pluralism system and culture (Bauman, 1998). This synthesis will undoubtedly enhance the degree of global connection and world integration, which is, at least, applicable to the part of population is closely linked to production the exchange of the world system, the world's communication and knowledge network. These new changes of globalization are undoubtedly a very important background conditions growing up of global cities in developing countries needs.

2.1.2. *Changes of competitive relationships between state and its cities, enterprises*

After the 1980s, the accelerating process of globalization, characterizing expansion of transnational corporations of developed countries into developing countries, has brought profound changes to the world economy in two main aspects: economy and space. One aspect relates to the concept of space, namely, regardless of whether the factors of distance are simply eliminated, globalization has reconstructed picture of the spatial constraints of their interaction (Cairncross, 1997). The other relating the world economic integration, that is, globalization has led to the liberation of movement of people, goods and services, which makes national and regional boundaries eliminated (Markusen, 1997). Obviously, these profound changes have a very important influence on this study when studying the global city, because they directly cause changes of competitive relationships between state and its cities, enterprises. Thus, a very important assumption made is that the importance of states as independent economic units decreases, while the importance of cities as economic units increases rapidly. Those major factors supporting this important hypothesis can be analyzed from the following.

The process of trade liberalization promoted by globalization restricts the nation-state's ability to intervene in national economy to different extents. As the study mentions earlier, flow of goods, trade flows, etc., all over the world, which constitutes contemporary globalization, are realized through intra-industry or intra-firm trade, with its ways and space of trade more complex than the traditional "single" pattern of trade between producing countries and consuming countries. In this process, the choice of production and trade partners is often guided by the company's strategy behavior, and thus less subject to the impact of national factors. Not only that, in the process of trade liberalization, various types of cross-border coordinating body come into being, such as the World Trade Organization at the global level and the North American Free Trade Agreement (NAFTA) and the European Union at the regional level. The relevant tariffs, subsidies, and other non-tariff barriers and treaties developed by these cross-border coordinating organizations lead to relative decline in influences of each nation-state on its domestic industries, regions, and other areas.

In addition, in the process, new changes such as the outward transfer of new technology-based industrial organization and economic policy liberalization have taken place. In this situation, the basic assumptions, based on state-centered spatial relationships emphasized by the traditional international trade theory, disinter some increasingly apparent fatal flaws, and hence the country factors in explaining contemporary international merchandise trade become more and more unimportant.

In relation to this, with the rapid expansion of international investment and diversification, cross-border mergers and acquisitions have increasingly become the main way of its global expansion. In the 1980s, the greenfield investment was a major way to enter the international market. After the mid-1990s, the new cross-border M&A investment begin to replace building new enterprises, becoming the main way to enter the international market. According to statistics of World Investment Report 2000, the value of M&A completed each year increases less than US $100 billion in 1987 and increased up to US $720 billion in 1999. The proportion of cross-border mergers and acquisitions in FDI flows in the world increases from 52% in 1987 up to 83% in 1999 (UNCTAD, 2000). The scale of cross-border mergers and acquisitions in 2005 remained at US $716 billion, accounting for nearly 80% of the world's US $916 billion FDI. The multinational companies or global companies rapidly expand the scale of their global operations through mergers and acquisitions and break the boundaries of the country when allocating resources, relying more on the world's major cities for their expansion. That is, the control and management of the international production and service activities of multinational or global companies mainly concentrate in certain big cities, and global corporations use them as important nodes to form a global production and service network. Especially, global companies locate world's major cities, completely breaking the concept of the home country (usually headquartered in the home country). For example, Sony Ericsson jointly ventured by Japan's Sony and Sweden's Ericsson doesn't headquarter in Japan and Sweden, but in London, while its research and development centers are located in Sweden, Japan, the US, Britain, and China, and manufacturing and procurement centers are located in China. Another example is the world steel giant, Mittal Steel, making a fortune in India, registering in the Netherlands and headquartering London, with its production facilities located in 27 countries worldwide. The development model of these multinational or global companies leads to new changes the global distribution of the world's wealth and updates the division of geographical border of center–periphery, showcasing a strongly changing distribution of the world urban system, urban functions, and the nature of urban life. This gradually adjusts the traditional production factors' role in promoting city economic development and makes the driving force of urban development and its elements more complex, thus challenging the traditional industrial location theory (Chen and Pin, 2000).

In the accelerating process of globalization, another significant change is the emergence of new large-scale global financial flows. In the past 20 years, with the development of economic globalization and financial liberalization, the developed countries and developing countries began to phase out most of restrictive measures of capital markets. Advances in communications and computer-related technology impelled the global FDI and foreign portfolio investment (FPI) to face continuous improvement of investment environment, and hence global capital flows increased year by year. According to IMF statistics, the global flows of FDI and FPI in 1990 were US $20.1 billion and US $25.1 billion, respectively, but in 2000, increased to US $1509.2 billion and US $1494.4 billion, increasing by 74.1 times and 58.5 times, respectively. In 2001, due to cyclical factors of multinational M&A, the global FDI dropped to US $797.8 billion, while global FPI remained essentially unchanged, at US $1.3005 trillion. In 2002, the global FDI further declined to US $650 billion and FPI also declined little, at US $1.0382 trillion.[2] These large-scale global financial flows also greatly weakened the status of national factors, dramatically changing the spatial relationship between economic activities.

In short, under the driving forces of globalization, the role of "nation" elements becomes a little weaker than before, and the gravity of its power moves down to the city. As Campell, of the World Bank Urban Development Headquarters pointed out, the world's trend is that the focus of decision-making power in various countries moves down, and a large extent of the power and public expenditure transfer from the central government to urban local governments. The decision-making scale of the urban local government is enlarged, and a considerable part of the public expenditure and decision-making power of urban development has been handed over to the city, which adds to policy levers and financial levers local governments can use. In terms of local taxation and land policy, the urban local governments have greater decision-making power than in the past. Foreign trade rights are being moved to the local, private-sector companies, leading to a substantial increase in urban local-government-led trade. The future direction of the city has basically is under the control of local government, with the central governments' intervention significantly reduced (Yu *et al.*, 2001).

[2] IMF, Balance of Payment Statistics (2002, 2004).

There are still differences in the view that globalization weakens the importance of the state as an economic actor, but most generally agree with this view. Therefore, an increasing number of researchers begin to turn their attention to the city, viewing it as an independent economic unit of the global economy. Kresl and Gappert (1995) notes that the city has the ability to operate basic resources and attract global investment, and this feature is very suitable for a highly competitive global economy. In a sense, the strength of the city often represents the strength of the state; international competition among countries has largely been specific to inter-regional competition, with city as the core (Hao, 2002).

In fact, in the accelerating process of globalization, the importance of cities (especially big cities) increasingly highlights this scenario. This is not accidental, but has inherent logic.

It is known that globalization is originated in regional economic expansion, and thus economic globalization geographically generates a complex duality: high degree of geographical isolation and high-degree of global integration in economic activity. As a result, this has led to a need to control and manage highly decentralized economic activities. Cities, especially big cities with unique location advantages are undoubtedly the best spatial nodes to implement such control and management, which determines that the phenomenon of globalization seems to be particularly obvious in the assembly points of regional economy — the city. In this process, the function, organization, and architecture of these increasingly globalized cities will also undergo dramatic changes. For example, the service industries gradually replace the manufacturing industries and become the pillar of urban industrial development and the level of innovation becomes a decisive factor of urban development, making the city into an innovation base. At the same time, the cities also become the centers of consumption and product sales. Through a series of qualitative changes, these cities will gradually evolve into main nodes in the global economic network structure.

Overall, globalization has increasingly highlighted the importance of the city as an economic unit, which does not mean that the city is a simple passive recipient of globalization, or that it passively accepts single globalization, an angle which is seriously neglected, or studied from a one-sided perspective, by the existing studies. Large numbers of research literatures on globalization usually assumes that globalization is a changing process in which local differences or local characteristics are eliminated but do not explain clearly why and how to eliminate local characteristics. The conclusion in this assumption must be derived: all cities can only have the same development model in the process of globalization, namely, they are bound to develop by the same model. In fact, in the process of globalization, there exists a very complex relationship between the global and the local; different regions and cities are involved into the process of globalization in different forms and intensity. Therefore, the understanding of globalization calls for an urgent transformation from an unconstrained phenomenal perspective to the theory based on time and space (Short *et al.*, 2000). It is very important for the study to make a comprehensive and accurate understanding of the relationship between globalization and urbanization, and the urban transformation and development in the process of globalization. What time- and space-based concept of globalization emphasizes is: the process of globalization is a kind of flow from different regions to the world and vice versa. A good example is the increase in types of national dishes, as well as the emergence of a variety of mixed dishes. Also, the process of globalization results from external stimulation, and the city's self-change is one of its stimuli. That is, the city changes in the process of globalization, in turn promoting the development of globalization, making it rise to a new level, which is the so-called reglobalization. Some scholars point out that reglobalization is sometimes based on the form of the city itself. In this sense, there are similarities between the globalization and the reglobalization of the city. What the city is experiencing is reglobalization rather than globalization (Short *et al.*, 2000). Therefore, the development of cities in the process of globalization, especially the formation and development of global cities, characterize the interaction with the globalization process, and in the process of interaction, their own development models and characteristics take shape.

2.2. Wave of Informatization and Cities "Space of Flows"

Since the 1980s, informatization brought about by the new technological revolution with information technology as the core is expanding all over the world through its extensive application and network effects. This new information and communication technologies and rapid air and sea transport lead to possibility of mankind's overcoming geographical constraints and reintegrating mankind's activities together. However, the disappearance of distance does not mean that there no longer exist differences between location models or leads to the disappearance of cities because, although a lot of information can be spread via cable or by the way of low cost in an instant, there is no possibility that a lot of tacit knowledge is transmitted through the encoding, for many activities can be completed only through face to face communication. As a result, there coexists spatial centralization as well as decentralization of human activity and residence at the same time. However, the centralization is not in the usual sense but is based on mobile spaces.

2.2.1. *Informatization is a major driving force of urbanization and urban development*

Historically, the city has always been an information gathering and exchange center. Because the city's basic function is to coordinate economic activities, information dominates various coordinating ways. Whether coordinating trade activities or coordinating research and innovation, product, finance, and all forms of goods, services, labor, capital, and land markets, information as a coordinating means is essential, which determines that the city must be the main place where information is gathered and exchanged. It is observable that information has been playing the primary role in cities from the ancient times till present. It is basically agreed that the city acts as the main center of the exchange and dissemination of information, even in the 19th century, when industrial expansion reached its peak (Hohenberg and Lees, 1995).

It is known that production, distribution, and flow of information resources follow the law of non-equilibrium operation. Research shows that the information index is significantly correlated to per capita income and urbanization index, whose regression line is a slightly upward curve. That is, the higher the level of a country or city's urbanization, the higher its per capita income, which is more conducive to the acceleration of normalization. What is more prominent is that, due to the role of the economy (e.g., trade), polity, and somewhat less important factors such as geography, culture, and history, a big city is often where highly concentrated information is originated and sent but also where the per capita supply and per capita consumption of information are relatively high. In short, informatization is strongly dependent on cities, especially large cities. At the background of informatization, the modern city is not only a point where material, energy, capital, and talent of its regions are highly concentrated but is also where production, communication, release, and delivery of all kinds of information are highly aggregated.

Informatization makes the decentralization of activity possible, but the law of gathering still remains valid. If Weber's classical industrial location model (traditional interpretation of raw materials and market concentration) is applied to the advanced service industry, it is an observable phenomenon that the flow and processing of information will be concentrated in some locations. The British Government Affairs in London has carried out a study of four cities of the world, showing a large number of information activities concentrated in four main areas:

(1) financial and business services, including banking and insurance, legal, accounting, advertising, public relations, and other business services as well as construction, civil engineering, industrial design, and fashion design;
(2) management and control, involving national governments and institutions, international agencies and multinational corporation headquarters, and other institutions;
(3) creative industries and cultural industries, including live performances, museums, art galleries, exhibitions, print and electronic media;

(4) tourism, including business and leisure travel (hotels, restaurants, bars, entertainment and transport services). All of these service industries with generation, transmission, and consumption of information as the core, due to the characteristics of immediacy and face to face communication of information activities, often are influenced by such a strong agglomerating force that they tend to be highly concentrated in some major cities. In other words, a lot of information activities are concentrated in the heart of some major cities. Large amounts of information are highly concentrated at some point a degree of aggregation, which seems that precious metals are successfully mined in a big mine (Hall, 1999).

Correspondingly, there is a significant "urban preference" in the geographical distribution of Internet activity (Gorman, 2002). When people make cross-regional electronic transactions using the Internet, the spatial distance does not work, but the location factors are still under consideration as for the layout of the Internet (Leamer and Storper, 2001). In fact, under the consideration of the economic interests, the Internet companies are bound to make the infrastructure of the Internet as close as possible to centers of production and consumption of information, and the size of the two as consistent as possible. Thus, by direct global and local connection, the location choice of emerging electronic infrastructure keeps pace with the original global city network (Graham, 1999). That is, the Internet activities still strongly depend on the city, especially large cities. For example, Malecki (2000) have found that the Internet network tends to locate the world cities around the world using the Internet backbone network bandwidth and the number of networks and other data in major cities worldwide. Moss and Townsend (1998) analyze changes of density of American cities' domain name in 1994–1997, finding that the growth of the city's domain name is correlated to its position in the national urban system, with growth of the city as the modern service center being the fastest.

In turn, the dependence of informatization also entrusts big cities with unique comparative advantages and has enormous impacts on the cities' development. Generally, informatization prepares new resources dependency for the city's economic and social development, which answers the question as to how the city carries out economic and social sustainable developments under the conditions of growing scarcity of natural resources. That is, the modern city, for the sake of its sustainable development, primarily depends on not natural resources but knowledge and information resources. The natural resource is only a necessary condition for the survival of the urban economy, but the city's economic development is promoted by knowledge and information resources. In economic development, if modern cities can make full use and exert their comparative advantage of knowledge and information resources, the economic instability that occurs in the competition for allocation of scarce resources will be significantly changed, showing the apparent regularity and trends of increasing returns rate. Therefore, in terms of modern urban development, knowledge accumulation and information transmission look even more important.

At the same time, the wave of informatization triggered by technology is rapidly changing the city's polity, economy, culture, landscape, and other aspects. For example, "electronic government", "EC", and "distance education" begin to appear, and the city's comprehensive information network also gradually takes shape. These new forces are quickly re-shaping and combining the original factors of city. On one hand, informatization strengthens and speeds up the accumulation and spread of matter, talent, technology, and capital, which further significantly strengthens the city's comprehensive functionality, resulting in the formation of the cross-border division of labor and separating location of different links in manufacturing industry chain. On the other hand, the city's function in the traditional industrial age has resulted in the city experiencing a profound change accordingly, playing a role by changing the city's land use rules or spatial pattern, making the city's development move toward the direction of adaptation of its production and lifestyle to the information society. It is also worthwhile to note that advances of information and communication technology enables a variety of "flow" to connect distant regions together and causes a revolution in trade, including fundamental changes in ways of inner-country and intra-country links, exchange, and interaction, which makes an important prerequisite for development of the mega-city (McGee, 1991), but also lays a solid foundation for the formation of the global city.

Obviously, informatization has become one of the important driving forces of urbanization and urban development. In this context, the pace of development of information technology is nonlinear so all the cities that have entered informatization age will grow faster and faster, showing the trend of accelerating development, and ultimately established the status of main information hubs and nodes, which help develop into global cities. Those cities that are not able to keep up with the trend of informatization will inevitably stagnate or decline and eventually become "forgotten cities", which is called "one backward step loses the whole game".

2.2.2. *The space of urban flow*

The more specific meaning many changes resulting from informatization gives the city is: a powerful capacity of information collection, processing, transmission, and regeneration transforms the city into an indispensable network node of international life networks. Aristotle once said that people flock to cities in order to survive, striving to live a better life after living in the city. In the past 2,500 years or so, the city did give full play to this role. But in the first 10 years of the 21st century, urban life is about to change. In the future, the city will not be the place where people live a better life, but the train station people pass through seeking a better life. The city is the intersection of population, information, finances, and goods. Once the city becomes a transfer station for international traffic, it will become an international center with a wide variety of activities, which are, most of the time, based on the knowledge industry.

Therefore, in the process of informatization, what is more important is the introduction of a new urban form, that is, informatization city. This informatization city is knowledge-based, organized around the network, and composed in part by the flow. It is not a form, but a process. In the process, the interactivity among local areas, which is subjected to much attention, breaks the spatial patterns of behavior, replaced by a mobile switching network. That is, functionally, urban space increasingly surmounts the physical proximity and becomes interrelated. For example, the city's new industrial space will be composed around the flow of information. According to different cycles and companies, these flows converge and disperse other regional components at the same time. And as the logic of information technology manufacturing trickles down from the producers of information technology devices to the users of such devices in the whole realm of manufacturing, so the new spatial logic expands, creating a multiplicity of global industrial networks whose intersections and exclusions transform the very notion of industrial location from factory sites to manufacturing flows (Castells, 1996, p. 393). Among these, the most critical are: the logic of urban space changes, from the local space into a space of flows. Space of flows became the space show of the dominant power and function in our society. Moreover, this is a global "space of flows". Castells thinks that, in the informatization process, "our society is constructed around flows":

> Flows are not just one element of the social organization: they are the expression of processes dominating our economic, political, and symbolic life. If such is the case, the materially support of the dominant processes in our societies will be the ensemble of elements supporting such flows, and making materially possible their articulation in simultaneous time. Thus, I propose the idea that there is a new spatial from characteristic of social practices that dominate and shape the network society: the space of flows. The space of flows is the material organization of time-sharing social practices that work through flows

The characteristics of urban space of flows are expressed by the establishment of functional connections across broad regions and existence of distinct geographical discontinuities. In this "space of flows", the interaction between cities is not limited by their physical distance, because the proximity between the nodes is not a necessary condition for the network structure and composition. On the contrary, empirical evidence shows that the geographical dispersion of the network structure brings greater efficiency (Kilkenny, 2000). Therefore, this "space of flows" makes a range of social and cultural mobility become more apparent. Appadurai proposes five major categories of mobility:

(1) technology, produced by the spread and flow of technology, software and equipment of multinational corporations, international organizations and government agencies;
(2) finance, produced by the rapid flows of capital, currency and portfolio, and expressed not only in the geographical concentration of financial services personnel but also in rapid changes in the location of capital inflows and outflows;
(3) the crowd, produced by flows from business people and foreign workers, tourists, migrants, and refugees;
(4) the media, generated from flows of the images and information passing through print media, television, movies, channels;
(5) concept, generated from the spread of ideas. Knox (2002) adds a kind to the above-mentioned, that is,
(6) commodities, generated by movement of products and services (with taste and characteristics of international brands and fashion) the high-end consumers are interested in. These flows are important to the global space organizations; just like rare materials, industrial products are important to the early capital accumulation.

Obviously, this "space of flows" essentially differs from space organization with long historical origin, and jointly experienced by us, namely, space of places. In the past urban development, this space of places is the spatial display of the dominant power and function in our society. Castells thinks that the place is a locale, whose form, function, and meaning are self-contained within the boundaries of physical proximity (Castells, 1996). Economic mobility often starts, concentrates, and diffuses on specific geographical areas or places with relatively fixed boundaries. This city based on space of places further characterizes visible producing or trading places or sites features.

Of course, in the process of informatization, the conversion logic of urban space does not completely deny the existence of space or places, still less meaning "the end of geographical position". Because the space of flows is built on electronic networks, which is connected to specific places, which has a complete definition of the society, culture, physical environment and functional properties. There does not exist a space of absolutely abstract service in cities and their networks. On the contrary, there are multifaceted geographical positions in the world, in which the city acts as a basic point of global capital flows. In this sense, a single global city represents key "area-globe" connections, and the world regions also represent "area-globe" connections in real geographical spaces. However, in this network, no place is capable of independently existing, because the position is defined by the flow and exchange in the network. Therefore, the appearance of space of flows is: place does not disappear, but the logic and meaning of place has been absorbed into the network. That is, the functions and powers of our society are organized in space of flows, the structural domination of whose logic is fundamentally changing the meaning and form of place. Although where the high-end centers of each period really locate is important to the distribution of the world's wealth and power, what is more important is the ability of the network modifications from the spatial logic of the new system.

The central city based on "space of place", in fact, is the network node of information transmission. Therefore, various high-level management and service institutions usually accumulate in these information nodes. Information, like a magnet, attracts economy to concentrate in these node cities, while information technology makes these node cities obtain a strong control over the coverage scope of information network. Combined with the interaction effect between information technology development and investment, node cities are of extraordinary significance (Pelton, 1992). They usually become the best sites of various multinational company headquarters and service companies. Thus, the city positioning in the global city system is not based on any model in the past, but only according to the information economy. The positioning of the city depends on its ability to create, process, and exchange information, in particular, quite professional information, which is always dependent on face to face communications (Hall, 1997).

In addition, the "space of flows" brings distant locations together through the telecommunications network and transportation network and integrates them into the global space, but again separating these locations from the other nearby locations in metropolitan areas, so the metropolitan areas' population and activities are highly decentralized along the transport axis and the entire metropolitan system features spatial sprawls (the formation of extended metropolitan areas) and the operation of network communications in the so-called the space of flows within metropolitan area. As Batten points out, in the information environment, a new type of urban form — network city — emerges in response to the requirement of the changing times. It is a collection of multicenter cities based on rapid transportation and communication networks and economies of scope, and full of more creativity and competitive advantage in comparison with the traditional central cities (Battern, 1993).

Therefore, the unprecedented "super convergence" (Tapscott *et al.*, 1999) resulting from the process of the world's informatization, in particular, large-scale internetization is causing reorganization of the original spatial pattern of resource centralization and diffusion, and transformation from the traditional "core and periphery" structure in to the vertical "global and local" structure, which leads to the emergence of a multilevel global city network. The development potential of space of flows–based global city will depend on: first, whether or not it could makes the node, density, and efficiency of all the physical entity (i.e., infrastructure) network linked to every quarter of the globe; the second is whether or not it could play a role in the global exchange of population, knowledge, capital, goods, and services in the invisible world's network system; third is whether or not it has innovation and adaptation ability to continuously develop potential synergies inherent in the network and set a superior style (Batten, 1993).

2.3. Information City and the Change of the World City System

The interaction between globalization and informatization makes more and more cities involved in global economic relations, resulting in the globalized city based on network structure, which leads to fundamental changes in the world urban system. The mainstream of the global city theory directly derives simple logic of global cities from globalization and informatization, which is not consistent with the above-mentioned and has bigger flaws in theory. Therefore, it is necessary to reconstruct the logic relationships of formation and development of globalization, informatization, and the global city, laying the theoretical foundations the study of globalizing cities.

2.3.1. *Changes of the world urban system from globalization and informatization*

The two major trends of globalization and informatization described above, in fact, interact. The new technological revolution, with information technology as the representative, becomes the technical support of economic globalization, causing global linkages being strengthened to an unprecedented extent, it is by means of electronic information technology, transport, and the network that the worldwide (except for some African countries) economic, political, and cultural exchanges pushed forward by the global trade and the internationalization of investment and production by multinational or global companies, and finance-dominated economic integration increasingly develop to an unprecedented extent. In turn, it is by means of the global flow of resources and factors that the extensive use of modern information technology and its internetization get popularized.

Differing from the mainstream global city theory, which only examines the relationship between globalization and global cities, what the study emphasizes here is that globalization and informatization not only create a few global cities but also have a significant impact on other cities. In the process of globalization, many cities through the capital flow, labor flow, goods flow, and service flow have relationships with the global city network. The emergency of these factors flow, goods, and services flow may result from the company's technical and organizational innovation, dealing with non-equilibrium relationship between market forces and strategic behavior at the supranational, national, regional, and local levels. Similarly, in the process of information, the exchange of information between the cities has also led to more complex urban systems. For this reason, some scholars question the relevance between Internet and the original global urban system. For example, Zook (2001) analyzes the dynamic mechanism production and consumption of global network information markets by presenting distribution pattern of Internet domain names in the global major cities through diagrams, and finally questioning: is the global urban system in information society "the old hierarchy or the new network?" Townsend (2001) finds that this new communication technology-promoted international connection between cities differs from the previous system in the analysis of the global Internet backbone network structure and spatial accessibility, meaning that more cities in different ways join the network, that is, some of the new "networking city" is on the rise. In this sense, the process of globalization and informatization leads to the majority of cities being, actively or passively, integrated into the global economic relationship. In this case, every city will become an integral part of the global system, being not only both the producer and market of goods and services worldwide but also the central link in the flow of personnel, capital, technology, information, and knowledge. Of course, the scale of the flow is different, so is its traffic volume passing through the central link. But the smaller size and lower traffic volume of global factors and goods does not mean that the city lacks the close ties with the world. As Marcuse and van Kempen (2000) point out, the process of globalization have a significant impact on all cities. Like the adjacent major cities, some "medium cities" also inevitably respond to the trend of globalization (Knox, 1996). Therefore, globalization and informatization not only create a handful of global cities but also necessarily entails the involvement of more cities in the world.

In short, the interaction between globalization and informatization result in:

(1) continuous enhancement of economic, cultural and political relationships between the global and the local;
(2) increasing reduction of role of nations as factors, and the increasing prominency of importance of cities as spatial carriers of global production and service networks. These double results jointly determine a new urban form, that is, the globalized city.

These globalized cities emerging in the interaction of globalization and informatization are directly involved in the global economy, becoming important international stages and the concept of integration into the global framework. At the same time, the globalized city's role in connecting the international economy and domestic economy will also be enhanced, thereby making it capable of more effectively promoting the development of human capital, organizations, and institutions that play a critical role. Therefore, these global cities are different from the average city in the past, and their main characteristics are:

(1) possessing high concentration of international activities;
(2) being internationalization-oriented, export-oriented;
(3) acting as the global network node with a high degree of external correlation. The global city is the general term for all cities included in the global city network, including global cities, globalizing cities, global cities, and general cities involved in globalization. That is, the globalized city is a broader concept; the global city being is just one part of it.

So, how do these globalized cities interact? This question will make people naturally think of the inner-city linkages within the nation, that is, so-called "national city hierarchy" mode. Do worldwide linkages between cities present a "world city hierarchy" like the way the "national city hierarchy" shows? It seems that the existing empirical evidence does not prove this conjecture. The traditional hierarchical structure's role is only limited in the concept of the global economy. Thus, the relationship among the globalized cities is a kind of relationship of the global city network with the "global–local" vertical links as the principle, completely changing the old world city system with the "central place" hierarchy system as the main framework. In the new world city system, these globalized cities are the nodes of the global city network. However, there are differences in the importance of the nodes, that is, the global city is central (basic) node of the world city network, and the other globalized cities are normal nodes. The specific content of globalized cities and relating city network systems will be elaborated in the next chapter.

2.3.2. *Theoretic defects in the mainstream global city study*

From the viewpoint of economic globalization, Friedmann and Sassen's "world/global city" hypothesis makes use of basic features of the concentration of multinationals' headquarters or international professional services companies in major cities when the production is globally spreading to explain the "world/global city", thus elaborating the logical relationship between economic globalization and global cities. However, this logical relationship ignores the important role of globalization and informatization in getting most cities actively or passively involved in the global economic relationship, and thus aid in their transformation into globalized cities.

The mainstream global city theory derives a simple logic of the global city, seeing economic globalization as a direct explanatory variable, which does not match the actual situation where globalization and informatization-led transformation of the world city system forces the disintegration of many cities into the globalized cites and into the global city network. This theoretic defect largely limits perspective and scope of its research and seriously impedes the deepening of the theory, leading to more controversy and criticism.

First, the simple use of globalization as the variable in explaining the formation and development of global cities makes the academes' attention of research concentrated in just a few global cities, that is, high-level cities in the world city hierarchy, with many other important cities are excluded. For example, Friedmann (1995) puts forward only 18 core and 12 semi-peripheral world cities, but not including more important cities in the world city hierarchy. Of course, the reason is lack of sufficient data, but mainly results from its theoretical framework.

Second, the mainstream research tends to separate global cities from the general city and excludes the general cities but pays more attention to the established global city, making an isolated or separated empirical analysis on them or static comparative study. At the same time, the mainstream research pays no attention to how the global city grows up, and then excludes the study of the globalizing city.

Third, because of no good explanation of the impact of as globalization and informatization on the world city system, so the world city hierarchy originated with Friedmann follows, to a large extent, the "national urban system" paradigm, constructing the hierarchal model among major cities from traditional functionalism (constructivism). However, observations drawn from the analysis shows that even the cities within a state do not mechanically form just a simple hierarchal model (Pred, 1977). From the transnational point of view, a simple hierarchal model becomes even more unreasonable (Taylor, 1997). Moreover, what is needed for the definition of the city hierarchy is not only the "importance" or the size and other factors but also "a number of factors" (Lukermann, 1966).

In response to the theoretical defects of this mainstream view, some scholars point out that globalization/urban studies should be extended to the relationship among the cities in the world and not just be limited to those global cities in existence, transferring the attention from the empirical measurement of the level of "global city" to the discussion of the impact of globalization on all cities (Short *et al.*, 2000). In order to find a wider understanding of the globalization city, Grant (1999) and Grant and Nijman (2000), based on the study of Africa and India, propose respectively the concept "gateway city" by which to illustrate the fact that almost all of the city can serve as channels of spreading economic, political, and cultural globalization, They make detailed analysis of how globalization affects the city by studying these channels. And even individual scholars understand and define the global city network from a broad perspective, such as, Townsend (2001a) proposes the Internet space allocation–based new "city network" system. Such nodes of Internet activities are distributed in more extensive information production areas than the global city hypothesis expects and are not entirely concentrated in a few global cities. Given information transmitters and some major information users all locate these important nodes, new employment opportunities will arise in these node cities, which are not included in the original research on global cities.

2.3.3. *Reconstruction of the internal logic of formation and development of globalization, informatization, and global city*

The study believes that fundamental changes in the world city system brought about by the interaction between globalization and informatization is essential. The products of these changes is the globalized cities based on the network structure, covering the existing global cities, globalizing cities, and general cities involved into globalization. That is, the global city is a special type of the globalized city based on the network structure, but there are many other forms, such as the globalizing city and the general globalized city.

Different from the mainstream global city hypothesis' direct derivation of the simple logical relationship among global cities from globalization and informatization, the logical relationship the study builds is "globalization, Informatization — changes in the world urban system (based on the global city network) — different types of cities including global cities, globalizing cities and general cities involved into globalization". Among them, the changes in the world urban system are important intermediate explanatory variables. In fact, only in the changes of the world urban system, can the global city get a complete description. Because in the context of the interaction of globalization and informatization, if the fundamental changes of the number of cities after their involvement into globalization and informatization are neglected, then a very real question to ask is: whether or not the formation of global cities and the significant changes of other cities are related? Due to the lack of this important explanatory variable, namely, the change of the world urban system, Friedmann and Sassen's "world/global city hypothesis" does not give a complete theoretical answer. In contrast, through introduction of the important intermediate explanatory variable, the study can explain clearly the logical relationship among the global cities, the globalizing cities, and the general globalized cities; that is, in the relationship based on structure, it is in the global city network that the global city finds a foothold and reflects its role and status. At the same time, the globalizing city, as a special form derived from changes of the world city system, is entirely relegated to the background of interaction between globalization and informatization and can be included within the analytical framework the study builds.

Therefore, reconstruction of the logic not only build the linkages among global cities, globalizing cities, and general cities (so that global cities and globalizing cities can get a more convincing explanation when placed in global city networks) but also help to more accurately reveal the dual properties of the general city (both global and local). More importantly, the use of changes in the world city system as an important explanatory variable will help the study to combine the diversity and characteristics of the global city with its dynamic process, grasping its different types in existence from the specific background, conditions and process in growing up, and further extend the research coverage to those globalizing cities.

Chapter 3

Global City Networks and Their Nodes

The previous chapter derives the proposition of the globalized city based on network structure from the background of globalization and informatization but does not specifically discuss this proposition. The global city network, covering the globe and including many globalized cities, is the network infrastructure by which the highly sophisticated global city maximizes its strategic coordination functions to the fullest and the globalizing city grows, especially, the network infrastructure by which many general cities involved into globalization operate. Therefore, the global city network taking shape in the interaction of the globalized cities is a central point of the study of globalizing cities (and the world cities). Without the network infrastructure, it would be impossible to study the globalizing cities. This chapter will specifically discuss the global city network and integrate the globalizing cities into the global city network framework, revealing its basic meaning and properties from the perspective of interconnected networks.

3.1. Global City Networks and Their Features

The global city network has been involved in the study of the global city. Because in the global context, urban system changes due to the interaction between globalization and informatization, the global city naturally has no ability to exist independently without the global city network; on the contrary, its pivotal position is exactly reflected in the global city network. A correlation between detailed explanations of the global cities and the definition of "the global network of cities" has been established (King, 1990). Some scholars have proposed new conceptualized instructions of "the global network of cities" in the light of the correlation of contemporary world cities.

Unfortunately, these conceptualized instructions do not make a clear definition of the global city network. Although Castells sees the global city as the middle level of "space of flow", he does not provide any other qualitative prescription for the "global city network". Because of the lack of definition of the global city network, the existing studies are incapable of making a detailed analysis of how the global city network operates, including its nodes, links between nodes, and how they form as a whole, and are incapable of determining its extension. Obviously, this is easy to produce a variety of ambiguities when understanding the global city network.

A more crucial problem is that these global city network studies focus on the analysis of the relationship between global cities, and the relationship among cities is more closely related to global cities from the perspective of the global city. That is, most researches that are put forward and empirically analyze the global city network are presented from the perspective of the global city. King (1990) originally put forward the concept "the global city network" to describe new forms of organization in which the "command center", caused by the activities of transnational corporations and acted by the global cities, plays the control and command role in the "new international division of labor". Later, Sassen's (1994) "transnational urban system", Lo and Yeung's (1998) "functional world city system", and Short and Kim's (1999) "global urban network" are basically the continuation of this idea. Therefore, these studies seriously neglected those general globalized cities with weak links and more extensiveness, which in fact is equal to exclusion of them from the global city network. These are related to the fact that the mainstream global city theory directly derives the simple logic from globalization and informatization and excludes the other cities.

Based on reconstruction of the logic between the interaction of globalization and informatization and the globalized cities, the study believes that the global city network does not mean that it belongs to "the global city", that is, it is constructed from the connections among some global cities. The global city network is formed by interknitting of all cities (globalized cities) involved in the process of globalization. In addition to global cities, the global city network also includes many other cities involved in the process of globalization and contact with other cities in the world through the various factor flow, goods flow, and services flow. In the global city network, every city with outside links is a network node and exists as part of the network. This concept of "node" means continuous interaction between cities. Although the degree of connection among these cities is different (or strong or weak), they are connected to the global city network.

It is natural to conduct a network analysis of the global city network. However, after having introduced the global city network for quite some time, what many scholars come up with is simply conceptual description, not really network analysis. There exists only the taxonomy analysis concerning "flow" before Smith and Timberlake (1995) promotes the use of network analysis as a "rigorous approach conceptualizing the theory". Only in recent years are Taylor and other researchers carrying out pioneering work on the basis of previous studies, making a theoretic analysis of the global city network.

In the full sense, the global city network is based on the relationship between the physical and non-physical properties. The former includes transportation, communications, and other infrastructure networks, whereas the latter includes trade, exchange, organizations, and other social networks. Clearly, infrastructure networks play an important and necessary role in supporting the global city network. However, social relations of the global city network present economic properties; particularly, the inner-city relationship constructs the world economy geographically (Taylor, 2001), and so its importance as a social network, as a form of organization, is of more concern and is thereby stressed. As a social network, the nodes of the global city network are operational units, and their connection is social.

It is noteworthy that, differing from general social network, the global city network is of its own peculiarities. Typically, the object most social networks analyze is individuals within the smaller-scale organization, and the global city network is a huge organization. But this is not enough to lead to the particularity of the global city network because the international nation-state system is also considered a social network with an even greater scale. Basically, the difference between the global city network and the general social network is that operational units of the former have their particularity.

It is known that a social network is generally defined as a node-composing unit level, but the activities of the operational units as nodes determine the connection itself. If the standard is used to study the global city, its network-operating system level corresponds to the world economy, while the node-composing unit level to the city itself. But the problem is the city itself is just a space environment, rather than an action unit. If there is no series of related activities of the corresponding action unit, the connection between cities isn't to set up, and thereby, the statement that the city acts as a network node will no longer exist. As it were, inner-city connections are achieved through the activities of the city government. Indeed, the city government as an action unit exercises its powers, such as establishing and implementing relevant policies, but most such activities that affect the urban environment itself, such as improving the city's investment environment or business environment, cannot affect connections among cities themselves. Although intergovernmental agreement or cooperation can also lead to individual or partial connections cities, it is impossible to achieve all the connections among cities. Different from individuals, the national governments, in the exercise of sovereignty, play a major role in other social networks, and the city government cannot be reasonably interpreted as the key players of network production and reproduction. Because of this, the global city network has become the social network, which is special and difficult to define.

However, as a network, the operational units of the node are indispensable. So, what are the operational units or critical roles of the global city network? According to Friedmann's concept that world cities act as the control and command centers, its key role is to serve as the base of multinationals, with the city itself being only the location or place where the control and command decisions are implemented. In this sense, transnational corporations' intra-city and cross-city actions or activities makes the city a network node, and the collective efforts of the global company's decision (not the city decision-makers) mold the global city network. Sassen's global city concept, in fact, talks about the "global service center" (that is, the center to satisfy financial and other business needs) composed of a group of offices of the specific high-end producer services, one of the most important features of which is providing advanced producer services. That is, these producer services highly concentrate their business or activities in certain areas of major cities both in order to produce good "cluster" effect, and in order to have a wealth of information for their effective operation, so as to stay leading in business activities. But the former does not necessarily make them concentrate in one or two cities with such "great service centers"; it is precisely the latter that will inevitably make them concentrate in those cities covering major regions and provide these services to the world. And, the development of modern information technology and network enables them to run as cross-border networks and provide seamless services for their company customers around the world (Porteous, 1999). According to Friedmann and Sassen's basic point of view on the world/global city formation, the primary role in the global city network formation is multinational companies and large global service companies, not the city itself.

The city itself should become the node level of the city network, but the city network node level cannot directly be defined by the city itself, which leads to a dilemma. To solve this problem, Taylor and others add a sub-node level composed of sophisticated producer service companies to the node level, thereby constructing the global city network which is internally interconnected and made up from three levels (see Figure 3.1), among them, being the world economy in which the network operates to spread services; the city in which knowledge is concentrated in order to facilitate the production of services; and the global service company, which produces services. The integration of these three levels can be formally defined as a service activity resulting to matrix *S*, which is qualified by the *n* cities and

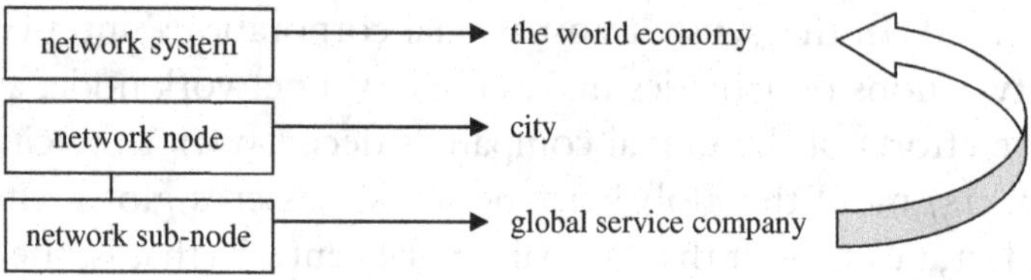

Figure 3.1. The Global City Network Structure.

m companies and composed of *s ij*, activities by company *j* in the city *i*. Therefore, this matrix, each column *j* represents the location strategy of the company *j*, and each row *i* represents comprehensive services provided by the city *i*.

In network analysis, this three-level structure is more special and is a type of network of boundary penetration and interlinkage. In these interlocking networks, all linked with one another, the city node is joined through the second-level node factors (producer service companies). That is, in the inner-city interlinkage of the world economy, the nodes (cities) themselves constitute an important promoting environment but not a key decision-making hierarchy in the three-level structure. The city government can design "promoting" policy to attract and retain the "leader" company, thus affecting the relationship between the nodes but cannot control the network relationship. In this three-level structure, multinational corporations and global service companies are the first operational units.

In the global city network, that multinational and global service companies become the primary units of action is determined by the special nature of their business or activities. The nature of the "control and management" activity by multinational corporations is universally known, so the study here analyzes the major characteristics of the global service company's activities. The producer service companies which are highly concentrated in the major cities, because their clients (companies) have expanded globally, have no choice but to adapt to provide global services, and need to keep abreast of when and where to provide the necessary services to their customers. Of course, they can also have another option, which is to outsource the companies' foreign business counterparts in other cities. However, in practice, this does not seem feasible for the producer service company, because in a field of processing information and knowledge, to create a service brand and maintain its brand integrity is very important, and largely determines its competitiveness. This has led to the necessity that large companies establish their own office networks in major cities in the world to in order to provide global services. The IT technology builds a new space relationship, which makes it likely to form new relationships between the enterprise and the market and is an important medium for enterprises to participate in global and local markets, but in a competitive market, local market information and close customer relationships are becoming increasingly important, so companies find it necessary to set up a body locally. That is, each company's success depends on its strategies of locating its offices in certain major cities. At the same time, in order to operate effectively and eclipse their competitors, the producer service companies must make their offices around the world carry out synchronizing actions, and avoid unrelated ones in global activities. This creates internal communication of all kinds of information, knowledge, ideas, plans, directives, and other aspects among them. It is this internal flow of all companies, including the flow of information, knowledge, instruction, strategies, plans, personnel, and other aspects, which provides a networking foundation. In the back of the internal links, the network relationships with broader forms, such as knowledge flow network, control network, energy networks, and cultural networks, play an important role in the formation of the inner-city relationships. In this sense, advanced producer services play a linking role in urban networks, linking up related cities through their activities.

The above-analyzed study shows that the global city service network is a complex mixture of a variety of a transnational company's office networks. So, Taylor (2001) defines the global city network as an interconnected network among cities composed of the internal flow by the advanced producer service companies in the world economy. The definition of Taylor should be supplemented by the fact that the flow of transnational corporations (its local branches) is one of the factors constituting interconnected relations among cities.

3.2. Nodes of Global City Networks

Previous analysis has shown that the global city network is a kind of page layout based on internal connections from a lot of nodes. Although the network concept has been increasingly used as a framework to explain social, economic, and spatial relationships, little attention is paid to the function of network nodes, which is, in fact, one of the core contents of the network concept. The clear understanding of the function of nodes is a precondition to fully understand the meaning of the global city network. Of course, only in the network, can the function of the nodes be revealed. Here, the study sees the globalized city as a node in order to better understand the status and special economic features of these cities in the global economy.

3.2.1. *The connectivity of network nodes*

Connectivity is the essential nature of the global city network nodes. Therefore, the importance of a city in the network depends on its relationship with other nodes and on "what are exchanged between them, rather than what they have" (Beaverstock *et al.*, 2000). In this sense, the level, frequency, and intensity of the flow among the globalized cities (nodes) determine their position in the global economy.

In fact, the exchange or flow is the inherent characteristic of the city. At any time in history, the main function of each city is to coordinate economic activity. This coordination is to facilitate the economic exchanges among the main bodies of the economy to effectively organize production, exchange, and consumption. Hohenberg and Lees (1995) think that, at least from medieval times, the city is part of the network organized to exchange personnel, goods, and information. Damette (1994) suggests that the city "provides the exchange of goods, money and information".

Gaschet and Lacour (2002) further stress that metropolises themselves are qualified by their overall capability of "attracting, organizing, filtering, and expanding a series of ever-increasing flow of goods, personnel and information". In such a coordination of economic activities, information is indeed the primary means of various forms of coordination. When the coordination depends on the exchange of information, the space externalities with important gathering effects will come into being (Guillain and Huriot, 2001). So when the city plays a role in the coordination of economic activities, it is bound to gather information and concentrate on the exchange of information.

However, as nodes of the global city network, the cities serve as interactive exchanges or flows not only for short distance but also long distance, meaning the interaction with the long-distance economic agents that live in different economic environments, with different cultures, different norms, different ways of doing things, more communication between economic agents, as well as more complex and uncertain exchanges. The increases in cities economic activities (especially long-distance cross-border trade, investment, finance and other activities) will form a network-type organization covering the traditional central location or hierarchical organization, making long-distance exchanges extended to these places far exceeding the original trade coverage. At the same time, the complexity of production and exchange calls for the combination of a large number of professional operations, a great deal of technology, a variety of high-level knowledge and skills, and in-depth use of implicit information, which further calls for the close interaction between economic agents through face to face contact. This co-existence of the short-distance and long-distance interactions of the economic activity of the globalized city is its first characteristic as a network node. More importantly, the combination of these two interactions promotes each other, thus becoming powerful causes of formation of global cities network nodes. And this constant process of accumulation leads to a locking mechanism conducive to improve the stability of the city network nodes.

Therefore, a network node city cannot simply be seen as an economic "central place" and should not be too much conceived as a place of trade, a port, a financial center, or an industrial city's role, but as a necessary component of complex networks circulating and the accumulating factors such as capital. Here, it is necessary to make a clear distinction between the city as a network node and the city as a "central place". A "central place" city is often a traditional single-center city, with the so-called central functions; the city as a network node is not isolated; it is linked with other cities to form a new multi-center city form-network city. Batten (1995) defines the network city as the city that, for the purpose of the realization of economic cooperation and to significant effects of economies of scope, two or more cities, independent of each other before, but with potentially complementary functions, evolves and forms by rapid and reliable transport and communications infrastructure. He further makes a comparative study of these creative network cities and single-center cities (also known as the central place cities), pointing out that the former has a clearer competitive advantage than the latter (see Table 3.1).

From the network point of view, the value of the city as a node lies in the correlation to other nodes. For it is the old and new contact to maintain the city and decide the city's position. Storper (1997) has put forward the concept "urban society", stressing that the city cannot exist and move toward prosperity in isolation, which is very reasonable. The more frequently a city is linked to other nodes, the more likely it gets the flow of information and knowledge, seizing opportunities for economic development through the innovation of production, distribution, and consumption. An important conclusion can

Table 3.1. Characteristics of the Network City Compared with the Single Central City.

	Central Place System	Network System
1	Centrality	Nodality
2	Size dependency	Size neutrality
3	Tendency toward primacy and subservience	Tendency toward flexibility and complementarities
4	Homogeneous goods and services	Heterogeneous goods and services
5	Vertical accessibility	Horizontal accessibility
6	Mainly one-way flows	Two-way flows
7	Transportation costs	Information costs
8	Perfect competition over space	Imperfect competition with price discrimination

Source: Batten (1995).

be directly derived from this proposition: in the global city network system, the links between the cities is the core issue of their development, which directly relates to their rise and fall. That is, over time, changes in the status of a city are determined by its interaction with other nodes. In general, the growth and development of the city is built on the basis of the extended contact; and when the city declines, the contact is also reduced. No contact with the surrounding city means its death.

It can be further inferred that, in the global city network, which the city as a node rises (or declines) doesn't necessarily results from its own material properties (such as size, facilities, material wealth, etc.). In this sense, the function of the city as a node appears to depend less on a variety of material resources, new technology, and its path dependence but more on its contacts in the city network. Of course, this does not mean that certain historical events or a special opportunity is not able to trigger the unique development process of the node as a specific region. But what can be asserted is that, in the city network structure, development opportunities of a city are more closely dependent on the interaction between strict structures and close links among nodes, rather than its own function.

Therefore, in the global city network, the most important measurement for each node is its connectivity. Taylor and others call the degree of "connection" of each city with the network the "global network connectivity". This global network connectivity can be measured by two methods: one is by calculating the size of the city as a node in the network system, represented by the number of network institutions in the city; the other is by measuring connections of these network institutions with other cities to measure the accessibility of the city network system. These measurements indicate the status and features of a city in the network system defined by the study. Taylor and others' measurement methods are of significant measurability and practicality, but confined to certain network institutions and their external connectivity, which is not enough to fully reflect a city's global network connectivity. From the theoretical analysis point of view, the relationship between the correlation among cities and their position in the network can often be measured in two dimensions: one is the correlation density, that is, the more and the more intensive the correlated levels are, the stronger the functions of absorption, transmission, and processing that the node can have, meaning the city will become more important. The other is the correlation breadth, that is, the more widespread the node links with other nodes, the stronger the interaction, meaning the node is at the more central position in the network structure. Of course, due to the lack of data or poor availability, these theoretical measures result in weak actual testability.

In short, in the global city network system, the strength and weakness of the city's links determines its energy levels. That is, the city with weaker links can only aim for a regional position and function in the region it locates; the city with stronger links can have a global status and function beyond the region in which it is located. Thus, the more extensively a city connects with the outside, the stronger is its connectivity and interoperability and the higher its energy level, meaning its position is higher in the global city network system; and vice versa. When the global spread and integration of economic activities result in space clustering of their top management and control, some large cities with good infrastructure and location, high energy levels may further evolve into the nodes where various factors extremely concentrate, thus becoming the location of global economic entities, playing a decisive role in the regional and global economic development, and increasingly dominating the global economy.

3.2.2. *The diversity of network nodes*

The basic properties of the node as the global city network are the same, and connectivity is its basic feature. However, these network nodes posses the diversity of forms, showing the different size, type, scope, weight, etc. The study of diversity of network nodes mainly reveals the different functions and status of the city in the global city network, thus helping the study further understand the definition and distinction of global cities, globalizing cities, and average globalized cities.

The issues that the nodes of the global city network involve in connection with the outside, in addition to the above-mentioned relevance density and relevance breadth, also include the relevance nature or relevance types, that is, the globe-oriented or region-oriented connection. The above-described general measurements of the city network connectivity only show the overall extent of the city's integration into the world city network, but cannot show the type of its contact. However, the nature or type of the external connection is very important for determining the significance of network nodes because the functions and status of the cities with different relevance nature or relevance types in the global city network are not the same. The node as a globe-oriented connection usually exerts a coordinating function of the global economy, being at a higher level in the network; and the node as a region-oriented connection usually plays a regional economic coordination function, being at a low level in the network.

Of course, there is some significance between the relevance and the connection. In general, external connections with higher relevance density and relevance breadth are usually connected with a relatively large range, thus more inclined to be globe-oriented; and external connections with lower relevance density and relevance breadth are usually connected with relatively small range, and are thereby having greater inclination to be region-oriented. However, there may be inconsistencies between the relevance and the connection. It is entirely possible for some region-oriented connections to form close linkage in the region, thus having higher relevance density and relevance breadth, or some globe-oriented connections are less contacted in the region, thus not necessarily having particularly high relevance density and relevance breadth.

So, based on the study of urban connection degree, Taylor further adopts technical means to determine the nature of urban connection (globe-oriented connection or region-oriented connection), thus distinguishing from the connection degree to the nature of connection. Of course, some scholars have questioned, such as Thrift (1998). He asks that "whether the idea of world cities as being in local or global space is now . . . even a sensible distinction in the contemporary world of movement, diaspora, and multiple but partial connection?" The study believes that it is still necessary to distinguish between globe-oriented and region-oriented connections in theory. The city as a global network node can indeed be divided regionally or globally in the space. Once the network structure dominates the inner-city interaction, these cities are global; on the other hand, some are regional, possessing multiple status in the global economy. However, there are some differences of the global weight or regional weight. Those cities associated with neural relevance to the global city network may bear more local features, while the cities at higher levels in the network will have a distinct specificity in the global system, so that these cities differ from their adjacent cities. In reality, it is seen that, top global cities like New York, London, and Tokyo often show their globalization through all of the activities. For example, in the UK, except London, other cities act very similarly in the globalization process, and London as a city most closely related to the global city network has completely different characteristics (Taylor and Hoyler, 2000).

Of course, these global cities have the corresponding multistatus. As Knox (2002) points out, global cities are the places where the globe and regions converge, and economic, cultural and social public service institutions in turn link national and regional resources to the global economy, and transfer the impetus of globalization to the national and regional centers. And more cities as network nodes are obviously playing multiple roles, that is, demonstrating their globalization in some economic activities though a variety of functions, with other properties displayed in particular local development path; acting as nodes in a certain network structure, but on the other hand, serving as the center of regional economic development. It is this dual potentials that give special status to the node, rather than turning it into global popularity (and homogenization) (Felsenstein *et al.*, 2003).

In addition, the nodes in the global city network also have two different types of power: control power and network power. Those cities with corporate headquarters tend to have strong control power because the corporate headquarters in these cities control regional headquarters or branches of companies in other cities. But the global city network does not simply operate in accordance with the order from top to bottom like a hierarchical system. Many cities in the network are often the places where the companies providing global services claim that they "must locate". This is expressed as a so-called "network power". Network power is based on the angle of the centrality, that is, to what extent the city is located in the center of the network. Three ways can be used to compute the centrality: orientation, tightness, and relevance. The higher a city's centrality in the network, the greater its network power. Those cities with great network power often called channel cities. For example, by acting as a bridge through which external customers enter the rapidly growing Chinese market, the lack of Hong Kong's headquarter functions and the "management and control" functions get compensated, which shows the great network power possessed by high-degree connectivity (Taylor *et al.*, 2002).

Another example is in Europe. Moscow is also the leading channel city, having attracted a lot of enterprises hoping to gain a foothold in the services market in the new Russia (i.e., locating corporate headquarters there), despite its lack of global service providers.

In reality, both control power and network power coexist in the global city network; the former is shown in the external relevance that many company's headquarters gathers in a city; the latter is manifested as the external relevance of "secondary domination" embodied in a large number of "ordinary" offices locating a city. In general, the concentration of control power is higher and mainly concentrated in a few cities. Thus, dominating cities only account for small number, such as New York and London, getting a good lead in the global dominance. In contrast, the city's network power is relatively scattered, and hence these channel cities are relatively large, widely distributed, and have their own characteristics. For example, three cities in northwestern Europe have special goodies: Dublin is a special place for back-offices; Brussels as "the capital of the European Union" has attracted large numbers of global services; and Zurich plays a role of a special financial center in connection with the center and periphery in the world economy.

Armstrong and McGee group cities in accordance with the strength of its connection with the world and sphere of influence, specifically describing the multiple statuses of cities as the global network nodes of the world economy. The global cities at the highest level gather the decision-making power of a transnational capital, and major international banks, financial markets, multinational corporations, communications networks, and other vital global service all locate these dominating cities in the world (London, New York, and Tokyo are named here due to their rule of the world's financial institutions). Some dominant cities get interested in specific industries, such as Detroit's auto industry and Houston's oil industry; the cities with political dominance include the national capitals such as Washington, DC, and Brasilia. Regional and local cities are characterized by lower-level company activities, which are increasingly subject to the impact of international trade and of industrial restructuring; the lower-level cities level in the global hierarchy bear the recruitment of labor migration, the extraction of natural resources and surplus value, the proliferation of the type of consumption necessary to the deepening of markets, and other tasks (Brain, 1996). The organizing principle of the global city system also provides room for the internationalization of urban functions in developing countries, such as export processing zones, offshore financial centers, international port city, and specialized production bases in manufacturing exports.

In addition, the functional specialization of the node city has become more prominent. This is very different from the central place model, which assumes that the cities at the same level in the city system have the same functions (Baskin, 1966). Camagni (1998) thinks that different cities in the world city system will have different functions, so their essential characteristics will be different. In the US, New York dominates in the banking, accounting, and advertising services, and Washington, DC, dominates in legal services, R&D, and associations service. High-tech industries such as Boston, Dallas, and San Francisco are superior to those in New York, Los Angeles, Chicago, and other global cities. In the computer industry, the most influential software company, Microsoft, is located in Seattle, while another influential producer, Dell, is located in Austin, and the city of San Francisco-San Jose dominates the industry. To take another example, Berlin is known as "design capital", with about 1.04 million people engaging in design as full-time work, along with freelance designers. Annual revenues of more than 600 design companies come to 1.4 billion euros, and the city has played host to many international achievements, from the design of Leica camera to the design of fashion shows. Also, Edinburgh is known as the "literary capital", Argentina's Santa Fe is known as "folk art capital", and so on.

It is noteworthy that, in the analysis of connectivity of network nodes, what is stressed mainly is the importance of economic exchanges or flows among cities, but as the carriers of contemporary economic, cultural, political, and social globalization and its derivation, the cities constitute an urban multinetwork system, and the economic flows between the global cities only constitute a pattern of multiple networks. Therefore, in the analysis of multiple attributes of network nodes, the role of other factors should also be under consideration. If the city's own distinctive feature, history of development, different cultural characteristics, environment, and many other factors are taken into account, then the diversity of the network nodes will have a greater tension and is displayed by different forms.

3.2.3. *The dynamic nature of network nodes*

The study already pointed out that connectivity is the basic properties of network nodes. In the global city network, the formation and change of the node are closely related to the flows of information, capital, investment, and other factors. In the long term, these flows of information, capital, investment, and other factors are inherently unstable. Every time some major changes take place in history, mainly including appearance of the new structure and organization of production, and new technical requirements, in particular, the progress of transport and communication, etc., the flows of information, capital, investment and other factors will occur, and sometimes often change irregularly, abruptly, forming new flows and flow direction, which makes the form and features of network nodes change significantly. Therefore, the cities of these network nodes are constantly changing to adapt to the changes of their environment. In this adaptation process, their coordination functions may be extended to activities of new industries, their structure and organization may be undergoing a fundamental restructuring, and their functions may be expanded spatially.

In this sense, these network nodes have dynamic characteristics, namely, instability and uncertainty. Some are progressively evolving, while some are changing abruptly. The nodes of the global city network result from a constant adaptation to the changes of environment and continuous movements. These continuous movements include the slow development and diversification of network nodes, and the growing influence of space. That is, in these continuous movements, the network node itself is constantly diversified, complicated, and continuously extended in space. Therefore, the changes in the global city network are displayed by such a scenario: some of the important nodes in the original, due to diversion of the factor flows, easily lose their status; at the same time, new nodes may also appear, and are in constant change.

In history, the dynamic changes in the status of the city are even more apparent. In the urban system at different times, there are some cities in the world that always have a clear leadership position. Even before the Industrial Revolution, a few cities were in the exercise of the important coordination function involving high-level activities and long-distance trade; its role will be reminiscent of the role of today's metropolis. For example, in the 17th-century London, Amsterdam, Antwerp, Genoa, Lisbon, and Venice were once metropolises. In the 18th century, Paris, Rome, and Vienna and other cities began to "rule the regions", while Antwerp and Genoa's influence declined. In the 19th century, Berlin, Chicago, Manchester, New York, and St. Petersburg have become international metropolises, and Venice and other cities became relegated to the background. Of course, that today's global city network nodes dynamically change is based on the completely different historical backgrounds and driving forces. In today's context of interaction of globalization and informatization, the key player of the international metropolis is no longer connected with the power, the empire, or the organization commerce, but with the operation of multinational corporations, international banking and financial sectors, supra-national politics, and international agencies (Knox, 2002). But what the above-said reflects is the dynamic changes of the city status. As Hall (1999) points out, due to technical, economic, political, and rapid changes, a city does occupy the absolutely advantageous position in the hierarchical structure. The cities of the global sub-location especially compete with the cities of the global location (such as Frankfurt with London and Milan with Paris).

To be objective, the significant diversion or changes of factor flows, to a certain extent, are linked to the transfer of the world's economic centers. When the transfer of the center of the world economy occurs, there will be major changes in the direction and scale of global factor flows, which results in changes in the function and status of urban nodes in the network structure. But in the process, the number of cities that will be subjected to the transfer of the world's economic centers and become the main channels and management and control centers of the new factor flows or the roles these cities will play in the flows of new factors are largely decided by their geographic locations, development foundations, and historical factors. What is necessarily made certain is that geographical location as a deciding factor is not just by chance, nor does it simply depend on the continuation of the history and traditions, but rather, efforts made by the participants assume importance. As Bourdeau-Lepage and Huriot (2003) point out, not all cities have the experience of being a metropolis. Only those cities that generate a faster and greater response to the modern technologies and economic progresses of the post-industrial era and have effective coordination and leadership functions can be classified as metropolises.

Therefore, the internal factors of the network node itself also play a positive role in the change of its status, which is displayed roughly by the following four aspects. The first is the changes in internal political environment. For example, Johannesburg lost its leading position in southern Africa owing to the international community imposing tough sanctions on South Africa during the apartheid regime, together with the ongoing internal unrest and political instability. Similarly, Rio de Janeiro once commanded a prominent position in the world city system, but after the government moved the capital to Brasilia, Sao

Paulo lost its edge in competition, and the significance of its status dropped greatly. The second factor is the city's creative ability to respond to external changes such as global economic adjustment. Whether or not a city can make successful economic restructuring, transforming from labor-intensive production to capital-intensive production, further to knowledge-intensive production, will largely determine its position in the world city system. In late 19th and 20th centuries, in the old industrial areas where many important heavy industries such as the automotive, steel, coal, metal products were located, many cities such as Manchester, Essen, and Detroit found it difficult to return to the previously important position as "world factories" because of the lack of such creativc ability in the knowledge economy. Third is the city's competition and cooperation skills. Cities that not only maintain their competitive advantages but also have a stronger ability to cooperate with the outside will create a strong attraction to the flows of global resources. Fourth is the city's sustainable development. Only those cities with beautiful environment and sustainable development ability can grow into global cities.

3.2.4. *Measurement of network nodes*

The preliminary analysis shows that globalization cities as the global city network nodes differ greatly not only in the degree of connectivity and the connection type but also in their functions.

In order to have a general identification and distinction of their differences, the study builds the corresponding measurement indicator system with accordance to the characteristics and functions of network nodes. Because each characteristic of network nodes can be looked at and fully reflected from their functions, it is necessary for the study to consider its connectivity and functions together, and on this basis construct an indicator system of measuring the globalization city's "globalization degree "or" urban globalization degree" (Table 3.2).

Each cell in Table 3.2 contains a number of representative indicators. The composite index measured from these indicators can be used to comprehensively measure its globalization degree and also determine the place of a specific city in the global city network system. Meanwhile, the

Table 3.2. Classification of Globalization City Indicators.

	CENTRALITY (Concentration of International Activities)	EXTERNALITY (External Orientation)	CONNECTIVITY (Linkage or Network)
Economic Functions			
Command & Control (management, finance, services)	TNC's HQ;FDI; financial center indicators; global service firms; proportion of producer services	Ratio of international to domestic figures of relevant indicators, e.g., TNC HQ/domestic firms HQ	HQ & branch offices network; FDI network of in & out origins and destinations; "global network connectivity" (GaWC)
Production, Transportation, Communication, Consumption, R&D	Patents; R&D institutions; telecommunication node; transportation hub; population; foreign labor	Ratio of international to domestic figures of relevant indicators; International communication/domestic communication	Air passengers network; telecommunication network; freight network; trade network
Other Functions			
Political, Cultural, Educational, Knowledge	National capital; Foreign residents & tourists; international organizations; international festivals, conferences, events; international schools; UNESCO cultural & natural heritage	Ratio of international to domestic figures of relevant indicators, e.g., foreign tourists/domestic tourists.	International network of these activities

Source: Hunmin (2006).

index decomposition can show the specific roles of a city in the global city network system, which can be used to determine the part type (management, transportation, consumption, production, or R&D) of the city node. Again, these indicators can also indicate the relative position of the city in the global economic, political, cultural, and other aspects.

According to this index system, the status and degree of connectivity of globalization cities in the global city network are different, and their relevance manners and link gateways differ greatly, thus showing a multilevel and diversity pattern, similar to a colorful mosaic. That is, globalization cities are not unified models but have different characteristics.

The different characteristics of globalization cities depend on the synthesis of determinants and a long-term cumulative basis. For example, London acts as a modern international metropolis with comprehensive functions results from many important factors at work. From a historical point of view, London has a good infrastructure and abundant knowledge, skills, language, and influence, which are the key factors of the business layout. From the control environment, London keep open for business and becomes the location choice of the global market because of appropriate controls, tax and employment policies and other advantages. From accumulation and economies of scale, London has Europe's most advanced knowledge and technology flows. And from the personnel and labor market, London has advanced technologies and professionals required for engaging international businesses and a multilingual and multicultural labor market. From the perspective of urban culture, in the "human capital-driven" economic activity, London is a city which is more suitable for living, which is very important for it to act as an international business center. The formation and development of respective characteristics of globalizing cities and general globalization cities also require these characteristics.

3.3. Globalizing Cities Based on Network Structure

From the perspective of the global city networks, the characteristics of global cities are expressed mainly by extensive and intensive interaction with other cities. In this regard, it is not fair to rank cities according to some important indicators such as economic strength and competitiveness. Instead, the method that is used to analyze the interaction by observing the flow between the nodes[1] appears more important. Similarly, the study also wants to adopt the same approach to reveal the stratum and characteristics of globalizing cities in the network structure.

3.3.1. *The globalizing city: the strata in the network structure*

According to the foregoing analysis, one thing that is clear is that the globalizing cities are those that are included in the global city network, and globalization cities with special forms and types in the network structure. But the problem is, for the globalization cities in the network structure, how does the globalizing city distinguish from the global city as well as other general global city? A common traditional way is to distinguish them through the division of the city strata. The ranking of cities has always been one of the hotspots of urbanology and the world city study.

Four main methods are widely used throughout the grading of the city, with each method representing research priorities and cores of different periods. The first method is to get multinational headquarters location as the main indicators. The more the city has multinational headquarters, the higher its level is in the global city system. This is the research method of early world city theories as represented by Friedman's world city hypothesis. The second method is to combine the performance of urban functions with the potential ability to economic development, not only considering the geographical distribution of the multinational companies' headquarters but also focusing more on innovation and decision-making capacity of the multinational companies, and taking them as the basis by which to grade the world cities. The third method is to take the degree of integration of the city

[1] "Flow" refers to the movement of capital, transportation, telecommunications, international investment, market information, culture goods, and skilled labor flows.

into the global economy, the ability to attract global capital and provide producer services as the basis by which to grade modern international cities. The fourth method is to select leading industries as the basis by which to grade the cities from the perspective of changes in industry structure and industrial restructuring. That is, in the context of speedy development of new technology and information industries, the significance of the traditional manufacturing industries gradually loses, and financial and advanced service industries have become the embodiment of urban internationalization. Obviously, the bases of these different periods by which to grade cities are based on the perspective of internal organization of the city and its properties. These traditional standards place too much emphasis on the content of the modern city itself, while ignoring its mutual connection and influence in the global city system (Knox, 2002). Therefore, using the traditional grading standards for the city to grade globalization cities in the global network itself is seriously flawed.

It is necessary to adopt the research methods and standards that can reflect the inherent requirements of the network structure when ranking globalization cities in the global city network. The foregoing analysis has pointed out that, as nodes of the global city network, a number of cities play the basic (central) node's role, some cities are sub-central nodes, and most of cities are the normal nodes. In addition, the structural features of the globalization city's internal organization of and its level of external connection clearly reflect that a number of cities are strongly linked, while other cities are overall weak; some cities are more strongly linked in many aspects and some cities are more strongly linked only in one respect. Therefore, grading globalization cities in the global networks take only what is necessary to adopt research methods which pay attention to the property of the city itself, but also consider the linkages between cities, and treat the global city system as the whole under the background of globalization.

The scholars of the Department of Geography, Loughborough University, London, conducted exploratory studies, which are fruitful. Based on four aspects of the main function of the global city and its network contact (international accounting, advertising, banking, legal services), they analyze 122 cities and deduce a three-level architecture (Beaverstock *et al.*, 2000). The 4 service functions of the 10 global cities at the first level all perform outstandingly, among which London, Paris, New York, and Tokyo are of the highest points. The 3 service functions of the 10 global cities, such as San Francisco, Sydney, Toronto, and Zurich, at the second level perform outstandingly. The two service functions of 35 global cities, including Amsterdam, Berlin, Miami, Osaka, Rome, and Washington, at the third level perform outstandingly.

According to the degree of the global network connectivity or network connection, the study summarizes that the nodes of the global city network are linked in three different ways. First is the cluster with a high-level global connectivity. Cities in a similar level and having complete connectivity often fall into this category. For example, New York and London, as the leading nodes, clearly belong to the members of the cluster. Second is the cluster with stronger regional connectivity. Cities with greater connectivity within the same region in the world often fall into this category. Third is the cluster with the trend of interaction between global connectivity and regional connectivity. Cities with global connectivity and regional connectivity are often included in this category. Members in this cluster, if they possess higher connectivity, tend to have less territorial limitations; and those having lower connectivity tend to be subjected more to geographical constraints. On this basis, the study can divide the network-structure-based globalization cities into different levels and types.

The first type is the cities with global connectivity of high degree and global coordination function, which have already transformed and matured into global cities. They have the most extensive and intensive global network connectivity, being the central (basic) nodes of the global city network. Currently, most of these cities are in the developed countries.

The second type is those cities whose global connectivity is gradually increased and global coordination function is taking shape, referred to as the globalizing cities. They have a more extensive and intensive global network connectivity, being important nodes in the global city network. Currently, this type of globalizing cities can be found in developed and developing countries.

The third type is those cities whose global connectivity and global coordination functions are both weaker, still belonging to the general globalization cities with development potential. They are just the general nodes of the global city network. These cities are relatively common, most of which are located particularly in developing countries.

Of course, the levels of globalization cities are dynamic. In this dynamic evolution of the global urban hierarchy, those global cities that maintained their dominant position may also be relegated to the background, with its global connectivity and global coordination function tending to decline. The general global cities with development potential, if they seize the opportunity to realize their full potential, may gradually become globalizing cities through continuous enhancement of its global connectivity and global coordination functions, and finally evolve into the global cities. It is possible for those globalizing cities to accelerate to become global cities or to stagnate, fall back, and are reduced to general globalization cities.

3.3.2. *Criticism of the traditional method of functionalism*

After making a relative distinction between globalizing cities, global cities, and general globalization cities between the post-globalization on the basis of ranking cities, the study should further research globalizing cities to reveal their basic properties and characteristics. But the first problem here is: what kind of approach should be used for research?

In urban studies, the theory of spatial distribution of urban centers occupying a dominant position for a long time uses the basic method of functionalism (and constructivism), that is, revealing the internal features and functions of the city through structural analysis, and thus defining its characteristics and determining its status. The empirical analysis usually uses important indicators like economic strength and competitiveness to give static ranking of city status. The mainstream global city studies also continuously follow the tradition of functionalism (and constructivism) and its basic method, with a considerable part of scholars focusing on defining the global city by mining its internal characteristics and functions. For example, Lo and Yeung (1998) proposes that the global city is of great significance because of its role in the global economy, and its ability to play this outstanding "role" results from its internal characteristics and functions. Fröbel *et al.* (1980) think that the "new international division of labor" results from great companies' global production strategy to develop new "global areas". This new global economy requires command and control centers to perform its functions, and the global cities are considered as such centers. After, Friedmann evolves this idea into the "world city hypothesis". This means that the internal characteristics of global cities are expressed as the sites of multinational headquarters, where multinationals play a role in organizing new international division of labor.

In the 1970s and 1980s, that a lot of multinational companies indeed headquartered in major western cities largely validated Friedmann's hypothesis. However, modern information technology, network development and new communications technology has rendered obsolete this necessity. In addition, in the 1990s, some company headquarters steer clear of Western cities and increasingly concentrated on the importance of capital flows in the so-called "emerging markets". As a result, multinational companies' headquarters are often decentralized to seek new (cheaper) locations (Castells, 1996). These changes show that the global city is no longer defined by the internal features of the sites, i.e., the presence of headquarters of multinational corporations. If the multinational headquarters are no longer the internal features of the global city, then what is it? To answer this question, Sassen (1994) proposes a possible answer, and explains why, despite the existence of the pressure of decentralization caused by modern electronic communications, some economic functions still remain in the city. The key to this answer is taking into account the advanced producer services, and defining these service activities as the performances that provide professional help for all types of companies to run the world economy. Many advanced producer service companies, such as banking, accounting, insurance, advertising, public relations, law firms, and management consulting and other departments, gradually develop into multinational companies through the implementation of global strategies, tailoring their business for global major customers and multinational companies. Moreover, such advanced producer services are highly specialized, and they need other service companies to provide services, that is, mutual exchange of services. So, the "global services" by this kind of global-oriented advanced producer services are more deepened than by the multinationals. Based on professional knowledge and with combination to different professional knowledge, these advanced producer services provide increasing number of new services products, including financial products, and advertising packages, diversified legal texts, so in order to accumulate and make use of this comprehensive professional knowledge, it is necessary for producer services to operate in a knowledge-intensive environment. Those global cities with a dense concentration of individual knowledge are to provide such an environment to facilitate the face to face exchange by professionals. Thus, in Sassen's eyes, advanced producer service companies' concentration is the internal characteristics of global cities.

While Sassen and Friedmann have different understandings of the internal characteristics of global cities and their functions, they actually start from traditional functionalism to examine the global city, putting arguments in the "assumption that main cities play a strategic role" (Sassen, 1994), and tending to describe the global city as "control center", the relationship of which with other cities is expressed in the global hierarchy of the core, semi-periphery, and periphery. This is highly consistent with the views of the mainstream world city theory. In relation to this, in the past, many standards of ranking cities and defining international metropolises are often limited to their internal features and functions. For example, Friedmann's seven criteria are: major financial centers; multinational headquarters; international agencies; rapidly growing business service sectors; important manufacturing center; important transportation hub; and population size. Some other studies also add some new standards, such as communication (Hepworth, 1990; Warf, 1989, 1995), quality of life (Simon, 1995), international affairs and cultural centers (Knox and Taylor, 1995; Rubalcaba-Bermejo and Cuadrado-Roura, 1995), and a destination for immigrants (Friedmann, 1995). What these standards emphasize is a variety of functions and their differences in global cities.

The studies of the city or global city based on the traditional functionalist places emphasis on the analysis of its internal characteristics and functions, which is bound to pop out the city's one-sided prominent "central" status and hierarchical structure, neglecting the new changes in its external network connection characteristics, placing too much emphasis on differences in the city's functions and ignoring the links between cities and their linkages with the globalization process. As some scholars criticize, too much emphasis on differences in the global city functions can only lead to neglect of the global urban network connectivity and plasticity. In fact, many changes are processed and communicated through the global city, and these cities are the nodes which keep in touch with the current world economy through a variety of linkages (Hall, 1996). Therefore, the study of the globalizing city in the global network structure cannot simply follow the traditional functionalist (and constructivist) approach, but combine the use of the method which analyzes their interaction by looking to flow between the nodes.

Different from the study of cities and global cities based on the traditional functionalist approach, what the study first wants to emphasize here is: in today's context of globalization and information technology, like other globalization cities, the globalizing cities have obvious external connection network characteristics. Although, in history, the trade cities and manufacturing cities also have more extensive external connections, it is definitely not comparable to the internetization in the current global "space of flows". In the present case, if a city does not enter the global city network, its coordination function is very limited, not evolving toward the globalization city. If a city is not in a basic (central) node of the global network, it simply cannot be called a global city. In this sense, the globalizing city is defined by neither its internal characteristics (such as labor, business, industry and the industrial structure), nor its functions (such as coordination, service, control, supervision); the same case applied to global cities as well. Castells (1996) clearly points out that the global city is not defined by its internal characteristics but its strategic position in the global "space of flow". Thrift (1998) also believes that "a global city cannot be considered limited national borders, or distinct, solidified continuum", it should be seen as "always in a process of interaction and things". Therefore, when revealing the nature of the globalizing cities, the study should start with research on the flow between the global network nodes and encircle the global connectivity as the core element.

3.3.3. *The nature of the globalizing city*

The global connectivity of a city comprises two parts: first is the city's extraversion, mainly expressed as its internationalization, with a relatively large role at the global level; second is the city's relevance, mainly close ties with the outside world and with the city itself, in the network contacts. Therefore, the external characteristics of the globalizing cities can be attributed to two factors:

(1) the globalizing city is an extraversion-oriented city, with internationalization as its characteristic;
(2) the globalizing city is a nodal city of the global network, with a high correlation with the outside world.

Of course, the globalizing city is seen as the "node" of the global city network, and the world economy emphasizes its external interdependence and liquidity, but not so as to negate its internal characteristics or completely separate them. The network features of the external connection of the globalizing cities precisely need the support of its corresponding internal features or require the adaptation of their internal characteristics to the external network features, which means both are in organic unity. The case is the same for issues of the global city. For example, the internal features, that is, the advanced producer services, mined by Sassen's study of the global city, can be unified together with the external characteristics, that is, the basic nodes of the global network, emphasized by Castells. Because, different from the multinational headquarters, advanced producer services companies are highly concentrated in major cities, and their global strategy is a process of global networking. It is by right of the global network of advanced producer services that the connectivity of global cities and their networks can be set up. Therefore, what the study wants to emphasize is that revealing the characteristics of the globalizing cities (including global cities) requires the study of the network features of the external connection and the analysis of its internal features, which are consistent with the former.

The study of the mainstream global city (Bosman and Smith, 1993; Clark, 1996; Cohen, 1981; Friedmann, 1986; Hall, 1966; Hymer, 1972; Reed, 1989; Sassen, 2000; Short *et al.*, 1996) has conducted extensive analysis of the internal features of the global city, which has boiled down to the city with a high concentration of international activities. The organizing bases supporting these international events are various types of global corporations and international organizations. Thus, the global city plays host to various global markets (commodities, financial futures, investment, foreign exchange, equity securities and bonds, etc.); a variety of advanced professional business services (especially international finance, accounting, advertising, real estate development, legal services, etc.) (Beaverstock *et al.*, 1999; Leslie, 1995; Moulaert and Djellal, 1995; Warf, 1989); highly centralized, large corporate headquarters of not only multinational companies but also major domestic enterprises and foreign companies (Godfrey and Zhou, 1999); a variety of domestic and foreign trade and other industry associations; a variety of NGOs (non-governmental organizations) and IGOs (intergovernmental organizations); media organizations (including newspapers, magazines, book publishing, and satellite television) with international influence; news and information services (including news editing and online information services); and cultural industries (including art and design, fashion, film, and television).

Since the degree of network connectivity of the globalizing cities is not on the same level as the global cities, the foregoing extensive description of the internal characteristics of global cities and their organization structure is not entirely suitable for the globalizing cities. But as the potential global city or future global city, the goal and position the globalizing city pursues are the same as the global city, with some differences in the extent, therefore, much of the foregoing inductive description of the internal characteristics of global cities can be used as the reference of the study of the internal characteristics of the global city. For example, multinational headquarters and international organizations are highly concentrated in the global city, whereas more regional or national headquarters of multinational companies and large corporate headquarters or their R&D and marketing headquarters are located in the globalizing city. In another example, the globalizing city is also location where several global markets or a group of the various markets with global influences, various senior professional business services, domestic and foreign trade and other industries associations, non-governmental organizations, and relevant organizations in the news media, information services, and cultural aspects have started locating their offices.

Although the internal characteristics of globalizing cities and their organization structure are not as sharp as the global city, they have come to possess the rudiment of the corresponding characteristics and organizational structures. Moreover, in real life, the above-mentioned organization structure does not necessarily get the complete expression in a globalizing city. Especially international non-governmental organizations and trans-governmental organizations (World Health Organization, the International Federation of Labour Organization, the Federal Bar Association, the International Union of Agricultural Producers, etc.) tend to be relatively concentrated in a few cities (see Table 3.3). Therefore, many of the global cities may not have the organizational element, but this does not affect the general description of the internal characteristics of global cities and their organization structure from the theoretical and abstract perspective. What is only emphasized is that the organizational basis of the globalizing develops toward the direction of the ability to support the international activities.

In addition, from the experience of the existing global city, the more complete the above-mentioned organizational structures are,

Table 3.3. The Distribution of United Nations Agencies and the Headquarters of Major International Organizations (Liaison Offices) in 18 Cities in the World.

City	Berlin	Brussels	Vienna	Moscow	London	Rome	Stockholm	Paris	Madrid
Quantity	6	60	15	14	57	31	14	208	5
City	Hong Kong	Mexico City	Singapore	New York	Seoul	Bangkok	Tokyo	Beijing	Shanghai
Quantity	3	4	4	21	2	13	16	2	0

Source: Li *et al.* (1996).

the stronger the synergy of them with each other is; contrarily, if the organizational structures just highlight a few aspects, their mutual synergy will become weaker. For example, New York has relatively complete organizational structures and their synergistic effects on each other are very obvious. New York attracts large multinational companies depending on its status of cultural and information center, and large corporate headquarters and the center of the global market attract a large number of high-end professional business services; in turn, the high concentration of headquarters of large companies, professional business services companies, and the central position of global markets form high-density, high-frequency flow of information, which also promotes the formation of its cultural and information central position. Therefore, New York is not only a global financial center and advanced producer services (accounting, lawyers, consulting, etc.) center but also the media, information, and cultural center. Early in the 1980s, there were 17 television stations and 39 radio stations in New York. The three major US broadcast networks: Columbia Broadcasting System (CBS), National Broadcasting Company (NBC), and American Broadcasting Company (ABC) headquartered in New York. These three media conglomerates control 2,139 radio and television stations, being capable of influencing to the news and entertainment around the country. New York is also the center of the US publishing industry: *The New York Times,* one of the three major US newspapers, and other US newspapers such as *The Wall Street Journal*, *The New York Daily News*, and *New York Post*, and magazines such as *Business Week*, *Time*, *News Weekly*, and *Foreign Quarterly* all publish from New York. Therefore, the globalizing cities should have the relative integrity of the organizational structure similar to New York, even if its level is lower anyway.

The internal characteristics of the globalizing cities and their organizational structures are intrinsically linked to the network features of their external connection, with high consistency between them. Each element in their internal organizational structures has its own global or regional network, which is very useful for the wide range of external connections required by the globalizing cities. In the globalization and informatization context, the impact and control of a city in the world urban system are realized through the production and consumption of high-level, advanced services. The key indicators to measure the network features of external connections of the globalizing city should be: whether or not the city can provide services, management, and financing for the market or the company's global operations; whether or not producer service companies of different sectors can have ancillary facilities of the global network; whether or not the city makes significant exports of producer services; whether or not foreign companies headquarter the city; whether or not there are financing institutions for cross-border operations in the city; whether or not there are the global markets in the city, whether or not they are part of the global equity markets, etc. Stanback and Noyelle (1982) make a study of the composition of the American urban system, dividing 100 major US cities into five main categories: the hub (which is divided into national, regional, and sub-regional hubs), functional hub, administrative centers, production centers, and residential centers. New York, Los Angeles, Chicago, and San Francisco are included in the four major national hubs. In their view, the hub is the highest level of the city system, which is characterized by: the sites where the company headquarters and related administrative and control functions are highly concentrated and where producer services, especially senior service companies, gather. These features serve not only the hub but also the entire urban system.

The globalizing city with an all-round development of the organizational structure has stronger global network connectivity not only in the banking/financial services and producer services but also in media and cultural and other aspects, which means that the globalizing city will tend to be at a forefront position in the overall global network connectivity. In contrast, if a globalizing city has outstanding development only in some aspects of its organizational structure, for example, in the banking/financial industry, but no corresponding development in business services, it means that the globalizing city will tend to be at a lower position in the overall global network connectivity. The obvious contrast between these two rankings, to a certain extent, reflects that the latter is not a globalizing city with "all-round development".

But most of the globalizing cities are in the "evolving process" and do not have the universal characteristics of the "all-round development", which often perform well only in one or more aspects in international exchanges, with their influences beyond the region, across borders, even spreading to the world. In the measurement of the connectivity of European cities in the global network, Taylor (2003) finds that the connectivity of the banking/financial aspects of European cities is graded at a lower position in the world than their overall ranking of the connectivity (this can be reflected from the relative important position of the bank/the financial industries of the Asia-Pacific regional cities). And in terms of the connectivity in the media, the European cities immediately show their particular importance: there are 16 European cities in the world's top 25. Conversely, if non-governmental organizations are seen as the factors to examine the city's connectivity, the European cities perform poorly, with only 6 cities in the world's top 25. This partially describes the varied importance of European cities in the global city network and also shows a unique form of the globalizing city in the "evolving process".

Based on the analysis of the internal and external features, the globalizing cities, and their organic unity, the study will further examine its main functions. It is well known that the city's basic function is its economic and social coordination. As sub-nodes of the global network, the globalizing cities, to a certain extent, control and carry interdependent factors of resources and financial and cultural flows, which jointly promote the development of globalization. They also provide a platform for global and regional interaction, comprising economy, society, culture, and institutional settings. They contribute to the integration of regional and metropolitan resources, thereby promoting the process of globalization. At the same time, to a certain extent, they act as the driving force of globalization on the region's political and economic development. Therefore, the globalizing city has gone beyond the scope of the national urban system, whose nodal location function and coordination function are more reflected in cross-border links between cities.

This important coordination functions based on global connectivity can be attributed to economic and non-economic coordination functions. In the modern economy, the most powerful economic coordination functions are mainly reflected in the control and domination of the global economy, and only the global city has this strategic coordination function. This function is reflected by global capital flows, transnational corporation headquarters, and global corporations and producer services worldwide. Although the globalizing city has not yet reached that level, it has begun to play an important coordinating function in the global capital flows, global industrial chain management, and global produce services. In addition, in the global economy, the role of the globalizing city as the center of world manufacturing or production, transportation, and communication centers, R&D centers, and consumption centers cannot be ignored. The globalizing city has relatively strong coordination function in this area, with certain advantages. Compared to the above-mentioned function of the domination and control of the global economy, the influence of coordination functions of the globalizing city are weaker, but these economic coordination functions of the globalizing city also plays an important role in its external relations, which are highly consistent with its global connectivity.

In the earlier urban studies, economic co-ordination functions are most frequently emphasized. It is noteworthy that non-economic functions, such as functions of politics, culture, education and knowledge generation, to which little attention was paid to in the past, are essential factors to assess the impact of globalization (Lever, 2002; Short *et al.*, 1996). Especially, knowledge-based cultural functions will be one of the main factors of the future global city. For the globalizing city, there is still large room for development of its non-economic functions, for those urban governments that plan to build their cities into global cities, it is of vital importance to pay close attention to the role of the non-economic coordination functions and continually strengthen it.

Chapter 4

Regions of Global Cities: A New Spatial Structure

Globalized cities, driven by globalization and information technology, are fully integrated into the network of regional, national, and global economy in all levels. An obvious trend is the close relationship between the globalized cities and their adjacent hinterlands, showing a so-called global phenomenon of urban areas. Global city region is the theoretical and practical extension of global cities and globalized cities, which more obviously evolves into a unique space in the international political and economic arena. It is of great significance for developing countries to support the rise of global cities. As environmental conditions change, the current rise of global cities in developing countries, perhaps unlike the early rise of the global urban space in developed countries, was born as a result of the global city region development. Therefore, in the analytical framework of globalizing cities, global city region will become an important component as a new space structure.

4.1. Regions of Global Cities: Basic Spatial Unit of Modern Global Economy

In the previous analysis, we particularly examined the impact of the interaction of globalization and information technology on the city itself, for example, it leaves most of the cities actively or passively involved in the process of globalization, from the "local space" into "space of flows", promoting the transformation of the world urban system, forming a global network of cities, and shaping the characteristics of globalized cities. However, various empirical analyses show that the process of globalization and informatization has a significant impact on the city itself and also penetrates into a wide range of urban areas. The global city region is becoming the basic spatial unit of the contemporary global economy and the geographical space base of the world's urban development.

4.1.1. *New changes in space*

In the traditional pattern of international division of labor and international trade conditions, the world's urban system is a type of the basic framework mainly based on the hierarchical system. In this framework, the strategic global cities in the global economy have the obvious tendency of cross-border space centralization, and to some extent, are cut off from its domestic and surrounding areas, the so-called "lamp black" phenomenon. As Sassen (2001) points out, there appears the serious imbalance of the economic ties between these cities and other cities, and similarly, the imbalance of the concentration of strategic resources and related economic activities.

The increasing depth of globalization and information promotes the creation of global markets, the rapid flow of capital, the transfer of global manufacturing, and the global extension of complex production chain, updating the geographical distribution of the central and the edge and strongly transforming the distribution of the world urban system, urban functions, and the nature of urban life. As Hall (1997, pp. 311–322) points out, despite the existing important economies of scale and agglomeration in the "center", working well, new regional development amendments under the control of international forces may be formed, such as the newly formed East Asian metropolitan area. In their studies, some scholars also find that the impact of globalization and informatization has widely penetrated into vast urban areas, greatly transforming the spatial distribution of the location of traditional industries. For example, Hodos (2002, pp. 358–379), in his study on Philadelphia, realizes that activities in the broader metropolitan area are just one part of the global economy. In many metropolitan areas, production activities, such as advanced manufacturing,

R&D, logistics, and warehousing transportation, are currently one part of its global functions, though located in the world outside the urban core areas. While studying Philadelphia as a city beyond its central area, he discovers that many companies have global operations, of which 12 have established their headquarters there, ranking in the 1999 Fortune 500 companies. In the chemical and pharmaceutical industries, 50% of the foreign employees worked for foreign companies. The area economy is clearly and globally market-oriented. Gertler, in his study of Toronto, finds out that there are important global industry sectors in the Greater Toronto Area, hence, being global-oriented. In addition to financial and business services in his general studies, he also points out that many activities, such as automobile industry, information and communication industry, engineering designing, health education, and cultural industries scatter through the Greater Toronto Area. O'Neill and Moss' (1991) analysis of New York, also observes the impact of globalization in the framework of the urban space. The New York global city region, plays host to 13 of the Fortune global top 100 companies' headquarters, 7 different service companies, and 38 research organizations. However, this study does not hold good when the original downtown area is taken into account. According to this observation, O'Neill and Moss, in their policy outlook of the industry, emphasizes that manufacturing — through the headquarters functions and R&D — will play a role in the future development of the region, suggesting that some policies be made to attract those industries in the region. Also, Markusen's (1999) study provides examples of the rapidly growing industry and employment in the sub-cities of the US, South Korea, Brazil, and Japan.

It has been increasingly noticed that the world city system is undergoing fundamental changes. The emergence of global cities increasingly based on the global network structure is changing the relationship between global cities, which occupy strategic positions in the world economy, and domestic and other regional cities. In particular, such megalopolises like New York, London, and Tokyo, are fully integrated into the regional, national, and global economy in all levels through the network of cities. An important aspect is to form a strong internal links with its adjacent or surrounding cities and totally integrate into the global economic system through a high degree of trans-regional communication and cooperation, including highly developed capital, information, and human resource flow. One can find a very complex and selective process of decentralization: some activities, in particular, the need for face-to-face communication, remain in the central area, and many other activities are often transferred out, not to the sub-important section of a large metropolitan area but to the area beyond the city. For instance, now in New York, the high-end service functions being transferred from the core Manhattan area to suburban Connecticut and New Jersey Center is obvious. In London, a similar phenomenon can be seen, as in west London or so-called crescent-shaped area, centering on Slough, High Wykang, Reading, Bracknell, Alder-shot, and Basingstoke: a progressive growth and development of a clear multicenter city area, including a network city of about 20 or 30 middle-sized cities is now attracting a large number of new investments in office facilities. Those office facilities are located in the town center, while some are located in the business district at the edge of the town (Baras, 1988). Except Bracknell and Basingstoke, which have been developed as planned, the rest are already established areas in history, only attaining new functions over time.

In fact, this new situation emerges not only in developed countries but also more apparently in developing countries. With the extension of global commodity chains and international industrial transfer, China, India, and other developing countries are undertaking international industry transfer in a massive scale. For example, China has undertaken a large number of international manufacturing transfers, thereby evolving into the processing base of the world. With the increase in foreign direct investment, the gradual extension of the processing chain in the processing trade, and the substantial increase of added value of products, the processing trade has gradually occupied a dominant position in the trade structure. In total imports and exports, processing trade accounts for 55%, of which foreign-invested enterprises account for more than 85%. Similarly, India undertakes a large number of outsourcing and software development and production, showing an obvious global production function. The global commodity chain extends to developing countries, not only centering in individual major cities but also gathering in areas with some of the major cities as their core.

In China, these external transfer of incoming global production activities mainly agglomerates in the Yangtze River Delta, Pearl River Delta, and Bohai Bay regions. Among them, the Yangtze River Delta region has the largest concentration of multinational companies in China. More than 400 of the global top 500 companies have settled in the Yangtze River Delta region. This region, besides Shanghai, Jiangsu, and Zhejiang provinces, has also attracted a large proportion of foreign direct investment, undertaking a large scale of international industrial transfer. Seen from the dynamic process, the actual use of foreign direct investment in Shanghai declined in proportion to total foreign direct investment in the Yangtze River Delta region, dropping from 46% in 1990 to 22.7% in 2003, while rising from 8.83 % to 26.38% in Suzhou, surpassing Shanghai. At present, many production activities or dominant production activities of the Yangtze River Delta region are all parts of the global commodity chain (manufacturing and processing), entirely driven by the international market. The Pearl River Delta and Bohai Bay area too have become a platform of participating in international division of labor and international competition.

All these have fully demonstrated that the process of globalization and informatization has a significant impact on the growing number of cities and regions, meanwhile involving them into the process of the global economic integration. In this process, various types of industries — whether manufacturing, service industries, high-tech industries or low-tech industries — are unprecedented for survival and development over the extensive contact area, meanwhile highly agglomerating in the wider urban areas. In this case, taking the "center" of a single city for the space unit has not fully explained the industrial competition and development in the age of globalization.

In short, in the context of the deepening process of globalization and informatization, many areas are under increasing pressure from global competition. Therefore, they are facing a choice: either passively submitting to such pressure or actively carrying out system construction and development of policies, absorbing as much as possible the benefits of globalization. At present the central government finds it increasingly difficult to deal with the various requirements from different regions under supervision. The global city region is undoubtedly an important choice, which contributes to the steady restructuring of state urban system, so many cities evolving into a comprehensive worldwide city of super clusters, namely, the global city region.

Currently, global-city-based regional urban system adjustment and reconstruction also take the trend of cross-border extension. Particularly, the European Union is vigorously promoting polycentric and balanced spatial development strategy concept, which bears the following strategic notion: faced with the ever-increasing competition of globalization, the joint development between the cities of the region can aid the European economy to function more effectively. For this to materialize, joint strategic development can be implemented in different scales. As the center of the whole Europe, the so-called "pentagon" of London, Paris, Milan, Munich, and Hamburg is considered to be a truly global economic integration area in Europe, and the cooperation between these cities will help to keep Europe advanced in the world. At the same time, in order to overcome such issues as overheating or over-crowding in the "pentagon" area — considered a threat to further attract investment, the regional collaboration and development between other urban areas should also be emphasized. Therefore, it is proposed that a strong east–west axis of trade development be set up in the north of England, connecting Dublin (currently one of the fastest growing city centers in Europe), Liverpool, Manchester, Sheffield, Leeds, Hull, and stretching into northern Europe.

4.1.2. *The provisions of the global city region*

At present, some scholars are beginning to notice that economic globalization has brought a new geographical phenomenon, an evolving global city region.[1] Based on economic ties and under the premise of

[1] Allen Scott, geographer/planning scientist, held the Global City Region Conference at Public Policy and Social Research Institute of Los Angeles School of the University

highly developed globalization, the global city region is a unique special phenomenon (Scott, 2001), an expansion and formation of globalized cities and those secondary ones with strong economy within their hinterland. It is distinct from the ordinary sense of the urban areas, but also from the city only a group of local contact form or the meaning of Megalopolis. The global city region has become the contemporary global economy, the basic spatial units (the so-called global economy, regional engine), although they are national or international level, and there is no formal, in particular, the political form of obvious consistency (especially in the US) (Scott *et al.*, 1999; Scott, 2001).

In order to have a more comprehensive and in-depth understanding of global city region, first, let us interpret a similar and somewhat related concept "urban area". Whether in theory or in practice, "urban area" is not a new concept. For example, from the year 1930 until 1960, the US proposed a series of concepts like "metropolitan area", "standard metropolitan area", and "standard metropolitan statistical area". In 1980, the US government further proposed a criterion for a "metropolitan area", with a population of 100 million or more.

In general, the urban area is the product of the urban development into the late stage. We know that, in the process of urbanization, there is always room for interaction between a pair of basic elements, namely the concentration and diffusion. Typically, the formation and development of a city in the geographical space can be seen mainly in its gathering process, that is, to attract various resources to concentrate on the urban area, causing the increase of urban population density. When developing to a certain extent, the growing economic radiation, economic scope will dominate the surrounding areas continuously, expanding the neighboring areas. As a city's diffusion effect, the expansion from point to surface is far beyond the city itself in space contact, resulting in urban regionalization.

---

of California in 1999, with 350 participants including scholars, government officials, entrepreneurs, AND community leaders conducting a wide-ranging discussion on the global city region.

Therefore, the concept of urban areas is primarily proposed as a product of urbanization process.

From its form, the urban area can be roughly divided into two types: single urban area and complex urban area. The former means the city itself is a region whose development is typical of both the expansion of the radius of urban areas and a combination of urban groups. Take London for example: starting from the smaller "London Town" to "Inner London", then "Greater London", and finally developing into a huge "London area". The latter mainly refers to the formation of urban areas: the sequential diffusion and jump diffusion after the centralized development of the city link many originally irrelevant or less relevant cities together.

Irrespective of the type of urban area, the concept "city region" reflects that the new boundaries can be the center of the existing jurisdiction of different urban, suburban, and neighboring regions and its hinterland, combined with the spatial scope of interest, whose economic, cultural, or political ties are far more closer compared to other areas. Obviously, this is different from the single city concept (including its suburbs) with a clear jurisdiction boundary. In addition, the foundation for the combination of urban, suburban, and neighboring regions and their hinterlands with different jurisdiction boundaries is mainly economic ties rather than simply geographical ones. Therefore, the urban area is not only the expansion of a city in space but also the geographical phenomena in the process of the upgrading city functions, industrial diffusion, and closer economic space ties.

It should be said that urban area is a concept of traditional urbanology, based on the basic theory that these cities are connected with their national, regional, and larger economic and social structures. In a closed system of a country (the traditional urban studies usually take this as a prerequisite), the urban economy is indeed exposed to the regional economy, often reflecting the characteristics of the regional economy. But the problem is that, in the case of the existing global cities in this city region, the global city is the world market-oriented with a high degree of cross-border space. Primarily, the city has extensive worldwide links, obviously expressed as supra-national relations, and is also domestically linked to other cities around the country, typical of domestic local relations. Therefore, just as Friedmann and Sassen describe, global cities' links with their second-tier hinterland cities are relatively weakened, which is considered contradictory to the main proposition of traditional academic studies on urban systems, which states that these systems promote regional and national economy to integrate geographically. It can be seen that the concept of urban areas cannot be used to explain the relationship between global cities and their surrounding areas and it is also in conflict with the global city as described by Friedmann and Sassen.

If the urban area is a concept put forward as a product of the urbanization process and, then the formation of the concept of global city region is not only the product of urbanization process, but the direct result of the interaction between highly developed economic globalization and informatization. The most critical difference is that global city region is a regional space (or global city functions) based on the mutual coupling geographical space within the global city.

Hall (2001, pp. 59–77) once raised a good point of view on how to define the global city region, believing that if the definition of global city is based on its information exchange with the outside, then the definition of global city region should be based on the internal relations within the region. But what should be further clarified is the nature of the internal relations within the region. If it is purely domestic local ties, then from the perspective of simple geography, we can say the global city region can be made up of some of the major metropolitan areas and peripheral or linked metropolitan hinterlands (which is itself a decentralized urban settlements of the place). Obviously, there are no essential differences from the concept of urban areas.

We believe that the prerequisite for the formation of a global city region is that the cities interconnected in this region are all involved in economic globalization processes. Here, not only are the metropolitan cities the main core of the region but also those intrinsically linked secondary cities are highly globalized cities. This means that most cities in the region are globally linked. Thus, the internal economic and political affairs between them will be linked in a complex way, constantly creating enhancing a more extensive supranational relationship. Obviously, this is completely different from the general interrelated areas of domestic relationship embodied within urban areas. In fact, only when the whole region is involved in the process of globalization are most urban cities transformed into globalized ones. The links between the core global cities and the secondary hinterland cities can be endogenously strengthened by embodying a super-state relationship. Clearly, be it the concept of global cities or urban areas or other metropolitan areas, none can reflect or reveal the intrinsic link of the supra-national relationship within the global city region.

Therefore, fundamentally speaking, the gathering of a growing number of global cities in certain geographical space, as a result of the interaction of globalization and information technology, prompts the rise of the global city region and development, which increasingly become the core of handling and coordinating modern economy and living. If we put aside the basic elements of global urban agglomeration in geographical spaces, we cannot define the concept of global city regions.

Seen from a realistic evolution, driven by globalization and information technology, the effects of spatial proximity and agglomeration on economic productivity and competitive advantage are increasingly highlighted. Conforming to this trend, some global cities form a loose club league, turning from the early expansion to the neighboring regions of space area (county, metropolitan area, city, etc.) in order to seek efficiency against the challenges and opportunities of globalization. With a high degree of economic links in these global city regions, adequate human resources, capital power, infrastructure, and related services support the production with global standards in order to become more competitive in global market competition, as large-scale enterprises or corporate network construction cluster geographic platform. Therefore, the great global city region has become a regional platform for enterprises to participate in the global market competition. These enterprises are rooted in the related resources of global city region (Scott and Storper, 2003, pp. 579–593). That is, the strong pressures of globalization and regional competition bestow a global city region of space with the more general economic characteristics. In this sense, the global city region is just a spatial structure to make globalization possible, or a spatial basis on which to promote the globalization. Thus, the global city region is not only the result of economic globalization but also one of the driving forces of the global economy. Globalization and the development of the global city region are just two different facets of a whole unity.

The increasing deepening of city regional economic ties with the world market promoted by globalization continues can stimulate economic growth, in turn, further encouraging specialization in the existing network. For example, Hollywood, Silicon Valley semiconductor, New York and London banking and financial services, and Paris fashion all have a flexible production networks on behalf of the cluster output, the fate of which is closely linked with the world market demand. That is, a network of local economic activity has merged into a more extended exchange of cross-regional competition and the worldwide network. Until now, in the world, through a large-scale reallocation of capital and labor, many leading industrial sectors have locally developed into intensive production clusters linked with the increasingly globalized market. The development of the global city region is closely linked with the globalization-oriented industry cluster. High degree of concentration of the globalization-oriented industries has become one of the most prominent characteristics in the global city region.

Furthermore, in the global urban areas, various global cities, characterized by the supra-national spatial relations as different global city nodes, have their own characteristics, status, and functions. Therefore, different from urban areas with a single core, the global city region is often a spatial structure of an urban expansion joint with multicore (center). There still exist controversies over this "multicenter" spatial structure, manifested as being a circle, or a band, or other forms. Hall believes that the global city region should have a multicenter circle spatial structure. The core is the central business district, such as the City of London, Chatelet, Marunouchi/Otemachi, etc. Located slightly outside is the new central business district, such as the West End, Paris district 16, Akasaki/Rippongi, etc., having a high concentration of certain types of office activities (especially, headquarters) and entertaining or cultural activities. Then is the inner edge city, mainly peripheral expansion of industrial and commercial sites, little away from the first and second levels of the center, such as La Défense, Canary Wharf, World Financial Center, Shinjuku, and Potsdam Square, highly concentrated with the new office space and entertainment venues; then further outside are outer edge cities, composed of some transport node towns, becoming a linking point of the central city's contact with the outside areas, such as London's Western Sector, Roissy, Kista-E4 Corridor, Amsterdam-Zuid, etc., the external part of which is called the "edge of the urban complex", concentrated with some of the main downtown business R&D departments or the "back offices", such as Crow Yin Dayton , Reading, Cergy-Pontoise, Omiya, Kawasaki, Greenwich (CO). In the furthest outer urban areas are present, specialized sub-grade centers in compliance with the division of geographical labor, which provide the central city and other spheres with education, entertainment, and business and exhibition services such as stadiums, amphitheaters, convention and exhibition centers, and theme parks), such as the Greenwich Millennium Dome, Paris Disneyland, Tokyo waterfront areas, etc. As for the "multicenter" spatial structures, as described by Hall, they can still be discussed further and brought into empirical investigation. But no matter what kind of form the spatial structure takes, there are several definite points, i.e., they create not the traditional single central city but a new polycentric urban form; they are located in some nodes, although fairly dispersed from the center to the edge; the multiple centers are based on the internal relations of specialization, respectively, playing different roles, not only cooperating but also competing with each other, forming a very unique urban areas in space. In this sense, the formation of the global city region of the circle and professional transformation of the circle is conducted simultaneously.

4.2. Interpretation of the Spatial Structure for Regions of Global Cities

In the context of globalization and information technology, the formation and development of the global city region has increasingly become the basic spatial units of the contemporary global economy, which is a very significant change. This change needs a corresponding theoretical explanation. The traditional city or global city theory is a single center-based geographical space, the analytical framework of which has been unable to expand the global city region to fully explain the unique spatial structure. Therefore, we must seek new theories and methods to analyze the global city region, to grasp the spatial structure of the new changes.

4.2.1. *Re-examining the spatial structure of traditional urban theory*

As we have pointed out earlier, the mainstream theory of global city derives the hypothesis of global cities directly from globalization, the specific context of information, and therefore the view of its research tends to focus on the impacts of globalization and informatization on the global cities. This not only ignores the general impact of globalization and informatization on ordinary cities (as previously commented earlier) but also actually implies the use of the concept "traditional single central city" and its further expansion.

Both Friedmann's world city hierarchy, and Sassen's discussion of New York, London, and Tokyo, are based on a single geographical space without exception, but this concept of central cities is more expanded (beyond the borders). In their view, a global city strengthens the transnational ties between the leading financial activities and business centers and weakens the link between its hinterland and national urban systems. In principle, a city should be embedded in a national urban system, linked with its hinterland and the national state. But the global city has continuously improved with regard to regional, transnational, and global links, and enhanced transnational links between them, leading to the weakened link between these cities and their domestic urban systems (Sassen, 2000, pp. 55–56). Although it is a significant change compared with the concept of the close relevance of the city and its hinterland in the traditional urbanology, the basic pattern of a single central city is not fundamentally altered. Even if the information city initiated by Castells is characterized by "space of flow", it is still the single center city and acts as a node of its network system. We believe that the mainstream global city theory is based on a single central city of territoriality, not accidentally, and as long as its own logic goes through the theoretical consistency, one is bound to rely on and strengthen the city center model.

It has been previously pointed out that the theoretical starting point of the global urban research production is based on decentralized production and globalized production of multinational corporations, which mainly analyzes the control and management functions in the process of decentralized production and the inevitability of high concentration of the corresponding service functions in the main cities, and make these cities as the basic nodes of the world city network with global functions. Clearly, this study provides us with an effective analytical tool to understand the spatial layout of multinational companies to implement their global strategy. But as is pointed out earlier above, one important flaw of the mainstream global city study consists in its far too narrow definition, mainly studying some of the top global cities (particularly those, manufacturing products and transferring to the large global cities such as New York, London, Tokyo, etc.), rather than bringing those more widely involved cities and their global city networks, with a complete sense in the process of globalization and informatization, into its analytical framework. Therefore, the mainstream study of global cities only focuses on the top headquarter control and management and producers' service functions in the global commodity chain while constructing the logical relationship between globalization, informatization, and global cities, taking this part as being self-contained, that is, network-based global cities with internal producer services. In a research of global cities, it is also pointed out that the headquarter control and management and producers' service functions are directly facing fragmented production but do not integrate this fragmented production into a particular analysis of urban space because of its narrow scope of definition and missing analytical framework.

We know that, with regard to the global commodity chain research, a good theoretical explanation of decentralized global production has been given. On the basis of Braudel's (1984) study, Hopkins and

Wallerstein (1986, pp. 157–170) proposed a "global commodity chain" concept, a complete network of labor, production, and finally the formation of commodity. Then, Gereffi's research provides the concept with a relatively complete paradigm. As a major tool of analyzing politics and economy, the theory of global commodity chains focuses mainly on the study of value-creation system of companies and other organizations, i.e., the control of transnational networks and the process of value creation and distribution, as well as a series of different stages of nodes of raw material extraction from the main processing to trade, service, and manufacturing process, to final consumption and waste disposal. Overall, the global commodity chain may be connected with different production, trade and service delivery process, organizational model, even including the external and internal market spillover effects (Gereffi and Kaplinsky, 2001; Pelupessy, 2001). The connection between these bodies has been conceived as a sequence of chains connecting imperfect markets, reflecting unequal value distribution caused by the non-equilibrium of market forces. It should be said that the global commodity chain research reflects the reality of economic globalization, providing an effective tool for analyzing the global strategy for multinational corporations and its global production system. However, in the mainstream framework of global city-specific analysis, this global dispersion of production cannot be accommodated; therefore, global commodity chain research is neither well absorbed nor combined organically.

Of course, there is also a major flaw in the global commodity chain research itself, namely, the absence of a comprehensive analysis of the commodity chain (Leslie and Reimer, 1999, pp. 401–420). In this study, regardless of the theory that the global commodity chain input is connected with those around the world, this input is simply believed to come from a specific place and provide output for different regions. Although it is also noted in the results of some studies that global commodity chains play an important role in promoting regional development and stimulating the local potential (Schmitz, 2000, pp. 1627–1650), its spatial concept has not shaped. In addition, in the global commodity chain analysis, there still exists a unique limitation, that is, the lack of an understanding of the key role of producer services in the establishment and maintenance of the global production networks. Although some scholars have originally called for exploiting a link between service sectors (Rabach and Kim, 1994, pp. 123–143), the global commodity chain analysis has not furthered into this sphere.

Thus, while the mainstream global city and global commodity chain research is based on globalization, with a common theoretical basis, i.e., the world-system analysis (of course, to varying degrees), they develop independently with almost the slightest cross-effects. As a result, both analytical frameworks are relatively good in proving the status of commodity chain or city network, but the relationship between them seems to be vague and hence the real problems in life cannot be well explained. For example, in their in-depth study of Mexico City and San Diego of Chile, some scholars have found that, on one hand, the data of the existing high-end production and rising levels of foreign investment show that the economy of Chile and Mexico is characterized by their increasing integration into the global commodity chain; on the other hand, there are indications that the economy of Mexico City and San Diego has close links with the transnational networks formed by organized global service producers (Beaverstock *et al.*, 1999, pp. 445–448; Derudder *et al.*, 2003, pp. 875–886). Studied separately, we know that Chile and Mexico are gradually being integrated into the global commodity chain, and global producers' service is being highly concentrated in Mexico and Chile, but we do not know the advanced producer services in the two cities are bound to show the relations of the two countries' production with the world market. Therefore, it is not enough to explain the space problems of globalization by using one of these theoretical models alone, and using these two theoretical models, respectively, is also problematic. That is, the lack of links between the study of global commodity chain and global city network is problematic.

In fact, when the commodity chain in the industrial manufacturing or processing of agricultural products is controlled by typical large multinational corporations, the global city networks provide advanced producer services for multinational corporations for their own interests, which are closely connected with the global commodity chain. It can be concluded that the combination of these two analytical frameworks is based on reality. The reason why mainstream global cities cannot properly absorb the research achievements of the global commodity chain or internalize it into its internal components of the analytical framework is not the researchers' negligence but is due to its inherent defects and limitations of its analytical theoretical framework, completely exclusive of the global spatial distribution of commodity chains based on the global production diversification, which will determine its only one stick on the basis of geographical space of the single central city. Obviously, the single city-based global city study cannot give an adequate and persuasive explanation of the industrial competition and development of supra-regional and extensive contacts and globalized urban areas in the conditions of globalization. When a theory cannot well cover more practical information and give a full explanation, it actually means the relativity or limitations of one's cognition, which is mainly reflected in the observation perspective of the geographical space of a single central city.

Hereby *et al.* (1996, pp. 1727–1743) point out that the increasing emphasis on decentralized model is still overshadowed by the traditional center model. Urban economic theory is still dominated by the analysis-inclined single-center model, so a convincing, alternative, more reality-predicting theoretical model has not been produced (in contrast with a range of fixed traditional styles of dealing with actual situation). Hall (1997, pp. 311–322) further states that cities should be based on the status of global information economy, rather than the traditional supply of retail services, manufacturing, and other activities, develop a separate set of urban development patterns, the geographic location (such as unique business centers), with Megalopolis linked to other places in the region, but also with other similar Megalopolis areas (does exist in other countries and continents) linked to other places within. A unique theory on exchange of information should include and evaluate the two links. The result is that a hierarchical structure of a new city center and sub-center should be formed according to the global positioning in the flow of information.

In short, by re-examining the mainstream theory of spatial structure of global cities, it can be clearly seen that the globalization of the urban spatial structure cannot be interpreted only by following the traditional model of a single central city but must be converted to the new viewing perspective, constructing a more inclusive analytical framework. Starting first from the impacts of globalization on all the involved cities, we extend to the widely affected urban areas, and then compare the global urban research and global commodity chains, two processes of contemporary globalization spatial model, breaking the limitations of a single central city model, examining the globalized cities of the global city network in the new spatial perspective. It should also be emphasized that it is the basic prerequisite to extend from the main globalized cities to the wider global urban research, increasing the tolerance of its analytical framework. Otherwise, it is difficult to accommodate the spatiality of the global commodity chains and combine urban development with a global geographical space.

4.2.2. *The spatial logic of the global city region*

We have pointed out earlier that a global city region takes the form of globalized space, showing the basic spatial unit of the global economy. Seen on the surface, globalization and the central role of urban areas, however, seem to be contradictory. Because globalization around the world is increasingly reinforcing close contacts with each other, emphasizing the regional weakening, coupled with the improving modern transportation and communication technology, it also helps to eliminate spatial barriers. Yet it is in this case that the global city space, as a very important phenomenon, emphasizes the importance of the region. So, how have these two seemingly contradictory aspects integrated each other?

Scott (2006, pp. 84–91) once explained the spatial logic of the global city region with the network structure (and related transactions). He believes that this network constitutes the basic framework of the economic organizations and social life, with its inherent duality: (1) the state as an entity, with clear signs of spatial structure, especially the performance of any bilateral or multilateral trade inevitably bringing about cost or the cost of dependent regions, namely, spatial transaction costs (including time and transportation costs); (2) its state as a social organization, with a clear way of specific combination and mutual links and often a strong synergistic effect (seen in Scott, 1998), the organizational contractual issue. According to the inherent duality of the network structure, we can, in theory, presume two simple extreme cases: one is high transaction costs of space, but simple organizational contract. In this economy, trading activity is purely linear, lacking coordination. It can be foreseen that the expansion of its trading activities to the urban and regional areas is rather limited; another case is that, in a purely virtual world, space transaction cost is zero, so the arbitrariness of its trading activities in the area can be foreseen in a country, whether the organizational contract be simple or complex. However, in our real world, the economic and social relations themselves are always broad in spatial distribution, so they will bear the transaction costs of space; and spatial transaction costs are different, usually with a lot of variables, sometimes high (i.e., a variety of face-to-face exchanges of information), sometimes very low (i.e., international currency in circulation), depending entirely on the type of production activities. Similarly, the organizational contracts are also diversified, ranging from the very simple, linear to highly synergistic transactions.

Based on the above assumptions, we analyze the current economic systems, usually two types of typical production activities and spatial transaction costs. One is a high degree of routine production activities, depending on regulated knowledge, machinery, and process, mainly as a pattern of repeated actions. The space transaction costs of such productions are lower, so it will not affect the efficiency of transactions even if there exists a lot of isolation space between producers. In this case, the effects of relevant inter-firm links on its choice of location may be quite limited. Therefore, the location choice of such production enterprises tends to be those relatively cheap lands or distant areas with associated companies.

In contrast, another type of economic activity has a huge uncertainty, and a strong interaction in between, with special requirements for the producers' abilities. For example, in high-tech industry, producers often face not only the rapid changes in basic technology itself, but also the ever-changing demands of customers for their products of different times. Another example is the professional business services and financial services, ranging from project-oriented to customer-oriented services, which require companies to implement a combination of different skills and resources to meet the specific needs of customers. Furthermore, since their own skills and resources (particularly human intelligence assets) of these highly specialized production activities have strong asset specificity, cannot be universally utilized. At the same time, these producing activities require a wider range of product differentiation and face high market volatility. In this case, the spatial transaction costs will increase with the expansion of distance, so regional spatial dispersion of the producers will lead to its rapid decline of efficiency. Obviously, when space transaction costs are very high, especially in frequent, unpredictable, and capricious face to face talks, a number of important economic sectors must rely on the parties being close to each other in order to make the transaction proceed smoothly.

We know that, in the past industrial age, economic activities tend to be more of a routine production mode, especially in manufacturing. But with the advent of the post-industrial era, and economic globalization, modern economic growth is dominated by the high-tech industries, new handicraft manufacturing, cultural products sector, media, and business and financial services. In addition, the economic environment tends to be more unstable than ever, forcing many departments to adopt a more flexible technical and organizational model. Moreover, there are also the factors of technological progress, for new information technology is now increasingly used in non-standard production processes to increase revenue and develop more varieties, and expand market share. Therefore, in the whole economic system, the second type of production becomes more and more universal, even if not currently occupying the leading position, but this flexible network system and value chain of production output and employment have accounted for an increasingly important share. In this context, the global city region becomes an important guarantee for lower transaction costs of space, interactive synergies, and enhanced competition. In many countries, those originally domestic market-oriented enterprises are faced with trade liberalization and removal of state protection and incentive policies. In order to turn to the international market orientation, to compete with imported products, the only way is to force them to use more urban areas in the world to have access to advanced production conditions. Through the dual nature of network structure (space transaction costs and organizational contracts), Scott points out the unconventional nature of the interaction becomes a stronger regional economic activity close to the global city region to explain the logic of space, which is more suitable for those used to describe highly developed urban areas in post-industrial era, because these areas are strong, interactive, and oriented toward economic activity.

But, as we have said above, the global city region is not restricted to the development process of metropolitan and regional areas in developed countries. In fact, this trend is occurring worldwide, including developing countries, where there is also abundant global city formation and development. The most prominent examples include Bangkok, Buenos Aires, Cairo, Jakarta, Lagos, Mexico City, Rio de Janeiro, Saint Paul, Shanghai, and Teheran. Clearly, in such urban areas of developing countries in the world, unconventional economic activities with strong interactions have not yet formed, despite a large number of routine production activities of a high degree of concentration, in particular, a large number of manufacturing activities. For this type of spatial logic of the global city region, Scott's theoretical explanation has some limitations. Because such production activities have lower transaction costs of space and weaker interaction, its location choice tends to be cheaper land prices and its related entities in areas far away, not producing close regional results. We believe that the spatial logic of the global city region can be fully explained only when the global commodity chain theory and the theory of industrial cluster are introduced, based on the interpretation of network structure.

First it must be noted, though still in the industrial age, economic activities in developing countries tend to be more routine, particularly in manufacturing, but in the process of integration into globalization, its routine production, particularly manufacturing, increasingly becomes a part of the global commodity chain. As the developing countries serve as the processing and manufacturing link in a global commodity chain, although their routine and basic properties of weak interaction do not change, the properties are even more weakening (due to a more specialized division of labor), and therefore there may be lower transaction costs of space. However, global commodity chain is a factor in the space allocation of global resources, so the location choice of direction and scope has taken on a fundamental change, i.e., the global location choice.

In terms of A-class global commodity chains of a single multinational companies, its global location choice in processing and manufacturing sectors may tend to be decentralized (distributed worldwide), but as an overall global commodity chain of transnational corporations, the global location choice in its processing and manufacturing links tends to be relatively centralized. That is, multinational corporations, driven by profit maximization, are always inclined to shift the manufacturing part of the commodity chain to areas having lower labor costs, high quality staff, good infrastructure, strong production ability, more active economic activities, and more stable social and political environment to obtain the maximum return in investment. At the same time, economic globalization is also enhancing the appeal of certain regions in developing countries to multinational companies at home and abroad. In the process, the space of manufacturing activities is relatively concentrated, so that industrial clusters of scaled economy, mutual support, and shared knowledge and information continue to show effects, which, in turn, becomes a catalyst for regional spatial concentration. Therefore, one node at one time, the international industrial transfer, especially international transfers in processing and manufacturing sectors, always tends to be centralized in geographical space, and even in areas of developing countries, even form large-scale global manufacturing bases.

On the basis of large-scale cluster manufacturing activities, many of the manufacturing activities relevant to research and development, marketing, logistics, technical services, and other service activities are bound to promote business and financial services, advertising, consulting services, accounting and auditing services, and legal service development. This not only promotes many unconventional and strongly interactive economic activities, but also greatly attracts the global services company, promoting the international transfer of services. Of course, those unconventional and strongly interactive producer service activities are usually more concentrated in urban centers in the region.

Therefore, global city regions in developing countries are typical of the coexistence of conventional and unconventional production activities, dominated mainly by routine production activities, interwoven and interactive. Although at this point, they are different from global city regions in developed countries, they still gather a large number of global enterprises or corporate networks for global market competition, increasingly serving as a geographic platform for the competitive global market. And, as globalization continues to expand the international market, further the production areas, the economy in these areas will also grow.

In short, on the basis of the network structure, the introduction of global commodity chain theory and the theory of industrial cluster interprets not only the spatial logic theory of global city regions in developing countries but also applies to developed countries, thereby having more theoretical integrity. In fact, in global city regions of developed countries, those dominant, unconventional, and strongly interactive economic activities are also one of the links in the global commodity chain, but the key sectors with higher added value, such as R&D, design, control, management, planning, marketing, and other activities as well as high-end producer services activities. Similarly, the spatial proximity of these production activities can better reflect the effect of industrial clusters, especially in the exchange and sharing of tacit knowledge. Therefore, the spatial logic of global city regions is based on the global commodity chain network structure and spatial configuration of the cluster spatial effect.

4.3. Regions of Global Cities and Globalizing Cities

From an analysis of the basic content of global city regions above, we can already see one of the basic premises for the formation of a global city region is the formation of city globalization, globalized cities and global city region is highly related. That is, the global city region is not existing independently of the element of globalized city, otherwise, it is, at most, a concept of city region. In this sense, global city region is a spatial agglomeration pattern of globalized city. Of course, this is not just the meaning of geographical proximity, but a spatial agglomeration based on the internal connection of network structure. Here I'd like to emphasize that, in contrary to the early progressive integration into the regional level in developed countries (to promote the formation and development of the global city region), the rising global cities in developing countries and global city regions shows a relationship of symbiosis, its formation and development being among global regional cities.

4.3.1. *The extension of the global commodity chain to the spatial distribution of the developing countries*

In the process of globalization, the extension of the global commodity chain to developing countries is one of the important levers shaping their involvement in the process of globalization. In general, this extension is not only rooted in national or regional network but also in city networks. However, because of different segments of global commodity chains, the spatial distribution of orientation is different, so where the spatial distribution of this externally embedded global commodity chains concentrates, to a large extent, depends on which part of global commodity chain it first undertakes.

Developing countries, however, usually undertake the "low end" processing and manufacturing areas in the global commodity chain. This "low end" process is linked with the input and output of low wages, low skills, and low profits. Moreover, this processing involves usually highly routine production activities, so the production of raw materials required for the variety of factor inputs and the number of inputs at a point of time is relatively immobilized, and bulk purchasing can be implemented but also can be conveniently obtained from a distance. This means that unit costs can be kept at a relatively low level. Therefore, in practice, the location choice of such conventional production is usually in accordance with cheap, low-skilled workers in line, sometimes far from the city center. Especially the "two out, in great quantities" processing trade production does not have high requirements for location and environmental conditions, but focuses more on low wage labor, cheap land prices, and convenient transport and corresponding preferential policies. Therefore, the "low end" part of the spatial distribution of global commodity chain is considerably dispersed.

At the same time, these processing and manufacturing activities also have industrial cluster effects such as coordinating production, scaled economies, transport, storage, and other platform sharing services, with information and knowledge being complementary. This seeks to further strengthen the close concentration of economic power, which could be partly interpreted as a kind of strategic response to economic competition, especially enhancing greatly the competitive advantage through industrial cluster. First, through some of the tight junction and spatial concentration clusters, different companies and participants can reduce their transaction costs, simultaneously increasing production space for flexibility and information effects, and thus helping to improve the overall efficiency of the economic system, so participants' efficiency is improved. Second, a huge flow of ideas and knowledge in insider trading links of local industry networks will appear, thereby strengthening the economic activities of learning, creativity, and innovation. Of course, it includes a diversity of different skills, emotions, and experiences embedded in labor, yet admittedly, interdependent producers gathering in one place will increase the formation of new ideas, new insights collision or the formation of practical possibility of knowledge. Third, compared with the location of distance separation, companies can obtain a more diverse supply channels and business opportunities, which would make companies more flexible, reducing excessive investment in inventory. Otherwise, in order to prevent the supply of strand breaks or very high risk of market outlets, we must increase the investment in inventory. Thus, the "low end" part of the spatial distribution in global commodity chains has focused on the objective requirements of corresponding concentration.

The "low end" spatial distribution in global commodity chain is dispersed and relatively paradoxical, which, in fact, is the inherent requirement for two balanced forces. The ultimate result is often more inclined to focus on certain areas and scattered in the area of the spatial distribution pattern in different cities. For example, a large number of foreign direct investments in China and its development zones are mainly distributed in the Yangtze River Delta, Pearl River Delta, and Bohai Bay area, where they are decentralized, mainly distributed in different cities. The spatial distribution of the "low end" links in global commodity chains generates an important effect of promoting the whole region's external economic ties, bringing many cities in the region into the globalization process. Because of this externally embedded processing of global commodity chain, there forms a "two out" large-scale processing trade activities in the region, leading to an influx of a large number of external resources (raw materials and energy, semi-finished products, components, etc.) and an outflow of finished products.

In this process, a more prominent change in the industrial structure may appear, namely, industrial isomorphism. For example, a considerable number of experts believe that there is a similar serious industrial structure in the Yangtze River Delta region, that is, the internal competition of similar products is too fierce while external competition is too weak, which will greatly affect the overall linking effects of the Yangtze River Delta, deterring the regional economic integration to a higher level. In this regard, some scholars provide certain reasonable explanations, with some believing that the industry structure is a micro-level problem and therefore one can rely on market forces of any of its industrial structure and orientation of the final decision while others are converging in a way that the industry can cause clusters, with the three industries clustering together (Chen, 2004). Still others believe that the Yangtze River Delta in the region is almost homogeneous in natural conditions, factor endowments, and technological conditions within the region, bound to make a convergence of the various sub-regional development (Zhu, 2003). These explanations do make some sense but do not touch the crucial issue. We believe that the most critical issues here are to determine whether the regional industrial structure is: (1) market-, domestic-, or international market-oriented and (2) endogenous or externally embedded. From the perspective of the global city region, the Yangtze River Delta region leads many production activities, or dominant production activities, as part of global commodity chain (manufacturing and processing areas), entirely driven by the international market. Moreover, most of its productions are foreign direct investments in externally embedded industry clusters. That is, multinational corporations are the main perpetrators to establish regional production networks. As multinational companies investing in China are mainly efficiency-seeking rather than market-seeking types, in order to minimize production costs, they not only break out of the production process a step or a link on the lowest production costs but also create scaled economies and complementary effects through industrial clusters. Currently, individual scholars have noted that the industrial structure in the Yangtze River Delta region is caused by the common acceptance of international transfer of manufacturing large products, and therefore it is reasonable. In some sense, it is precisely the industrial structures in the global city region that participate in the international industrial division and the obvious feature of international competition as a regional platform.

So far, we have revealed the spatial distribution of the "low end" part of global commodity chain, but its analysis does not end here. Developing countries, in the process of accepting international industrial transfer, on the whole, are at the "low end" of the global commodity chain (processing and manufacturing sector). However, processing depends on the smooth progress of activities related to supporting producer services, including R&D, design, technical consulting, maintenance, transportation and warehousing, advertising, marketing and accounting, auditing, and legal services, coupled with large-scale regional industrial clusters and the huge potential domestic market demand, which will attract "mid-range" and even "high end" link parts of the global commodity chain to enter. Of course, as embedded by the external processing in the global commodity chain, because of its R&D, design, and marketing, the "two out" part of coordinating producer services comes from abroad or achieves its coordinating services abroad. However, with the manufacturing of large-scale field of foreign direct investments and regional industrial clusters, those multinational corporations for the management and control of global commodity chain, regional or national headquarters for R&D and procurement centers and multinational corporations for professional business services and financial services will pour in to provide corresponding services. The high end of the process of global commodity chains, is closely associated with the input and output of higher wages, technology, and profits.

In contrast to processing and manufacturing activities, this type of producer services often involves non-routine activities, requiring a more stable business relationship with other related companies. This determines service companies of this kind must pay close attention to market changes and adjust the configuration of its internal resources. For this, these service activities are highly dependent on high-level access to a variety of information and resources. Although information technology can speed up the transmission and processing of information, the knowledge potential in these processes is often very hidden, so timely acquisition of such useful economic knowledge depends on interpersonal relationships and the ability to interpret the information in a read-between-the-line way. In addition, the degree of specialization and flexibility of producer service activities tends to be constantly improving, and its enterprises are facing rapid changes in network transactions, appearing in the new contract negotiations and adjusting their buying and selling relationships, or the rapid flow of human capital, so a high degree of expertise and complementarity is called for. Insurance is also required to deal with major emergencies or unexpected input needs (an important feature of a flexible economy is that it is very difficult to develop a long-term production plan). Therefore, an intricate network or a professional association between them has strong collaborative relations of production. Many of the interdependences of trade and non-trade are usually implemented in the form of the network by the individual producers. In this extensive network of trade relations, there are not only some obvious high spatial transaction costs but also supplement for the effect of a large amount of increased income (such as many modern and flexible financial capital sectors). In a strong collaborative relationship between the producers and a need for "face to face" information exchange, in order to reduce the high transaction costs of space, these industrial activities tend to be situated close to each other. The resulting aggregation occurs not only in a large number of domestic transactions but also in multilateral trades with foreign customers. As a place for many highly concentrated interdependent activities, a city is also a place for a new stream of social interactions and experience, where every day a lot of information is created and disseminated, it naturally becomes the most appropriate place for this type of producer service activities. Especially the central city, more suitable for producer services activities naturally becomes the concentrating place for producer services sectors.

In addition, a new change in trend is: with the acceleration of technological progress, increasingly fierce competition between companies, opening of new markets and company-specific enhancement of liquidity lead to a change in motivation of TNCs' global production, which is FDI for creative assets target [2]. As Dunning (1988) pointed out, in the past 10 years, the most siginificant change of FDI motives is the rapid growth of the creative asset-seeking FDI. Then FDI scarcely emphasizes the specific advantages for use of existing land ownership, yet more attention through the acquisition of new assets, or establishing partnerships with foreign companies to expand their advantages. In part, this FDI is similar to early natural resources-seeking FDI, but the choice of their location there is a huge difference. Part of the reason is the availability of creative assets, such as technical knowledge, learning experience, management expertise, and organizational capacity mainly concentrated in advanced industrial countries and larger developing countries. So those who prefer to build advantage through FDI companies will look for opportunities

[2] Creative assets, also known as strategic assets, are knowledge-based assets acquired through efforts on the basis of natural resources, include intangible assets such as information on the stock, trademarks, business reputation, intelligence, skills, abilities, and the relationship, as well as tangible assets, such as stock of financial assets, communication facilities, sales networks, and the like.

to invest in a particular location and to access and use creative assets required for the company. In developing countries, where the goal is to create assets, FDI will be more concentrated in major cities.

Thus, different from the choice of location in manufacturing activities, the "high end" part of global commodity chain externally embedded usually tend to concentrate in a few major cities, because these cities can play a most advanced part in connecting the global economy as the main node. Obviously, this gathering of the city, as a learning, creativity, and innovation center, will have many positive effects on the improvement of functional capacity. When this uncertainty, flexibility, and complex-network-based producer service clusters appear in a large urban center, it will help to consolidate and focus on the dynamic use of space.

4.3.2. *The rise of globalized cities among the development of global city regions*

As said above, the large-scale extension of global commodity chain to some areas in developing countries, according to the "high end–low end" of the border, constitutes a chain of value added and profits in the unequal access to the spatial distribution of the formation of a high-end process-oriented place (i.e., high-production areas) and the low end of the process leading to the place (i.e., low-production areas). Of course, in reality, the spatial distribution of the global commodity chain is more complex.

First, the meaning of "high" and "low" changes greatly based on time and space. The same is true with the process behind the specific operational mechanisms as well. Historically, a feature of these two processes is that they are both moving in the direction of centralization and decentralization. Among them, the evolution of market forces, entry barriers, and chain control mode will have a significant impact on its development. In addition, the so-called "high end" and "low" is not a pure single process but a mixed process. A production chain of any part of the mixing process is mainly based on the dominant process and experience, which are classified as "high", "middle", and "low". Therefore, the so-called "high-end production area", also contain a large number of (even a small number of) low-end process; while in the "low-end production area", also contain some of the high-end process. For example, the Yangtze River Delta region undertakes the extension of global commodity chain. Although Shanghai attracts multinational regional headquarters in China and producer services and finance, a high concentration of "high production areas", it also undertakes a large number of low-end manufacturing process; and Suzhou, Kunshan, Wuxi, and other cities undertake the processing and manufacturing in global commodity chain but also introduce some high-end process. Therefore, it is obviously not simple to define a "dual world", but a social model based on very complex interweaving of the reverse process of the most complex geographical space. In some areas, if the two opposite processes are generally in equilibrium when aggregation or dispersion effects have not been fully produced, this situation may be considered as "mid-structure".

In a region, the global commodity chain, in accordance with the "high end–low end" of the unequal distribution structure, often goes hand in hand with a high degree of a consistent city-level system. A center city has its "high-end process" (such as the supply of advanced producer services) leads the node, corresponding to "high-end production areas". Of course, there are low ends of the internal processes, manifested as social polarization effects, such as those serving the professional tradition of advanced producer services sector in the low-wage, low-technology process. In large cities, there are professional services and other high-paying job, and while they are not dominant, there is a high-end and low-end production chain mixing process, in which a low-wage, low technical and economic process is also important. Medium and small cities have "low-end process" as their leading nodes, corresponding to the "low-end production areas".

In short, when the global commodity chain extends to some regions in developing countries, on a large scale, the region's cities are likely to integrate into it. Even if they are just "general" cities, they also play a peripheral role in entering the global commodity chain, but close contact already starts to occur in this space of flows into the world economy. That is, the global flow of goods in the branch nodes can be obtained from these cities to increase the value and further generate revenue streams in these cities. The major cities in the region are specific and critical nodes in the extension of global commodity chain, embedded in its production process by advanced producer services. In this sense, the main city is a service node in a chain, thus having a comprehensive central position. The producer services provided through major cities not only support the city network connection but are also indispensable in connecting decentralized aspects of production and consumption points and therefore essential to the smooth operation of the production chain, because they provide the key elements of input, from the initial bank loan to production, until company's services to facilitate use of advertising in the final consumption. As a result, these service agencies provide a global commodity chain and a global point of intersection between the urban network (Parnreiter *et al.*, 2005), so as to establish a link between the two. Thus, high-end, mid-range, and low-end production areas are formed and maintained by the spatial structure of global commodity chains, which in turn form and keep going through global city networks.

Externally, we can see the embedded global commodity chain, on the basis of promoting globalization of cities in the region, as a "high-end production area"; the center of the city and its neighboring region as a "medium and low production areas"; and the general city inherent between the global contacts as a "headquarters and producer services — processing and manufacturing" division of labor and cooperation in the area function model. Without this extension of global commodity chains formed by large-scale regional processing and widely distributed manufacturing activities, there will be no demand for comprehensive services to promote high-end part of global commodity chain (control and management, advanced producer services) embedded in the major cities of the region's production process to make it as a service node in global commodity chain and become a comprehensive center. Conversely, if none in these regions can act as a special node of multinational and large domestic companies, the large-scale extension of the global commodity chains to this region is difficult to carry out smooth and sustainable development. Basically, the global flow of goods is included in the core formation process, regardless of where its production is located. These core processes and the implementation of production chain control is necessary. This region in the wide range of foreign economic ties, usually takes a major global city network as an intermediary node city; and large-scale economic flows formed by regional industry clusters also flow through the service function of major network cities.

From the above analysis, we can describe globalizing cities from the "path dependence" perspective as follows: the extension of global commodity chains to developing countries, concentrated in certain regions under the conditions of aid, with the cities in the region based on a wide range of globally external economic ties, relying on the interactive large-scale economic flows within and outside the region, serving as a bridge to connect the domestic economy with the world economy, plying economic, financial, and central trade and shipping functions, and then evolving into major node cities in the global city networks. That is, the rise of global cities in developing countries is based on the regional urban globalization, with regional development among global cities.

Chapter 5

Rise of Global Cities: Prerequisite and Positioning Strategic Target

In the previous three chapters, we analyzed the background conditions, the network foundations, and the new spatial structure of a globalizing city. In addition, based on rectifying and developing the main theories of a globalizing city, we constructed a theoretical framework to analyze a globalizing city. After that, we exploited this framework to further study the development modes and path-choice of a globalizing city by taking China as an example. In this chapter, we will explore more problems regarding the fundamental preconditions, strategic requests, realistic differences, strategic target location, and target tendencies of the globalizing cities in China.

5.1. Deeply Melting into the Process of Globalization

As pointed in the former analysis, globalizing cities are usually the basic panel points in the global economy network, which are, to a great degree, the outcome of the deepening process of globalization. In return, they are the main force behind globalization. Basically, this means that the rise of the globalizing cities cannot be dissociated from the process of globalization. The extensive opening-up of China's economy means it is integrated to globalization process and is playing an increasingly important role in the world economy, which is one of the basic preconditions for us to explore the rising of the globalizing cities.

5.1.1. *Opening-up and independency on outgoing economy*

The reforms on the economic system in 1978 can be considered as the symbolic turning point: China overturned its closed and autonomous economic structure, which was in place for a long time and began to open up to the outside world, participate the division of international industries, carry on the relative links of the global commodity chain, seek the cooperation and exchange with world economy, and integrate gradually to the process of globalization. Especially after its entry to the WTO in 2001, China largely improved with respect to its systems and mechanisms and extended its all-around opening-up policy to the outside world. In the following five-year transition period, China promulgated and revised more than 1,000 laws and regulations, which decreased the average tariff tax rate from 15.3% in 2001 to 9.9% at present. In addition, China reduced or eliminated a number of non-tariff barriers, relaxed the market access conditions to international services providers, and enhanced the transparency of the government program, which ensured that China conformed to the provisions of the WTO in trade systems.

A country's opening-up to the outside world is one of the preconditions for it to enter and participate in the globalization process. In fact, the degree of its opening-up to the outside world reflects the size of its "door" to participate in the process of the economic globalization. Generally speaking, a bigger door means its bigger scale in entering and participating in the process of globalization and vice versa. Therefore, the degree of opening-up to the outside world in economy is one of the important indexes to see if the country enters and participates in the process of globalization. With the deepening of China's opening-up to the outside world, there is an increasing expansion of the outgoing economy. China's present economy is characterized by its opening-up in a wide range of areas, which means China's economic activities are increasingly related closely to the world market. In a horizontal comparison, China's opening-up is greater than that of other developing countries such as India and Mexico, and it is also higher than that of developed countries such as the USA, Japan, and the UK. For example, although the opening-up of the Japanese economy has improved since the 1980s, imports account for only 11% of its GDP; while that of China was as high as 29.6% in 2005, its total amounts of import and export was as high as 63.9% of its GDP.

In the process of opening-up to the outside world, one of the main goals is to introduce the foreign direct investments (FDIs) or to bring in the global commodity chain. Initially, China attracted FDIs and introduced the global commodity chain into the country by the system arrangements or favorable policies such as the establishment of economic special zones in the coastal cities and various development zones. After 1992, China's government further released, and even eliminated, the limitations on the domestic selling of foreign-invested enterprises. With the high-speed growth of China's economy in this period, the transnational companies are stimulated to invest in China and share its massive market. An increasing number of foreign investments from transnational companies came to China successively. According to the statistics, the number of the foreign-invested enterprises approved by China from 1979 to 2004 was 508,941 throughout the country; the contractual foreign investment amounted to US $1096.609 billion, while the actually paid-in capital was US $562.105 billion, and more than 400 of the top 500 transnational companies in the world established their branches in China. In 2003, China replaced the US as the biggest capital in-flow country in the world. In 2004, 43,664 foreign-invested companies were newly approved by China, the contractual foreign investment reached to US $153,479 billion, the actually paid-in capital reached was US $60,603 billion. In 2005, the actually paid-in foreign capital was more than US $70 billion. The percentage of the total FDI is more than 40% of China's GDP, which is much higher than that in the developed countries and the Asian countries or regions.

By attracting FDI, especially from the transnational companies, China gained fundamental conditions such as capital, technology, and sales network. The collocation ability of China's manufacturing industry was improved, and the development of China's industry and regional economy was promoted. In addition, China was pushed to embed into the global value chain and merge into the global industry system. At present, China has entered into the overall layout of industrial division of the world; and its assembling and processing industries have become the main links in the international industrial chain. As the dual bases of world factory and market, China has become the most attractive hosting country to the whole world. Though the salaries and relative costs tend to increase in China, it has the industrial gathering, which is not available in other countries, and thus it is more attractive to the foreign investment. According to the survey conducted by Japan Cooperation Bank on Annual Survey of Overseas FDI in 2006, as the expected investment destinations in the following three years, China ranked the first place (but the percentage of obtained votes decreased from 93% in 2004 to 77% in 2007), followed by India, Vietnam, and Thailand.

With the large amount of FDI to China, the international manufacturing was transferred to China and resulted in the rapid expansion of the trade scale in China. According to the statistics, the total amount of China's import and export increased from US $20.64 billion in 1978 to US $509.65 billion and rose to US $1421.91 billion in 2005, surpassing US $1.7 trillion in 2006, which was three times as much as that in 2001. In particular, the exports increased from US $18.12 billion in 1980 to US $593.36 billion in 2004, its percentage in China's GDP steadily rose from 6%, in its lowest level, to 36% in 2004 (see Figure 5.1). The percentage of the value of exports in China increased from less than 1% of that of the world in 1979 to

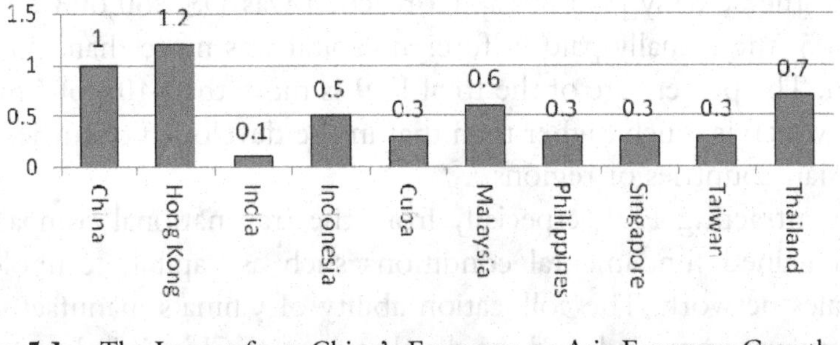

Figure 5.1. The Impact from China's Economy on Asia Economy Growth if it is Increased by 1%.

Source: The analyzed result by CitiGroup using Newton Economic Prediction Model.

6.5% in 2004, which ranked third in the world. Since the 1990s (except the year 1993), the trade deficit in China was transferred to the trade surplus (see Figure 5.1). The trade surplus of the successive 10 years and the large-scale flow of foreign investment rapidly increased China's foreign exchange reserves. In 2006, the foreign exchange reserve of China reached to more than US $1 trillion, which equaled to 45% of the overall economic production in the same year.

In view of the dynamic process, this massive trade development tendency is increasingly strengthened with the transmission of the trade structure. Between 1980 and 2005, the percentage of China's export of primary commodities gradually decreased from 51.6% to 6.4%, while that of industrial products increased from 48.4% to 93.6%. The internal structure of the export of manufactured goods changed drastically, and the export of machineries and transporting equipments increased rapidly, with its percentage in the overall export increasing from 10% in the 1990s to 42.9% in 2004. At present, this percentage of China's manufacturing goods is higher than the average level in the world and is at the same level as that of Germany. In addition, the surplus of industrial manufacturing goods is higher while there is a great deficit in primary commodities. The surplus of import and export of industrial manufacturing goods increased from US $41.9 billion in 2001 to US $200.7 billion in 2005, and the deficit of primary commodities increased from US $19.4 billion in 2001 to US $98.7 billion in 2005.

In view of the future development, based on the global productive system, massive trade activities will possibly be sustained. The reason is that, in view of per capita, the level of China's trade development is still at the level of a developing country. In 2004, the percentage of China's export value was 6.5% in the overall export value in the world, while its population account for one-fifth of the world, which means that the per capita export level of China is only one-fourth of that in the world, while the per capita export level is several times as much as that in the world. In this sense, China has a great potential in the growth of export. If the world export trade continues to increase by 5% each year, and China's export trade continues to increase by 12%, China will needs another 15 years before it can

Table 5.1. Percentage of China's Export Value and its Trade Balances Between the Years 1980 and 2004 (in the Unit of US $100 Hundred Million).

Years	Export Value/GDP (%)	Export Value	Import Value	Trade Balance
1980	6.0	181.2	108.9	−11.4
1985	9.0	273.5	422.5	−149.0
1990	16.1	620.9	533.5	87.4
1991	17.7	719.1	637.9	81.2
1992	17.6	849.4	805.9	43.5
1993	15.3	917.4	1039.6	−122.2
1994	22.3	1210.1	1156.2	53.9
1995	21.3	1487.8	1320.8	167.0
1996	18.5	1510.5	1388.3	122.2
1997	20.4	1827.9	1423.7	404.2
1998	19.4	1837.1	1402.4	434.7
1999	19.7	1949.3	1657.0	292.3
2000	23.1	2492.1	2251.0	241.1
2001	23.0	2661.5	2436.1	225.4
2002	26.0	3256.0	2951.0	305.0
2003	31.0	4328.3	4127.6	254.7
2004	36.0	5933.6	5613.8	319.8

Source: The Yearbook of Foreign Trade and Economy in China, in the Corresponding Years.

account for 20% of the world overall export value. In other words, at least in the future 15 years, China's export trade will possibly increase by more than 10%.

For a rather long time, China was involved in the process of globalization by implementing the "bringing home" strategy, but in recent years, it reinforced the strategy of "going out", which resulted in the rapid development of overseas investments and acquisition. According to the statistics, over the past five years, China increased its overseas investment by 86% each year. By the end of the year 2006, China's accumulated total of FDI reached to US $73.33 billion. In the same year, the non-financial FDI of China reached to US $16.13 billion, which increased by 31.6% year-on-year; its position in FDI globally rose from 17th in 2005 to 13th in 2006. Originally, China's FDI was focused on the mining industry, while it transferred to the manufacturing industry recently. In 2004, the mining industry accounted for 52.8% in the non-financial FDI of China; the business service industry, 26.5%; the manufacturing industry, 13.5%; the wholesale and retailing industry, 3%; the other industries, 4.2%. In 2005, the percentage of the manufacturing industry increased to 13.5%, while that of the mining industry decreased to 28.7%; the percentage of information transmission, the computer services, and software industry was 26.3%; the business service industry, 5.2%; the wholesale and retailing industry, 3.2%; the transportation industry, 2.2%, the industries of farming, forestry, animal husbandry, side-line production, and fishery, 1.8%; the architecture industry, 1.7%; and the other industries, 1.9%. In the modes of foreign investment, the domestic competitive enterprises invest overseas by merger and acquisition. For example, PetroChina succeeded in purchasing oil fields in Kazakhstan and Ecuador; CNOOC purchased oil fields in Nigeria; Sinapec purchased Udmurt Oil Company in Russia; CHALCO purchased bauxite mines in Australia; and Minmetals group set up joint ventures enterprise with Codelco, Chile, the world's largest copper company. In addition, China's Lenovo group acquired IBM's personal computer business; TCL group acquired the television manufacturing business from Thomson Company; China Blue Star Group Corporation purchased Rodia company in French, etc.

In view of investment regions, from the regional perspective, Africa has become another preferred region for China's overseas investments after the ASEAN countries. For example, China opened factories in Kenya and Mauritius, with the total amount of investment amounting to US $6.3 billion in 2006. Also, China began to invest in other fields of service, for example, in September, 2006, China Mobile claimed to purchase a mobile telecom carrier in Ethiopia. According to the statistics, in 2006, China realized US $4.74 billion FDI by means of merging, which accounted for 36.7% of the total FDI of China in the same year.

It is predicted in the research report by Deutsche Bank that, in the future 15 years, the annual growth rate of China's FDI will possibly be over 20%, and the total amount of its FDI will reach to US $60 billion in 2011. China will be the country with the largest FDI in Asia, and FDI in the resource industry will account for two-thirds of the total investment, followed by the wharfs, automobile, banking, telecommunications, and electronics industry.

5.1.2. *Highlights of Chinese elements in the global economy*

For a globalizing city, increasing participation and merging into the process of globalization is the only essential, but not sufficient, condition. As pointed in Chapter 3 about the analysis of the global urban network structure, the changes in the world economy are the key factors influencing the changes of urban panel points in the network structure. In detail, there are several aspects as stated in the following:

(1) changes in the development levels of the world economy, for example, the promotion of the level of overall economic strength, the transmission from the industrial economy to the service economy, the expansion and structural change of world trade and investment scale;
(2) changes in the global space expansion in world economy, such as the transferring of international industries, the space extension of the global commodity chain, the changes of the space distribution of world market;
(3) changes in the world economy situation, such as the replacement of the growth engine, the transferring of growth weight, and the changes in the growing balancing strength. These changes can result in the changes of flowing direction and paths in the global resources, elements, commodities, service, etc., and it will further result in the re-collocation of the global network panel points and their changes. Generally speaking, in those urban panel points which are in the flowing direction and flowing paths of the global resources, elements, etc., their higher connection with the global network implies their increased importance;

while, in urban panel points that are far away from the flowing direction and the flowing paths of the global resources, elements, etc., their lower connection implies their declining position. One conclusion drawn from this is the following: some cities, on the basis of higher participation and emergence in the process of globalization, will possibly become common globalizing cities; however, because they are not in the flowing direction or flowing regions of the global resource elements, they will not necessarily rise as a globalizing city. In this sense, if a city wants to be a globalizing city, the transferring of the world economic center and the strength of its home country are the sufficient conditions.

Dunning (1981), in his theory of investment development level, tried to explain the relationship between the economic development level of a country and its international direct investment position in the world in a dynamic view. He analyzed data of direct investment flow and the economic development level of 67 countries between 1967 and 1978 and concluded that the out-flow quantity and in-flow quantity of the direct investment of one country were closely related to its economic development level. The investment developing paths of Dunning are illustrated well in China. In the process of opening-up to the outside world, China enjoyed the fruits of globalization, promoted its rapid economic development, and expanded its overall economic scale. In the 1990s, the average growth rate of China's economy was 7.5–8%. In the 21st century, the economic growth was stimulated further, especially since the year 2003, when China's economic growth rate was increased by 10: it was 10% in 2003, 10.1% in 2004, 10.4% in 2005, and increased to 10.7% in 2006. In view of the overall economic scale, according to the data from the Bureau of National Statistics in China and the World Bank, the GDP of China in 2005 reached US $2.235 trillion, ranking fourth globally. The percentage of its share in the world economy rose from 1.8% in 1978 to 5% in 2005, only after that of the USA, Japan, and Germany. The more important thing is that the rapid growth and the overall scale of China's economy means it has more influence on the world economy. According to the data of the World Bank, between the year 2000 and 2004, China's economic growth contributed 15% in each year to the growth of the world economy, only after the USA, and it has become the most important accelerator in the world economic growth. The report released by IMF pointed out that China would contribute the most (25%) to the world economic growth in 2007, a quarter of the overall. The analysis of the growth structure showed that rapid economic growth comes from the accelerating development process of industrialization under the context of opening-up, mostly, the rapid growth of the manufacturing industry. According to the statistics, since the year 1979, China has witnessed the fastest growth of the manufacturing industry (see Table 5.2). China's industrial product index increased as much as 1.86 times between the year 1985 and 1990 and by 3.75 times between the year 1991 and 1996, while the other manufacturing countries such as the USA grew at a lower rate, with Japan even experienced a negative increase in the late 1990s. In the growth tendency, China took up more shares in the manufacturing industry globally. During 1980 to 1997, China's percentage of the added value of the global manufacturing industry rose from 1.4% to 5.9%, which was 0.26% per year on average. After rapid development of more than 10 years, China ranks the first or the second in the production of many key industrial products, such as the manufacturing of electric appliances, telecommunication equipment, textile, mechanic equipment and

Table 5.2. The Comparison of the Industrial Production Indexes of the Key Countries.

	1985	1990	1991	1996		1985	1990	1991	1996
China	176	328	111	416	USA	112	126	98	117
Israel	120	132	107	151	UK	108	123	97	108
Japan	118	148	102	98	Denmark	121	133	100	117
Malaysia	138	236	111	87	Australia	114	126	100	110
Korea	164	302	110	163	France	101	144	99	100
Philippine	231	451	115	168	Finland	16	132	91	121
Canada	115	128	96	114	Brazil	9	100	97	112

Note: Compared on the Basis of the Index 100 in 1980 (1985–1990), and the Index 100 in 1990 (1991–1996).
Source: *The Yearbook of International Statistics* (1998).

chemical industry. All of these show that China's manufacturing industry has become a newborn strength of the world.

The more important thing is that the operation of China's economy not only relies on the global development space but also participates into the economic balance of the world. At present, the world economy is in a multipolar balance, in which China's economy has become one important pole. In East Asia, at present, China has gradually transformed into a new economy-integrated country. In 1990, China attracted 18.7% while ASEAN countries attracted as much as 66.4% of the total FDI in Asia. However, in 2004, China's percentage increased to 58%, and that of ASEAN countries decreased to 22.2%. In addition, China has become the base of the world's manufacturing industry; it replaced the USA and became the biggest export market of Korea and Singapore in Asia and became the key of the manufacturing network in East Asia. Between the years 1992 and 2002, bilateral trade between China and Japan increased by 300%; that between China and Korea, 700%; China and Thailand, 800%; China and India, 1100%; China and the Philippines, 1800%. The countries or regions in East Asia enjoyed a huge trade surplus from China, but this surplus was actually transferred from Japan, Hong Kong, Taiwan, Koreas, and the ASEAN countries to China. Under this context, China's economic impact is increasingly expanding its impact on the Asian country (see Figure 5.1).

In addition, the economic balanced relationship between China (and the other Southeast Asian countries) and the USA is becoming the key factor influencing the overall world economy situation. This relationship is embodied as the following:

(1) the increasing trade deficit of the USA corresponds to the increasing trade surplus of China (and the Southeast Asian countries). The regular account deficit of the USA in 2005 amounted to US $800 billion, which accounted for 6.5% of the GDP of the USA and it is expected to exceed 7% of its GDP in 2006;
(2) the increasing expanded negative savings of the USA correspond to the increasing net savings of China (and the Southeast Asian countries). The total foreign debt of the USA in 2005 exceeded US $2.5 trillion in 2005, and the saving rate in the USA is as low as 0.3%, whereas the foreign exchange reserve of the Asian countries

exceeded US $3 trillion and the saving rate keeps growing. Among them, the foreign exchange reserve of China amounted to US $1 trillion, the saving rate of the people is as high as 46%;

(3) the strong and growing requirements of the USA correspond to the strong and growing supplies of China (and the Southeast Asian countries), see Figure 5.2. At present, imported material products of the USA amounts to 40% of the domestic material product consumption, most of which are from China. For example, 80% of the 6,000 global suppliers to Wal-Mart are in China. In 2005, the imported Chinese products by Wal-Mart amounted to US $20 billion. However, in 1995, only 5% of the sold products by Wal-Mart were from China, today one of two products sold by Wal-Mart is from China.

Between the two totally different economic structures, one is the high consumption and low savings in the USA and the other is the low consumption and high savings in China, the corresponding relationship

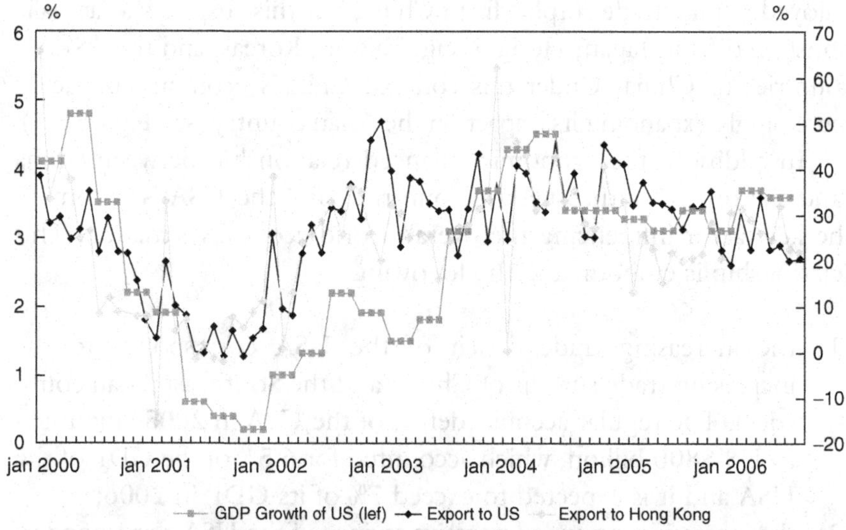

Figure 5.2. The Relationship Between the Economic Growth of the US and China's Growth in Exports to the US and Hong Kong.

Source: CEIC Data Com. Ltd.

relies on a kind of recycling mechanism to a great degree. FDI from developed countries such as the USA greatly improved the production ability of China and supported its export growth, which resulted in the huge trade surplus to the USA and allowed China to accumulate a huge amount of foreign exchange reserve. These foreign exchange reserves were used to buy the American bonds. According to the data from the Ministry of Finance of the USA, by June, 2005, the Chinese public and private sectors had at least US $527.3 billion worth of American bonds, including long-term American national debt or governmental bonds worth US $450 billion. These capitals are flowing to the USA successively, making up the huge deficit of regular accounts in the USA, lowering the long-term interest lower and increasing the asset price, supporting the consumption requests of the US government and the private sectors by financial effects, and making it become the main driving source of the American economic growth. In return, this will help stir the export growth of China (see Figure 5.3)

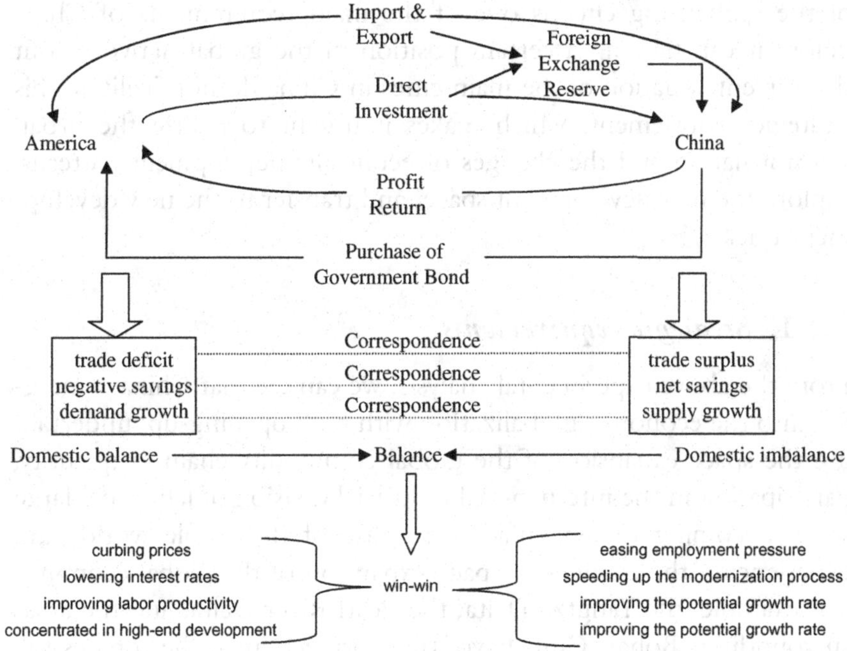

Figure 5.3. The Economic Balanced Mechanism Between China and the USA.

In the recycling system, the two sides are in a win-win situation in mutual restriction and become the "engines" in promoting the growth of the global economy. Similarly, once the mutual restriction dysfunctions, the economic growth of the two countries will be influenced mutually and the global economy will be struck greatly. Thus, since the year 2005, the American policies aimed at China underwent huge changes in view of strategies, the US transferred its policies of pressing and blocking to those of communication of cooperation, which require China to undertake more responsibilities in the global system.

5.2. Strategic Requirement of Globalizing Cities

China is comprehensively involved in economic globalization, and the elements concerning China are becoming more obvious in the global economy, which necessitates strategic requirements, that is, the rise of the globalizing cities. That is to say, no matter it is in the view of the global strategy or the development strategies of the country, the rise of the globalizing cites is one of the main requirements of China before it can take up a certain position in the global network. But the current situation of the main cities in China do not facilitate this strategic requirement, which makes it urgent to realize the urban transformation and the changes of economic development patterns, explore the new development space, and transfer to the new development track.

5.2.1. *Strategic requirements*

From the above experimental analysis, we can see that China is merging into the economic globalization with high opening-up, undertaking the space expansion of the global commodity chain in quantity, participating in the international industrial division of labor in a large scale, becoming the manufacturing base of the whole world, and experiencing the changes of space expansion of the global economy. For example, the Yangtze Delta, the Pearl River Delta, and the areas surrounding Bohai Gulf have transformed into the processing factories of world's industrial products, which are closely and extensively related to the outside economy, especially the processing trade of increasing exports, which results in the large-scale economic flow. In 2004, the imported and exported goods in the area of the Yangtze Delta accounted for 36% of the total of the country: the area exported 30% of the country's total manufacturing goods and 31% of the total exports of the foreign-owned enterprises (Hu, 2005), its interdependency of foreign trade reached 182.6%. In this area, the most internationalized industries include manufacturing industries of electronics and communication equipments, garments and other fiber-related industries, and electrical machines and devices. In 2004, the export value in these manufacturing industries accounted for 78% of its total industrial products, which stands for the position and function of the manufacturing industries in the area of the Yangtze Delta in the system of international division of labor in international manufacturing industries.

On the basis of extensive opening-up and participation in the global economic recycling, China's economy is increasing successively and its scale is expanding rapidly, which result in a huge economic flow with respect to both its domestic and outside relations. At the same time, the huge economic flow is closely related to the country, one of the engines of the world economy growth, and one of the balanced strengths of the global economic growth. According to international practice, the huge internal and external economic flow is usually related internally to the transferring of the international economic center. When one country has a huge economic flow in its connection to both internal and external economies, it will increasingly undertake the functions of the panel points of the global network. Thus, in the rapid growth of the flow scale in China's connection to both internal and external economies, some central cities will surely be entrusted with the responsibility of undertaking the functions of the panel points of the global network.

At the same time, what the integration to the economic globalization brings is the increasing influence and the rapid growth of the economic scale in the connection to internal and external economic connections, which, in fact, is transforming the urban functions in China, promoting the development of the cities and urging them to transform into globalizing cities. Thus they are the necessary conditions and realistic foundations for the rise of China's globalizing cities. Castelles (1996) and the others considered the city as a process. And Jacobs (1970) pointed out further that this was the process of the expansion of economic life. Jacobs thought that the process in which imports replaced the newly created jobs was actually the process in which the cities were promoted to develop further. Apparently, China is enjoying continuous and rapid economic growth because of its integration to the economic globalization, which will greatly promote urban development and profoundly change the urban functions.

In the process of China's opening-up and its integration to the globalization, the cities, especially the developed coastal cities, are playing more and more important roles. As is well known, in the modern economy, as the development center of the regional economy and the base of scientific and technological innovation, the city is usually playing a key role in the development of the national economy. For example, at present, 50% of China's total industrial production, 70% of its GDP, and 80% of its national tax revenue are from the cities. Thus, in the process of opening-up to the outside world, the cities are attracting more FDI and becoming the main space carrier of the extension of the global commodity chain. The reasons are obvious: the cities have better environment conditions, such as advantageous locations; solid economic foundations; convenient and accessible transportation; complete infrastructure; mating of industries and related services; developed culture, science and education; gathering of professionals and qualified labors; intensive exchange of information and knowledge, etc. In particular, the coastal cities are experimental units to open up to the outside world: they attracted a large sum of FDI, thus promoting the development of urban economic society, expanding its connection to the outside economies and improving the economic extroversion and the level of urban internationalization. For example, the 15 cities (excluding Taizhou,

Zhejiang Province) in the area of the Yangtze Delta have 37 state-level parks of various kinds, including 6 new technological development zones, 11 economic and technical development zones, 1 finance and trade area, 13 exported-oriented processing zones, 3 bonded areas, and 3 scenery resorts, which account for 21.8% of the total in the country. Some scholars analyzed the space concentration of the manufacturing industries in 16 cities of the Yangtze Delta and found that 92% of gross output value was from the industrial parks and economic and technological zones in these central cities (Hu, 2005). Meanwhile, in the trade activities in large scales, the cities are becoming the doors or passageways connecting to regions at home and abroad.

In the process of opening-up and integration to the globalization, the cities themselves are developing rapidly, especially showing great changes in their urban functions. For a long time, bound by the traditional systems, the urbanization process in China was relatively hysteretic and urban development is comparatively slow with respect to its industrial development level. The market-oriented reforms on systems broke through the system barriers, binding urbanization, and formed the internal system to mutually promote the urbanization and the industrialization. But it is noted that the export-oriented economic development based on globalization is the catalyst in this process. Since the reform and opening-up, especially since the 1990s, the process of China's industrialization has accelerated, closely related to the transferring of international manufacturing industries and it became a powerful support to speed up the process of industrialization, requiring the effective integration and better collocation of the resources in the cores of the cities. And moreover, it resulted in the economic development in the surrounding areas, and even expanded regions, by the function of integration and radiation of the cities. Thus the regional and national economic coordination and operation system was constructed. The process of urbanization was accelerated, and the positions of the cities in economy and politics were promoted rapidly. In this context, the present China focuses on the spatial structure of economic development on the cities. The rapid economic growth promotes the rapid development of the cities; in return, the rapid development of the cities becomes the source of motive power and the supporting bases.

What is more important is that, in the process of China's economic integration to globalization, the cities are integrated to the concept framework of world as the main spatial carriers of the expansion of the global commodity chain in China, which are becoming increasingly important international stages. Differing from the international trade, by creating jobs and direct participation to the mutual internal economic activities, FDI contributes to the mutual economy and society in a direct way. Therefore, the attraction of FDI and participation in the international division of industries as one link of the global commodity chain helps in the easier formation of mutual involvement and function between the internal economy and the external economy. With the deepening of China's participation in the international division of industries, the penetration and interaction between the internal economy and the external economy is becoming increasingly obvious. As important spatial carriers, the cities are playing an important role in the penetration and interaction between the internal economy and the external economy as bridges and channels. In return, in the interaction between connecting the internal economy and the external economy, the cities' function as a global strength are more and more obvious; they are evolved to globalizing cities and integrated to the global urban network. There is a new change at the present stage, that is, the cities connect more to the outside world and exert more impact by overseas investment. For example, Shanghai invested on only 34 overseas enterprises, with an investment of US $32.74 million in 2004; while, in 2006, this number increased to 75, with the investment of US $329.77 million, and the average compound growth rate between the year 2000 and 2000 reached to 31.3% (see Table 5.3).

According the present leading document of the research on the globalizing cities, it cannot be confirmed which cities are the most important globalizing cities in China finally and comprehensively for the time being, let alone the exact position of a certain city in the country and the global urban network. Some scholars think that some

Table 5.3. The Number of Overseas Enterprises and the Investment by Shanghai in 2000–2006.

	2000	2001	2002	2003	2004	2005	2006
The number of Newly Increased Enterprises	34	32	64	81	91	59	75
The investment ($ ten thousand)	3274	5384	13494	17200	32824	68775	52977

Source: The website of Shanghai Statistics and the Bulletin of Shanghai's national economy and social development in 2006.

main cities in present China are just the central cities in the country and that they cannot meet the requirements of the globalizing cities (Yeung, 1996, 1997). At the same time, they point that these main cities have the potential to become globalizing cities due to China's rapid development in the global economy. The most competitive cities among them are Hong Kong, Beijing, and Shanghai. Hong Kong may continue to be the bridge and window for China to connect to the globe. Beijing and Shanghai are the two potential competitors of Hong Kong, and each has actual strength to be a potential globalizing city. The advantage of Beijing is that it is China's capital, which is the gathering center of decision-making on national economy and management and supervision institutions and organizations. Before 1949, Shanghai was once the important financial center in the Far East. At present, with the support from the central government of China, Shanghai has regained its position as the economic center of China, which locates Shanghai's prime position in the ranks of domestic cities and improves its position in the global urban system.

It is noticeable that both Beijing and Shanghai are characterized by obvious globalization in their connections to the outside world. On the basis of differentiating the connection degree (linking degree) and the connection (the classification of connection, namely, the global connection and the local connection), Taylor (2006) experimentally analyzed the Asian cities. The results showed that Beijing and Shanghai had their own features in the global urban network, that is, they have better connection than the other cities which have the same connection degree. Though the connection degree of Beijing and Shanghai is similar to that of Kuala Lumpur and Jakarta, their connection classification is more globalized and less localized. Their globalization is similar to that of Hong Kong, Tokyo, Singapore, and other cities. The global-oriented index of Shanghai is 1.167, which is bigger than that of Hong Kong, 1.110; Tokyo, 0.949; and Singapore, 0.640. Irrespective of whether these remarks are consistent with the reality, the rapid economic growth in the process of China's integration to the globalization, the rise of its position in the global economy, and its rising as a globalizing city have surely become the necessary strategic requirements.

5.2.2. *The strategic requirements and the realistic differences*

In the system of traditional economy, by the planned collocation of resources, some main cities in China have become manufacturing cities with mono-functions. When China's door was closed to the world at that time, these cities became domestic manufacturing entities in the typical and closed country. Since the reform and opening-up to the outside world, with the promotion of the process of marketization, the urban development was injected with new elements and energies. In particular, the urban potential economic energies are released greatly since the marketization of the elements such as capital and land, influx of foreign investment, reforms on production and rights, and reforms on the financial system characterized by the separation of powers, which became a strong and powerful impetus of the urban economic development. On this basis, the urban functions are changing greatly, especially, the urban comprehensive service functions are strengthened consecutively. The cities are playing a core role in the regional economic development as the bridges to connect the domestic economy and the international economy, but there is a long way to go before they can meet the requirements of the rise of the globalizing cities. Even the main central cities, such as Shanghai, which strategically aimed to construct a modern international metropolis, have a lot of catching up to do. In the following, we analyze and illustrate a case study by taking Shanghai as an example.

Since the 1990s, Shanghai's economy successively increased in a rapid speed. To a great degree, it can be attributed to the release of system energy after the reform and opening-up. However, the economic increase is based on the original urban development modes, which is displayed by the rapid growth and accumulation of investment-driven urban material capital and wealth and the lack of modern service industries. The experimental analysis showed that, since the 1990s, in the three variables influencing the economic growth, the consumption contributing to GDP does not fluctuate much, stabilizing the percentage to 41–51%. It reached a peak of 45.4% in 2002 and began to decrease to some degree; for example, it decreased to 43.78% in 2004, which was only 2.4% more than that in 1998, 41.38%, the lowest percentage in the past years; the contribution rate of the investment underwent a larger fluctuation, it reached from 42.55% in 1990 to 66.44% in 1996 rapidly, and it decreased at the same speed to the lowest point, 44.55% in 2002. But in 2003 and 2004, it began to rise, and the contribution rate of the investment to the economic growth reached 48.42% in 2004. There was an opposite tendency for the contribution rate of the net outflow to the economic growth, and it reached 9.6%, the lowest point, in 1996, and then began to rise. The rate of its contribution was down from 10.05% in 2002 to 7.81% in 2004. If compared to 15.57% in 1990, the contribution rate fell by almost 50% (see Figure 5.4).

From Figure 5.4, we can find some valuable messages: (1) since the 1990s, investment has become the main driving force to promote economic development, but its contribution rate fluctuated less: it reached a peak of 66.44% in 1996, and began to fall in the following years, though it rose a little in 2003 and 2004, but it was not as obvious as before; (2) the contribution rate of consumption reached to the level, 43.19%, in 1991, it retained the same in the following ten years, and more, it was lower than the average of the country, which showed that the consumption energy level was restrained to a great

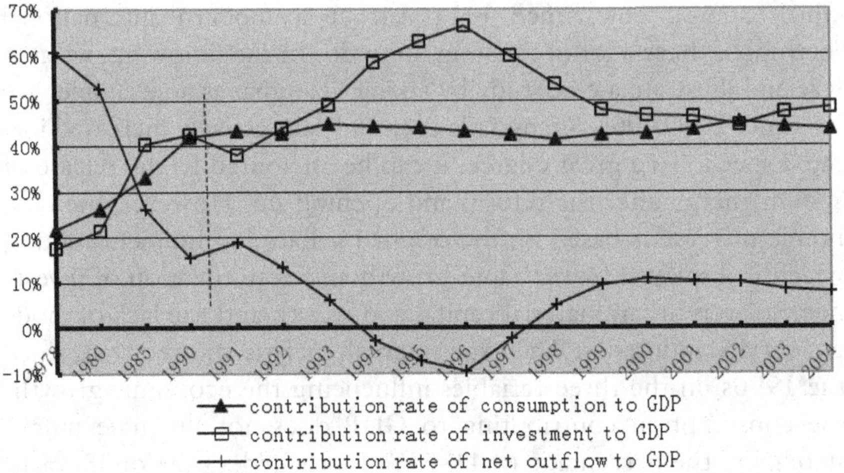

Figure 5.4. The Contribution Level of Consumption, Investment and Net Outflow to GDP.

degree; (3) the contribution rate of net outflow decreased greatly, however, it reached to 60.77% in 1978, which showed that the radiation and influence began to fall rapidly.

In addition, from the analysis on GDP calculated by income (see Figure 5.4), we can find that the rate of the labor's pay in GDP began to decline since 1993, it reached to 32.8% of the GDP in 2004 (while, the average percentage in 2003 in China was 49.62%), the net value of the depreciation of fixed assets and the production tax accounted for more and more GDP, and the corresponding percentages in 1990 were 12.29% and 19.74%, which were reached to 14.61% and 26.64% in 2004; but the earned surplus, which is the index to reflect the enterprises' profit, was increasing year after year in the successive 20 years: the percentage reduced from 56.69% in 1979 to 35.71% in 1990 and reached to 25.91% in 2004.

By the analysis on the information shown in Figure 5.4, we can draw the outline of the basic profile of Shanghai's economic growth: the reduction in labor pay. The increase in the net value of the production tax showed that more and more GDP was taken by the government, which was returned in the form of investment to the

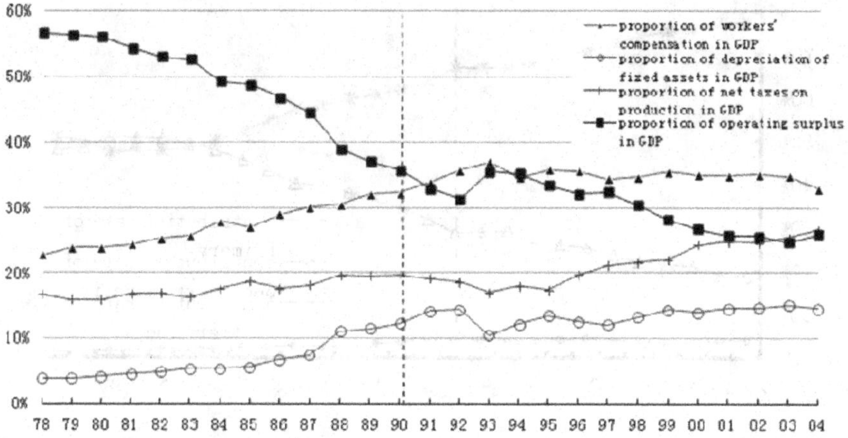

Figure 5.5. Workers' Compensation, Depreciation of Fixed Assets, Net Taxes on Production and Operating Surplus to GDP (%).

recycling process of social reproduction, the increase of investment percentage resulted in the direct increase of the depreciation of the fixed assets. Due to the fact that Shanghai had entered the stage in which the marginal profits of investment was substantially increasing, macroscopically, the contribution rate of the investment is decreasing year after year, whereas microcosmically, the enterprises' profit continues to be low successively.

In the economic growth driven by investment, Shanghai witnessed great changes in its industrial structure: the secondary industries contributed to the economic growth declined successively since 1978, while the tertiary industry was in the opposite track (shown in Figure 5.6). It surpassed the secondary industry for the first time in 1999, when the contribution rates of the secondary industry and the tertiary industry were 49.59% and 48.43%, respectively. But when they reached 50%, the original motive power of the industrial development was obviously weakening, the rate of the secondary industry did not decline any more, the rate of the tertiary industry did not rise as expected and they entered into the stage of adjusting and strolling. In addition, the transforming of the industrial structure resulted in the surface phenomenon to a certain extent, that is, the relationship

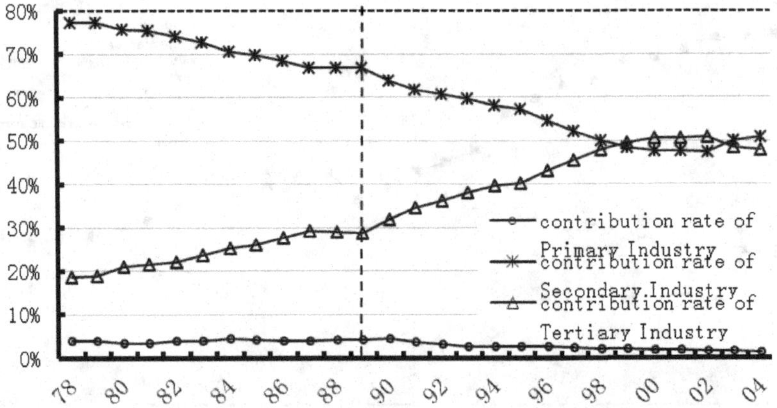

Figure 5.6. The Ratio of Industries Contribution to GDP (%).

between the production value of industrial sectors and the employment rate is being changed, whose internal structure is still dominated by the traditional industrial sectors and the low-added-value industrial sectors. Both are low in technology and intelligence. Accordingly, the industrial organizations retain the traditional and hierarchical organization structure, and the market structure is based on the traditional division of industries. Superficially, it is easier for this kind of industrial structure to cause instability of the rate relationship, and the structural relationship between the secondary industry and tertiary industry is reversed sometimes.

The massive promotion by investment in the original urban development framework, due to its own problems, will bring negative impacts on the later growth, and with the passage of time, the promotion effects will decline and cannot continue in future, which is shown in the following aspects:

The investment structure is not reasonable. In the massive promotion driven by investment, the investments to the fixed assets in the whole society went to infrastructure and real estate, and the percentage of the overall investments rose from 39.82% in 1992 to 74.57% in 2003 at a rapid speed. The overall investment to the real estate rose most rapidly, with the percentage rising from 3.59% in 1990 to 38.11% in 2004.

The effects of the marginal decreasing by degrees are more obvious. Since 1990, the added value corresponding to each unit of fixed assets began to decline comprehensively. From Figure 5.7, we can see that the tendency was shown in the overall economy and the tertiary industry to different degrees. The added value of the overall economy reduced from 0.64 yuan RMB in 1990 to 0.44 yuan RMB in 2004, down 31%; the added values in the first, secondary and tertiary industries reduced from 1.52 yuan RMB, 0.60 yuan RMB, and 0.68 yuan RMB to 0.73 yuan RMB, 0.47 yuan RMB, and 0.41 yuan RMB in 2004, down 52%, 22%, and 40%, respectively. The added value corresponding to each unit of the fixed assets can be considered the index to measure the investment efficiency of the fixed assets. From the data in Figure 5.7, we can see that the investment efficiency in Shanghai's first industry is the highest, while that in the tertiary industry is the lowest. This shows that there is great gap between the development degree of Shanghai's manufacturing and service industries compared to that of the developed countries, and the industrial development level and urban functions of Shanghai remains at a lower stage, and the part of the high-added-value in manufacturing industry and service industry is not developed well. The share of the high-end sectors, particularly in the service industry, is not so large, and is driven mainly by the investment. The lower investment efficiency shows that the position of the modern service industry undertaking the urban service functions does not match that in the globalizing cities.

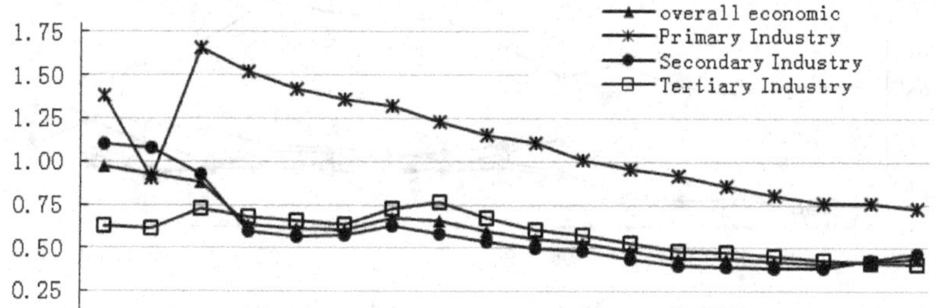

Figure 5.7. The Added Value Corresponding to Each Unit of the Fixed Assets (RMB Yuan).

The increasing effects of income and consumption are weakening. According to Shanghai's statistics, between 1999 and 2003, the overall average of the residents' disposable income increased, and its growth speed was basically parallel to that of the GDP. But if we analyzed the income level in different groups, it is not optimistic, for the disposable income of the medium-income residents lags behind that of the GDP. Even since 2001, the disposable income of the low-income residents is increasing negatively. On the other hand, the research on the residents' expense on consumption shows that the urban residents of Shanghai will not increase their expense on consumption with the overall increase of the disposable income. That is to say, the increased income of the residents does not automatically translate into an increase in their consumption. The successive decrease of consumption results partially from the distribution of the national revenue to the finance and from the income gap between the residents due to the unjust distribution of income. Therefore, there is a serious weakening link and congestion in the recycle "the increase of residents' income — the growth of expense on consumption — the promotion of economic development — the creation of more jobs — the further increase of residents' income level".

The growing driving power of the key industries tends to slow down. Figure 5.8 lists the developing tendencies of the five

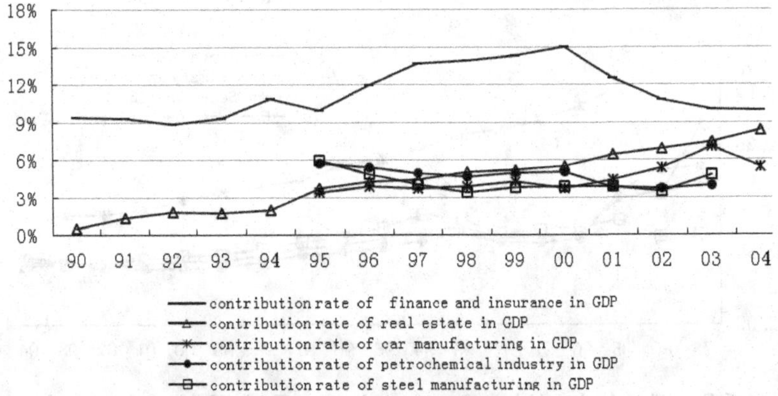

Figure 5.8. The Contribution of Several Major Industries to GDP (%).

key industries in Shanghai, which shows the banking industry has the biggest fluctuation in Shanghai, whose contribution rate began to rise, reached the peak in 2000 and then returned to the level in the early 1990s. The contribution rate of the real estate to the overall economy keeps to increase, which rose from 0.5% in 1990 to 7.24% in 2003. But its rapid increase is restrained by the land supply and cannot remain at such a rapid speed when it reaches a certain level. And moreover, the macro-adjusting policies from the country exerted more pressure on the growth of real estate industry. Obviously, the economic growth relying on real estate industry cannot last for a long time. The growing motive power of the three pillar industries in the field of industry is not as strong as before, among which, the contribution rates of oil and chemical industry and the steel manufacturing industry to GDP began to decline since 1995. The rates were 5.72% and 6.00% in 1995 and 3.95% and 4.80% in 2003, and the falling ranges are 31% and 20%, respectively. The contribution rate of the automobile manufacturing industry is always increasing, rising from 3.38% in 1995 to 7.06% in 2003. But its added value began to decline rapidly, whose contribution rate to the economic growth reduced to 5.42% in 2004. In comparison, the information industry and the manufacturing industry of complete equipment (not marked in the figure) are increasing at a stable speed, and the contribution rate of the information industry to GDP increased from 7.4% in 2000 to 11.4% in 2004. The contribution rate of the manufacturing industry of complete equipment to GDP increased from 2.9% in 2000 to 4.3% in 2004. These two industries can become the important economic growing points in Shanghai in the future years. But by the observation on the structure of the information industry, we can see that the main body of the information industry in Shanghai is still the manufacturing industry of information products, whose proportion did not fall but rise after the four years' development from 57.9% in 2000 to 58.2% in 2004. The Shanghai information industry did not break away from the development mode of the manufacturing industry, which limits the promotion of Shanghai's urban service functions to a great extent.

By the above experimental analysis, we can see that the performance and situation in Shanghai before 2004 is actually an objective reflection of the traditional development mode. In recent years, this situation is being changed; especially since 2006, there is an obvious change in the tendency of the economic growth. But as a whole, there is a long way to go to meet the strategic requirements of the rising globalization. It is also the case in the other cities in China such as Beijing and Guangzhou.

5.3. Positioning Strategic Target of Globalizing Cities and its Trend

The aim for the globalizing cities in China is to play a globalized role. In the background of the global network, its globalized role is increasingly relying on its ability to connect to the outside world and its connectivity and its position in the global network, which is decided by the urban energy level. Therefore, what the globalizing cities are seeking is not the regular urban development. And more, they cannot follow the traditional development path to expand the economic scale and strengthen the economy. They have to realize the overall urban transition by their strategic target location, that is, they have to realize the transition from the industrial and commercial city to the economical central city; from the manufacturing production city to business service production; from the mono-function city to multi-function city; from the localized city to the globalizing city; and from the single-point city to the regional city. Only by this profound urban transition can the urban energy levels be improved. The cities can merge into the global network and become the globalizing cities.

5.3.1. *The target location of the globalizing cities*

The target location for the globalizing city is not a very complicated problem. Some main cities in China have put forward and made clear their development strategic targets. For example, Shanghai put forward its strategic targets to build four centers and a modern metropolitan city in the 1990s, that is, to build a new industrial system to match the core as a metropolis and an infrastructure system with three harbors and two networks as a core and the social undertaking system with the promotion of overall human development as a core in order to become the centers of international economy, finance, trade and shipping. This strategic target is also approved by the State Council of the PRC and thus it has become a national strategy.

But the problem is that the connotation of the target location has to keep pace with time and be deepened. In the 1990s, Shanghai put forward the targets to build the four centers and become a modern metropolis, whose connotation focused more on the hierarchical concepts and relationships to compete with each other, with the most prominent one being to concentrate the controlling function. For example, after more than ten years of development, by its special location advantage, historical foundation and the development and opening-up of Pudong District, a strong concentration was formed in Shanghai, and large amounts of resource factors were attracted to the city. In return, Shanghai's urban construction and development were promoted. However, in the process of massive inward agglomeration Shanghai's fostering and function in external radiation were not sufficient. For example, Shanghai is incapable and lags behind in the external industrial transferring; the export of the factors such as technologies, capitals, talents, management and brands; the construction of external network; and the service outflow to the other places in the country and the world.

However, as pointed out in the above analysis, the coordinative functions of a globalizing city are included and embodied by the global connections. To see if a city can be an international economic center and a globalizing city is decided neither by its scale and shape nor its resources or capital, but its location as a panel point in the global urban system and its massive and available economic flow. In this sense, the globalizing cities, in the time of globalization and informatization, are actually the main panel point cities in the global network, which emphasize on the external connection and the competitive and cooperative relationship based on the network, the most important function is the service coordination. Therefore, the target location of the globalizing cities has to be established on the network with global connections, which is usually characterized by the distant interaction and can be illustrated by the following: (1) the coordination activities are usually intangible, individual, globalized, and information-intensified, which concentrate on the advanced professional service and have the high-level functions of coordination and service; (2) the multi-polarization and the special structure of the different poles are formed in the cities, that is, the advanced professional services are concentrated in the central city area and the new professional service belts are created in surrounding area; and (3) they are gradually prominent in the system of the global network, the coordination function itself is global and keeps pace with the world.

In fact, even a city that has already become a globalizing city needs to deepen their cognition and understanding of its connotation by the requirements of the time, the development and the changes and enrich and perfect their target locations. For instance, Tokyo's development plans targeting the year 2050 in Japan did not consider the numbers about urban scale or economic power as its seeking targets, what it focuses on is the transfer from the quantity to quality, from the simple targets to diversification and individualization aiming at a charming and prosperous international metropolitan at the leading position in the world. Guided by this general target, the five development target concepts are established in Tokyo:

(1) to maintain and develop urban vitality with international competition;
(2) to create and develop the environment to maintain persistent prosperity;
(3) to create an urban culture with its own characteristics;
(4) to create a safe, healthy and comfortable living environment with high quality;
(5) to form a development body with diversification and mutual coordination among citizens, both in enterprises and non-governmental organizations.

All in all, the target location of China's globalizing cities does not lie in the corresponding concepts or slogans put forward by the cities but their correct understanding of the basic connotations and requirements of the time. If they cannot understand the basic connotations well, target deviation will surely appear and mistakes will be made in a series of key problems such as the basic construction of the urban development, the choice of the urban development mode, the adjustment of the urban development patterns and the spatial expansion of urban development. Thus, we are requested to start from the requirements of globalization and informationalization, stand on the requests by the national interests and national strategies, deepen our cognition of the connotations of the target location, grasp correctly and scientifically the development of the globalizing cities and continue to enrich and perfect their contents of the target location.

5.3.2. *The target tendency of the globalizing cities*

The basic connotations of the target location of the globalizing cities are always embodied by their corresponding forms, especially the development tendency with certain representativeness. Though we may not understand the complete connotations of the globalizing city after one attempt, we should understand the target tendency from the very beginning and understand the connotations gradually in practice. If we are wrong in target tendency, there will be a miss as good as a mile in promoting the rising of the globalizing cities. Actually, the profound understanding and grasping of the target tendency of the globalizing cities will also be helpful to understand the connotations of the target location in reverse.

As far as we are concerned, the target tendency of the globalizing cities is to enhance the urban energy rank drastically, to take the key position as a panel point in the global urban network; to supply an interface between the cities and the world in economy, culture, organization, and institute; to introduce the resources in the country or in the regions to the global economy; and in return, to introduce the world resources to the country or regions. The enhancement of the urban energy rank will be established on the basis of economic servicization, intensification, and networking. Only by this way can the participation in a large scope be involved in the world economic process and integrated further to the division of labor in international industries and the world urban system.

In the present economic network system, as a main panel point, the city has more attributes of flowing space, and the level of the urban energy rank is decided by its flowability, concentration, and radiation. Therefore, the promotion of the energy rank level of a globalizing city requests economic servicization. More modern service activities must be supplied, especially the services aiming at the producers. In the process of the economic servicization, there will be two significant changes. On one side, more and more manufacturing industries will be intangible, custom made according to the individual's taste, and the business pattern is changed from manufacturing of one kind of a product to the supply of one kind of a service. On the other side, many service industries are characterized by their mass production, which connects the economies of scale to the individual service. Meanwhile, services can be expanded to places which are far away from the final markets. For example, finance, entertainment, education, security supervision, secretarial, accounting, and gaming services, and especially, distant medical services, can be produced and sold in places that are away from the final users.

As we all know, by its special location advantages, the city attracts all kinds of resource factors to concentrate. But if the city cannot collocate these resources However, if the city cannot collocate these resources intensively but only expand its urban space and accumulate massive capital, it is more difficult for the city to radiate to the outside world. Therefore, the promotion of the globalizing cities in their energy rank needs a main foundation of economic intensification. There will be two great changes in the process of economic intensification. On one side, due to the massive resource collocation beyond the city region, it is requested to relatively integrate the distributive functions in order to promote the industrial cluster and shape a better industrial economy ecosphere. At the same time, the main urban functions should be deepened and strengthened to highlight its features and form the core competition. On the other side, the intensification of the economic operation should be strengthened further, say, improve the exploitation degree of the resource factors, reduce the consumption of the resource factors, improve the efficiency of resource collocation and promote the efficient flow of the resource factors.

Due to the fact that urbanization is expanding massively in the background of economic globalization and informatization, the cities, especially the bigger cities, are merging into the global conceptual framework, and the rapid flow of the factors between the cities makes the connections between different cities closer and closer, which results in a multipolar and multilevel global urban network system. Therefore, the promotion of the urban energy rank in the globalizing cities is surely to develop in the direction of the economic network. Two great changes will take place in the process of economic network. On one side, the economic network requires mutual connection and interaction, and the main panel points in the network need an extensive external connection, which needs the cities to open in more aspects and focus on their own connections to the outside world more extensively. On the other side, as an important panel point in the economic network, the cities will undertake more functions in the flow of various resource factors in the network system in the development pattern of urban flow economy.

At present, some main cities in China, such as Shanghai, Beijing, and Guangzhou, are equipped with the basic conditions for the promotion of urban energy rank based on their present foundation and their levels in the development accumulation, with each of them having a strong internal driving force. First, the hardware framework and shape are initially formed in these cities, which are stable in politics and social environment. Second, these cities have the corresponding creative reaction abilities when facing external changes such as the global economic adjustments. They are undergoing the transformation from the labor-intensive production to capital-intensive production and then to the intelligence-intensive production and the adjustments of their economic structures. Third, the comprehensive service functions of these cities are intensified, which is improving the influence and expanding in a wider scope. Fourth, the development potentials in these cities are great, with better growth and the corresponding sustainable development abilities. In addition, development opportunities, such as the Olympic Games in 2008 in Beijing, the

World Expo in 2010 in Shanghai, the comprehensive reform pilot in Pudong District in Shanghai, and the completion and opening of the Yangshan Harbor, are becoming the driving forces for the promotion of the energy ranks of these cities.

But the problem is to see if these cities can make clear the target tendency of the globalizing cities; grasp each opportunity; and take on, develop, and promote the process of the economic servicization, intensification, and the networked system. At present, due to the limited land usage and the controlling of land rank difference, more output of each inch of land is requested, which has become one of the most important indexes for the cities to choose the industries on the market. Furthermore, the business cost is improved rapidly, and the cities are adjusting their industries and the lower-profit industrial sectors are being driven out of the cities. The uncompetitive industrial sectors are extinguishing due to the strong competition extrusion from home and abroad and the surrounding areas. Obviously, the main urban industrial sectors have to be updated, replaced, and renewed, which will focus more on internal contents, namely, the new industrial sectors will replace the traditional ones, the high-end or high-value-added industrial sectors will replace the low-end or low-added-value ones; the high-tech and high-intelligence industrial sectors will replace the low-tech and low-intelligence ones. Adapting to the contents in the industrial structure requires corresponding changes in the industrial organization structure. In the process of integrated development between the advanced manufacturing and modern service, new changes, such as the operation overlap between different sectors and market overlap, allow the enterprises to break the boundaries of their own division of labor and get involved with each other. The relationship between different enterprises involves not just the competition but also coordination and cooperation, which makes the enterprises flexible in the organization structure based on industrial automation and intelligentization and revolve into the atomic organization structure to adapt to the quick and changeable market organization structure.

With the expansion of the economic scale and the transformation of the urban functions, social development will play increasingly important roles. International practice shows that, at a certain stage of economic takeoff, rapid economic growth will bring many social problems, especially, structural unemployment, the lagged education level of the labors, expanding gaps in income distribution, pauperization of the vulnerable groups, etc. The solutions to these social problems are directly related to the lasting length of the rapid economic growth. For the globalizing cities, with the reorganization of industrial system and the changes of urban shape, the social system of the city will be profoundly transformed. International practice tells us there will be three outstanding transformations as stated in the following:

(1) the incomes and social status of the urban residents will be changed and differentiated due to their different degrees of participation in the process of globalization;
(2) the overall employment scale will be expanded and result in the tendency of "two increasing ends with decreasing middle";
(3) the social power is transferred to the transnational organizations with increasing influence;
(4) two new polar populations will emerge in the community layout, that is, the international community related to globalization and the public community related to localization;
(5) the contrasting thoughts in culture will shape globalism and nationalism, and the existing problems in the process of urbanization will be expanded in the process of internationalization. Therefore, for the globalizing cities, the development problems in the society will be part of the city's agenda, which include urban management, community construction, social security, employment, education, and culture development. The urban economic growth will be promoted after duly handling and solving the social problems, which will be interactive to the economic development.

Chapter 6

Path Dependence of Globalizing Cities

International experience shows that the basic premise and condition of the globalizing city are substantially the same, the pursuit or location of its objectives may also be convergent, but because of differences in the context, foundation, location, history, and corresponding path dependence of every global city, different global cities often show a variety of development models. Therefore, the global city is not a standard evolution model (including the already formed and emerging world/global cities), and there is no so-called "development model" of the global cities. New York, London, and Tokyo have shown obvious differences in their development models. These established and emerging differences between the global cities should be attributed to different historical and geographical environment, path dependence, the internal institutional capacity, and different structures of practical behavior (through strategic actors). In this chapter, the study will focus on the study of the major constraints and path dependence China's globalizing city faces, initially describing the model of the growing up of China's global cities.

6.1. Main Control Conditions: Involved in the Process of Globalization

Foregoing analysis has shown that the interaction of globalization and informatization is one of the main driving forces of the formation and development of the globalizing city (including the global city). As the construction of space of flows progressively integrating into the global network, the rise of global cities must be dependent on new impetuses like globalization and informatization. In addition to the level of development of globalization itself, that in what kind of starting point and by what kind of the manner a country or city participates in the process of globalization and what role a country or city plays in the globalization is also usually reflected in the main binding conditions of the rise of global cities. As for participation in the globalization process, there are many differences in the initial basis, time, space, environment, conditions, etc., between China as a developing country and developed countries. Overall, China participates in the globalization process at a lower level of development and by a passive way, which largely decides specific binding characteristics of the rise of global cities in China.

6.1.1. *The main features of passive participation in the process of globalization*

It is known that, based on their highly developed national economy and enterprises, developed countries participate in the globalization process by way of continuous outward expansions, including initiatively making foreign direct investment (FDI) and distributing production globally. Especially after the 1980s, with the acceleration of the globalization process, the traditional international geographical trade patterns determined by location of the natural resources have been broken, with the organization and spatial structure of their economic activities gradually undergoing a deep restructuring, and the new pattern of international transactions with financial and specialized services as the main content, with FDI as the main approaches and with the internationalization of production and services as the main features comes into being. The formation of new pattern of international trade strengthens the extension of the global commodity chains of the developed countries' multinationals to developing countries and transferring of global manufacturing location to developing countries. Thus, so far, economic globalization is still dominated by the developed countries.

As a developing country, China gets access to and participates in the globalization process on the basis of the low level of per capita income, weaker overall national strength, obvious dual structure, low level of modernization, and lagged urbanization. In terms of attitude toward the globalization process, China has taken a proactive opening-up policy, such as throwing open more fields to the outside world, vigorously developing foreign trade, and actively attracting foreign investment. However, because its economic strength and enterprise development are still at a low level, and there is an absence of stronger national and enterprise competitiveness in the global economy, both in the traditional pattern of international trade or in the division of labor in the contemporary pattern of global commodity chains, developing countries are always in a "passive" situation. In international trade, developing countries participate in the international division of labor based on low value-added commodity exports; in the global commodity chains, they are mainly involved in the global division of labor of intra-industry and intra-enterprise, with processing and manufacturing industries as their main business. Therefore, as far as the participation and contribution of developing countries in the globalization process are concerned, they are highly passive and participate mainly by the way of attracting FDI, receiving low value-added processing and manufacturing areas in global commodity chain by using their comparative advantages such as cheap labor, huge potential markets, and undertaking processing trade with "a flood of exports as well as a flood of imports" as characteristics. In this sense, China is involved in the globalization process. This "involvement", with the positive implementation of opening-up to the outside world as the premise, can therefore be called the "passive participation in the globalization process" to distinguish it from developed countries' active participation in the globalization process.

Like other developing countries, China participates in the new international division of labor mainly through attracting FDI and undertaking the expansion and extension of global commodity chain led by multinational corporations to developing countries. In this process, the asymmetry of international direct investment flows is very obvious, that is, the inflow of FDI is massive but China's FDI outflows are very little. For example, in the first half of 2005, the net inflow of FDI was US $26.4 billion, while the net outflow of China's FDI was US $3.9 billion, a difference of 9 times. Moreover, compared to the same period the earlier year, the net inflow was reduced by US $51 billion, with net outflow increasing by US $29 billion. It can be imagined that there are more differences between the two in the previous years. Therefore, international direct investment essentially shows the basic pattern of a one-way flow.

Further, the massive inflow of FDI and transnational corporations is combined with the expansion and extension of the global commodity chain led by multinational companies to China. It is known that, depending on their own different factors advantages, every country occupies different production processes with different value-added contents in the international industrial chain, which is led by multinational companies based in developed countries. As a developing country witnessing rapid industrialization, China has attracted an increasing number of multinational companies that choose China as the manufacturing base for global markets depending on its advantages like low-cost, high-quality labor, excellent infrastructure, strong industrial support systems, a vast domestic market, stable social and political environment, and increasingly open foreign trade and FDI institutions. Data show that most of the large-scale FDI inflow into China is in manufacturing. By the end of 2003, based on the total number of FDI projects, the secondary industry accounts for 75.265%, accounting for 67.01% of total amount of the contracts (see Table 6.1). The first half of 2005 saw that foreign capital still invested in the manufacturing field. FDI in the manufacturing sector accounted for 71%, followed by real estate and rental and business services, accounting for 9% and 6%, respectively. The situation was not changed until 2010, when foreign investment actually used in tertiary industry rose to US $58.962 billion, a little more than the US $53.860 billion FDI in the secondary industry.

From the view of dynamic process, this extension of the global commodity chain to China is manifested as the process in which the manufacturing sector gradually develops from its low-end links to high-end links and from the spare parts production to base production. The 1980s witnessed the transfer of mainly labor-intensive processing and manufacturing industries from the developed countries and regions to the Chinese coastal areas. After the early 1990s, the

Table 6.1. The Industrial Structure of FDI (as of 2003).

Industry Name	Item Number (a)	Proportion (%)	Contract Amount (US $ billion)	Proportion (%)
Total	465277	100	943.130	100
Primary Industry	13333	2.87	18.036	1.91
Secondary industry	350170	75.26	632.010	67.01
Tertiary industry	101774	21.87	293.084	31.08

Source: Investment Guide Online. Available at: http://www.fdi.gov.cn.

traditional labor-intensive manufacturing FDI stagnated, while the labor-intensive, high-tech manufacturing FDI, such as electronics, telecommunications, and computer assembly FDI began to transfer to China. For example, between 1997 and 2000, the contractual FDI attracted by the textile industry increased from only from US $11.43 billion to US $19.88 billion, with the actual inflow of FDI experiencing an absolute decline (down from US $18.59 billion to US $13.68 billion). At the same time, the contractual and actual FDI of electronic and communication equipment manufacturing sectors all experience rapid growth. The former increased from US $29.44 billion to US $11.36 billion, while the latter rose from US $26.59 billion to US $45.94 billion. In the electronic and communication equipment manufacturing industries, contractual FDI of computer and electronic devices increase from US $870 million in 1999 to US $1.88 billion in 2000, increasing by 80.06% and 64.63%, respectively. After that, the developed countries and regions began to transfer part of the production chain of capital-intensive heavy industries (such as petrochemicals, etc.) to China. Experience has shown that, in the transfer of industries (especially manufacturing sectors) from developed to developing countries, whether vertical or horizontal, the output industrial technology is usually more advanced than the host country's industrial technology. Without this fall between levels of industrial technology, it is difficult to form the potential energy of transfer of industries. Therefore, in the international industrial transfer, base countries hold the right to make more active choices, making use of the industrial technology advantage, namely, deciding what kind of industries or which links of the production chain should be transferred, and the sequence and timing of the transfer. In contrast, host countries receiving the industrial transfer are usually in a selected position, being characterized by obvious passive acceptance.

Further investigation shows that most of the FDI belongs to the extension of the global commodity chain to China, adopting the production process whose "two key links are operated abroad", that is, most of the relatively high-tech components and technologies are provided by foreign countries, and a large number of finished products are exported to Europe, America, and other countries, with the processing and assembly link based in China. For example, in the Yangtze River Delta region, more than half of manufacturing enterprises are concerned with processing and assembly. Although this mode of production will bring GDP growth, because its production link does not further expand along the industrial chain, without finer division of labor, the promotion and proliferation of domestic industries and the surroundings of center areas are limited. However, the processing trade derives from this large-scale production model. With the increased FDI, the gradual extension of the domestic processing chain within the processing trade, and the more substantial increase in the product added value, the processing trade gradually dominates in the trade structure. The first half of 2005 saw that the import and export of processing trade accounted for 47% of total imports and exports, which is more than 43% of the general trade.[1] In addition, foreign-invested enterprises gradually dominate the import and export sector. The share of foreign-funded enterprises in total exports has increased from 1% in 1985 to more than 50% in 2004. The first half of 2005 saw the foreign-invested enterprises involved in import and export accounted for 57% of total imports and exports, being much higher than the proportion of 27% of state-owned enterprises, which greatly contributes to China's large-scale foreign trade activities based on the global production system.

[1] Analysis group of balance of payments in State Administration of Foreign Exchange: "The First Half of 2005 China International Balance of Payments Report", *Financial Times*, November 28, 2005.

The FDI of one-way inflow into China is mainly concentrated in the field of processing trade, whose strong selectivity of location makes it mainly flow into some economically developed and the first opening areas. Particularly, China's regional development is in the non-equilibrium state, and the eastern coastal areas take the lead in the implementation of the opening-up policy, which makes the regional concentration of FDI more obvious. For example, the development level of the Yangtze River Delta, the Pearl River Delta, and the Bohai region is relatively high, accounting for 6.3% of the national land area and 24.2% of the national population, but producing 48.3% of China's total GDP, and with perfect infrastructure such as transportation and communication, and good geographical advantages, which makes the FDI inclined to locate these areas, forming high regional concentration of FDI. In 1993, the FDI and other investment of three core areas accounts for 71.03% of provinces, municipalities, and regions; by 2001, the proportion has increased to 77.55%, increasing by 6.52 percentage points.[2] The first half of 2005 saw that the foreign capital actually used by three regions of the Yangtze River Delta, the Pearl River Delta, and the Bohai region accounted for 87% of the national total amounts, increasing by 16.4% compared with the same period; their import and export trade accounts for 77% of the national total amounts, increasing 23.94% compared with the previous year. Especially, the foreign capital actually utilized by the Yangtze River Delta region (Jiangsu and Zhejiang provinces and one city) accounts for a higher proportion of the national total, usually accounting for over one-third of the total; in 2003 and 2006, it was as high as 50.65% and 48.12%, respectively. In this large-scale introduction of FDI, the Yangtze River Delta has become the most concentrated areas of transnational corporations (see Table 6.2). More than 400 of the Fortune 500 companies have settled in the Yangtze River Delta, with nearly 300 in Shanghai, more than 180 in Jiangsu, and close to 60 in Zhejiang. Meanwhile, the Yangtze River Delta region is also the most important gathering place of domestic large enterprises: in 2005, more than 120 of China's top 500 enterprises are in the Yangtze River

[2] He and Sun (2005).

Table 6.2. The Actual FDI by JiangZheHu and China and Its Share Over the Years (Unit: 0.1 US $ billion/%).

	2004	2005	2006	2007	2008	2009
JiangZheHu	25.36	27.756	33.427	40.19	45.26	45.80
China	60.630	72.440	69.470	74.768	92.395	90.033
% of JiangZheHu in China	41.83	38.32	48.12	53.75	48.99	50.87

Source: *Statistical Yearbooks* of the provinces and the *China Statistical Yearbooks*.

Delta area alone, including 44 in Shanghai, 42 in Zhejiang, and 40 in Jiangsu. According to "Research Report On 2005–2007 Transnational Industry Investment Trends In China", released by the Ministry of Commerce on February 27, 2005, in the next three years, multinational companies will expand general investment in China. With respect to the location, the Yangtze River Delta becomes the preferred investment region by multinationals by an overwhelming advantage of 47%, with the Bohai Sea region accounting for 22%, PRD 21%, and other regions 10%. Domestic and international resources and industries stream to these key areas, transforming them into the world's most vibrant and dynamic economic regions and forming the "industry gathering place" with the world's fame.

In the key economic areas where FDI mainly gathers, many cities, and even organic towns, possess the environmental conditions required for attracting FDI in processing trade, so the distribution of FDI flowing to the cities tend to decentralized, both flowing to large cities or major cities in the region, and a major chunk flowing to medium and small cities or the general cities. For example, in the Yangtze River Delta region, the distribution of FDI in the city is relatively decentralized. After 1990, when the total actual use of FDI in Shanghai accounted for 46% share in Yangtze River Delta, Shanghai's inflow of FDI has tended to decline, dropping to 21.59% by the year 2003, with the proportion increasing a little in 2004 and 2005 but again plummeting in 2007 to 19.71% (see Table 6.3); and Suzhou's inflow of FDI is more than Shanghai, increasing from 8.83% to

Table 6.3. The Actual Use of FDI by Shanghai and the Yangtze River Delta Region Over the Years and Its Share (Unit: US$ 0.1 billion).

	2004	2005	2006	2007	2008	2009
Yangtze River Delta Region	60.630	27.756	33.427	40.19	45.26	45.80
Shanghai	6.541	6.850	7.107	7.920	10.084	10.538
% of Shanghai in Yangtze River Delta Region	25.79	24.68	21.26	19.71	22.28	23.01

Source: *Statistical Yearbook* of the two provinces and one city.

26.38%. In Suzhou New District, 52 sq km of space holds more than 800 foreign investment projects from more than 30 countries and regions, hosting a number of investment projects worth over US $100 million and 188 or more investment projects worth with over US $10 million. In Wujiang, a developing zone of 20 sq km has been built, bringing together more than 300 foreign-funded enterprises, 90% of which produce mainframe computers, monitors, notebook PCs, and supporting products relating to electronic information, with the local matching rate above 90%.[3] Thus it can be seen that the global manufacturing bases in China and their spatial distribution characteristics, i.e., the regional concentration and the urban decentralization, are decided largely by FDI location choice, resulting from spatial arrangements of the multinational's global commodity chain.

6.1.2. *The specific binding characters of the rise of China's global city*

The foregoing analysis has pointed out that China receives international industry transfer mainly through attracting FDI, thereby extending the global commodity chain to the country. In this process, every upgrade of international industrial transfer always shows that

[3] Institute of Contemporary Shanghai (2005).

the level of externally transplanted industries is higher than the domestic industry level, thus contributing to increase in the level of development of domestic industries and the upgrading of industrial structure. That is, China's industrial development is the externally transplanted industries-oriented industrial upgrading model.

This environment where the overall industrial upgrading is promoted by externally transplanted industries has important influences and specific restrictiveness on the globalizing cities, which search for new economic functions and form new urban systems based on the positioning in the world city network. As a developing country, the base and overall level of China's manufacturing industry is not high, there being a big difference compared with the developed countries, so are some large cities as the domestic manufacturing centers and processing bases. Of course, in a closed economy, some of China's major cities acting as the manufacturing centers or domestic processing bases are perhaps capable of transferring manufacturing activities to the surrounding regions and whole country based on high level of industrial development. For example, before the reform and opening-up, Shanghai's manufacturing level was in a leading position in the country, there being many famous domestic brands, so Shanghai is capable of transferring its manufacturing activities to the surrounding region and across the country. Even at the beginning of the reform and opening-up, the development of private enterprises in Zhejiang and Jiangsu provinces largely benefits from the "informal" and localized transfer of Shanghai's industries (such as equipment rental in the name of economic cooperation, "Sunday" engineer and retired professionals' technical output, etc.). But in an open economy, the gap between the levels of domestic and the developed manufacturing industries is completely explicit. Foreign technology and equipment are much more advanced than the domestic technology, in some cases, with the former even taking the lead by several generations. Therefore, the original advantages of industrial development maintained by the big cities, as the domestic manufacturing and processing bases in a closed economy, disappear. In this case, through the direct introduction of advanced technology and equipment from abroad, and accepting technological innovation diffusion from the outside, they can quickly reach a new level higher than other domestic cities. Moreover, even those places that originally did not have any industrial base can promote the rapid development of manufacturing activities through the shortcut. Therefore, it has become the best choice to realize the leapfrog development of economy and industry. When the surrounding regions as well as within the wider areas of whole country develop the manufacturing sector through shortcut methods, forming a burgeoning trend, the so-called "highland" of manufacturers, these big cities that were originally occupied are razed down to a "flat" version, or even collapse as a "depression", presenting a decadent trend in the face of strong domestic and international competition. This study compares the situation as the "sinking island" effect.

In addition, the environment where the involvement of the globalization process is by the way of one-way inflows of FDI, in combination with large-scale trade activities, has a major impact and specific restrictiveness on the rise of the global cities and their position in the global city network. China mainly takes in external technology, capital, equipment, management, and other resources, receiving the global allocation of resources, and therefore, in the global links, the cities serve as the bridge of external resources inflow and outflow of finished goods, even playing a role that combines outside resources (capital, technology, etc.) and local resources (labor) for further production and processing. Of course, with the one-way flow of resources, corresponding service flows will form, such as investment information services, brokerage services, consulting services, accounting and auditing services, and legal services, but these service flows expand relatively slowly. In addition, the one-way inflow of FDI will form the corresponding service flows through large-scale trade activities, especially modern logistics services, various types of transfer services, maritime services, and support services, However, because the mutual relevance formed by trade activities is not much stronger than that by two-way FDI, its service flows expand the relatively slowly.

Due to the lack of such interactive flows of capital (direct investment) and elements, these central cities like Shanghai and Beijing are difficult to become interactive nodes in the global economic coordination, only important "transit" nodes with the global influence, serving as the coordination/transportation center responsible for the acceptance or delivery of inflows of capital. Relative to the global city of developed countries, these cities are connected with the global economy only to a limited extent. Of course, these cities play an important role, because, in a country, they are in a special location, where they have much to do with the global space of flows through the operations of key actors and institutions (Meyer, 2000). However, the establishment of these urban external links is embedded, and more often dependent on external inputs, rather than resulting from the active external (global) output and extension.

Also, the pattern of regional concentration and urban decentralization of FDI and the environment in which external capital inflows promote local economic development and enhance the global connectivity have significant impacts and the specific restrictiveness on the rise of China's global cities and the path dependence. In the traditional planning system, China's cities are mainly connected with their hinterland, which is similar to the "core–periphery" model, with weak economic links between cities.

Moreover, such economic ties are implemented mainly through the strict planned allocation mechanism. After the reform and opening-up, the market-driven economic ties tend to expand and deepen, but the administrative and regional division does not make a unified national market really formed, so economic links between China's cities is not sufficient, and the relationship between them not very close. In China's opening-up to the outside, the pattern of regional concentration and urban decentralization of FDI first leads to the increase in the global links of these regions and cities, which means that more cities tend to internationalize, creating global linkages, which, on the other hand, means that these cities have only limited external linkages, without any city forming a very prominent global links. Therefore, in this process, although the central city's global connectivity is further enhanced, its position in the global connectivity is not to be further polarized, but relatively weakened, with the increase in the global connectivity of other cities.

It must also be noted that China is still in the stage of investment-driven development, and the introduction of FDI is highly correlated to economic growth. This largely strengthens the heavy reliance of the economic development on foreign factors like capital, technology, equipment, and management; international markets; external marketing networks; and information networks. At the same time, when external resource inflows are present within the regional centralization and urban decentralization, it is necessary that many cities in the same region develop rapidly, with each having large economies of scale and higher level of development. For example, more than 10 cities around Shanghai such as Suzhou, Wuxi, Hangzhou, and Ningbo are develop more rapidly than Shanghai, with their overall size and level of development gradually close to Shanghai, forming the overall pattern of rapid development. Among them, the per capita GDP of Suzhou reached Shanghai's level in 2003. According to a rough prediction, before 2010, the per capita GDP of Wuxi, Changzhou, Hangzhou, Ningbo, and Shaoxing will be close to or reach Shanghai's level (Zhuo, 2005). Although the per capita GDP is not the main explanatory variable of a city's economic strength and function, to some extent, it reflects that the level of development, starting point, and competitive strength of Shanghai's surrounding cities are similar to that of Shanghai, which has resulted in a decline of the latter's long-time polarization status in the Yangtze River Delta. For example, the proportion of Shanghai's tertiary industry in Jiangsu, Zhejiang and Shanghai fell from 41.2% to 26.9% from 1978 to 2003.

Therefore, these cities are not very closely linked domestically but show growing global linkages, which objectively develop a centrifugal force on the domestic central cities, forcing them relatively to shake off or dissociated from their dependence on the linkages between domestic cities, especially relatively weakening their dependence on domestic central cities. This state may even develop to an extreme situation in which the extent of international linkages of these cities is stronger than their domestic level. Obviously, this will have a greater negative effect on the polarization of central cities. This state is called by the study the effect of generalization of the global linkage.

6.2. Path Dependence of the Rise for China's Global Cities

The specific restrictiveness on the rise of China's global cities resulting from passive participation in globalization means that China cannot fully follow the logical process of the rise of developed countries' global cities, duplicate constructing models of global space of flows global cities like New York, London, and Tokyo have, or imitate their unipolar development patterns. The specific restrictiveness, to a large extent, determines the path dependence of the rise of China's global cities.

6.2.1. *The logical process of transformation of urban functions: with the help of the global commodity chain*

It is known that new impetuses like globalization and informatization promote the gradual loss of the city's traditional functions, mainly in the manufacture and processing of goods, and the mushrooming of new functions, such as the creation, exchange, and use of information, and thus forming complex urban systems linked by people flow and information flow. Various components of the urban system are similarly involved in the process in which old activities are rejected, and new ones are obtained (Gordon and Richard, 1996). Global cities such as New York and London experience the transformation of economic function conversion and the process of updating the city system, being realized mainly through the outside (domestic and international) transfer of manufacturing activities and enterprises, while retaining and gathering a large number of the management and service institutions directly related to their decentralized manufacturing activities, sequentially completing the transformation from the manufacturing center to the financial business service center.

In developed countries, the transformation of the economic function of global cities is naturally evolved, a very important prerequisite of which is that their manufacturing industries are highly developed internationally and are fully equipped with an outsourcing ability (such as technology, brand, marketing network, management recipes, etc.).

Thus, globalization and informatization promote these cities to continue to outwardly transfer manufacturing activities and distribute production bases globally. The control and management functions of these manufacturing activities as well as supporting producer services are maintained and developed in these cities and are highly concentrated, forming powerful long-range coordination functions. It is based on this that producer services spring up, with the proportion of service industry ever increasing, which replaces the old economic function by the service economy. It is (thus) clear that the loss of the cities' traditional manufacturing function largely results from the active outward transfer of manufacturing activities, rather than their decline or disappearance.

Differentially, due to China's passive participation in the process of globalization, the impact of externally transplanted industries on the domestic industries leads to the "sinking island" effect of big cities' manufacturing industries, which gradually lose their ability to externally transfer and radiate. In this case, these functions of management and control of manufacturing activities do not exist any longer, which results in massive base loss of the development of supporting producer services, which means that the new economic function by which to replace the lost old economic function does not grow from within. As a result, when their economic strength drops, these cities tend to decline.

If not reconciled to sink, these cities are bound to have to improve the level of manufacturing industries and enhance their competitiveness through the introduction of foreign advanced technology, equipment, and management. Shanghai puts forward the building new heights of industry during "the 10th Five-Year-Plan", which is, in fact, its strong response to the effect of "sinking island". Obviously, this can only further strengthen its existing manufacturing capabilities, forming the confrontation of the old and new functions during a longer period. Therefore, the "sinking island" effect resulting from externally transplanted industries usually will form an "inversely forcing" mechanism by which to force the transformation of economic functions of these cities.

Therefore, the rise of China's global cities, on one hand, have to go through the process in which the new economic function replaces the old one, and the emerging economic activities replace the traditional ones, which ultimately leads to the formation of the industrial structure system based on service economy and the urban comprehensive service system; but on the other hand, the impact of "sinking island" effect by externally transplanted industries and the specific constraints of the "inversely forcing" mechanism means that the conversion of the cities' the old and new economic functions do not have the naturally evolved endogenesis. That is, the logical process of developed countries' urban economic function cannot be realized under China's current conditions. In this case, the conversion of urban economic functions required by the rise of China's global cities must be carried out with help from the global commodity chain increasingly extending to China, and by means of ways different from the developed countries.

(1) When the city cannot develop the new economic function from within to replace a lost old economic function, one way to make up is to externally transplant the new economic function as a substitution. Specifically, the way is to attract multinational regional headquarters and their R&D centers, foreign financial institutions, and various types of producer service companies (such as accounting firms, law firms, consulting firms, and other intermediaries) to settle in cities. The entry of these institutions brings a number of new economic activities (mainly service activities), and their global or regional networks also bring a large-scale people flow and information flow. So these new bodies and their activities promote the rise of local service activities (a lot is its supporting service activities), which will be able to give the city new economic functions. Singapore and Hong Kong, to a certain extent, belong to this type, relying on large externally portable economic functions as a substitution, and thus developing into global cities. However, unlike some major cities of inland of China, which are almost lost in the capacity of the external transfer of manufacturing in the face of outside impact, they are capable of externally transferring a considerable part of the manufacturing industries. For example, the majority of Hong Kong's manufacturing industries

have been transferred to the Pearl River Delta. However, the limited numbers and sizes of these transfers are not sufficient to constitute the status as management and service centers, mainly relying on externally transplanted new economic functions.

Of course, these management and service institutions get access to some of the major cities not haphazardly but going with much of their direct investment, which has formed large-scale production activities, namely, the spatial extension of the global commodity chain is a prerequisite for these institutions to enter. Although, like Singapore and Hong Kong, the global commodity chain itself does not directly extend to these geographical spaces in which the large-scale production activities are formed, the global commodity chain has extended to their neighboring regions, which results in the possibilities that a number of foreign management and service agencies will locate in these geographical spaces. If the global commodity chain does not extend to Southeast Asia and China, Singapore and Hong Kong cannot attract large numbers of foreign management and service organizations to locate. In addition, an even more important sufficient condition is whether or not these cities' environment can guarantee the effective functioning of these external management and service organizations. In addition to the city's location, other factors such as infrastructure, transport and communications, office buildings, availability of professionals, living conditions, and other environmental conditions are important. Also of significance are some "soft" factors like the degree of control, economic policies, and market order. If the appropriate environmental conditions are found to be lacking, these organizations will not easily enter, and even if they do so (for the strategic layout under the long-term considerations), they cannot operate effectively.

The actual situation in China is that large-scale international manufacturing is being transferred to China, making the Yangtze River Delta and other regions as the *de facto* manufacturing bases of the world, which shows that China has basic conditions needed to receive the spatial extension of the global commodity chain. As for environmental conditions, some large cities such as Shanghai also have a good location, relatively good infrastructure, convenient transportation and communication, A-class office and star hotels, qualified professionals, and better living conditions. Therefore, they already have the appropriate conditions needed to attract the regional headquarters of transnational corporations and other institutions, forming an important basis for the development of headquarters economy. By the end of 2006, 154 regional headquarters of multinational companies, 150 foreign investment companies, 196 foreign R&D centers, and more than 200 national corporate headquarters have settled in Shanghai. But it must be seen that there are big gaps in soft environments such as control degree and market order; especially, the level of Shanghai's financial liberalization is low. For example, subject to restrictions on the fund management, multinational corporations located in China find it difficult to exert a unified control over funds of subsidiary companies in different provinces, which will seriously affect their management and service functions. The lack of such environmental conditions seriously affects the speed and size of the transferring of foreign management and service institutions to China. Among the regional headquarters of multinational headquarters as well as business and other financial services companies that have been currently stationed in Shanghai, Beijing, and other big cities, a considerable number of them are purposed to race to grab these cities' markets for competition, with limited energy for their operation, resulting in difficulties in providing these cities with new economic functions. Therefore, it is very urgent for these cities to improve the soft environment by strengthening legislation and enforcement, enforcing deregulation, and rectifying market order.

(2) When the city cannot give birth to new economic functions after the loss of the old economic functions, and lacks appropriate environmental conditions affecting external implants of new economic functions, it has no alternative but to resort to seek the help of the global commodity chain to upgrade the manufacturing level, develop advanced manufacturing, and enhance the capacity of external transfer of manufacturing through independent innovation, gradually transforming into the service-industry–dominated economic structure. What matters here is not whether the city should retain manufacturing industries but rather how to develop the manufacturing sectors.

There are some defects in the existing researches on this issue. Most researches on global cities demonstrate a tendency which simplifies the function of the global city as the financial center which also provides specialized services for the company. The study does not deny the importance of a financial center and a business service center in the functioning of a global city, but it must be clearly recognized that global cities and metropolitan areas continue to play an important role in the development of manufacturing industries, being particularly core sites of knowledge-based production chains and innovative production clusters. In addition to the links between enterprises within metropolitan areas, from a global perspective, the innovative leading enterprises of "knowledge clusters" in these cities are highly dependent on the links between them and innovative enterprises in other urban areas. Transnational connections between industries in urban areas and service clusters might be the basis for the phenomenon of globalization (Krätke and Taylor, 2004). Therefore, in the rise of the global city, it is also equally important to foster innovative leading enterprises in manufacturing industrial sectors and form production clusters of innovation by the structural upgrading of the manufacturing industry, and the development of advanced manufacturing industry.

Judging from international experience, there are such precedents. Different from New York and London, Tokyo, with its rapidly developed service sectors, is still one of Japan's most industrialized cities. After 1955, Tokyo's industrial development continued into the 1970s, and the employee scale increased from 76.47 million in 1955 to 140.45 million in 1965, and then began to decline, reverting to the scale of 1955 in 1990, with employees in 2000 being only 55.56 million.[4] In the 1980s, Tokyo was Japan's largest industrial center, although the succeeding industrial external transfer resulted in the decline of its industrial position in the national economy, Tokyo is still an important industrial city in Japan. In 1987, the number of factories and total industrial sales in Tokyo accounted for 12% and 7.3% of the country, respectively, second only to Aichi, Kanagawa, and Osaka,

[4] Liu *et al.* (2003).

ranking fourth in Japan.[5] So, as a leading global city of the world, Tokyo cannot do without a strong manufacturing base built up in the stage of industrialization.

But it must be seen that Tokyo has two distinct characteristics in its manufacturing industry: First is the considerable concentration of industrial distribution, and the presence of five major industries, including publishing and printing, electrical machinery, transport machinery, food, and general machinery. Since the 1970s, these five major industries have played the leading role, with their proportion in Tokyo industry increasing, especially the publishing and printing industry and the electrical machinery industry, with their sales value ranked in the top two, accounting for over half of Tokyo's total sales since the 1990s. Second, fashion and information-based industries play an increasingly important role in the industry, with the relative proportion of 15% in 1955 increasing 32% in 2000, and the proportion of technology-intensive electrical motor, communication machinery, precision machinery, and transport machinery in industry gradually increases. The general machinery industry and food industry gradually declined; steel industry and chemical industry retreated from the list of five leading industries in the 1950s and 1960s. These two features show that the manufacturing industries supporting the construction of modern international metropolis are highly concentrated in a small number of advanced industrial sectors suitable for urban features, eventually evolving into departments with central management functions with their energy levels constantly increasing on the basis of innovation.

The rise of China's global cities can use Tokyo's case as a reference. In today's China, it is not realistic that some major cities be called to abandon manufacturing and only develop service industries. In fact, in this particular situation, some major cities giving up the manufacturing sectors cannot help the service industry; in particular, producer services develop, only leading to urban economic decline. Of course, it is no use continuing to maintain the existing development model of manufacturing. Therefore, at the same time, when

---

[5] Cai *et al.* (1955).

vigorously developing service sectors, these cities should focus on changing their manufacturing development model with the help of the extension of the global commodity chain, breaking the all-round development pattern of manufacturing industries, selecting the key industries with comparative advantages, and vigorously developing advanced manufacturing satisfying urban characteristics. These cities should shake off their sole reliance on the introduction and reintroduction of foreign technologies, and instead focus on digesting the introduced technologies, eventually realizing innovation by imitation, innovation refinement, integrated innovation, and original innovation, thereby improving the manufacturing level by enhancing the ability of independent innovation. These cities should shake off the path dependence on the general low value-added production and processing links in the global commodity chain, going to the high end of the value chain in which these cities create own brands and the function of the producer service is enhanced.

In accordance with China's current situation, it is entirely possible to attract outside management and service organizations to station in its major cities with the help of the extension of the global commodity chain and its position as the global manufacturing base, but it is not feasible to completely depend on replacement of the old economic functions with externally transplanted economic functions. So, it is also necessary for China's cities to promote and develop advanced manufacturing with the help of the extension of the global commodity chain and realize outward transfer of production on the basis of innovation and strengthening own management and service functions. In short, the rise of global cities in China must get the aid of spatial extension of the global commodity chain, and achievement of their urban transformation will be through externally transplanted and internally bred new economic functions.

6.2.2. *The structural model of the space of flows: depending on large-scale trade flows*

Since their formation and throughout subsequent development, global cities of developed countries establish extensive connections with other cities mainly through the external expansion of service flows, having stronger external connectivity. The headquarters of multinational companies highly concentrated in global cities realize their control and management over the global commodity chain mainly through service flows, including technology, design, brand, sales, and network; similarly, the large-scale supply of professional business services highly concentrated in global cities is realized through service flows such as information and knowledge. In fact, the service flow plays a major role in the node connections in the entire global network of cities. The global cities with the widest and the most intensive external connections are naturally important nodes of the most frequent service flows. For example, in London, the proportion of employment in the service sectors is as high as 82%, and exports of services make an outstanding contribution to the British international trade balance, with only lawyers, medical services, and cultural entertainment industry's net income up to £2.7 billion, and the insurance industry contributing more than £4 billion pounds to the UK economy. But the prerequisite is that developed countries have the allocation capacity of global resources, having both large inward flows of global resources and outward flows of domestic resources, especially two-way flows of financial resources. For example, in 2003, FDI flowing to the EU in US outward FDI accounted for 65%, and FDI flowing to the US from Europe is nearly 75%. In this two-way flow of capital, the US and Europe's corporate assets show the spatial cross distribution. In 2001, 60% of US $5.8 trillion assets of the US are in Europe; and nearly 70% of European corporate assets are in the US, reaching US $3.7 trillion. One of the correlating indicators is the level of sales of overseas affiliates, such as the sales of locally produced goods by the subsidiary in the US of a European company. In 2001, the commodity sales by the US subsidiaries of European companies account for up to 51% of total sales of foreign affiliates in the USA, with total sales of their services as high as 54% of those of foreign subsidiaries in the USA. Different from commodity trade, FDI forms direct economic and social ties through job creation and direct involvement in the internal economic activities between host and base countries. Two-way flow of FDI usually forms deep bilateral economic integration. Therefore, the interactive flow of resources not only forms large-scale service flow but also naturally transforms the host city receiving these service flows into an interactive node, evolving into the global city.

Different from the above-mentioned, one-way inflows of FDI resulting from China's passive participation in the globalization process make it difficult to directly form large-scale service flow. In this situation, China's cities are more frequently dependent on external inputs from global cities, but less interactive, more impossibly promoting the outward flow of capital (or information) serving global economic development. But it must be noted that the commodity trade flow brought about by the production processes of processing and assembly from FDI is an important variable in the rise of China's global cities.[6]

The analysis concerning globalization has pointed out that, differing from the traditional (core and peripheral) pattern of world trade, modern international trade is based on the global commodity chain, which forms different trade types. The first is the highly monopolized trading activity based on specialized knowledge and skills, which is the support of the position of London and New York. The second is the well-known trade type formed by international division of labor, which, in practice, represents the transfer of production from high-paid countries to low-paid countries. The third is the trade type based on horizontal specification. In many countries, technologies of flexible mass production or diversified quality production of a large number of manufacturing or service industries are almost the same, which means that a range of countries and regions may participate in the exchange of products and services based on specialized knowledge and skills, and local companies can engage in the important global production.

[6]The mainstream of global urban studies usually leave merchandise trade aside and focuses on the study of the impact of service trade on the global city formation and development. We believe that this has certain limitations, and it is necessary that modern trade theory was introduced into the global urban research.

In China, current large-scale trade mostly belongs to the second type of trade, but also partly the third type of trade, which has been completely different from the traditional trade of "core–periphery" relations.

Formally, in this trade activity, the developing countries not only export local raw materials and energy in exchange for manufactured goods in developed countries but also import a large amount of raw materials, energy, and large manufactured goods, forming large-scale global production-based trade flows. However, this new model not only reduces labor costs, reflecting the comparative advantage but also, importantly, facilitates the existence of complex knowledge flows, because "the local partners of transnational corporations in developing countries engage in production in accordance with international standards ... [and] the flow of knowledge and accompanying experience would have an important impact delocalized activities" (such as activities re-deployed to the third world countries). In these associations, the study and use of knowledge from an industry to many other industries enriches simple trade effects, which means that some countries and regions can develop by receiving the global commodity chains and bagging projects in the process. The experiences of Taipei and Singapore are good examples, and in the near future, Shanghai and Guangzhou are possible candidates that can replicate their success (Storper, 2000). This means that, unlike traditional trade theory, what dominates the economic and trade activities is not only a few cities and regions in a small number of countries but maybe also cities and regions of more countries.

As the flows of goods trade are realized mainly through urban nodes as the trade center and shipping center, large-scale flows of goods trade based on global production will be instrumental in allowing these cities to play an important role in the global economy and trade and also promote them to greatly expand their external relations. Foster has proposed a method measuring impact of trade on the city.

On the basis of blueprint of American cities, Foster discusses whether or not the impact of the global trade center (usually as a institutional reflection of the importance of local trades) is reflected by the impact of global linkages of 90 cities in the USA and Canada, and their location in metropolitan areas. Although the activities of global trade centers and the trade centers around the world are very different, she finds that 48 metropolitan areas with global trade centers participate in the global trade on a bigger scale and to a deeper extent. They have higher per capita exports, more "sister" cities, more overseas visitors (and more air passengers per capita) than 48 metropolitan areas without global trade centers, and are more likely to be included in the list of the immigrants' candidate cities. Although the method measuring global linkages is relatively crude, the conclusion is very important, emphasizing the important role of the trade in producing the locale external linkages, accounting for the gateway role in global linkages the trade plays in a broader sense.

In general, a city's dependence on foreign trade is highly correlated to its internationalization. The higher the dependence on foreign trade, the more closely the city relates to international markets together, and the stronger its influence on surrounding countries and regions and attractive power on their economy. Therefore, if a number of global cities have the service flows, they also have a high dependence on foreign trade. New York, London, and Tokyo's dependence on foreign trade come to more than 500%. Hong Kong's dependence on foreign trade in 1990 was 220%, increasing to 352% in 1998, while Singapore's dependence on foreign trade in 1995 was 180%, increasing to 230% in 1998. Some of China's major cities' dependence on foreign trade is rapidly increasing in recent years, which is significantly higher than the national level. For example, it can be found that Shanghai's dependence on foreign trade has increased over the years. According to observation data, in 1996–1999, its dependence on foreign trade increased steadily from the 62.6% to 76.3%; in 2000–2001 it remained at 95%; and again in 2002–2004, it rapidly increased from 104.8% to 164.1%. Shanghai's total imports and exports of foreign trade come to US $227.489 billion in 2006, an increase of 22.1%, with its dependence on foreign trade reaching 174.9%, 111 percentage points higher than the national 63.86% (see Figure 6.1). According to statistical standards on ports, the import and export of goods in Shanghai Port amounted to US $428.75 billion by 2006, an increase of 22.3% in comparison to last year, accounting for 25% share of the national total

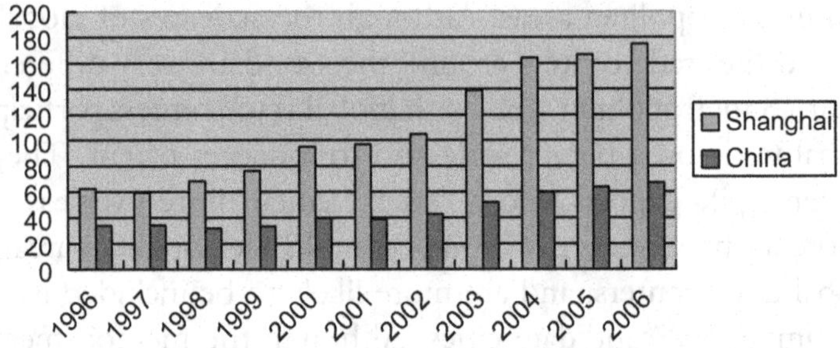

Figure 6.1. Comparison of Shanghai and the National Dependence on Foreign Trade.
Source: Shanghai Statistics Network.

imports and exports,[7] with its dependence on foreign trade as high as 331.9% (based on calculation of 2006 annual average exchange rates price 7.9718 level).

It is (thus) clear that, unlike major cities in developed countries that witness rapid expansion of flows of services based on two-way flow of capital, the rise of China's global cities relies more on one-way inflows of FDI and the resulting large-scale trade flows. China's global cities should expand their external connections through the commodity trade, and relate to global space of flows, expanding service flows with the help of flows of goods trade, forming interaction of flows of goods trade and service flows, more deeply integrating into the global network of cities.

6.2.3. *Development shape: residing in the global city-region*

It is known that, when initiatively participating in the process of globalization, the developed countries' big companies are increasingly developed into multinational corporations. Based on the decomposition of their value chains, these corporations seek the countries or regions with the lowest cost to organize their production, outwardly

[7] Shanghai Municipal People's Government Development Research Center, *Shanghai Economic Yearbook 2007*.

transferring a number of links of their production and processing, with their headquarters and supporting advanced producer services highly concentrated in the central cities in these countries. These original central cities transform into major management and coordination centers of the world economy system. For example, because their countries' economy is highly developed and outwardly expanded, and the local large enterprises evolve into transnational corporations and decentralize their production, New York and London establish their positions to control or dominate the world economy with the help of tremendous economic traffic like global provision of advanced producer services, the global flows of financial capital, and the control and management of the global commodity chain. Although Japan is a newcomer compared to developed countries in Europe and America, Tokyo's road to the global city is also like New York and London. The "Plaza Agreement", signed in 1985, lead to the appreciating of the yen and the dollar depreciation, which greatly contributed to Japan's FDI and the country's success in lowering production costs. With Japanese FDI flows to other countries, including Asian, European, and other countries, Japan has developed into a multinational economic system. Tokyo, which was the economic center of Japan in the past, became the center of the multinational system and began to act as the management and coordination center of the Asian economies and the world economy. This function of Tokyo gets further promoted with the help of transnational flows of financial capital, with its position to control or dominate the world economy being consolidated and strengthened. Similarly, unlike New York, London, and Tokyo, which have such comprehensive and top-level positions, the other global cities in the developed countries also form and develop following the logical path.

It can be seen that it is entirely possible for the developed countries actively participating in the globalization process to transform some of their central cities into global cities through their decentralization of production and functions of global management control centers and high centralization of related producer services. Around these central cities are some other cities with low extraversion and less global contact, which do not affect their evolution into global cities by virtue of constant polarization development depending on their traditional factors or specific locations. For example, the status of New York and Tokyo as the economic centers of Japan and USA, respectively, is hard to shake. In comparison to their surrounding cities and other cities, these cities are obviously located at the top of the social ladder. The population of New York accounts for 61.6% of total population of New York City metropolitan area, with its contribution to the GDP being 60.3%, which is around 1.2 times the total of surrounding regions. Tokyo has lower proportion in total population, but its GDP accounts for 54.9% of Metropolitan Tokyo, with the tertiary industry accounting for 60.8%, according to 2002 data. Thus, emerging global cities (such as New York and London) in the 1970 and 1980s are outstanding in many aspects among cities (like "a crane standing among chickens"), being characterized by "powerful" externality but weak internality, namely very strong global links but relatively weak linkages to their surrounding cities and domestic other cities. That is, although global cities with high global links have existed in this region, other neighboring cities are not globalized, among which the domestic mutual contacts are formed. Especially in the USA, in addition to New York and Miami (an important mixed city connecting Latin America), no inland city is significant enough to exceed its own country in global connectivity, which results from the USA's large-scale, long-term, well-developed economies and also from its broad financial and business service markets. This allows enterprises that lack incentives to "go global" so as to achieve the same status of global service to other regions. This actually reflects the unity of the global cities in the regional space, there not being a single global city-region with global cities as its core.

In this sense, early formed global cities in developed countries usually present unipolarized development patterns, namely, an individual single city develops into a global city, which is not born at the same time when the global city-region generates. In fact, the early formed global cities in the developed countries get integrated into the region level through their spatial expansion in the process of deepening globalization and informatization, which leads to the formation and development of metropolitan regions. At the same time, other cities in these metropolitan regions are increasingly globalized and integrated into the global network of cities, establishing a wide range of external links. Based on regional globalization, these global cities and their neighboring cities begin to form closer economic linkages, which promote the development of the global city-region.

Different from the developed countries' active participation in the process of globalization and informatization, developing countries cannot copy their early formed development patterns, nurturing the evolution of some central cities into global cities with the help of the global decentralization of production, the establishment of management and control centers, and high centralization of related producer services. On the contrary, in the context of today's globalization and informatization process, developing countries undertaking the extension of the global commodity chains first promote the development of global cities in regional scope, and the rise of the global city-region based on these global cities.

FDI-oriented economic activities of most developing countries are usually highly concentrated in certain cities. These cities themselves are often the centers of their domestic economy, for example, Bangkok, having only 13% of the population but producing 86% of the gross national product (GNP) of the national banking, insurance, and real estate sectors and 74% of manufacturing GNP; Abidjan (the capital of Côte d'Ivoire), having only 15% of the population, but achieving more than 70% of national economic and commercial trade; Lagos, accounting for only 5% of Nigeria's total population, but creating 57% of the total added value in manufacturing, and having 40% of the national high-tech workforce.[8]

So, the high concentration of FDI-oriented economic activities in these cities promotes the development of big cities (including the mega-cities), extended metropolises (such as Jakarta-Bandung, Rio de Janeiro-Sao Paulo) in the form of corridors, or expanded metropolitan areas like Bangkok. Similarly, China also receives large-scale extension of the global commodity chain, forming a highly externally oriented economy, especially in the Yangtze River Delta, Pearl River

[8] See Kasarda and Parnell (1993).

Delta, and Bohai regions. Massive inflow of external resources forms global links of China's cities in an embedded way, which will not only lead to internationalization of many cities in the region but will also form a pattern, with more cities simultaneously rapidly developing, showing multipolar development of cities within the region. In this process, many cities in the region not only rapidly achieve high industrialization but also increasingly act as a "gateway" for external resource inflow and finished products outflow, with their external linkage become increasingly wide and close, ultimately evolving into the global cities from national or local cities.

Without such embedment of the global commodity chain, these national or local cities cannot form a wide range of external economic ties in such a short time, rapidly evolving into global cities. Different from developed countries, local companies in developing countries are less competitive internationally, especially in R&D and international marketing, which relatively limits the development of their foreign trade. It is more difficult for local companies go abroad to expand their global dispersed production, evolving into multinational companies. In this situation, it will take a relatively long time for cities in developing countries to evolve into global cities with the help of external economic linkages developed from their internal power. But large-scale extension of the global commodity chain helps the cities in this area establish global linkages in a relatively short time, evolving into global cities and integrating into the global networks of cities. Particularly, in the regions in which the global commodity chain cosmically embeds, the evolution of local cities into global cities is not an individual but a general phenomenon. For example, in the Yangtze River Delta region, in addition to Shanghai, other cities such as Suzhou, Wuxi, Nanjing, Hangzhou, and Ningbo are moving toward becoming modern international metropolises, so are the Pearl River Delta and the Bohai Bay area.

Of course, the formation of globalized cities is driven by external forces in those regions, and whether those regions could further develop into the global city-regions depends on other factors. But according to the past facts and experience, the generalization of global linkages within the regions will, in turn, promote inter-city relationships within the regions. Because enhancement of these cities' global linkages results from the extension of the global commodity chain to China and reflects regional globalization. These cities' global linkages resulting from the extension of the global commodity chain to China are not isolated, or completely separated, but intrinsically linked. It can be seen that, at present, China's Yangtze River Delta, Pearl River Delta, and Bohai Bay region have not only become "the world's factories" but are also gradually forming large, dense, and polarized (or multipolarized) labor and capital clusters, which are brought into the world system. These industry clusters within these regions are distributed mostly across administrative divisions. For example, the electronic information industries in the Yangtze River Delta region form the spatial structure with Shanghai, Nanjing, and Hangzhou as the centers, distributing along train lines such as Shanghai–Nanjing and Shanghai–Hangzhou–Ningbo; the equipment manufacturing industries will also form the overall spatial structure with Shanghai as the leader, distributing along train lines like Shanghai–Nanjing, Shanghai–Hangzhou and Ningbo–Taizhou, and the rivers; the petrochemical industrial clusters locate both sides of Hangzhou Bay between Shanghai and Zhejiang provinces. Within the regions, these industry clusters themselves have internal requirements, enhancing inner-city economic ties.

And, as the study points out in Chapter 4, the high-end, mid-range, and low-end parts of the global commodity chain are also intrinsically linked. Further extension of the global commodity chain to China, especially transfer of the "high-end process", is bound to achieve the integrity and systematization of "high-end production areas" and "low-end production areas" within the regions, forming a division of labor and cooperation model with "headquarters and producer services and processing and manufacturing" functionally separated, so as to make central cities as "high-end production areas" and their neighboring average cities as "medium and low production areas" that are closely linked with the "high-end production areas", with the status of central cities remaining constantly polarized. This enhancement of urban external linkages in turn promotes deepening of urban internal linkages and is an important counteractive mechanism for the rise of China's global cities.

Therefore, the enhancement of external linkages of China's cities and the polarization of their status will suffer from the specific constraints of generalization effects of regional global linkages, which renders China's cities unable of copying the unipolar development pattern of New York, London and Tokyo. It is impractical to try to develop individual central cities into global cities without the development of the global city-region. China's global cities must arise from the globalized cities in the region. In this sense, the rise of developing countries' global cities depends on the development of the global city-region, featuring a symbiotic relationship between them. If developing countries can be consciously aware of it, they should strengthen relevant cooperation and coordination based on these global city-regions, and actively build regional alliances (either top down or bottom up), collaborating the stated collective orders. Developing countries should jointly seek to enhance regional capacity dealing with administrative and policy issues, forming some available new spaces as regional platforms, by which enterprises participate in the global market competition. This will allow these global city-regions to adapt to the changing world system and increase their global competitiveness and economic benefits.

At present, some of China's economically developed regions and cities are beginning to realize the importance of regional cooperation and coordination and are taking the some necessary actions. For example, Guangzhou and Shenzhen have developed a new North–South strategy, which considers Hong Kong, Macau, and Guangzhou as the centers to form a golden triangle based on Guangdong Hong Kong, Macau, and Hong Kong. The urban groups in the Pearl River Delta have made a great progress and will expand their industries by using western and inland resources. In this process, based on economic ties, these globalizing cities will unitem surrounding secondary cities with more abundant economic strength. The secondary cities, on one hand, will serve as important nodes in the global network of cities, and on the other hand, as regional economic development centers, playing an important role in coordinating and integrating regional resources and strengthening regional economic ties to integrate into the global network.

Chapter 7

Relations of Competition and Cooperation During the Rise of Global Cities

Urban development is always accompanied by inter-city competition based on convergence and proliferation. To some extent, this competition between cities promotes urban development, but the more complex context of contemporary globalization means urban development and its success or failure are not simply determined by the competition between cities. In the global network of cities, cooperation between cities is as important as the inner-city competition. The external cooperation of global cities which are integrating into the global network of cities is particularly important. Therefore, competition between cities is not simple but involves the twin facets of "competition and cooperation" that promote the important driving forces of global cities development. The rise of China's global cities is in the face of international and domestic competition and cooperation, so they acquire strong driving forces only by establishing collaborative mechanisms for multiple participants.

7.1. Popular Trend of Thought and Theories of Competition among Traditional Cities

All kinds of indications show that the rise of China's global cities is affected by the popular trend of thought and traditional theory, with urban competition as the driving force. The information revealed by many literature researches shows that the rise of global cities can be realized apparently only through urban competition and at the expense of suppression of other urban development. This induces some cities to place unilateral emphasis on urban competition and improve the competitiveness, in practice, particularly strengthening urban gathering capabilities and economic strength in a one-sided way, which leads to vicious competition among cities. In fact, this vicious competition between cities, which is equal to the zero-sum game, is neither in line with the requirements of urban development based on the global network of cities nor is helpful for the rise of China's global cities. Therefore, it is necessary for the study to provide a reflection on the prevalent trend of thought and theory of traditional urban competition.

7.1.1. *The trend of "think global, act local" based on urban competition*

The trend of "think global, act local" based on urban competition was internationally popular in the 1980s and 1990s, which is generally pursued by policy makers and politicians. The emphasis on the trend is not accidental, but related to the upgrading of urban status, function, role, and globalization of urban competition in the globalization process.

According to the macro level analysis, urban competition has increasingly reflected inner-state strategic contention on the global resources. It is known that economic globalization is the spatial reconfiguration of all kinds of economic resources. The global allocation of resources breaks the boundaries of the country (meaning the status and role of national borders are weakening), to make cities as nodes of the global network directly involved in the global economy, So that cities or regions out as the main participants in economic competition instead of countries. In this process, it is realized that urban competitiveness is the key of strategic contention on the global resources. Therefore, national and urban governments around the world are actively engaged in cultivating and enhancing their urban competitiveness in the hope of the success in strategic contention on the global resources in the new century.

According to the analysis of micro levels, urban competition is mainly reflected in the effects of geographical concentration of industries and enterprises. Globalization and technical changes in production, transport, and communications lead to dramatic changes in the spatial relationship of economic activities, forming the new inherent characteristics of market factors — the high global flow. It is the high global flow that makes some decisive factors (such as high-quality human capital, capital, technology and knowledge) in the urban development more accessible to the urban agglomeration and also more easily influence urban development by "vote-with-their-feet" approach. At the same time, enterprises can change their location in the city or region at any time in accordance with their strategy formulation. Therefore, the city's strategic planning in the future, infrastructure construction, investment environment, and comprehensive services play a major role in the concentration of industry, new business formation, healthy development of SMEs, and effective technical communication among universities, research institutions, and enterprises.

It is in this context that policy makers and politicians of every country generally follow the trend of "think global, act local" based on inter-city competition, and the theory and practice based on regional basis come into being, that is, local economic growth strategy is emphasized, with global competitive advantage considered to result from local economic growth strategy (Hillier, 2000, Savitch and Kantor, 1995, Senbenberger, 1993). The main means and ways of getting global competitive advantage are through urban development (usually large-scale infrastructure and project construction) based on resource-driven strategies to enhance the status in the global city hierarchy. In practice, the city government tends to pay attention to increase in capital stock, accumulation of material wealth, and urban environmental improvement, emphasizing the dependence of urban competitiveness on local assets (such as lands, banks, companies, etc.), which makes these cities more attractive to global investment than their rivals, that is, maximizing the urban attractiveness on the flow of capital through the operation of the "local assets" (Savitch and Kantor, 1995).

Although this trend has been increasingly questioned and reflected in foreign countries, it is still popular in China. In addition to the above-mentioned background conditions, its prevalence in China results from some basic conditions in a particular stage. For example, the local decentralization in reform results in the availability of more resources, especially land resources under the control of the urban government; that governmental reform has not yet in place results in routine asymmetry in political and financial power between the central and local governments; and the evaluation of administrative merits takes GDP as the standard, and local governments are in pursuit of economic growth speed. To some extent, these factors become fertile grounds for breeding such trends, which not only forces local governments to accept but also enables the governments to execute such policies. Owing to the impact of this trend, in the formulation of economic and social development plans, many cities have prioritized "to take the enhancement of the urban competitiveness as the main task", strengthening the role of urban competition; some strengthen the urban ability to gather resources in the name of "city management".

Of course, there is a widespread one-sided understanding of the concept of urban competition. For example, it is believed that urban competitiveness is the ability of a city to attract, scramble, own, control and convert resources and scramble, control and occupy markets to create value and provide benefits to its residents compared with other cities, and that urban value is created by urban enterprises or resourceful business people, and the collection of urban advantages is urban competitiveness (Liu, 2002). Some also believe that, in the context of economic globalization, a city's competitiveness will largely depend on its ability to attract multinational companies and related capital inflows (Cai and Xue, 2002). So a city's competitiveness will largely depend on local endowments advantages (such as lands, banks, efficient enterprises), which make it more capable of attracting foreign investment than other cities. In some examples, the city "comparative advantage" is considered to result from local economic growth strategy. Some people see the urban competitiveness as the result of the urban business leaders' promoting the development strategy. Some people think that government shape a city's competitiveness by means of intervention.

So, in practice, the enhancement of urban competitiveness is often interpreted as a simple contention of external resources (especially foreign capital), such as attracting foreign investment through a variety of preferential policies like tax breaks, artificially lowing land prices, and rent concessions and excluding capital flows and industrial transfer among regions. This often results in excessive competition between cities; serious local protectionism; lack of effective support and connection among major infrastructure such as railways, highways, shipping, aviation, and other facilities; coexistence of waste of resources and shortage of facilities; lack of effective space control; unreasonable space development and order of division of labor; lack of convergence of regional policies; and difficulties in establishing the coordination mechanism of market- and business-led regional competition. This vicious competition among regions and cities has brought great difficulties to the national level foreign policy adjustment and industrial restructuring, rendering it difficult to adjust the national strategy for its effective implementation in local areas. In the process, the urban government's policy leverage is local, and infrastructure construction (new buildings, airports, telecommunications investments, etc.) to attract foreign investment is focused on a single city, which also causes ignorance of the global network of cities itself and the importance of its connectivity in deciding urban success.

7.1.2. *The theoretic core of traditional urban competitiveness*

The emergence of the above-mentioned trend not only has the necessity of reality but also has a profound theoretical basis, that is, traditional mainstream theory of urban competitiveness. The traditional theory of urban competitiveness usually sees the city as a local space-based material region in which production and life are highly concentrated, which results from the accumulation of large investments or solidification of large factors, sequentially, paying much attention to the relationship among factor conditions, business strategies, structures and competition opponents, demand conditions, and related pillar industries, with the belief that urban competitiveness results from presence of production clusters in local areas. Many literatures hold the belief that the concept of urban competitiveness is formed based on the internal characteristics of the city and define and elaborate the basic connotation and core issues of urban competitiveness based on the "output capacity", "factor capacity", and "process capacity".

The American scholars Kresl and Gappert (1995) think that urban competitiveness is the ability of the city to create wealth and increase revenue, the measure of which is as follows: the ability to create high-tech, high-paid jobs; the ability to produce environment-friendly products and services; the ability to concentrate production in products and services with a certain ideal characteristics, such as products with high income elasticity of demand; the ability to link up economic growth and full employment, preventing market from overloading; the ability to engage in the business which is helpful for the city's future; and the ability to strengthen the city's status in the city hierarchy. Gordon *et al.*, point out that urban competitiveness is the ability of a city to create more income and employment within its borders than any other city. In China, many scholars hold similar views. Some believe that urban competitiveness is the ability of a city to create wealth and value with more outcomes, higher speed, better quality, and less cost in the competition and the development process compared with other cities. Whether a city can get access to value gain, and if so, the extent to which it gets access are decided by the ability of the city to create value and the city's competitiveness (Ni, 2003, pp. 40–50). Some believe that urban competitiveness is the ability of a city to produce goods, create wealth, and provide services to meet the demand of the regional, national, or international market, and the ability to improve net income, improve quality of life, and promote sustainable social development (Yu *et al.*, 2001). These views further materialize the content of "creation of wealth and value gains".

These views emphasizing urban output capacity and performance often further reveal the strength and weakness of urban decisive competitive factors. Based on distinguishing the performance of urban competitiveness (dominant factor) from the decision urban competitiveness (decision factors),[1] Kresl distinguishes between the different attributes of decision factors from the mode of impacting urban competitiveness, namely, economic determinants and strategic determinants, the former including factors of production, infrastructure, location, economic structure, urban suitability; the latter including government efficiency, urban strategy, public and private sector cooperation and system flexibility, etc. He builds the model of urban competitiveness, namely, urban competitiveness = f(economic determinants + strategic determinants), believing that the role of strategic determinants is not directly exposed, but shown by the linkages to relevant departments like local universities and research centers. Similarly, some scholars in China believe that urban competitiveness is the comparative advantages and comprehensive potential of a city, reflected in the comprehensive expression of productivity factors, the level of productivity training, and development mode selection and system innovation at the stage of internationalization and marketization (China City Development Report, 2001–2002, p. 257). That is, the strength and weakness of urban competitive factors are boiled down to urban comparative advantage and overall potential.

In addition, some studies emphasize the city's process capability. The British scholar Begg (1999) delineates the relationship between the "inputs" of urban performance (top-down sector trends and macroeconomic impact, corporate characteristics, trade environment, innovation, and learning capacity) and "outputs" (the level and quality of life determined by employment rate and production) through a complex "maze". This relationship depends largely on the size of urban process capability (see Figure 7.1).

Deas and Giordano (2001) construct a linear input–output structural system, taking two factors of economic activity and "place"

[1] Kresl believes that urban competitiveness is of no direct measurement, only being capable of estimating its quality and quantity by the shadow it casts. According to this idea, he constructed a set of variables (indicators) to represent the urban competitiveness: urban competitiveness = f(Δ manufacturing value added, Δ retail sales, Δ business services income). These are the dominant factor, rather than decision factors.

Figure 7.1. The Urban Competitiveness Maze.

feature into account, making a dynamic analysis of the assets of urban competition and corresponding potential outcomes. They see urban competitiveness as the unity of competition assets and the corresponding outcomes. Among them, the urban competition capital is composed of economic environment, institutional environment, and physical and social environment, and the competition results are reflected at the enterprise level and workplace level. The competition assets are a prerequisite for the competition outcomes, and the competition outcomes are the embodiment of practical application of the competition assets, presenting a transformation process between the two, but they are interactive, thus ensuring the durability of the process (see Figure 7.2).

In the above-mentioned definition and modeling of urban competitiveness, scholars place emphasis on the structure among urban internal factors, especially on the enhancement and integration of urban internal "output capacity", "factor capacity", and "process

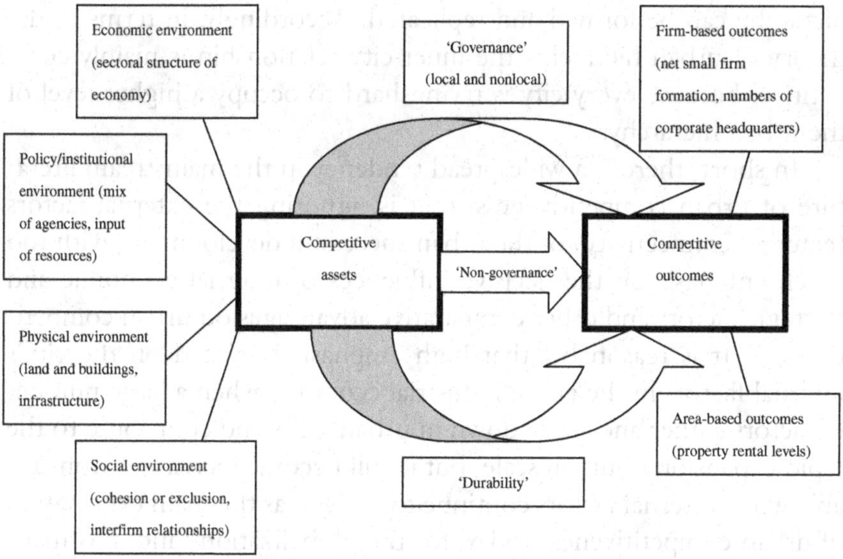

Figure 7.2. The Relationship Between Assets and Outcomes.

capacity". Kresl's urban competition theory is an extreme representative of such views. In his view, the way of measuring the city's economic and strategic factors can be used to compare the urban competitiveness, while the city's economic and strategic factors belongs to the city itself. Therefore, it is necessary to separate the external factors from any explanation of urban competitiveness, the reasons of which are: there are differences between the competitiveness of a city and its capabilities to globalize, with the former involving the city itself and the latter emphasizing its external linkages. In his view, a city can be highly competitive without exchanges with other cities, as if a city in the urban system does not have any competitiveness. It is possible for a city to dramatically increase its competitiveness, even its international competitiveness in the absence of international status.

In addition, the competitiveness of these cities is defined and analyzed from different points of views but based on the basic concept of urban hierarchy, which, in fact, is a hierarchical analysis, using an urban hierarchical model based on competitive relations. It is based on the competitive relations that the basic structure of urban hierarchy can be formed and replicated. Accordingly, in terms of the theory of urban hierarchy, the inner-city relationship is mainly competitive, because every city is trying hard to occupy a higher level of the urban hierarchy.

In short, there is a widespread tendency in the mainstream literature of urban competitiveness, that is, ignoring the external factors (external connectivity) of the urban successful development, with too much emphasis on the decisive influences of internal economic and strategic factors and other comparative advantages on urban competitiveness. It is reasonable that high emphasis is placed on the city's internal factors in the era of industrial economy when a large number of factors gather and settle down in urban areas and contribute to the rapid expansion of urban scale, but it will become increasingly unsuitable when internal factors continue to be seen as the main explanation of urban competitiveness today, for the globalization- and informatization-motivated urban economy is mainly dependent on the inner-city interrelations and flows.

7.2. Competition and Cooperation in the Network of Global Cities

The study discusses the thoughts and defects in the studies of traditional urban competitiveness but this does not simply deny urban competition, rather it tries to further consider how to accurately understand the basic meaning of urban competition, especially how to define significance of urban competition in the context of globalization and normalization, and the relationship between competition and cooperation in the global network of city. Therefore, the study looks upon the historic evolution of urban competition from a dynamic perspective, especially digging the basic connotation of urban competition from the inherent track of the global network of cities development in the context of globalization and informatization, and positioning the city appropriately in urban development, elaborating the relationship of intercity competition and cooperation using the theoretical framework of the global network of city and network analysis.

7.2.1. *The historic evolution of and its role of urban competition*

It is known that urbanization always means that man seeks for the capability to compress time and space. From ancient to modern days, there is a continuous and gradient-like increase in human activity radius (reflecting space compression capabilities) and human speed (reflecting time compression capability). Formation and development of the city typically reflect improvements of human space–time compression capability in his long history (China Urban Development Report, 2001–2002, p. 13). The process of urbanization reflects the high convergence of human power to get access to material, energy, and information, with the growth of social wealth accompanied by the improvement of man's space–time compression capability. When resources are established, the urbanization-led high concentration is bound to spawn competition for resources, which constitute the intercity competition.

In this sense, the competition between cities has been on for quite some time, being a very common phenomenon. However, the essential attribute of urban competition is shown by a particular manner and form. Acting factors of urban competition vary with different stages of urban development, which makes the contents and methods changeable. As Berg and Braun (1999) point out, the city's competition depends largely on its development stage. That is, the city's competition has different contents and performances in different stages of its development.

It is known that, in the early stage of urbanization, the formation of cities and towns relies on spatial concentration of a large number of factors, which makes their functions of concentration prominent and diffusion relatively limited. In addition, these cities and towns that are forming and developing have not yet become relatively independent functional units, which lead to limited scope of their concentration and diffusion and relatively weak contacts with other cities and towns. Therefore, the inner-city complementarities and competitions become relatively weak.

After urban development comes into the age of the industrial economy, the large-scale development of urban manufacturing leads to urban expansion from central areas to suburbs. This forms the coexistence of a certain range of urban diffusion and a wider range of manufacturing concentration. In this situation, greater changes take place in urban competition, which is mainly reflected in the city's contention of factor concentration of the particularly relatively intense competition with the surrounding cities. With the further development of the city, the highly concentrated urban energy forms a strong diffusion, so that concentration and diffusion are deepened, and their scope expanded. These largely expand the scope of urban competition, forming the city's wide area competition, which means that big cities not only compete with their surrounding cities but also with other long-distance major cities.

At the same time, it should be noticed that urban connectivity with the outside world is not only an objective reality but also an essential prerequisite of urban development. In terms of cities as nodes, the high energy and energy conversion resulting from high compression of space and time is bound to form the connectivity with the outside world. The more tense its spatial and temporal compression, the stronger the city's connectivity with the outside world. The city's connectivity with the outside world is realized through the two-way interaction flows of a variety of tangible and intangible factors. In this sense, competition and cooperation between cities have always been simultaneous. In the context of globalization and informatization, the city achieves greater regional adaptability in using its space, which provides it with greater flexibility in its layout choice, scale structure, and industry selection. At the same time, the city's concentration and diffusion are wider and deeper, and some urban soft factors such as quality of life, environment, cultural services, and access to knowledge have become important location factors. More importantly, along with formation and development of the global network of city, any city must face the normative external world, and impossibly break away the network relationships. As the global network of city is a combination of many individual cities and is built based on cooperative relations, without this basic relationship, any network will lose its function and fail (Powell, 1990), the global city enters the global network of cities through the networks, so, "the city is considered a wide range of connections" (Thrift, 1997). In this sense, the global city's interest is not a fixed position in the inward and stable system (Virilio, 1999), but serve as the entry and exit points, and contraction and expansion of the acceleration and deceleration (Jameson, 1984). Therefore, the city integrating into the network has a wider range of connectivity with the outside, highlighting the function and value orientation of the urban value flows.

7.2.2. *Criticisms and innovation of the theory of urban competitiveness*

The traditional studies on urban competitiveness place too much emphasis on the role of urban accumulation and internal factors, neglecting the external linkages that decide urban competitiveness, which cannot meet the realistic demands that the city needs in integrating into the global network of cities in the context of globalization and informatization. Therefore, the traditional theory of urban competitiveness has been questioned from all angles. Krugman has criticized that the multivariate evaluation system established by Kresl does not fully absorb the results of international trade theory. In his view, opposite to the intuitive judgments, the best option of the city's prosperity is its active participation in international division of labor. Other scholars have also held a similar view that urban competitiveness and economic growth are based on regional trade and exports, and determined by the terms of trade outside these regions, with the terms of trade increasingly as the basis of innovation in the process of production and trade. In their view, that industries and enterprises "cluster" in the city is the result of the external performance of competitiveness, rather than its source. Under this view, the competitive cities are those cities "gateways" or "nodes" in the global economy, such as London, Paris, New York, and Tokyo. Hall and Hubbard (1998) more harshly criticize Kresl's views, stating that his study is short-sighted and separates competition from cooperation.

Currently, an increasing number of scholars have noted that the external linkages and internal factors of the city are of equal importance, both having a major impact on urban competitiveness. For example, Webster and Muller (2000) distinguish two types of different factors in the analysis of urban competitiveness:

(1) "economic activity" factors, such as finance, tourism, computer manufacturing, the role of the informal sector, technology, innovation, etc.;
(2) "place" factors, such as location, infrastructure, natural resources, amenity, cost of living and doing business, an urban region's image, human resources, business culture, and governance and policy frameworks.

They believe that urban competitiveness is jointly decided by places and urban activities. The former is more associated with the externality, being the performance, process, and results of the city to compete with the real world; and the place is non-transactional (non-tradable), largely reflecting the internal characteristics of the city. "Place" factors decide where and how activity factors are able to work. For example, human resources, regional endowments, and institutional environment determine the location of urban activities and their extension or compression. In addition, in the construction of urban competitiveness models, Sotarauta and Linnamaa (1998) do not focus on individual aspects of business and employment but sees the city as a whole, consciously highlighting the city's core competitive advantage, in particular, by placing too much emphasis on the role of the network and its management. Linnamaa thinks that the city organizes its various functions and activities by networks, rather than purely by hierarchical approaches and market approaches. In this process, there is both intense competition and close cooperation between cities. Urban development pattern is largely based on cooperation and networks, with network management increasingly becoming a decisive element of urban competitiveness. Thus, in his six elements of urban competitiveness, he emphasizes the institutions and policy-networks, and memberships in networks (see Figure 7.3).

Some scholars (Cox, 1997, Cox and Mair, 1988) put forward more clearly that urban competitiveness is significantly from external influences. They believe that urban competitiveness is related to the improvement in the flow of value in local social relations, involving

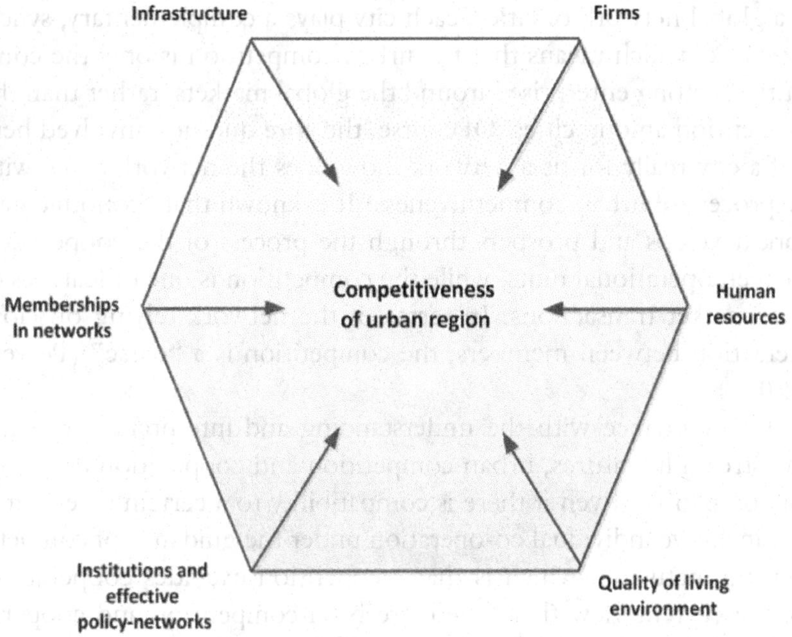

Figure 7.3. The Elements of Competitiveness of Urban Regions.

cooperation of agencies, institutions, and practices of different spaces. These views lack empirical evidence of inner-city relationships but realize that inner-city mutual relationships are the core of urban competitiveness. After investigating the relationship between London and Frankfurt, Beaverstock *et al.*, (2001) clearly point out that the competition between cities is harmful to the business stream, which leads to necessity of international collaboration.

7.2.3. *Compatibility of urban competition and cooperation*

It is a very important advancement that the network analysis has replaced the traditional, static model of urban hierarchy in the study on urban competitiveness. According to the network analysis method, urban competitiveness should be seen as a systematic phenomenon and be based on the interoperability of the global urban system. The competition between cities is part of the forming process of the global network of cities, but only a small part of the process (Kresl, 1995).

In a global network of cities, each city plays a complementary, synergistic role, which means that the urban competition is only the competition among enterprises around the global markets, rather than the competition among cities. Of course, the core question involved here is, if a city really forms a network, how does the network agree with the process of urban competitiveness? It is known that economic network develops and prospers through the process of the cooperation between operational units, while the competition is one of features of open market transactions. In terms of the network relying on close interaction between members, the competition is a "curse" (Powell, 1990).

In accordance with the understanding and interpretation of the mainstream literatures, urban competition and cooperation are really not compatible. Even if there is compatibility to a certain extent, it is only inclusive individual co-operation under the guidance of competition, the nature of which is that competition excludes cooperation. So, the current view that "there are both competition and cooperation between cities" (Begg, 1999, pp. 795–809) has gained increasing acceptance, but academic studies generally emphasize urban competition, almost not intending to involve urban cooperation (Lever and Turok, 1999). Therefore, rather than being based on the industrial economy like the mainstream literatures, the study of this core problem should focus on today's context of globalization and informatization, the method of which cannot follow the theoretical framework of urban hierarchy model, but rather use the theoretical framework of the global network of cities and network analysis.

From the perspective of urban network, the city's prosperity is not decided by "competitive advantage" preponderating over its rivals, but by the cooperation with its rivals, because only the cooperation can form network relations and massively expand network flow. Sassen (1994) points out that if cities only compete with each other in the global business activities, they cannot constitute a cross-border system. She also specially describes a model of cooperation between London, New York, and Tokyo from the perspective of the different roles played by the cities in finance and investment, showing that the relations among cities are not only simple business competition.

Camagni (1993) more fully describes the global network of city as a chain network, providing a means by which to explore "cooperative" relationship among cities and showing that the extensive intercity cooperation is increasingly important. Therefore, it is essential to define the city's economic success by the quantity and quality of its linkages to other cities. In other words, the city's success depends on connections in the global network of cities (Beaverstock *et al.*, 2002). In this situation, urban competition increasingly presents the nature of global competition, being accompanied with the trend of more extensive cooperation among cities at the same time. If a city lacks a broad, external cooperation, its competitiveness is difficult to effectively improve. Some empirical studies also show that many cities implement positive activities and design so-called international comparative advantages to enhance their international competitiveness, but achieve so little, the main reason being the lack of appropriate economic, social, and cultural foundations that are absolutely essential for cities to connect the global network (Loftman and Nevin, 1998).

Moreover, in the global network of city, the "urban competition" the study researches has a particular meaning and cannot be equated or confused with the general market competition. Krugman (1994) points out that the concept of economic competition should be limited to the main bodies that directly involve in market competition. Because the real competition means that, should it fail, the main body actually disappears from the market, which is reflected in the absolute failure through bankruptcy and the relative failure by taking over. Clearly, the market will not make the country disappear and will not force the city into bankruptcy. From this perspective, it is the only companies that compete in world markets. States and cities provides favorable conditions for their companies' success in world markets but themselves not constitute separate main bodies of market competition, only acting as a subsidiary part of the real market. Cities take part in "urban competition" in attracting foreign investment and inflow of key resources, but the real competition takes places between companies.

Inner-city cooperation is also reflected in communication and cooperation agreements concerning the various economic, cultural, and social aspects, signed between urban governments or other ways such as setting up of sister cities, but its basis lies in deeper network relationships between enterprises. So, in order to understand the cooperation between cities, it is necessary for the study to elaborate the influences of corporate competition on the inner-city cyberspaces after studying the competition between enterprises on how to influence the enterprises' location choices.

In modern conditions, each business has different market characteristics but all businesses are faced with the contradiction between globalization and localization. This fundamental pressure resulting from the contradiction influences the inner-city network spaces (Beaverstok *et al.*, 2001). The globalization–localization pressures subject enterprises to a series of contradictions in organizational structure, knowledge creation, business operations, location choices, and other aspects and force them to adopt new strategies and policy measures. For example, the international market expansion of enterprises across geographic spaces will cause the merger and union of enterprises so as to rationalize their organizations; but at the same time, in order to maintain their the core competitiveness, enterprises also emphasize the enhancement of core functions (non-core functions are from external purchases) and show their flexibility in the market, thereby in turn producing reverse forces to break the traditional vertical organizational structure of enterprises.

These pressures that prompt enterprises to find suitable market positions in the upstream and downstream of the industrial chain may promote the continuous reconstruction of commercial relations between different cities. Again, business service industries that provide knowledge products are subject to a similar contradiction. As professional and technical staff and their business knowledge are the core assets of these industries, they compete in the labor markets to scrabble for professionals and try to seize service market shares, which will lead to both specialization and diversity (only in this way, can enterprises provide services which are different from competitors). The competition for knowledge and skills will lead to the formation of new business models, strategic alliances and market diversification between cities. Also, there is the tendency of decentralization and centralization in terms of business operations: on the one hand, the pressure for enterprises to control risk and reduce cost makes their business operations tend to centralize; on the other hand, IT technology makes some of their functions can be placed almost anywhere in the world. This allows companies to put their important global functions in some of few major cities, but also to set up branches in other cities in order to achieve their organizational goals. Even in location selection, businesses also subject to a similar contradiction. On the one hand, competition forces enterprises to transfer their partial functions from expensive international cities to the places with relatively low costs (labor costs and space costs); on the other hand, economic concentration featuring face to face directly linkages and high-density dissemination of knowledge between cities in the world all have a stronger driving force on geographic concentration of business operations.

These contradictions triggered by globalization and localization place double pressures on enterprises. On one hand, the demands for international services power businesses to expand their markets. If this expansion fails, it will seriously affect their business development and competitiveness. So, they feel that it is absolutely necessary to set up branches in cities of other countries. On the other hand, globalization of market competition necessitates enterprises to approach their customers and actively participate in the local markets. This dual pressure leads to the expansion of the enterprises' scale, so as to serve global and local markets and be able to offer their customers comprehensive "seamless" cross-border services. It is the enterprises' location selection, and spatial distribution of network-style that provide interdependent foundations which are essential to operation of urban networks. That is, inner-enterprise competition in international markets leads to growing inter-dependence among cities.

It fully supports an important point: only in the global network of cities can the inter-city relations be correctly understood. There is more interdependence, but a little weak "subsidiary competition" among cities (nodes). Of course, it is also important for the city improve the environmental conditions to attract businesses, which, compared to the overall forming process of the global network of cities, can only be regarded as a very unimportant feature. Many empirical analyses also show that inner-city cooperation is of great complementarities. For example, London's competitive advantage relative to Frankfurt will not endanger the latter's status in European space flows. London succeeds not at the expense of Frankfurt, since they constitute the integral part of the European network of the world cities. On the contrary, highly concentrated market technology and experience in London is useful to the business activities in Frankfurt. That Frankfurt strengthens ties with London is very important to the development of Frankfurt's international business activities. Similarly, growing importance of Frankfurt as a "fortress" from London to European market is also beneficial to London.

In practice, an increasing number of cities have cognizance of the fact that, with more cities entering the global network of city system, the development of globalization-based economic ties, especially the exchange of science and information, will be unprecedented. Therefore, inter-city cooperation will help improve the public welfare in safety, environment, and overall quality of life. For example, Paris thinks that the inner-city science and information exchanges will help develop unity and cooperation. As part of its global urban development strategy, Paris includes it as an important strategic development plans to cooperate with the rest of the world cities (Moscow, Los Angeles, Rome, Madrid) and France's Marseille, Lyon, and other cities, actively promoting cultural and technical cooperation with world's major cities, particularly EU cities, continuously increasing the frequency of exchange and making it standardized. Therefore, the city government of Paris has signed cooperation agreements with 20 major cities, signing friendly agreements with three cities of Washington, Madrid, and Athens, whose core contents is to actively promote international cooperation, strengthen the dialogues, consolidate dynamic partnerships, and promote cultural cooperation.

7.3. The Rise of Global Cites Driven by Competition and Cooperation

The foregoing analysis shows that, under the conditions in the global network of cities, the driving force of global city development is not simply the urban competition but competition and cooperation.

Different from the early development of global cities of developed countries, the rise of China's global cities takes place at the time when the global network of cities has formed and perfected and has extended to China to a large extent, forming a global city region in space. This situation makes the rise of China's global cities completely driven by double competition and cooperation, which requires concerted mechanisms of multiple participation to ensure the implementation of mutual benefit and win-win from competition and cooperation.

7.3.1. *The globalizing cities: facing dual competition and cooperation*

The rise of China's global cities will face double urban competition and cooperation. One is competition and cooperation with international major cities, mainly reflected in their role and function in the global network of cities beyond their motherland; the other is the competition and cooperation with domestic cities, mainly in reflected in their role and function in the domestic network of cities. There are both differences and relationships between the two.

The above analysis shows that the urban competition and cooperation is an organic whole, which cannot be separated. However, the degree of competition and cooperation, namely, their weights may be different: either the degree of competition is higher, or the level of cooperation is lower, and vice versa. There exists simply pure competition or cooperation in the extreme poles of the "spectrum" of competition and cooperation. Of course, there may not exist this definite state in reality, but in theory it is feasible to make such assumptions. So, according to the dual international and domestic competition and cooperation pattern, the study can build a simple theoretical model (see Figure 7.4).

Interval B indicates that a city has a stronger competition with domestic cities and has a competition with foreign ones, but with cooperation of at least two dimensions. In this situation, it must have a strong domestic and international competitiveness, otherwise, it will be impossible to intake the domestic resources and international

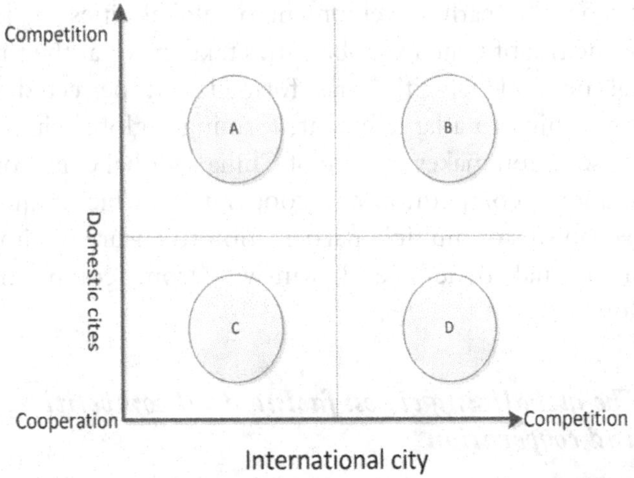

Figure 7.4. Dual Model of Urban Competition and Cooperation.

resources. To say the least, even if a city intakes the domestic resources and international resources by virtue of its special advantage, at most, it develops into a giant city or a super city, rather than the global city based on the network linkages. Obviously, too much emphasis on competition and neglect of cooperation does not constitute the driving force of the rise of global cities, which is criticized by the study.

Interval C indicates that a city has a stronger cooperation, but little competition with both domestic cities but also with foreign cities. In this situation, it will develop into a typical "gateway" city connecting the home and the outside, because of its weak ability to draw domestic and international resources and smaller size and strength. In reality, this wide range of domestic and international cooperation is restricted by the various conditions, therefore not having a strong practical universality.

Interval C indicates that the city has a stronger competition with domestic cities, but maintains more cooperation with foreign cities. In this situation, it competes for not only domestic resources with domestic cities but also inward foreign resources with domestic cities. If the city is more competitive than other cities, it can gather domestic and foreign resources. Its growing size and strength can transform it into a city with a higher degree internationalization, even a global city.

Interval D indicates that a city has a stronger domestic cooperation with domestic cities and simultaneously has a stronger competition with foreign cities. This situation will lead to two possibilities. If it does not form a stronger international competitiveness on the basis of its cooperation with other domestic cities, it will develop into the core city or central city in the national urban system. If it forms a strong international competitiveness on the basis of its cooperation with other domestic cities, gathering a large number of international resources, it will likely become the core city in the global city regions.

The above theoretical analysis starts only from the perspective of a single city, if considering *N* cities in a country are to become global cities, a different angle will be used to analyze the relationship between urban competition and cooperation. Here the study will start from the perspective to analyze the possible state of urban competition and cooperation and its impact on the rise of global cities.

First of all, it is necessary to distinguish the different effects of big country of economies and small country of economies on urban competition and cooperation. A big country of economies has a larger domestic market size and larger space for the flow of domestic resources and forms a relatively complete national urban system, so in addition to a few cities with a high degree of external connectivity, the considerable cities focus more on domestic competition and cooperation, with more domestic linkages and less external connections. For example, in the USA, except the global cities like New York and Chicago, the other cities mainly focus on domestic urban competition and cooperation, and their external connectivity is lower than European cities. In contrast, the major cities in small countries of economies are generally more inclined to participate in international competition and cooperation, with higher external connections.

Second, it is necessary to further consider the influence of a city's functional orientation on urban competition and cooperation. Because of their political, economic, and cultural functions, capitals or economic center cities of big countries as well as economic center cities with higher regional integration usually evolve toward the direction of the integrated global cities, such as New York, Tokyo, and London. The small- and medium-sized cities in small countries or general cities in big countries, such as Geneva, Amsterdam, and Brussels, because they do not have very strong overall advantage, and often only select the way to professional internationalization.

If *N* cities in a country develop themselves into modern international metropolises with comprehensive functions or similar professional capabilities, there is more mutual competition than cooperation. To achieve their objectives, these cities intake significant domestic and international resources and investments. And these global economic and cultural flows often has been directed into a particular globalizing city before they further venture toward and (or) are assigned to other cities in the country. Therefore, while the particular globalizing city potentially competes with other domestic cities, the other cities also, to some extent, challenge the particular globalizing city. Assuming that, in the context of international competition and cooperation, there is the possibility of global cities development, the mutual competition of domestic cities often results in the fact that only a city or a few cities can develop into global cities because, to a certain extent, the competitiveness of a global city is determined by its role and function in the global network of cities beyond specific regions and countries (Coe *et al.*, 2003). Once a global city in a country has such a strong competitiveness, it is also very difficult for the country's other cities to become dominant global cities. For example, in the UK, only London can become a global city, because it holds such a strong influence by adapting itself to act as a strategic node for the global economy. In this situation, it is virtually impossible for other UK cities to compete with London. Of course, it also depends on the contrast of primary nodes power and the possibility of its change in the global network of cities, that is, whether there is the possibility that the original global cities with integrated functions can be replaced or adds new comprehensive global cities to the network system.

Therefore, in a country, there is usually only one dominant, comprehensive global city, although it has important connections with other cities in the country. This is mainly because it competes with other cities of the country. Similarly, a country usually has only one global city with the same type of professional functions. This level of interaction between cities is of great importance to understanding why a country almost has the several similar dominant global cities at the same time.

If *N* cities in a country, which are to become global cities, differ from comprehensive functionality orientation to professional functionality orientation, or significantly differ in specialized functionality orientation, they are more in mutual cooperation than competition. Because these cities set up mutually complementary development paths, operate on different levels, and root in different spatial economic networks (although with some overlaps), they participate in less domestic interaction (competition). In this situation, all *N* cities are likely to develop into global cities with different specialized functions, if the conditions concerning international competition and cooperation allow. For example, in the USA, there are several global cities with specialized functions at the same time: New York is a major financial global city, San Francisco is the major global city in high-tech industry, and Los Angeles is a major global city in the cultural industries (Abu-Lughod, 1999). These three cities are to become the dominant global cities because of their clear positions in the global economy/culture, forming a globally diffusing and radiating economic system based on the global network of cities. That is, all global cities/global city regions mainly depend on more domestic and international markets to maintain their survival (Hill and Kim, 2000).

Therefore, China's future global cities must set up clear functional positioning, concerning which cities are positioned to be functionally integrated, and which cities are professionally orientated, with mutually complementary development paths. The formation and development of integrated global cities require a fairly long process of accumulation. For example, the formation of the global city of New York is the result of continuous accumulation and innovation for several decades. Of course, factors such as major historical events, global economic restructuring, and the shift of regional development focus often are important opportunities for those cities with some basis to speedily develop into integrated global cities. In contrast, the rise of professional functional global cities do not need the accumulation of such a long period, especially in the context of the acceleration of economic globalization today, the internationalization of an aspect or a function of a city can rapidly take root and form in a short time. But no matter what type of globalized cities China's cities hope to become, they should further increase external connections, change the prevailing situation of competition gaining the upper hand over cooperation, strengthen cooperation with domestic cities, especially close cooperation with their surrounding cities, form stronger international competitiveness, and strive to become the core cities of the global city regions.

7.3.2. *Multiparticipators of urban competition and cooperation*

The preceding analysis shows that the rise of global cities results from the shift from adversarial competition to collaborative competition. This collaborative competition puts much emphasis on win-win, integration, correlation and joint consultation system (Ning, 2003). So, by what mechanism does urban competition and cooperation based on the urban network achieve? This requires first study on participators and their mutual relationships.

At the mention of urban competition and cooperation issues, people often first think of city governments. The reason is simple: the perpetrators who improve investment environment to attract enterprises to locate (the so-called city competition) are city governments; similarly, they are the main bodies in charge of the signing and implementation of the cooperation projects between cities are city governments. Moreover, in the process of globalization, there appears a shift of national power down to cities, which empowers city governments to have appropriate physical resources (including land and infrastructure), political resources, and other resources and makes a difference in urban competition and cooperation. The central and local official separation of powers in China's economic restructuring allows city governments to actually control many available resources and have a greater say in urban competition and cooperation. Therefore, according to the public, the city government is the only main body that implements urban competition and cooperation. However, this assumption is wrong. Participants of urban competition and cooperation are multivariate. In addition to city government, the state and its departments, enterprises are also important implementers.

In the traditional study of global cities, there is the mainstream view of denationalization, namely, with the deepening process of globalization, the role of nation-states in the implementation of accumulation tends to weaken. For example, as representatives studying the global city, Friedmann and Sassen all agree to the view of denationalization, but think differently: the former defines it as the "national extinction" process, and latter considers "system interruption" (Brenner, 1998). Friedmann (1986) believes that the way and extent of a city's integration with the world economy and its given functions in the new division of labor will play a decisive role in the structural changes taking place in it. In his view, the global city and country are two diametrically opposing "political-economic" units. The rise of global cities is bound to weaken the nation-state's influences, especially at the local level (Friedmann, 1995). Therefore, he predicts, it is a process of gradual national extinction. Sassen (2000, p. 13) is relatively modest in his approaches, putting forward the "system interruption" to emphasize the incremental effects. She believes that in the past world economy, there are close relationships between leading industries of a country's global city and its national economy's overall growth, but now there is significant asymmetry: the conditions permitting the growth of global cities includes important factors that lead to the decline of the USA, United Kingdom, Japan, and other countries, resulting in an increase in governmental and corporate debts. So, she concludes that there possibly is "system interruption" in the relationship between national economic growth and its form thought by people, which necessitates global city formation and cities' separation from their respective states. In other words, these global urban systems with more prominent economy are interpreting their own logic, and breaking away their countries, meaning that the global cities break away from their national urban system, becoming part of the global urban system, which leads to the global cities' separation from their national urban system and the nation-state. These global cities together constitute a system, not just competing with each other. Therefore, what benefits economic growth in the global network of cities does not necessarily benefit the national economic growth (Sassen, 1991). For example, what benefits London and New York may not be similarly beneficial to the United Kingdom and the USA.

Obviously, this logic will underestimate the role of the state (government) and large enterprises in actively building and participating in the global city. In fact, in the context of the global economy, the enhancement of the city government's status does not mean the complete loss of the state's role. Weiss (1998, pp. 70–80) has analyzed the state's role in the globalization process, pointing out the four key dimensions:

(1) management support: the solid collaboration mechanism between the government and enterprise will maximize the effectiveness of public resources, which are used to upgrade products, lower prices, or expand exports;
(2) the resolution of public risk: to win the cooperation with the relevant producers, the public sectors absorb all or most of risks and often mediates between producers and consumers in the domestic market;
(3) governance of private sector: the government "abducts" the ability of economic and social self-government, coordinating private sectors, acting as "the last coordinator";
(4) innovation alliance of public–private sectors, involving the policy of getting, enhancing and proliferating technology, public–private technology partnerships, and networks servicing the training capital, and the regulation of public liability by designing performance criteria. Clearly, these aspects also have influences on the global city. Although the globalization has resulted in finance and producer services being embedded in strategic places (nodes) in the network, these strategic places are still embedded within the boundaries of the nation-states. The enterprises operating around the world also need the host country's effective property rights protection and enforcement of contracts, while the state's legal system is to ensure a reliable property rights and contract enforcement.

It is known that, regardless of how national power tends to shift down to cities in the process of globalization, the "urban economy" is not the "national economy" with the autonomies. Regional and urban development strategies and regulatory frameworks designed by countries will make the city run in a specific manner. For example, the UK's global city operates in an environment different from that of USA. Therefore, countries with different systems and organizations play a crucial role in the global city formation process and its governance. In the study on formation of European global cities, Brenner (1998) points out that it is impossible to fully understand the formation of global cities unless the role of their country is examined. Douglass (2000a) holds a similar point of view, in that the ambiguity of interaction between nations and the global city is related to a more mysterious question, namely, how a currently identified central area to build a global city truly becomes a global city.

The country's role in the rise of China's global cities or the "national strategy" may be even more important. The preceding analysis has pointed out that the prerequisite for the rise of global cities is integration into economic globalization and informatization. In China, it is the central government that implements conscious, purposeful, and planned opening-up strategy to promote the national economy and urban economy into the globalization processes. The state has always played an important role in China's metropolitan areas into the global economy. In addition, the central government also sees building the global city as the strategy practice connecting its economy with global economy, such as a clear position to build Shanghai into a modern international metropolis, and offer support from all aspects (including development and opening up of Pudong, the international financial center construction, etc.), which upgrades Shanghai's strategic position so rapidly. Obviously, this national strategy plays a decisive role during the rise of China's global cities.

Moreover, in the process of the rise of China's global cities, due to the tremendous impact of the central government, including controlling the bonding process of potential global cities and global urban system, there does not appear a weakening of relationships between global cities and their countries just like some scholars have predicted. Increasingly close relations between Shanghai, Beijing, and other Chinese cities and the global urban system is rapidly improving their status and role in the national urban system, which is basically consistent with the tropism of the national urban systems (including national policy and practice). Global economy and multinational corporations' development in China, improved China's position in the world economy, and the Chinese government's efforts to promote the major cities as bridges by which to connect the global economy have largely contributed to the rise of China's global cities. Even if unbalanced development, isolation, and detachment are the inevitable results of the formation of global cities and global urban system, like many people said, the central government's conscious control of the process can reduce these negative effects. Timberlake and Xiulian (2006) point out that the global city formation results from both global and local factors and also the interaction of global and local (e.g. national) forces. The majority of these judgments are especially true for the rise and fall of Chinese cities under the control of the highly centralized authority for decades.

In short, the state plays a very important role in the formation of global cities (Brenner *et al.*, 2003). Because the country plays a very clear role in the rise of global cities and is able to respond to changes of urban competition and cooperation, it is one of important participants of the rise of global cities and their competition and cooperation mechanisms. If the special nature of its industrial management is taken into account, and its impacts of urban competition and cooperation are studied in depth, the country can be further broken down into central government and government departments.

In addition to the role of the country in urban competition and cooperation mechanism, the important position of enterprises also must be taken into account. As the preceding has already proposed, the city's real competition is from the competition among enterprises: the city government itself does not constitute a real competitor. Similarly, inter-city cooperation does not only mean the cooperation between the city governments. In fact, the inter-city linkages are mainly based on inter-firm linkages in different cities, and inter-city traffic is mainly from business activities and concrete business between enterprises in different cities; therefore, many projects reflecting urban competition and cooperation are started at the enterprise level on the effects of the market mechanism. In the context of globalization, there exist more close business linkages among enterprises. Especially, the business of advanced producer service companies is usually beyond their geographic scope, but because it is difficult for many services to trade in long distances, most producer services companies must locate foreign markets serving their local customers through a wide range of branches, which results in the formation of connections between cities. Therefore, enterprises, especially global companies, are undoubtedly important participants of urban competition and cooperation.

In addition, in a mature market economy, the government as a "night watchman" does not directly interfere with business activities. The government cannot impose special effects on inner-firm business and economic ties and mutual competition and cooperation. In this regard, a variety of industry associations and other organizations usually provide regulatory frameworks, their products (services) and professional standards to manage companies' activities. The importance of such institutions is particularly pronounced in the advanced producer services, whose taxation, standards, and business activities are managed by trade associations, especially professional organizations. Due to their different properties, different producer service sectors have different thresholds through which to join in. Law firm professionally operates differently from insurance companies, and advertising companies have different areas of specialization from within the accounting agencies. In general, those sectors (such as accounting, legal, investment banks, etc.) directly related to the financial system, real estate development, and financial-related professional services are both subject to articles of their association and to strict management from industrial standards of members. But other some producer services such as advertising, administrative inquiries, and real estate agents and other departments are more dependent on industrial self-regulation, undertaking business activities in accordance with the relatively loose domestic and international rules.

Thus, the formal and informal admittances, practices, rules, habits, and traditions in each industry affect the behavior of each company within the industry and instill them special values and characteristics.

Because these institutions have a greater impact on trans-regional, cross-border business activities (i.e., help or hinder the business of trans-regional or global operation), in a way, they are also important participants of urban competition and cooperation. Of course, in China's economic transition, state-owned enterprises (including state-owned holding companies) especially carry out nominal separation of administrative functions from enterprise management, but the fact is that the government can still impose special influences on these enterprises, intervening in their operations such as the appointment and removal of representative of their investors and asset restructuring. At the same time, industry associations and other institutions play a limited functionality. Therefore, the role of such institutions as the participants of urban competition and cooperation is not obvious.

Perhaps the study can be summed up as follows: the city government does play an important role in urban competition and cooperation, standing on the shore, but not the only participant. Competition and cooperation mechanism in the city, there is a "development coalition" comprising multiparticipants who include countries (including governmental departments), the city government, businesses, and trade associations.

7.3.3. *Achieving mechanisms for urban competition and cooperation: the synergy between participants*

Beaverstock *et al.* (2002) have proposed a synergy model of the global network of cities, which includes four categories of actors (cities, companies, industry sectors, and countries) and can be created, supported, and changed through two ligaments (i.e. city–company, country–the industry sector) and two groups (i.e. national city, company within the industry sector), emphasizing that the four categories of participants promote the global network of cities through the synergies. Among these, cities, companies, industry sectors, and countries constitute a heterogeneous combination, and their respective networks play an interactive role in the creation and support of the global space of flows. From this, it is deduced that the relationship between the participants has a direct impact on the basic pattern of urban competition and cooperation, and ultimately decided the city's success or failure in the global economy.

Therefore, the kind of urban competition and cooperation formed in the rise of global cities involves not only the city government's strategic direction and development policy but also the behavior of participants such as businesses and industry sectors.

In general, only when the behaviors of these participants contribute to the creation of synergies, can they adjust and improve the relationships between urban competition and cooperation and promote the rise of global cities. That the synergetic power is strong or weak is directly related to the speed of the rise of global cities. The so-called synergetic power refers to the ability arising from the interaction of the closely linked actors through a combination of specific cultural, economic, social, and political relations, which is more than the sum of individual ability. So, how to form this synergetic power in the rise of global cities and urban competition and cooperation? According to international experience and China's current situation, there are following several aspects.

When it comes to the direct impact of national policies on the city, two main aspects should be paid attention. First, promoting the rise of global cities should be labeled as the national strategy in order to acquire persistent support. Currently, many countries are very concerned about the global city construction and support, the intention of which is to use these cities to embed a country's economy into the world economy, usually using a very strong political and institutional will to list it as a "national strategy" and allocating it substantial resources to cause its adjusting changes (Robinson, 2002). A country's persistent support for these specific cities is a key condition for them to become global cities. To a great extent, this clear national strategy actually avoid the vicious competition with each other, which results from the unclear positioning of domestic urban development. At the same time, the rise of global cities is coordinated and guided by the national-level regional development planning so as to make these cities more mutually cooperative based on dislocated development. Second, the city government should be more empowered to create synergies between the state and city. In the modern economic society, based on public duty, government action must meet the local requirements, and be adapt to local resources and local opportunities. And clear decentralization will lead to possibility that provide public services and quality of life and local competitiveness. In this sense, moving power from the state down to the city, to some extent, is the important step the country takes to promote the rise of global cities. Under these conditions, the city will have more room and potential for development.

As Brenner (1998) puts it, the European experience shows that, in the era of globalization, global cities increasingly are in harmony with re-regionalized government agencies and powers, whose intention is to raise the global competitive advantage of main city areas through the reconstruction of the "global" regional government.

In terms of the interaction between the national system and industrial sectors, the content mainly related to include the following. First is the greater impact of the country's regulatory framework on industrial sector activities. The relatively liberalized national law and economic policies are perhaps the keys to promote the flows among global cities; otherwise, the flow between global cities will halt. For example, different from the UK's banking system, Japan's financial control system is still very tight, hence, in competition with less regulated markets in Europe, Hong Kong, and the USA, foreign financial institutions located in Tokyo usually suffer from more activity constraints. Second is the greater impact of changes in national economic policy, especially the amendment of legislative frameworks for financial transactions on institutional culture of the industry sector and its businesses. Supra-national (e.g. EU), national (central governments), and regional policy-making, such as encouraging certain economic patterns of behavior and conditions-based support for those projects with externalities, perhaps has an impact on business activities and their culture. Thus, industrial policy of some countries will largely and imperceptibly influence the corporate culture of a particular industry sector (Beaverstock *et al.*, 2000).

In terms of the city authorities, a city's competition policies should be based on the belief that each of the global cities is an integral part of the global network of cities (Taylor, 2001), focusing on the policy improving the general business environmental conditions, rather than competitive measures with other cities, and lobbying the central government to obtain support. In fact, most multinational corporations may not be much interested in sacrificing city A to promote city B. For the city authorities, the most important thing is to provide a handful of world-class arena by creating a good environment for domestic and foreign enterprises. At this arena, there must be first-rate "actors" (i.e. corporations) to perform or play no matter where these official award-winning actors are situated: local, domestic, or foreign. In other words, the best "actors" of a big city are those companies or organizations that make this city become important, although these leading companies or organizations may be mostly foreign rather than domestic. This is not only suitable for New York, London, Tokyo, Frankfurt and other global cities, but also for Hong Kong and Singapore, where almost all large companies manufacturing high-end services are foreign.

In this sense, a city's international competitiveness is mainly expressed in its business environment and first-rate companies or organizations located in it. In addition, given the rise of China's global cities lives in the development of the global city-regions, the city authorities should explore the road to urban development from the regional level, forming own core competencies in the regional cooperation. At present, people are increasingly aware of the importance of regional cooperation and coordination and are beginning to take more action. For example, in its "Eleventh Five-Year Plan", the city of Taizhou in Jiangsu Province established the basic idea of "developing itself by complementing, cooperating and combining with other regions". In practice, there are a number of successful explorations and experiments in regional cooperation, such as two cities of Jingjiang and Jiangyin, which has broken administrative barriers to engage in joint development zones: brands and personnel are provided by the Jiangyin, land is provided by Jingjiang, and the two cities share taxes and GDP.

From a prospective business perspective, the key is that the company has its own networks and branches in major cities and forms a connection in urban networks, which results in a mutually beneficial relationship with the city. For example, a US law firm's offices in London perhaps get their big gains by continuing to maintain an excellent original lead position in the global cities. Similarly, the advertising or media organizations in UK's provincial capitals can perhaps operates in London's urban network, especially those companies which have their main service branches. For local businesses, the key is to "go out", concentrating on international expansion and setting up their branches in major cities at home and abroad to establish contact with other urban networks. The foregoing analysis has pointed out that, at this stage, it is difficult for China's enterprises to "go out", but, sooner or later, they will go "abroad". At present, those globalizing cities relying mainly on "bringing in" should make choices when making efforts to introduce into companies and organizations, giving priority to the introduction of organizations or institutions with corporate networks, especially the global networks, rather than focusing on the size of their funds and how much value they can bring. The size of the funds brought by these companies is not great, but it will bring global linkages and the wealth of flows in information and personnel, which will greatly promote the position of the city in the global space of flows.

In short, in the rise of global cities, enterprises, departments, cities, and countries interact through linkages. Although, in this process, they may be contradicted and conflicted, they carry out joint operation by means of the consistency of the global network of city. It is the belief that the rise of global cities results from the various types of participants jointly creating a corporate network (which is connected with the departmental network) and an urban network (which is connected with the national network) to jointly create specific cultural, economic, and political relations. Therefore, the belief that the rise of global cities only results from the urban growth strategy implemented by the "entrepreneur-typed" urban politicians (Savitch and Kantor, 1995) does not agree with the perspective that national mandatory intervention is necessary to ensure the success of a global city (Yeung, 2000). For the same reason, defining a global city simply using the number of foreign companies or producer services clusters locating there is not agreeable. On the contrary, the analysis suggests that the global city is defined only depending on its attributes in the global network of cities, with its rise supported and maintained by synergies among city, companies, departments, and country.

Chapter 8

Strategy Oriented by Flow Expansion and Its Development Mode

With the interaction of globalization and informatization, the local space of the cities is transforming into flowing space. As the main panel points of a global network, the flowing economy has its new connotations and characteristics and thus result in the large-scale economic flow (information, knowledge, currencies, cultures, etc.). According to the international practices, the existence and development of a globalizing city are realized by the large-scale flow based on the communication in the globe. The main tasks of a globalizing city are to extend the global communication, construct the panel points of a global network, strengthen the economic flow based on the gathering of extensive interaction, and set the realistic base of taking the load of a large-scale flowing. Therefore, a globalizing city usually advocates the guiding strategies and development modes of flow extension based on the correlative network.

8.1. Strategic Orientation of Globalizing Cities

For a globalizing city, whatever its relying path is, it usually has the problem of guiding strategies. The guiding strategies are the choice of the development strategies and modes which are suitable to the target location of a globalizing city. Proper development and clear guiding strategies guarantee the realization of a target location.

8.1.1. *A globalizing city based on the flow extension*

At present, the target location of some globalizing cities in China is increasing clear, for example, Shanghai will be basically constructed by envisioning it as a major international economy, finance, trade, and shipping center and a socialist modern international metropolis by 2020. The target setting and target location may be biased in reality and can be deemed as too impractical and idealistic for future development. However, these problems can be adjusted and amended in the dynamic development. The more crucial problem is to choose clear and suitable guiding strategies. If the strategies are not clear, the target location will not be clear either, and the former will be reduced to impractical slogans or labels. Choosing improper guiding strategies will result in impossible or even opposite target location.

From China's experience, it is clear that the guiding strategy of a globalizing city is being explored and the Chinese authorities are not yet clear about the measures, let alone the clear targets, of natural implementation. In reality, we observed that we are following the traditional development strategies and modes and deviate from the knowledge of a globalizing city. For example, when talking about a globalizing city, we usually refer to a first-class city with immense mass, large scale, solid force. In our subconsciousness, these cities are founded and accumulated on the abundant material wealth and capital, which are based on the large-scale solidification and gathering. Dominated by this idea, what many places focus on are the extension of city scale and physical mass, the wealth accumulation in their own cities, and the extension of material capital. What these city stress are the enhancement of economic aggregate or economic force and their rising in the proportion nationally. What happens next is enlarging the city scale, extending the urban space in all directions, advocating for urban spatial structure with multimasses, expanding the city size, increasing the population, and extending the urban size a few times or double or triple the urban population. At the same time, blindly following the first-class standards, a large-scale capital was invested in urban infrastructure such as more buildings, bridges, or roads. It is not suitable and seasonable to construct and develop the super squares, theaters, gyms, luxurious complexes, fashion blocks, senior residential areas, and top-grade entertainment places with the so-called high standards. For the improvement in urban economic force and material wealth, the industries which bring in high productive values or wealth were attracted, gathered, and developed in the limited area regardless of the location and economy of the city.

These guiding strategies are not in accordance with the essential attributes of a globalizing city and run counter to the development tendency of a globalizing city, which is deviating the target location of a globalizing city. Therefore, the first necessary and urgent task of a globalizing city is to explore and define the guiding strategies. As a globalizing city in the developing countries, we have no successful example to follow and need to accumulate more lessons of guiding strategies. It is a brand new issue and a natural process to study and research, which includes the acquisition of laws to develop a globalizing city, the learning lessons from a globalizing city in developed countries, and the exploration in the construction practice of a globalizing city.

From the earlier analysis, we know that the dynamic mechanism and process of a globalizing city are universal and have the essentials of global communication under the context of globalization and informatization. For a globalizing city, the keys are its degree of merging with various network systems globally. The entry and merger of a globalizing city with the network and its extensive relations with the outside world will result in a large-scale economic flow in a wider scope and more effective resource collocation, expand the sources and channels of available resources such as information and knowledge, improve the ability to transfer and collocate the resources and promote the economic growth and urban development. In this sense, the urban economic growth is increasing reliance on the quantity and quality of the city's communication and relations with other international cities.

Furthermore, a globalizing city should have a higher position in this network system. Its position is based on the scale and scope of economic flow to great extent. This means a bigger scale and wider scope of economic flow will result in the city's higher position in the network system, or vice versa. In essence, the scale of the flow in the network system is actually the network power. The more extensive communication of the city with other cities in the outside world will ensure its center and potential power in the network. If the city has a higher inner attraction, it means that the city is more outstanding and has more advantages, thus it is followed by the other cities. If the city has a higher outside attraction, that means the city needs more communication with the outside world, which shows that the city is more influential and need to be able to communicate with the other cities or make the other cities care about its ideas. Apparently, in the cities that have higher inner attraction and outside attraction, the scale of the flow is naturally larger and it has more network power and a high position in the network system. For example, they have more ways to meet their own requests and weaker reliance on the other individual cities; they can gain or apply more resources in the network and have more development potentials and space; they can be the third party or medium in trade and get benefits from it (Hanneman and Riddle, 1988). This is the reason why the globalizing cities in the first layer or second layer in the system play a more important role on the international stage, develop more international markets, participate international division of labor, expand international influence, and stimulate the development of the domestic cities than the other central cities in the large system of international economic recycling.

In effect, as a globalizing city in the first or the second layer of the global urban network, though as the global or regional center of international finance and trade, international control and decision, international culture and information exchange, the difference of economic flow has direct impact on its control force and influencing in the world economy and politics. For some people, compared to New York and London, Tokyo has relatively weak control force and less influence, one of the most important reasons is its relatively less economic flow. For example, the annual movement of Narita Airport, Tokyo in 1998 was 127,600, compared to John Kennedy International Airport, New York, 362,200; Heathrow Airport,

London, 451,400; Charles de Gaulle Airport, Paris, 791,000; and Changi Airport, Singapore, 177,400. Another example is that Tokyo welcomed 2.5 million overseas visitors in 1998, compared to Paris, which played host to 12 million visitors in the same year; even Singapore and Hong Kong welcomed more overseas visitors, with the former welcoming 6.96 million overseas visitors in 1999 and earning international tourism income worth US $6.501 billion in 1998, while the latter earned US $7.114 billion through international tourism in 1998. Comparing the rate between the urban population and the number of foreign visitors, the obvious gap can be found in Tokyo. The rate in Paris is 1:5, while in Tokyo it is only 1:0.2. In addition, 63 international conferences were held in Tokyo in 1999, while, the number of international conferences in New York was 88; it was 140 in Singapore, 160 in London, and 247 in Paris. The other data also demonstrated that 260,000 foreign residents lived in Tokyo by the year 2000 and it accounted for 2.2% of the whole population in Tokyo. However, the percentage early in 1990 was 28.4%. It is obvious that the gap between these economic flows has direct influence on its control force and influence in the world's politics and economies, which decides the global urban competitiveness.

Even though globalizing cities have no comprehensive or complete economic flow like in New York, London, and Tokyo, their role as superior panel points in the network can help to shape the large-scale economic flow in certain aspects and give rise to critical competition. The practice shows that, in some cases, the places which cannot be changed to central panel points due to their special history can result a specific network with their special region features. Some examples are Rochester in Minnesota, USA, and Villejuif in the suburbs of Paris. Both regions have become the interactive central panel points in the global network of advanced medical and health research, because Mayo Clinic is located in Rochester and the French government's main cancer therapy center is located in Villejuif. Combined with their specific regional characteristics, the complexes with knowledge production and advanced medicine are established due to an occasional historical background. Since their establishment, they attracted the researchers, doctors, and patients globally, formed the panel points in the world medical network and resulted in the large-scale flow in medical treatment.

For a globalizing city, an important problem is to determine if it can enter into the global network, and if so, to what degree and in what position, which finally decides the city's destiny to become a globalizing city. If a city cannot merge into the network and gain coordinate effects, it will be marginalized, its economic development will be limited, and its competition will be weakened to a great degree. In this sense, a globalizing city is not decided by its properties, capital stock, or scale, but by the degree to which the city merges into the global network and the coordinate effects. The reason is that the coordinate effects based on the global network will increasingly strengthen the city's competition and thus have more competitive advantages than other cities. Several central cities in different countries put forward the strategic targets of international development and describe the complete designing of future development. The aims are to merge into the global network, reshape the functions of panel points in the network, extend economic flow, and raise the city's position in the future global urban systems.

Overall, the rise of a globalizing city is a process of gradual merging into the network. By producing and consuming high-quality and advanced services to promote urban development, the city can connect to the global network and become its main panel point. In such a process, one increasing obvious feature is the forceful flow and the large-scale flow, which are based on the panel points in the network. For a globalizing city, the first critical problem is to expand its connection to the outside world actively, construct the flowing space connected to the global economic functional properties, merge into the global network, and expand the flow scale which is based on the panel points.

8.1.2. *The flow expansion based on the flowing space*

The economic flow based on the connection to the locations (or places) is the inherent essence of the city. But the expansion based on the panel points in the network is a new form of economic flow developed in the flowing space. It does not equal the circulating events in economy, or the economic flow demonstrating in urban gathering and distribution, but is in accordance with the urban economic essence — the economic flowability — in the new conditions of urban spaces. For a further understanding of this problem, we will review the development process and the economic flowability in historical perspective.

In the sense of the city's production process, the essence is flowing economy or circulating economy and is the combination of the city and market. The city is the outcome of the gathering of resources and the accumulation of wealth, which is a form or a hull. The market resulting from economic flowing or circulation is the city's main content. Only based on the thriving business exchanges can the city be rid of the form before it can realize the actual market exchanges. From this, we know it is commerce revolution that causes the thriving and development of the city. In the general survey of the historical process of urban development, the ancient cities relied more on the convenient transportation in which the trade with liquidity was increasing greatly and consolidated their central position in the region by gathering various kinds of products, while the modern cities relied more on the conditions such as region and environment and established their central position in business and economy by the flowing of different factors. The present cities rely more on technologies and network and exchange knowledge and information in high-density before they can form the global urban network. In such a process, the main line is the economic flowability in a wider extension in the flowing scope.

Of course, in the development process of urban economy, abundant resource factors such as fixed assets, infrastructure, and relatively stable human resources will be condensed or solidified in large scale in the cities. While these stocks mainly form the material base of urban economic flowability, they cannot become the sole resource collocation in economic flowability. That is to say, the value growth and scale enlargement of the factors rely on effective operation platform, suitable operation environment, gathering of resources, integration and operation, and regional expansion. In this process, the urban economic scale tends to be increasing and thus promote the development of urban economy.

In the definition of urban functions, the economic events of supplying goods and service to the outside can be termed as "basic functions" or "basic events" while those to the city itself, the non-basic functions or non-basic events. Hirsch discussed the outside functions and inside functions of the city and defined them as "non-central local functions" and "central local functions". He said, "When the strength related to production and the strength related to demanding interact and stimulate the urban economy, some non-central functions will be increased, that means the local basic events will increase concerning industries, commerce and transportation serving the bigger markets". Due to the fact that the development of urban economy is always related to the growth of its functions, especially the non-central local function, the economic flowability is sure to increase in the process of urban development.

However, for a long time, economic flowability was realized by space of places, which had a historical origin and the space as we experienced. Based on the space of places, the economic flow is usually the unilateral flow between points and points or multilateral flow between the points and places: it has obvious and physical consecutiveness in region and is thus limited by the transportation ability to a large extent. With changes of urban space logics, the base of urban economy is changed and its flowability is placed in the flowing spaces. In the development of urban economy based on flowing space, the main domination process is combined in the network which connects different places; different specific roles and power are distributed in the layers of wealth production, information processing, and power creation. The city's entry to the network means its extensive economic relations to the outside and a large-scale economic flow within the network. That is to say, the features of flowing space establish the functional connection beyond the limitation of territory but they have obvious non-consecutiveness in physical territory. Apparently, this enlarged the scale of urban economic flow, what is more important is to change the mode of economic flow fundamentally which spans the consecutiveness of physical territories.

Therefore, the space of places is changed to flowing space, and urban economic flowability is promoted further in contents, layers, forms, etc. When economic flowing is located in the flowing space, it is related to the resource flowing in large-scale and the flow expansion with effective collocation based on the panel points in the network, it differs greatly from the traditional economic flowability in base of space of places and has different features.

Based on the space of places and with the city as the medium, the traditional economic flowability attracted and collocated the various resource factors inside the territory, promoted the development of relative industries; formed and expanded the economic energies, including the factors such as products and service; and influenced the surrounding regions or even remote regions. Based on the flowing space, the city is only one panel point in the network system, or one panel point with extensive outside relations. By this panel point, the various resource factors are reformed, integrated, promoted, and collocated in most economic time and spaces in the flowing process. This endowed a new definition to the economic flowability, which is not the gathering and collocation in one panel point but the flowing in the network. It is not the resource flowing in the collocation of urban industries but the resource factor collocation in the urban flowing. This economic flowability in the flowing space consists of the basic features of urban development oriented by flow expansion.

The feature of flowing space spans the functional connection constructed on the extensive territory and surpasses the consecutiveness of the physical territory and does not depend on the economic development levels of the surrounding areas, thus expanding the scale of urban economic flow. The more important thing is that it is an economic mode oriented by the added value of various resource factors in the flow. Though some resource factors are deposited in the flowing process and collocated in the local industries, most of them are rationally collocated and exploited in a more wide scope by one panel point. Apparently, compared to the economic flow, which depends on the collocation and development of urban industries, it has a more bigger flowing scale, a high rate of flowing, and a more wider flowing scope than anytime in the past. Therefore, the multiplication of urban economic flow by the flowing of resource factors in a large scale is another important feature of urban development oriented by the flow expansion.

As an important panel point in the network system, the city is loaded with an economic flow in a large scale, with the high openness of the system as a prerequisite. In addition, differing from a common economic system which exchanges for its own energy transmission, the urban development mode oriented by flow expansion attaches more importance to promoting and boosting the flowing of various resource factors and thus requests a more open system, an extensive channel of connection and flowing. So, it is a must to keep the high openness of the urban system and to promote the flowing of various resource factors in a wider scope of time and space in the urban development oriented by flow expansion.

However, to ensure more effectiveness collocation and exploitation of the economic flow of a large scale, a coordinated inner system and a cooperative outside system are necessary in the panel point of the city. If the inner system is not coordinated and the flowing channels are blocked, the effective recollocation, integration, and promotion of resources cannot be realized and thus influence greatly the expansion of economic flow; if the outside system is not cooperative, the origins and outlets of the flowing of resource factors will be a problem, which will fundamentally result in the shrinkage and drainage of economic flow.

Differing from a traditional urban network system, the new system is based on the flowing space and has an electronic network. The application of modern information technology and the information facilities (for example, the Internet) make the flowing of resource factors break the limitation of physical time and space and realize the instant flow in a large scale. The electronic network has become an important material foundation and technological means of the flow expansion of urban economy.

All in all, the urban development oriented by the flow expansion inherits and arches the essential attributes of urban economic flow and is developed in an advanced form in the context of globalization and informatization. In this development process, the city, as an important panel point, is a blender, which means the more effective collocation of various resource factors in the urban flowing; meanwhile, the city is an amplifier, which means to realize the multiplication of economic energies after recollocating various resource factors.

8.1.3. *The relationship between the flow expansion and outside connection and network linkage*

Based on the above analysis, we know that the essence of a globalizing city is to merge to the global network and become the important panel point in the network in order to strengthen the economic flow based on the flowing space. It involves the enlarging of outside connection, the promotion of network connection, and the expansion of flowing scale. Then why do we describe the strategic guidance of a globalizing city as the expansion of economic flowing, but not the other concepts such as the enlarging of outside connection and the promotion of network connection? To study this further requires the analysis of the relationship between the flow expansion and outside connection and network linkage. If the relationship is clear, this problem will be readily solved.

Though the flow expansion of a city involves the strengthening of its inner flow, the more fundamental drive is the strengthening of its outside flow, especially the flow expansion based on the flowing space. It is no doubt that this flow expansion is based on the prerequisite of outside connection. And more, as a whole, the outside connection tends to move in line with the flowing scale. That is to say, with the unchanged flow of outside connection, the expansion of the outside connection will definitely enlarge the scale of economic flow; or with the deepening of outside connection (that is the promotion of relevance), with no expansion of outside connection scope, the general flow scale will be enlarged accordingly. But the outside connection and economic flow are different concepts and are not in accordance with each other in reality. For example, the outside connection scope of a city may be not extensive (limited quantity), but its frequent economic exchanging with each related city will enlarge its flow scale. On the contrary, the outside connection of a city may be comparatively extensive, but its less economic exchanging with each related city will result in a flow in a small scale. The following is observed in our reality: though many cities have more outside connection, some of them enjoy a higher flow in the network; only a few of them has a higher relevancy (Timberlake and Xiulian, 2006). In this sense, the flow expansion can reflect the practice of the city's merging into the global network better than the outside connection.

Likewise, the flow expansion which is based on the flowing space is closely related to and based on the network connection. The theoretical research on globalizing cities has transformed from the traditional feature analysis of globalizing cities (the theory of Friedmann) to the network analysis, the most outstanding research result is those which concern about the analysis on the degrees of network connection. For example, the research on the network system of globalizing cities by Alderson and Beckfield (2004), which is based on the office locations of the Top 500 of the world transnational corporations; that by GaWC, which is based on the network of productive and service companies (Beaverstock *et al.*, 1999), and so on. Taylor once used a mathematical model to indicate the degrees of network connection. There are *m* advanced productive and service companies in *n* cities, the service value of the Company *j* in the city *i* is defined as the importance degrees of the office location of the city in its office network, which is indicated by *Vij*. One set of service enterprises $n \times m$ constitutes the service value matrix *V*. The basic relationship in the service value matrix *V* is indicated by the following.

$$r_{ab,j} = \mathrm{v}_{aj} \cdot v_{bj} \qquad (1)$$

This is the basic relationship between the company *j* in city *a* and the company *j* in city *b*. They can totaled up, and the connection between the cities can be indicated by the following:

$$r_{ab} = \Sigma_j \, r_{ab,j} \qquad (2)$$

There are n–1 (at most) connections in every city, and these connections are corresponding to the office location of the companies in other cities. The general connection of the network in every city can be indicated by the following:

$$N_a = \Sigma_i\, r_{ai} \quad \text{(here } a \neq I\text{)} \tag{3}$$

Here N_a is the connection degrees of the global network. The higher connection degree of the global network is, the better the city is merged into the global economy. Apparently, the measurement of this network connection degree is significant in reality. First, the connection degree means that the global service is developed well in the city to a great degree. Second, it reflects that the service enterprises in large scale are developed well, which shows the economic development of the city where the enterprises are located. The most important is that the analysis of the network connection degree reflects well the basic features of the globalizing cities on the condition of flowing space, in a certain degree, and it reveals the flowability of the economy. Equation (1) shows clearly that the flowing of the two small office locations in the network is less than that of the two big office locations. But this analysis on the network connection degrees has its advantages, one of them is that the flowing of the globalizing cities is based only on the service flowing of the advanced productive and service companies, and furthermore, it is the inner flowing of the companies. Here, what we measure is the inner connection of the companies, which means the flowing of information, knowledge, instructions, plans, originalities, suggestions, and personnel inside the companies in different countries and different cities. Therefore, the analysis of the network connection degrees cannot reveal the overall perspective of the development of the network flowability in the globalizing cities.

In the globalizing process, with the shaping of the new regional layout of the international industries, the global products chain between the different countries introduces more and more developing countries and cities to the globalizing process, which establishes the network relationship such as the one in production, technology, marketing, etc. Meanwhile, with the rapid growth of the global trade, the scale of the productive flowability is becoming bigger, and the global and local economic relationships are becoming closer. Therefore, the function of the global product flow in the shaping of the globalizing network cannot be ignored. Whether in theory or in practice, this is significant in the globalizing cities, especially in the main cities of the developing countries. In fact, more cities, particularly the cities in the developing cities, enter the global urban network by global trade and global production chain, attract and gather the advanced producing service companies globally and merge into the global urban network completely by their inner network. Thus, we think that, besides the advanced producing service companies, the advanced manufacturing companies in the global production chain, especially the high-tech enterprises, are the components in the minor-nodes of the urban network. That is to say, the global urban network can be defined as the jointly connected network based on the urban relationship composed by the inner flow between the advanced producing service sectors and the advanced manufacturing sectors in the world economy. The various material flow and information flow across the geographical space connect the globalizing cities.

If we put aside the limitations of the model of the network connection degree by Taylor and his followers, we can find that the concept of the network connection degree actually includes the actual contents of the network flowability. In this sense, the network connection degree is identical to the expansion of the flow. But the network connection degree cannot reflect the identity between the essence and phenomena of the flowability of the global urban network fully and exactly. Just as Jacobs (2000) pointed, a vigorous city is surely the one with strong connections, an unconnected city will ultimately become a lifeless city. However, the strong connection does not mean the absolute vigor of a city, but depends on what the people who are involved in the urban connection will do inside the city. Anyhow, the economic motivation is defined by the process of the urban operation.

So we think that the flow expansion, as a specific development form, is penetrating the operation process of the cities, which can reflect the identity of the essence and phenomena of the network flowability of the globalizing cities comprehensively and reveals the network connection directly as well. The larger scale of the node cities means the stronger economic flowability and the higher network connection, or vise versa. Of course, this flow analysis has the fatal limitation, that is, it lacks the data to support it. Though some scholars are trying to evaluate the relative position of a city systematically by the flow analysis, for example, Shin and Timberlake (2000) and the other scholars measure the globalizing degree of a city by standard network analysis based on the number of flight passengers between the cities. But it is obvious that number of the flight passengers is only one part of the urban flowability, which cannot measure the network flowability roundly. However, what we stress here is not the practical flow analysis, but the strategic orientation of the globalizing cities starting from the basic connotation of the concept of flow expansion, which is not a significant problem.

8.2. Spatial Structure Model of Flow Expansion

Based on the network nodes, the urban economic flow itself is considered as a special urban spatial structure. However, we cannot explain the traditional theories of traditional spatial structure in the theories such as growth-pole theories, the developing theories of point-axis, the theories of core-edge, and the theories of concentric zones in a simple way. These traditional theories of spatial structure are usually based on the physical regional space when researching the spatial organization relationship between the different systems and factors in the regional economic system. And furthermore, these theories focus on mutual places, mutual relevance, interaction, resembling degree, and resembling scale of these factors in space, and the regional comparatively balanced relationship between different regions. These theories answer the questions concerning the generation, motion, development of these factors in space, and ways in which they are combined to form the spatial entity of the productive forces. On the contrary, the spatial structure of the network flow expansion is founded on the basis of flowing spaces. The basis itself is the fundamentally subversion of the basic footings of the traditional theories of spatial structure. Though these traditional spatial theories describe the fundamental operation status of the network flow expansion in the function mechanism and effects resulting from the flowability of resource factors, as a whole, a new spatial structure theory is necessary to explain the spatial structure of the network flow. Here, we construct an elementary theory model which reveals the basic components and the structural system of the network flow expansion, sketches the operation mechanism and its basic features of the network flow expansion, and describes the evolution process of the spatial structure of network flow expansion.

8.2.1. *The structural system of network flow expansion*

The core of network flow expansion is the expansion of connection scope, the deepening of the interrelationship, and the concentration of the cities which are the panel points in the global network. The connection, linkage, and relevance of the network are realized by the flowability. The flowing tangible or intangible elements (or the objects) are the carriers of this flowability. The flow which measures the connection degree between different cities is composed by these flowing elements (or the objects).

The flowing objects have many different categories, they are mutually related and they form a complicated complex. There are different ways to categorize them due to the different researching intentions and the orientation of the target objects. In China, the scholars divided them into the following: material flowing, energy flow, information flow, currency flow, and talent flow (China City Development Report, 2001–2002). Smith and Timberlake (1995) divided them into two categories in a totally new angle, namely, the form flow (talents, information, and material) and the function flow (culture, economy, politics, and society). And they constructed a new type of the connection between the different cities. If we divide them according to the resource factors, the flowing object is made up of the cargo flow, the capital flow, the talent flow, the technology flow and the information flow (see Figure 8.1). As the material carrier of network

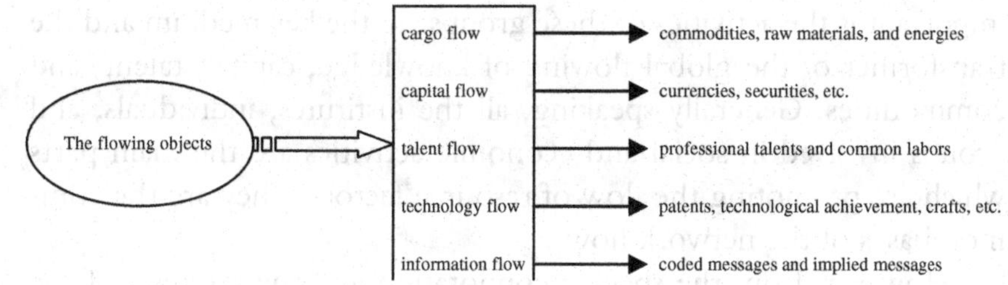

Figure 8.1. The Composition of Flowing Factors.

flow, it is noticeable that the flow of the resource factors is based on the network relationship and it is the flow inside the network. This network relationship is comparatively complicated and can be categorized in different angles and different levels. For example, the network relationship between different countries and regions, the one between domestic cities and regions, and the one within cities. And more, it can include the network relationship between different industries, the one between different enterprises, the one between the consumers, the one between individuals, etc.

As an objective target, the flowing of the resource factors is realized by the activities of the institutes, individuals, and groups. The activities and behaviors of any institute, individual, and group generate or contribute the flow of resource factors to a certain degree.[1] As the special places in the contemporary world economy, there are talented elites living in the globalizing cites, who are actually the reflection of successful economy (Storper, 1997). According to Thrift, the concept of reflection means the core. He considers that the world is the place where the individuals, institutes, and talented groups are working to construct and maintain connections. The more

[1] In a complete sense, the activities by any organizations and individuals, including the behavior of market activity and non-market activities, will produce flow of resource elements in different levels, but under the conditions of market economy, resource factor mobility by the non-market activity behavior is a very small portion, especially for the flow of the economy, being completely negligible. Therefore, the activity behavior of the mentioned in text is specially referred to market activity behavior.

important is the activities of these groups are the key medium and the transformer of the global flowing of knowledge, capital, talent, and commodities. Generally speaking, all the institutes, individuals, and groups involved in social and economic activities are the main parts which are promoting the flow of resource factors. They are the common bases of the network flow.

However, from the specific connotation and the requests of the network flow, we can see the institutes and organizations are playing an important and particular role and bring or promote the economic flow in a large scale. These institutes and organizations are networked; they are undertaking the networked operation, and thus the flow expansion of the network is the indispensable and stable main parts. The networked institutes and organizations can be divided into the following categories:

(1) **The large-scale corporation groups, including the productive corporation groups and investment companies.** The production and operation of the productive corporation groups are large scaled, which require large amount of input of resource factors and result the output in large scale. The activities of their production and operation themselves result in a certain amount in economic flow, especially the cargo flow, such as the raw material, the intermediate products, and products include relevant capital flow, information flow, technological flow, etc. In particular, the large-scale and export-oriented corporation groups can bring great economic flow because of their extensive relationship in supply and demand with the outside world. But in view of the network flow expansion, the important role that these enterprises playing is not the producing or manufacturing process, but the two ends of the productive chain, that is, researching at the upper end and marketing at the lower end. That is to say, the two ends with more added value in the smiling curve of the productive chain. The R&D and marketing of these enterprises are involved in the network system, which is extensively related to the outside and forms the information flow, technological flow, talent flow, and capital flow in high density. The investment

activities of the large-scale investment companies are also related to the outside, their financing, equity trading, investment, and operation and management resources can also produce a greater economic flow, especially capital flow.

(2) **The headquarter of the corporations, mainly the ones of the transnational enterprises including their regional headquarters, the headquarters of domestic large-scale corporation groups, the headquarters of domestic financing institutes or the headquarters of business execution.** As for the domestic institutes, once the headquarters of the corporation groups are settled, the function sectors such as management, technology, marketing, etc., will be followed, which results in the flow of capital, talent, technology, information, and partial entity. As for the overseas institutes, if their regional headquarters or investment institutes are settled in a certain city, the central city will become the investment base for them in a wide regional scope. A large-scale investment will enter this central city at an early time and then flows to other regions. Some of the resource factors invested in this region will be reorganized and generate a greater economic energy before it spreads to the outside. Particularly, because of their global investment and selling network, the entrance of the large-scale organizations and institutes will play an active role in the development of the flowing space of the key factors and will promote the flow economy throughout the world. For example, 60% of the Top 500 of the global enterprises have established their agencies in Hong Kong; the number of the transnational companies which established their offices in Hong Kong is more than 3,200; and quite a few international purchasing institutes are assembled in Hong Kong, all of which play an important role in undertaking the large-scale economic flow in Hong Kong.

(3) **The service organizations and institutes, including the market intermediary institutes and trade associations such as the R&D institutes, the finance institutes, the accounting firms, the lawyer's offices, the assets evaluation offices, the enterprise consulting institutes, etc.** In the practical economic life,

the organizations and institutes which supply the relative services to the trade and flow of the key factors have an extensive network relationship. They develop their business in the frame of the network relationship and exert an impact on the flow of the key resource factors. They are indispensable organizations and institutes in network flow expansion, which are embodied in two aspects: First, their business can drive the flow of the key resource factors; for example, the businesses of the finance service institutes can bring the flow of capital and information in large amounts; Second, the business is operated in a regulatory market. It serves the enterprises and residents in the form of marketing agencies, creates the market opportunities, improves market efficiency, and promotes the rapid flow of the key resource factors in indirect ways. These service enterprises are playing an important part in promoting the flow of the key resource factors and improving the operation efficiency of the whole market system.

(4) **International organizations, including United Nations institutions and the headquarters or liaison offices of international organizations.** Though these institutes are mainly non-economic organizations, some of them such as the World Bank and the International Monetary Fund are economic institutions. Due to their extensive connection in the international network, they can bring large-scale flow of information and talent and promote the network flow expansion directly or indirectly.

(5) **Media organizations, including newspapers, magazines, book publishing, movie and TV companies; online information services; and the culture transmission and originality institutes such as art designing and fashion.** These organizations and institutes usually have an extensive network relationship and large-scale business, which brings large-scale information flow and promotes the corresponding flow in capital and talents. For example, the ground satellite and cable broadcasting operators supply a variety of broadcasting by more 170 channels; more than 130 international media have established their offices in Hong Kong.

The above-mentioned organizations, institutes, individuals, and groups promote the networked flow of the key resource factors by their activities with their own purposes. Their business is operated on their own corresponding platform. These operation platforms are the soft infrastructures, hard infrastructures, or the places for the flow and effective collocation of the various key resource factors in the node of the city. The platforms construct the most important support for the network flow expansion and can be divided into three categories according to their different functions:

First, the fundamental operation platform, which refers to the basic infrastructure and hard infrastructure for the flow of the key resource factors such as transportation infrastructure, the ports and docks, the airports, the information communication infrastructure, and the places for office and residence, which are the necessary passageways for the key resource factors to flow in space and time. The large-scale network flow expansion needs the complete, convenient, effective, and safe infrastructure. For example, London has the underground system with the length of 400 km and carries more than 3 million passengers each day (Xiong, 2000). Paris has the track transportation network with the length of more than 1,000 km, and the number of the commuters on the suburban trains is over 1 million. The quick track transportation line in Tokyo city circle is as long as 2,000 km, there is a ring elevated railways inside Tokyo is as long as 35 km and carries as many as 3–4 million passengers daily. There are 3 international airports in New York, the number of the flight passengers domestically and globally is more than 60,000 daily; the bus line is as long as 2,735 km and carries as many as 1.7 million passengers daily; and the subway line is as long as 1,179 km and carries as many as 3.7 million passengers daily (Bai, 1996).

Second is the dealing operation platforms, mainly the dealing platforms which are helpful in the transferring of property rights and thus make the key resource factors transfer and flow on the platform. The platforms include the commodity markets, capital markets, future markets, technology markets, and talent markets. The large-scale network flow expansion needs a highly developed market dealing system. This system includes the complete market system, efficiently operated market institutes, and the soft and hard infrastructure for the dealing of the key factors between the different possessors. Not to say the high-developed world markets of the globalizing cities such as New York, London, and Tokyo, Hong Kong is the tenth greatest banking center worldwide with 263 licensed banks from more than 40 countries, and 79 of them are on the list of Top 100 banks globally. The total assets of these finance institutes amount to HK $6.7 trillion, the total deposit of the clients is as much as HK $3.35 trillion, and the total loan is close to HK $2.5 trillion (Guang, 2005).

Third is the service platforms, which mainly refer to the operation systems that serve the transfer of the property rights of the key resource factors and their actual shifting, including finance, transportation, business, visa, intermediate, technological policy, and information services. The varied, high-quality, overall, and consistent service on the service platform becomes the lubricant in promoting the rapid flow of the key resource factors. Besides the well-facilitated service institutes, according to the experiences of Hong Kong, the construction of the service platform needs the international first-class service supplied by the professionals to the business world in consulting, trade, finance, insurance, marketing promotion, R&D, product designing, laws, accounting, project, consultant, PR, etc.

The above three platforms are integrated and indispensible. Due to the transforming of the property rights in the flowing of the key resource factors, the operation platform which facilitates the trade activities is the core. The fundamental operation platform and the service platform supply the necessary conditions for the actual flowing of the key resource factors (see Figure 8.2).

When developing their own operational business on the corresponding operation platforms, the organizations, institutes, individuals, and groups are limited by the outside environmental conditions. These outside environmental conditions are not only embedded in the operation platforms but also related to the software level of the operation platforms, which will influence the behavior patterns of the organizations, institutes, individuals, and groups. Thus, the favorable or unfavorable environmental conditions are directly related to the flowability

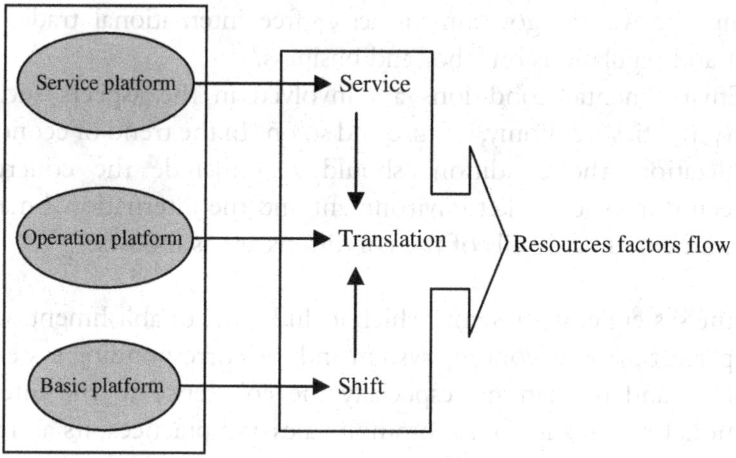

Figure 8.2. The Operation Platform of the Network Flow Expansion.

of the network and decide the expansion speed of the network flow. For example, the reason why such great economic flow is present in Hong Kong, a tiny area, is inseparable from its superior environmental conditions. Hong Kong is a member of the WTO and a complete free trade zone as well, so there is no limits and customs duties to the imported goods except some special items; the foreign exchanges can be converted and passed in or out freely without any controlling. The passports of Hong Kong Special Administrative Region are visa-free in more than 130 countries, it is free to enter or exit; the laws are complete, an excessive government is invalid, and the court is independent of the Bureau of Legislation and Administration. Business laws are also very perfect and the businessmen can develop their economic activities in the protection of the fair and just legal environment. The government is incorrupt and highly efficient, the business services institutes are completely facilitated, and the businessmen can easily obtain the necessary information for business development. So Hong Kong has been awarded as the world best city for business environment in 7 years successively and named the world freest economic system by American Heritage Foundation for 10 years in a row. Hong Kong is always leading the way in government scale, free international trade, and credit and regulations on labor and business.

Environmental conditions are involved in the aspects such as society, politics, economy, culture and so on. In the trend of economic globalization, the conditions should also include the coherence between domestic market environment and the international market environment. The details of the conditions are as follows:

(1) the system environment, which includes the establishment of the perfect market economy system and the corresponding system of laws and regulations, especially the coherence to the international markets in some common rules and practices, its aim is to eliminate the system obstacles in the international flowing of the key resources factors.
(2) The governmental management, which includes governmental control, public management, and economic adjustment and control. The administrative regulation sectors are always efficient in operation, the modes and the tools in adjustment and controlling economy are comparatively perfect, the policies and regulations of the government are usually transparent, which supply the better environment and conditions for the flow of the key resource factors.
(3) The market environment, which includes various kinds of market rules and behavior standards, the better social credit base focusing on reputation and goodwill to construct a fair, open, and just trade environment. The better market environment strengthens the behavior definition of market bodies, decreases the trade fees, improves the information symmetry and economic performance and thus helps to promote the business activities and the flowing of the key resource factors.
(4) The social culture, which includes historic culture, tradition and custom, architecture style, city features, the civilization level, social atmosphere, etc. The urban culture with deep cultural deposit, inclusiveness and variety, originality, and tolerance to failure is surely helpful to the flowing of the key resource factors.

To sum up, the flow expansion as the network nodes, in theory, involves basic elements such as the flow objects, the subject bases, the

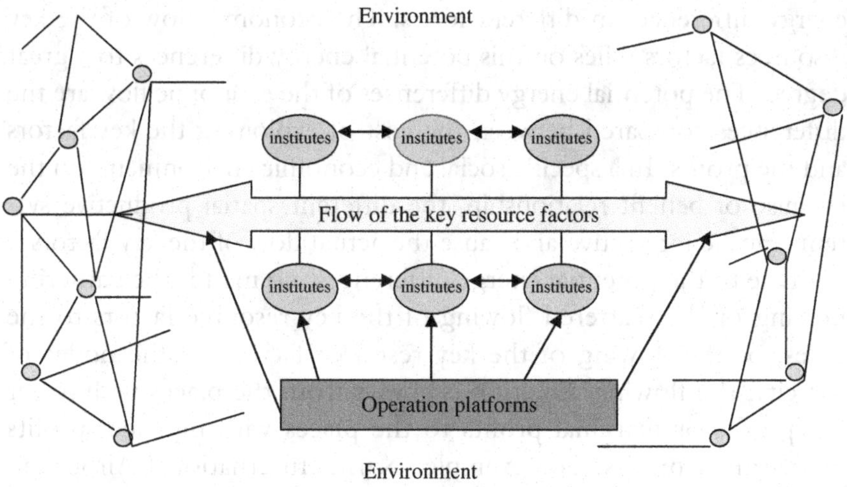

Figure 8.3. The Organization System of the Network Flow Expansion.

operation platforms, and the outside environment. These elements are related closely, interdependent, and function jointly, which forms the following organization system of the network flow expansion (see Figure 8.3).

8.2.2. *Operation system of the network flow expansion*

We have to admit that the flowability of the factors is related to the attribute of factors. Generally speaking, the flow of the global factors is deviated in the system. That is to say, the flow of the superior factors is sufficient, for example, the ultimate flow of capital, technology, excellent talents, standards, brands, transnational operation network, transnational enterprises or institutes, and so on. The flow of the inferior factors is not sufficient, for example, the common labors of the processing trade, and the lands and the natural resources are not flowing. The differences of the key factors in flowability will always cause the assembling of the productive abilities from the countries with senior factors to the countries with inferior factors.

Setting aside the flowing of different key factors, the flow of the same key factors is involved in a problem of drive in flow direction. As we know, the natural flow of any object is caused by the potential energy differences in different levels. The economic flow of the key resources factors relies on this potential energy differences to a great degree. The potential energy differences of the economic flow are the differences compared between the cost of exploiting the key factors and the profits. In a specific social and economic environment, on the premise of benefit relationship, the different spatial productive systems can be interactive and cause the actual flow of the key factors.

Due to the potential energy differences, no matter the gathering flowing or the scattered flowing of the key resource factors to the cities, or the flowing of the key resource factors by the nodes of the city, the flowing direction is always from the places with lower net profits or marginal profits to the places with high net profits or marginal profits. For example, Narita International Airport in Japan, that we mentioned previously, has less landing times than John F Kennedy International Airport in New York, Heathrow Airport in London, and Charles de Gaulle Airport in Paris. The reason is that Narita International Airport has only one runway in 20 years since it was opened and the airport is not all-weather, though it later constructed a 2180-m runway. The main reason is that the airport charges a higher landing fee to the flights. Take Boeing 747 as an example, Narita charged 950,000 yen for each landing, while Hong Kong charged only 410,000 yen; New York, 540,000 yen; Paris, 330,000 yen; Frankfort, 170,000 yen, and Seoul, 310,000 yen (converted by the average exchanged rate of the year 2001). The differences between the cost and profit constitute the potential energy differences. In similar conditions, more people and cargo by air tend to land in the airports in New York, Paris, not in Japan. Of course, the potential energy differences of the flowing inside a city are much more complicated in the components.

In the past researching of urban economy, the potential energy differences were explained by comparative advantages, such as regional conditions. That is to say, the city usually has comparatively high potential energy than other areas, the main reason being that the city has relative advantages because of its geographical conditions, which is more beneficial to the integration and collocation of the key resource factors and thus the efficiency is much higher. Later on, the potential energy differences are explained further by the competition advantages. That is to say, due to the accumulation and ability fostering of the city itself, including the economic structure adjustment, the updating of the industrial structure, the development of the enterprises and the institutes, the gathering of the knowledge and talents, the cultural deposits, and so on, all of which result in competition advantages such as scale economy, gathering effects, and moreover make the key resource factors more efficient for collocation and exploitation inside the city. In the network flow expansion based on the flowing space, this kind of comparative advantages and competition advantages still plays a role, but what is more obvious and important is the network advantage of the city. The externality of the network increases its value according to the growth of the node expansion of the network. A bigger network means more potential value. Obviously, the extensive connection and the network relationship supply more space and opportunities for the collocation and exploiting of the key resource factors and thus result in their potential energy differences in the flowing of the key resource factors in the node of the city. Therefore, as for us, the comparative advantages, the competition advantages, and the network advantages jointly construct the foundation of the network flow expansion and result in the potential energy differences of the highly economic flow.

Based on the potential energy differences of the space, the benefit motivations of the network flow expansion can be described as the following:

(1) The promotion of the trade events in scale, variety, and levels improves the success rate of the trade events, reduces the trade cost, and improves the net benefit of the trade. The pursuit of the comparative benefits results in the flow of the key resources factors in the node of the city and gains the comparatively high net benefit of the trade.

(2) A bigger possible space (including the city and the scope outside the city) and more choice opportunities are supplied for the collocation of the key resource factors, which is helpful to the reasonable combination of the different key resource factors and

thus result in "price to value and best use of everything". At the same time, this can enable the different key resource factors to find reasonable collocation or mating and arch the complementary effects such as the scale economy, the industry gathering, the expansion of the value chains, etc. The pursuit for these complementary benefits results in the flow of a large amount of the key resource factors and gains the corresponding added values.

(3) The positive or negative effects between the key resource factors are strengthened; they are supported or promoted mutually and result in a large sum of positive economic externality. The pursuit of the mutual benefit results in the flow of the key resource factors inside the city and gains consecutive added and supplementary benefits.

Here the benefits refer to the set of benefit order which includes the comparative benefit, namely, the benefit relationship chain of "comparative benefit — mutual benefit — interactive benefit", they construct a social motivation structure in the process of the network flow expansion. These benefit motivations promote the reorganization, integration, and exploitation of the key resource factors in flowing, make the city more attractive in markets and result in the radioactive flowing, which is the internal motivation of the network flow expansion.

In addition, the flow of the factors goes through many chains and procedures. In this process, the flow of the factors possibly encounters technological, systematic and economic barriers, or the factor trade cannot be found or realized with insufficient information. Usually, the intermediate institutes are necessary in promoting with the help of a set of service systems. This system constitutes the transmitting system of the factor flow. The developed factor trade and the correspondent factor flow are not carried out directly between the two parties: they are realized by a set of intermediate institutes, especially when the laws regulate that certain trade chains and trade procedures have to be undertaken by the intermediate institutes. For example, the trade companies are playing an important transmitting role in import and export trade; in Hong Kong, there are more than 100,000 trade companies contributing HK $4 trillion in export or re-export trade.

All in all, the network flow expansion based on the urban flowing space highlights the basic features of the urban economic flowability, which is realized by its unique motivation systems and transmitting systems.

8.2.3. *The dynamic process of the network flow expansion*

The network flow expansion is embodied not only in the growing flow scale but also the dynamic process from a lower pattern to a higher pattern. In effect, the size of the flow scale is closely related to the development of the patterns. To some degree, the size of the flow scale is decided by the development of the patterns. In the change of the patterns of the network flow expansion, the flow scope, the flow control and influence, and the leading flow jointly compose the main identifications of the measurement. That is to say, the large flow scope, the stronger flow control and influence, the higher leading flow will mean the high patterns of the network flow expansion. However, they are closely related, mutually influenced, and restricted.

As for the flow scope, it is divided into four levels: First, the lowest level is the flow scope of the surrounding areas, the diameter of the flow is limited, and the flow scale will not be too big; the next, the flow scope at home, the flowing nodes are growing, the flowing lines are longer, and the flow scales are growing larger and large; and then, the flow scope in the neighboring countries, the flow penetrates the bounders of the country and is internationalized, the flow network spreads and expands to the outside, the flow scales are dramatically enlarged, especially the international flow scale is gradually enlarged or even exceeds the flow scale inside the country; and the last is the flow global scope, the flow network covers the whole world, it can communicate any area in the world and begins to have a global flow scale.

The size of the flow scopes is related to the flow control and influence. The more control and influence of the factor flow means the bigger flow scope or vice versa. In return, the bigger or smaller scope of the flow scope means the stronger or weaker flow control and influence. The control and influence of the factor flow is the flow abilities decided by the quality, level, efficiency, and radiation of the flowing factors. Generally speaking, the rich knowledge content, the high technology levels, and other qualities of the flowing factors will mean higher efficiency, large radiation, and stronger flow control and influence of the flowing factors and the combinations of these factors.

From this, the control and influence of the factor flow can be divided into three levels.

(1) The lower-energy level: As the center of the gathering and collocation for the key factors is established in the city, the operation efficiency and the collocation efficiency of the flowing is obviously higher than those in the surrounding areas, it has a certain radiation, and it has more obvious control and influence on the flow of the key resource factors.
(2) The mediate-energy level: Based on the network flow, more networked institutes and organizations, especially the international ones, came into being on the perfect operation platform with an optimized environment, the flow control and influence are spreading the other countries. Both the attraction to the factors and the radiation of the energy are becoming more internationalized.
(3) The higher-energy level: The construction of the structure and system in the network flow is becoming perfect, the efficient operation and favorable environment are attracting more and more world high-level resource factors to gather and collocate more effectively. The radiation of the resource factors reaches to any country or region in the world, and the flow control and influence are spreading throughout the world.

The flow scope and the control and influence are connected to the evolution of the leading flow with the network flow expansion. Although various kinds of factor flows are mingled in the structural system of the network flow, and the flow of any factor will result in the flow of the other factor, a leading factor flow is always playing an important role, that is, the leading flow. This leading flow means the relevance of the flow or the flow scale, or the flowing energy is the core of the various factor flows. Historically speaking, the evolution of this leading flow can be divided the following three stages.

First, the stage is led by the cargo flow. At this stage, the massive cargo flow brings the corresponding information flow and capital flow, but it exerts less impact on the other factor flows. Under special circumstances, the initial capital flow will result in the cargo flow, the talent flow or the other factor flows, but it is only a temporary phenomenon. The massive cargo flow relies on the developed transportation of the city, such as the railways, highroads, shipping, and air transportation. Thus, as the leading flow, the cargo flow is limited more by the special attribute of the physical network, the scale of the economic flow is comparatively smaller and its level will be lower too.

Second, it is led by the capital flow. At this stage, the flow scale of the capital is expanding rapidly, transferring from passiveness to taking the initiative, which brings more talent flow, technology flow, and information flow than those brought by the cargo flow. The massive capital flow relies more on the developed financial system, the settlement means, and the information technology service platform. Therefore, as the leading flow, the capital flow is less limited by the physical network. It will result the rapid expansion and the higher level of the flow economy.

Third, it is led by the knowledge and talent flow. Pushed by the world economic globalization and knowledge economy, the R&D of the globalization is another important tendency in the world economy integration after trade globalization, production globalization, and finance globalization. In the late 1980s, only a few transnational corporations began their R&D globally. But after 1990s, the global R&D of the transnational corporations began to thrive. According to the statistics on The Report of World Investment in 2005, the R&D input of the foreign branches of the transnational corporations increased from US $30 billion in 1993 to US $67 billion in 2002, the percentage of the input rate of the R&D in foreign countries increased from 10% to 16% (UNCTAD, 2005). In addition, the R&D of the transnational corporations in the other countries does not meet the requests of the local market; however, it aims at the global market, which merges into the process of the knowledge creation of the transnational corporations. When the technology and knowledge are playing more and more important roles in the development of the economy and society, knowledge experts and talent resources will control the initiatives of the development in various aspects, and the other factors will revolve around the talent factor and flow along with knowledge and the talent factor flow. As Bauer (2002) stated, during the industrialization era, gaining raw materials was the basis of urban development, but this tendency is changing. In order to attract more brains and capital to assist economic growth, a city has to attract them with a certain lifestyle or culture style. The economic flow brought by the knowledge and talent flow is great, in particular, the large-scale capital flow and information flow. The economic flow dominated by the knowledge and talent flow mainly relies on the information network, whose flow is so convenient that the scale of the flowing economy is much larger.

Based on the analyses of flow scope, flow control and influence, and the leading flow, we can see that they have a corresponding relationship and construct the main stages of the dynamic expansion of the network flow (see Figure 8.4). At the beginning stage of the network flow expansion, the flow of other factor flows is led by the cargo flow with limited flow scope and small-scale economic flow and

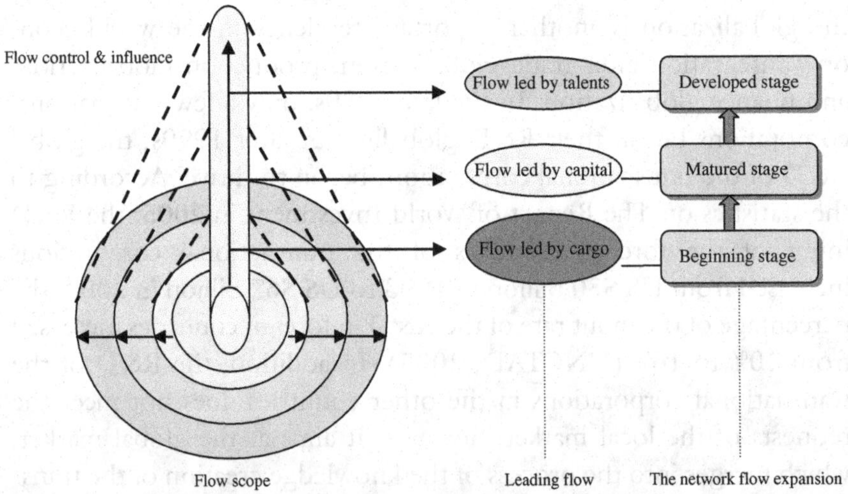

Figure 8.4. The Dynamic Process of the Network Flow Expansion.

thus the flow control and influence is limited in the surrounding areas and, inside the country, the energy level of the network flow is lower. At the matured stage of the network flow expansion, the flow of other factors is led by the capital flow with an expanded flow scope which breaks through the boundaries of the countries. The scale of the economic flow is expanding, the flow control and influence spread in the other countries, especially the surrounding countries and regions and thus the energy level of the network flow is promoted. At the developed stage of the network flow expansion, the flow of other factors is led by the knowledge and talent flow with a global flow scope. The scale of economic flow is so massive that the flow control and influence is penetrating every part of the world, the energy level of the network flow is much higher.

8.3. Developmental Strategy and Mode Oriented by Flow Expansion

As a globalizing city, one of the most important tasks is to transform the traditional development strategies and modes, the ones oriented by the network flow expansion should be carried out. That is, on the base of the flowing space, the city has to construct an extensive connection to the outside. As an important node in the network system, the city has to attract and organize the consistent and recycling flow of the resource factors such as materials, capital, talent, technologies, information, etc., in order to gain the flowing added value with the coordinated effects of the network system and promote the promotion of the energy level and globalization of the city. In such a gradual process, the city has to attach more importance to the keynotes and breakthroughs at its present stage and promote the city's evolution in globalization.

8.3.1. *Handling the relationship between flow expansion and stock accumulation*

International practice shows that the formation and development of a globalizing city are realized on the basis of the flow expansion of the global network, such as the flow of information, knowledge, capital, culture, etc., and not on its stock condensation, such as the shape and scale of the city. Some traditional super-cities with large population, economy, and a vast territory are not globalizing cities. If we cannot recognize this and pay more attention to the stock condensing, such as the expansion of the city shape and the enlargement of the city scale, we will make mistakes in orientation and even serious errors in our actual promotion to a globalizing city. Certainly, as for a globalizing city, it is not realistic to consider the problem of flow expansion, putting aside the urban stock accumulation.

Though the city scale and mass is not the indispensible stand to evaluate a globalizing city, and wealth accumulation and stocked capital in the area are not the fundamental means in a globalizing city, the corresponding city scale, wealth, and power accumulation are the main important conditions for a globalizing city. The problems to expand the city scale and improve its comprehensive strength cannot be totally excluded in the construction of the urban flowing space, especially when China is still in the lower level of economic development, urbanization is lower, the urban construction and development are comparatively lagged behind, the urban infrastructure and environment conditions are imperfect, and the various kinds of service facilities and conditions are in shortage. Otherwise, it needs the basic and fundamental conditions when merging into the global network, connecting to the world, and expanding the flow in the nodes, and it is difficult to undertake the pressure from the internal flow of the outside resources, let alone the bidirectional flow with the outside world.

In a more abstract theory, the emergence of the flowing space to connect to the world in economy does not deny the existence of the places or the sites, and it does not mean "the termination of the geographical location". It is internally related between the flowing space of the city and the place space, the flow interaction and the stock condensing. The professional public service and infrastructure needed by the flow interaction has the requests on the minimum scale, because they are in accordance with the theories of scale economy. If there is no considerate scale, massive flow is impossible. Of course, it does not mean the great urban space is surely has the massive flow interaction.

In addition, in the view of the history of the metropolitan's development, the city scale is beneficial to the concentration of the coordinated functions, especially when the operation of these functions is in the state of increasing returns. The concentration of economic activities brought by the city scale is helpful for the flourishing of high-level business activities, because they find the expanded market there. In the end, the metropolitan area creates new activities which are impossible in other places. In return, the diversity of the urban functions is strengthened. Thus, the larger the city scale, the more diversified are the functions. This diversity in function means the concentration of various activities, the complexity of the trades, and the main coordinated function of the metropolitan are developed well. At the same time, this diversity is one of the conditions for the stability of the metropolitan city. As stated clearly by Hohenberg and Lees (1994), one city involved in the only overwhelming activity is not stable as the one with complete functions. The latter city is usually the one with main coordinated functions. Therefore, the immense scale and complete functions are the key factors in the coordinated functions in the complex economic activities operated by a globalizing city in the extensive space scope both at home and abroad.

In effect, a globalizing city is a dual complex: on one side, it is the interaction center for the flow of various and massive factors in the world scope; on the other side, the city itself is a material, dynamic, and multifarious complex. For the cities in the developed countries, the corresponding scale and complete functions are formed in the interactive development process between industrialization and urbanization. After entering the post-industrial era, on the above base, its key is to construct the flowing space connected to the global economic functions. As the globalizing cities in China, they cannot skip this lesson for they did not undergo the fostering of a complete industrial era, the corresponding scale, and the fundamental material conditions are not shaped.

However, differing from the urban development mode, which is pursuing the scale expansion and stock condensing, this kind of urban expansion and wealth accumulation is helpful to promote the connection to the outside world and to meet the requests of large-scale interaction. That is to say, this kind of urban scale expansion and wealth accumulation is developed in the framework of the construction of the flowing space, which is related to the advanced service, the production center, and the global network market. Considering most cities in China grow and develop as the manufacturing and processing bases underground the background of the industrial era, the city scale expands with the development of the manufacturing. This is not only the problem of scale expansion but also the adjustment in urban scale and structure in order to form the reasonable function division, the spatial structure and industrial layout which are suitable to serve the economy. All in all, the rising of China's globalizing cities has reshaped the place space in the construction of the flowing space with the expansion of flow interaction and stock accumulation as the focuses.

8.3.2. *Breakthrough choice of the flow expansion*

According to the above analysis and the international practice, the expansion of the network flow is an evolutionary process in which the scale is gradually enlarged, the energy level is gradually improved, and the leading flow is gradually transmitted. In the process, there are different leading network flows in different stages. Therefore, in the rise of China's globalizing cities, the development strategies and modes oriented by the expansion of the network flow should be implemented, with the focus on different stages in the expansion of the network flow and the breakthroughs of the development based on the requests at the stages of the economic development, the realistic fundamental condition's and the system environment.

In the process of economic growth in high speed and the deepening of reforms and opening to the outside, the globalizing cities such as Shanghai and Beijing are connected to the outside world to some degree and have a massive network flow. But their developments are still in the transmitting stage, from the late industrial time to the post industrialization. The development of the modern service industry is not complete and matured, the development level of the domestic overall economy is still low and is limited by the finance systems, and the development conditions and environment dominated by the capital flow are not available. As a whole, they are still in the initial stage of the network expansion, the stage of flow expansion led by the cargo flow.

As for the flow expansion led by the cargo flow, the globalizing cities in China have not only the corresponding bases but also the significant and perfect conditions. At present, China is still at the stage of the massive industrialization, especially the coastal areas became the processing center of the world manufacturing in the process of the world industrial transferring and the massive flow of commodities and materials were requested. Though the value of China's foreign trade accounts for only 7% of the total in the world, its logistic amount accounts for 40% of that in the world. Besides the massive amount in the flow of foreign trade, the flow between different provinces is huge too. The requests for the large-scale cargo flow supplies the powerful supports to the expansion strategies of the network flow in the globalizing cities in China.

Accordingly, the infrastructure of the logistic transportation is gradually complete and perfect. For example, the berths in deep harbors are increasing and the international flights are growing. Maersk Logistics, one of the largest container liner corporations in the world, has four of the five Asia–Europe lines and six of the seven Pacific liners to China. At present, the Top-20 shipping companies in the world have the lines to Shanghai Harbor. In 2006, more than 30 international lines in Shanghai Harbor, covering more than 300 harbors in more than 200 countries and regions. There are more runways in the airports and the landing time of the flight is increasing rapidly. At present, more than 300 flights land in Shanghai Airport each day. According to the new plans, Pudong Airport will have 5 runways, with 1 runway at present, and will compose a U air terminal complex with 3 air terminals. In addition, Hongqiao Airport will construct a second runway, and the planned west air terminal will connect to a highly integrated transportation complex which assembles flights, CHR, the track transportation in Yangtze Delta, and the urban underground system. Meanwhile, the transportation conditions between different regions are increasingly perfect, and convenient and accessible transportation network is formed. For example, the trend of the transportation flow between different regions in Yangtze Delta has changed from the original with provincial capitals as the center to the connection to Shanghai, which focuses on the connection between the cities.

With the improvement of the transportation conditions, the cargo-flowing abilities are obviously strengthened. In particular, Shanghai is becoming the main important path in international logistics. With the efforts of a decade, the present Shanghai Harbor is at the world advanced level in the functions of gathering and distribution. From 1978 to 1998, Shanghai Harbor's cargo handling capacity reached 3 million standard containers. Within 3 years since 2000, it rose from 5 million to 10 million standard containers. In 3 years from 2004 to 2006, it realized the leap from 10 million to 20 million standard containers. In 2006, the handling capacity of the containers in Shanghai Harbor reached 2,171 standard containers. In recent years, the handling capacity of the containers in Shanghai Harbor is at the third place consistently, and in 2005, its cargo-handling capacity ranked the first in the world. It is predicted that the handling capacity of the harbors will reach 30 million standard containers. In 2015, the passengers landed in the two international airports of Shanghai will reach to 110 million, and the cargo-handling capacity is expected to reach 7 million metric tons.

Therefore, at present, the globalizing cities in China are implementing the development strategies and modes oriented by the network flow expansion, which start from realistic bases and comparative advantages; focus on the expansion of cargo flow; foster the city's gathering and distribution, service, industries, and management; and improve resource collocation. Certainly, all kinds of economic flow are penetrated mutually and overlapped in the development of modern economy: it is a tendency in which the economic flows are merged. This makes the new and mixed modes possible with the expansion of cargo flow as a focus in which the capital flow and the information flow are developed jointly. The globalizing cities in China have the conditions to foster capital flow, information flow, etc., with the rapid expansion of the cargo flow. By the development of the other factors such as, finance market and information resources in order to promote the scale and level of the cargo flow, a new development layout with parallel development and mutual promotion of multiflow is created. At the same time, starting from the surrounding areas, various resource factors are gathered and distributed at the different levels nationally and globally; the development of flow economy is promoted from the external flow to the internal flow in different levels. In this process, the economic development of the main cities such as Shanghai and Beijing will undergo the following changes:

(1) The obvious and dynamic changes will be possible in the core factors of the flow expansion. On one side, as the leading economic flow, the cargo flow will be improved and optimized; on the other side, in the merging to the capital flow and the information flow, the cargo flow is gradually improved in energy and set a good example for the flow of other resource factors. At the same time, the cargo flow and information flow are rapidly fostered and developed, and its position and function in the overall flow expansion will be promoted consistently.

(2) With the accumulation of the resource factors, the full-playing and strengthening of the radiation, the speed of the factor flow is becoming rapid, the scale is enlarged, and the energy level is further promoted, thus the central position of the collocation of the resources is formed and the advantage as the regional center is gradually established. Related to the modern logistics, the main cities such as Shanghai and Beijing have become the most important domestic centers of the exposition and business information, the order center and the delivery center of trade at home and abroad, and the center of the management and control of the business capital operation domestically and globally. For example, there are more than 3,000 exhibitions in China in each year, which makes China rank the first place in the countries involved in exhibitions. In the span of the 10th five year planning, Shanghai held more than 300 international exhibitions annually, among which about 100 international exhibitions were held by foreign enterprises or enterprises from other provinces and cities; the annual exhibition area is more than 4 million sqm; the

annual number of the exhibitions of more than 50,000 sqm is 20, which accounts for the half of that inside China.

(3) With the full development of modern logistics, the advantageous and related industrial sectors involved in information service, professional service, shipping service, and the others are developing rapidly. The knowledge, informatization, and network degrees are strengthened and result in a service shape and industrial structure to adapt to the development of the logistics. These main cities will become the places where the headquarters of the domestic service and trade enterprises and intermediary institutes are located, the key bases for the enterprises such as those in foreign finance, trade, transportation and etc., to distribute their businesses inside the country. The service trade will become a new backbone industry gradually. For example, by the end of the year 2005, Shanghai had more than 610 various financial institutes, including 231 banking institutes, 110 security institutes, and 269 insurance institutes. The total asset of the foreign banking institutes in Shanghai accounts for more than 50% of that in the country, and the total assets of foreign insurance companies account for 30% of that in the country. The financial asset reaches to 3.2 trillion, which accounts for 9% of that in the country.

(4) The rapid development of various market organizations, the joint development of commodities and factor flow, and the collocation of the domestic and foreign resources in the central cities result in the perfect producing organizations and management and service function. These main cities will gradually become the gathering and distribution centers of the commodities; the hotspots for traveling and shopping; the domestic centers of the precious metal trade; the centers for agricultural product futures, price discovering, and main short-term capital trade nationally; and the centers for long-term capital market and free on board financial business. For example, at present, Shanghai has a financial market system that is characterized by the multilevel of trade places, the abundance of the trade products, and the diversity of the trade mechanism. In 2006 more than 70% stock trade, foreign exchange trade between the main banks and the inter-bank lending, and at least the half of the futures are

traded in Shanghai, Shanghai has become an important center of capital trade in China. According to the incomplete statistics of Shanghai Headquarter of the People's Bank of China, by the end of November 2005, the loans from Shanghai to Jiangsu Province and Zhejiang Province account for 55% of the overall loans in different places. Almost one-third of the newly increased loans to the enterprises in the financial institutes of Shanghai flow to the enterprises in other places.

To summarize, with the maturing of the various fundamental conditions and the improvement of the overall environment, especially when the transition period is over according to the WTO rules, China will be more open, and the system innovation in finance and trade will be strengthened. The leading mode dominated by the main urban flow expansion in the cities such as Shanghai and Beijing will be changed to the mode dominated by the capital flow in a few years.

Chapter 9

Industrial Base of the Leading Service Economy

The new form of flowing expansion of a globalizing city is supported by the relative industrial bases. The properties and features of urban industrial structure decide the basic attributes of urban development and functions to some extent. In the context of global service economy, the industrial base of the globalizing cities, without exception, is oriented by the service economy. However, the globalizing cities have to face confusion in transforming the industrial bases; the critical problem is the opportunity cost in the process of transformation. It is pointed out that the industrial bases dominated by manufacturing bases or manufacturing centers should be created or transformed by a special path with the minimum cost. By the development of service economy based on the industrial integration, the globalizing cities can give way to the leading function of modern service industry in order to strengthen their urban comprehensive service function and the global coordination ability.

9.1. Transition of Industry Base in Globalizing Cities

What kind of industrial bases do the globalizing cities depend on? In terms of the reference system of the existing or matured globalizing cities, this answer is obvious. Namely, they rely on the industrial bases dominated by service industry. However, the current conditions of the globalizing cities are the industrial bases dominated by industrial economy, which is facing fundamental transformation in industrial bases. In the transforming process of industrial bases, the series of opportunity cost and actual-paid cost plus the non-synchronism of the expenditure cost and profit always result in confusion in the globalizing cities. Anyway, the only choice for the globalizing cities is to construct industrial bases dominated by the service industry.

9.1.1. *The great transformation of industrial bases the globalizing cities are facing*

As pointed out in the above analysis, the city's position in the global urban network is directly related to its energy level rank of the urban economic flowability. As a globalizing city, it has to solve the most important problem, that is, to promote its energy level of economic flowability. The energy level of urban economic flowability is the representation of internal comprehensive qualities, position, and function, which can be represented by urban service function, urban modernization level, pattern of urban economic growth, city's influence and controlling power, etc. These aspects are actually closely related to the industrial bases dominated by service economy.

Even in the view of urban economic growth, the industrial development dominated by service economy is the main driving force. That is to say, the economic growth of modern cities is mainly rooted in the development of modern service industry, which can be demonstrated by many international examples in this aspect. For example, the percentage of service industry in the GDP of the countries in OECD increased from 52.6% in 1960 to 68.2% in 1995, the employment percentage in service industry increased from 43.1% to 64.4. In the 1980s, 95% of the 65 million jobs newly created in the OECD countries was supplied by the service industry. In the development of the service industry, the modern service sectors are growing rapidly with expanding scales. The economic growth of the globalizing cities which lie at the higher positions in the global urban network system rely more on the production of highly professional service and financial products.

A globalizing city, irrespective of the angle or aspect, has to establish industrial bases dominated by the service economy. But the reality is, though the service industry is developing rapidly, the globalizing cities are resting on the industrial bases dominated by the traditional industrial economy as a whole, which makes the energy level of the urban flowability comparatively low. There are many comparative research analyses on this problem in China, here we just make a simple comparison by the example of Shanghai. However, as an administrative division, Shanghai has a large non-urbanized area. To a certain degree, it has non-comparability to the globalizing cities abroad, but its absolute magnitude of the added value in service industry seems to be small scaled; and the internal structure of its service industry is still low. Compared to the abroad globalizing cities, the key sectors in the employment structures in New York, London, and Tokyo are those in the governmental public management organizations, financial service, health, social security, and social welfare, while Shanghai's key sectors are manufacturing industry, commodity trade, storage, and even agriculture (see Table 9.1).

Even compared to the other main cities in Asia, we can find that the added value of the service industry in 2000 in Tokyo is US $620 billion, which is 22 times as much as that of Shanghai; the added value of the service industry in Hong Kong is US $140.5 billion, which is 4.2 times as much as that of Shanghai; and the added value of the service industry in Singapore is US $63.1 billion, which is almost two times as much as that of Shanghai (see Table 9.2). In terms of the internal structure of the service industry, the four cities' percentages in commerce, transportation, posting service, finance, insurance, and real estate industry are almost the same, but the gaps between Shanghai and the other cities such as Hong Kong, Tokyo, and Singapore are mainly in the social service and other service industries. These industries involve the extensive fields such as social service, medical service, education, culture, and information consulting, which are characterized by knowledge and production services. The percentages of these sectors in service industry in Shanghai are obviously lower than those in Hong Kong and Tokyo; the sectors in Shanghai are lower in development level and limited in service space. The percentage of service industry in sectors such as trade service, information service, medical service, law service, and designing consulting are still lower, thus the features of the modern metropolitan cannot be demonstrated well.

Table 9.1. The Comparison of the Top-5 Sectors in Employment Percentage in New York, London, Tokyo, and Shanghai.

	1	2	3	4	5
New York (2004)	Governmental public management organizations (14.2%)	Health, Social security and welfare (13.4%)	Retail trade (9.9%)	Technology service (7.8%)	Finance and insurance (6.5%)
London (2001)	Finance and commerce service (33%)	Hotel service (22.2%)	Education, social worker service (14.4%)	Transportation, storage and communication (8%)	Other industries (7.1%)
Tokyo (2005)	Governmental public management organizations (20.2%)	Wholesale and retail trade (18.9%)	Manufacturing industry (13.8%)	Hospital and welfare industry (8.62%)	Construction (7.7%)
Shanghai (2005)	Manufacturing industry (31.72%)	Wholesale and retail trade (15.1%)	Resident service and other service industries (9%)	Agriculture, forestry, animal husbandry and fishing (7%)	Communications and transportation, storage and post service (5.6%)

Source: RUPRI, "Demographic and Economic Profile, New York", p. 10, July (2006) and *The Yearbook of Shanghai Statistics* (2006).

Table 9.2. The Comparison in Service Industries Between Shanghai and Tokyo, Hong Kong, and Singapore.

		1983	2000	2001	2002
Shanghai	Percentage of service industry (%)	23.6	50.6	50.7	51.0
	Added value of service industry (100 million USD)	179.8	278.6	303	333.2
	Per Capita GDP (USD)	1514	3725	4520	4914
Hong Kong	Percentage of service industry (%)	67.3	85.7	86.5	87.4
	Added value of service industry (100 million USD)	175	1350	1349	1405
	Per Capita GDP (USD)	5120	24782	24211	23797
Singapore	Percentage of service industry (%)	62.0	71.0	74.2	72.5
	Added value of service industry (100 million USD)	107.8	649.6	630.1	630.8
	Per Capita GDP (USD)	6484	22769	20544	20877
Tokyo	Percentage of service industry (%)	—	81.7	—	—
	Added value of service industry (100 million USD)	—	6200	—	—
	Per Capita GDP (USD)	—	38903	—	—

Source: *Yearbooks of Shanghai Statistics* in previous years. See the websites: http://www.info.gov.hk, http://www.metro.tokyo.jp, http://www.singstat.gov.sg for statistics concerning Hong Kong, Tokyo, and Singapore, respectively.

There is a long way to go for the service trade in Shanghai to become the leading power to bring the development of Shanghai's economy similar to the position it enjoys in cargo trade.

The current conditions, with small economic scale and lower level, are surely influencing the city's energy levels. Thus, in the rise of China's globalizing cities, they have to face realistic problems, such as the transformation of industrial bases, formation of the industrial structure dominated by service industry, and the promotion of urban comprehensive service function and the energy levels.

9.1.2. *The confusions in the transformation of industrial bases*

In the developed countries, the transformation of urban industrial bases may be a natural process. When the development of the service economy in a country reaches a certain level, the country itself has better bases for the development of service economy. But for the globalizing cities in the developing countries, they have to face a great confusion when transforming their industrial bases, which has typical significance at least in present China.

Here is a story that goes around in Shanghai. In the early 1990s, Shanghai put forward the guiding principle for the industrial development in the order of "tertiary industry first, secondary industry second, primary industry coming last", with the development of the tertiary industry as the core. Since 1978, the added value of the service industry in Shanghai increased year after year. Except the years 1988, 1989, and 2003, the added value of service industry accounted for an increasing percentage of GDP in a rapid speed (see Figure 9.1). That is to say, the percentage of service industry increased from 20% to 30% in 10 years (1981–1990), from 30% to 40% in five years (1990–1995), and from 40% to 50% in 5 years (1995–2000). Especially, the percentage of the added value of service industry in 1999 accounted for as much as 49.5% and surpassed that of the secondary industry by 1.16%, which broke the industrial structure of "secondary industry > tertiary industry > primary industry" and formed the new structure to promote the economic growth jointly by the secondary and tertiary industries.

However, the development of service industry began to decrease in the following years. The added value of service industry increased by 10.9% in years from 2001 to 2005, which is lower than the yearly average growth rate 15.5% in years from 1996 to 2000, and it is even

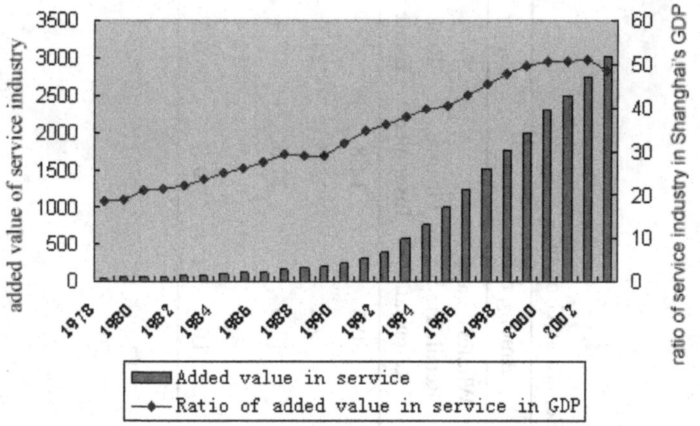

Figure 9.1. The Added Value and Its Percentage in Shanghai's GDP Since the Reforming and Opening-Up.

lower than that in years from 1991 to 1995 (at 12%). At the same time, the secondary industry is developing much more rapidly. In years from 2001 to 2005, the yearly average growth rate of the added value of secondary industry is as high as 13.3%, much higher than that in years from 1996 to 2000, 9.7%, up 2.4% than the yearly average growth rate of service industry in the corresponding period. In particular, the contribution rate of the secondary industry rebounded rapidly in 2001, which is even higher than that of 1995, with slumping contribution rate of service industry (see Table 9.3). In 2002, the production value percentage of the secondary industry decreased slightly, while that of the service industry increased slightly; however, the declining scope of the contribution rate of the former two industries is bigger than that of the production value, while the increasing scope of the contribution rate of the latter is bigger than that of the production value. By the end of the year 2006, the growth rate of the added value in secondary industry (12.8%) and the contribution rate to economic growth (51.7%) were higher than that of the tertiary industry by 1.3% and 3.4%, respectively. During this period, the percentage of the added value of service industry in GDP did not continue to increase and was only

Table 9.3. The Contribution Rate of Shanghai's Industries to Economic Growth.

	Contribution Rate	Secondary Industry	Industry Among Them	Tertiary Industry	Among them: Transportation, Storage, Communication	Wholesale and Retail, Trade, Restaurant	Finance, Insurance	Real Estate
1990	100	**49.4**	43.1	**45.9**	22.9	0.5	14.8	
1995	100	**55.2**	49.2	**43.8**	3.8	9.8	3.7	21.5
2000	100	**42.3**	41.0	**57.0**	9.1	11.3	21.5	7.4
2001	100	**56.0**	51.1	**43.5**	6.0	16.4		11.4
2002	100	**52.6**	49.8	**46.9**	7.3	10.6	0.3	8.5

Source: Zheng (2004).

Table 9.4. The Structure of Shanghai's GDP (1999–2006), Unit: %.

	Primary Industry	Secondary Industry	Tertiary Industry
1999	1.8	47.4	50.8
2000	1.6	46.3	52.1
2001	1.5	46.1	52.4
2002	1.4	45.7	52.9
2003	1.2	47.9	50.9
2004	1.0	48.2	50.8
2005	0.8	48.6	50.5
2006	0.9	48.5	50.6

Source: *The Yearbook of Shanghai's Statistics* (2006); *The Yearbook of Shanghai's Economy*, (2007).

slightly higher than the percentage of the secondary industry. As a whole, the percentages of secondary industry and tertiary industry stayed even for a long time (see Table 9.4).

The phenomenon has been explained as follows: it is not the service industry that is developing too slowly, but it is the manufacturing industry that is developing too rapidly. After thinking it over, we find this explanation reasonable. Generally speaking, the average growth rate of the service industry by more than 10% is not slow. But why is the manufacturing industry developing so rapidly? Here is a realistic basic reason: many cities in China are used to being the centers or the bases of manufacturing industry, and under the background of industrialization and urbanization at present, there is a strong demand for development in China. For example, the selling proportion of Shanghai's industry product at the local market, the home market, and international market is roughly 3: 4: 3. The local market accounts for 30% of the whole market, which includes the consumer and investment goods markets. At present, with China embracing Western-style development, rise of the middle China, and the accelerating development in East China, there are more demands for infrastructure construction, the input in industrial production, etc., especially the construction of the electric power and the power grid in rural areas, which supplies an opportunity for Shanghai to expand its production of power station equipments. That is to say, all of these factors support the development of Shanghai's manufacturing industry.

The combination of the two factors promoted the rapid development of Shanghai's manufacturing industry to some extent and further strengthened its contribution rate to GDP. On this occasion, the transition of industrial bases is facing a realistic uncertainity: If the comparative advantages and profits of the manufacturing industry are abandoned, it is certain that the urban economy will begin to decline at least in the short term; but on the contrary, the transition of industrial bases will be stopped. Thus a core problem is involved, which is actually the problem concerning the cost payoff in the transition of industrial bases. Apart from the actual transition costs such as sunken cost and the replacement cost, the most important is the opportunity cost in the transition of industrial bases.

One realistic problem we have to face is: Does the abandonment of development of manufacturing industry mean the lasting and consistent development of service industry? Or can the development of service industry support the growth of urban economy in place of manufacturing industry? We cannot answer this question with a simple "yes" or "no", what we should do is to see if there are enough conditions for the lasting and consistent development of service industry. As we know the modern service sector was controlled by the government in term of admittance, operation and pricing. International practices show that, in the expansion of the modern service industry, the adjustment of the government's controlling policies play an important role, which decides the opportunities of market entrance, market structure, and competition degrees. Therefore, since the 1980s, the policy choice of many developed countries is being transformed to the loose controlling and the adjustment of policy frames, which include the permission of mixed operations, business overlapping, etc. The modern service industry is granted more developing space and freedom, which results in more enterprises with more investment and competition. In turn, the development of the modern service industry is promoted greatly. For example, the overall productivity of telecommunications in Germany, France, and Spain was promoted by 40% because of their reform in the concerned laws and regulations. At present, China's service industry is controlled seriously, for example, highly concentrated controlling in finance and insurance shows insufficient endophytism in the development of these industries. To some extent, we can say that the local governments are very limited in improving their functions in the service industry. It means that the abandonment of the development of manufacturing industry and the insufficient development of service industry will contribute to the depression of the overall urban economy. Therefore, one precondition is involved, that is, the adjustment of controlling policies in the field of service industry. The lack of this precondition can mean great opportunity cost in the transformation of industrial bases.

Even though the above precondition were established (the adjustment of controlling policies in the field of service) in order to guarantee the endogenic development of service industry, there is a problem of opportunity cost, namely, the cost payment brought by the low productivity of comparative labor. As we all know, the income elasticity of industries and the comparative cost are the decisive independent variables in the transition of industrial structure. Usually, the industrial sectors with the increasing income elasticity and the decreasing comparative cost can replace those with the decreasing income elasticity and the increasing comparative cost, and finally they can play an increasingly important role. For example, in the transition of industrial bases dominated by the industrial economy, there will be increasing income elasticity in the manufacturing industry, which is higher than that of the agriculture. In addition, promoted by the technical advancement, the comparative cost will be decreased and the productivity will be increased. Therefore, it is possible for the industrial bases dominated by industry economy to be transformed with the consistent and rapid economic development. But it is quite different in the process of transforming to the industrial bases dominated by service economy. Though the income elasticity of service industry is increasing with the enhancement of per capita income, the higher income elasticity of the industries means the more share in industrial structure, but the decreasing comparative cost in the service industry is not remarkable. Thus the productivity of comparative labor in concerned sectors is much lower.

Triplett found that the productivity and growth rate of many sectors in service industry was quite low or even negative. And more,

Kuznets, Chenery, and the others discussed the particularities of service industry from the point of view of the evolution of the industrial structure: the increasing employment rate and the labor productivity stagnate or decline because of the invariant production value. The relative data also show that, because the employment rate is usually higher than that of the production value of service industry, the labor productivity of service industry is lower than that of the other industries in developed countries. For example, the index ratios of the labor productivity of countries such as the UK, Canada, France, and Australia are as low as one (see Table 9.5), which means, compared to the scales of other sectors, the contribution of the service industry is

Table 9.5. The Comparative Labor Productivity in Service Industry in Some Countries (by %).

	1980	1985	1990	1995	2000
USA	0.97	1.01	0.99	0.99	0.99
UK	0.92	1.00	0.95	0.94	0.96
Canada	0.88	0.93	0.92	0.89	—
France	1.07	1.10	0.97	0.97	0.97
Australia	0.89	1.00	0.96	0.94	0.97
Germany	—	—	1.07	1.08	1.06
Italy	1.10	1.15	1.07	1.10	1.10
Mexico	2.38	—	1.60	1.24	1.24
Japan	1.04	1.04	1.00	1.07	1.06
Korea	—	—	1.02	0.94	0.87
India	—	—	2.41	2.20	—
High-income countries	1.04	1.10	1.00	1.00	1.01
Medium-income countries	2.47	—	2.04	1.96	2.29
Low-income countries	—	—	2.05	1.50	—
Worldwide	—	—	2.07	1.88	—

Source: Calculated by the data released by World Development Indicators Database.

Table 9.6. The Yearly Average Growth Rate of Productivity (Per Capita Output) in Service Industry in Some Countries.

	1971–1980	1981–1990
Germany	2.6	2.0
France	2.6	1.9
Japan	2.3	1.9
Italy	0.6	1.4
Canada	1.5	1.0
UK	1.7	0.8
USA	0.2	0.1

Source: US Department of Commerce, Service Industries and Economic Performance (1996), p. 13.

limited to the overall productivity. The survey in 1996 showed that, with the growth of the service industry, its productivity in the developed countries before the 1990s was declining sharply (see Table 9.6).

How does the compared lower labor productivity in the service industry sectors influence the transition of industrial bases in the cities? In 1967, Baumol put forward the model of cost disease (also called the unbalanced growth macroeconomic model in the two sectors), which explained the theory well to some extent. He presumed that there were two sectors, the stagnant sector and the progressive sector. The former's growth rate of labor productivity was zero, mainly referred to the service sectors, while the latter's growth rate of labor productivity was positive. He presumed that labor is the only factor input, and that the labor incomes in different sectors are the same, with the nominal wages increasing at the same speed as the average labor productivity, shown by the following production function:

$$Y_{st} = aL_{st}\ ;\ Y_{pt} = bL_{pt}e^{rt}$$

Here Y_{st} and L_{st} are the output and labor input when the stagnant sector is at t, respectively; Y_{pt} and L_{pt} are the output and labor input when the progressive sector is at t, respectively; a and b are technical parameters; r is the productively growth rate of the progressive sector; according to the assumption, $r > 0$ and wage $W_t = We^{rt}$.

Baumol's model of the cost disease showed that, in the unbalanced economy (urban economy) in the process of productivity growth, the realization of the balanced economy means the growth rate of the overall economy will tend to be zero. That is to say, increasing labor will be chanelled into the stagnant sector, and the economic growth will tend to be stagnant at last, because the balanced growth means E^* remains unchangeable, the overall economic aggregate is recorded by

$$Y = Y_{st} + Y_{pt} = [L(E^*a + b)e^{rt}]/(1 + E^*e^{rt}),$$

and the growth rate of overall economic aggregate is recorded by

$$G_Y \equiv (dY/dt)/Y = [L(E^*a + b)re^{rt}/(1 + E^*e^{rt})^2]/[L(E^*a + b)e^{rt}/(1 + E^*e^{rt})] = r/(1 + E^*e^{rt}).$$

Obviously, $\lim_{t \to \infty} G_Y = 0.$.

Hence, the model is sure that the transition from the industrial bases dominated by industrial economy to the ones dominated by service economy will influence the changes in the development speed of urban economy and the economic growth will slow down to a great degree. Sheets *et al.* (1987) found that most big cities in the USA underwent a deep economic transition since the early 1960s, which brought economic distress for a long time, and the large-scale adjustment in economic structure and the great changes in employment and income opportunities for the urban residents.

9.1.3. *The only choice for the globalizing cities*

From the above analysis, a question can be raised: can the globalizing cities have their own specific choice in industrial bases? That is, can they be established on the industrial bases which lay equal stress on both the secondary and the tertiary industries? And if so, are such industrial bases strong enough to support the rising of the globalizing cities?

Let us start from the relationship between the urban development and the development of service industry: we have to answer the question: are they necessarily related to each other? The assumption put forward by Singlemann (1987) tells us that, with the development of urbanization, the service sectors is sure to expand. In fact, Sabolo (1975) found this relationship as early as 1975 from the empirical analysis on the developing countries. But some researches show that there is no stable relationship between the urban development and the development of service industry. For instance, based on the two sets of section statistical data of the 81 economic entities from 1977 and 1981, including 17 low-income economic entities, 28 medium-income economic entities, 18 upper-income economic entities, and 18 industrialized economic entities, Riddle (1986) tested and examined the assumption by Singlemann. The results show that, during 1981, there is an obvious positive correlativity between the urban population proportion (representing the urbanization level) and the proportion of service industry in GDP (representing the development level of service industry) only in the upper-income economic entities. But if we analyzed the same on 1977 data, the above relationship is not obvious. This shows that, even in the developed economic entities, the relationship between urbanization and the development of service industry is not stable either. And moreover, Riddle found that, in every developing country taken as the sample, the urbanization is related to the per capita GDP, it has nothing to do with the growth rate. Though the slowing-down in the growth of GDP in the industrialized economic entities is positively related to the speeding-up of urbanization, to the developing countries, the expansion of service industry is not necessarily related to the growth of GDP.

There may be common views in this regard, that is, the cities are not the gathering places for the service industry and may be the gathering places for the manufacturing industry, because there is a problem concerning industrial location and division of labor in different industries in the cities. The research by Sheets *et al.* (1987) on America's urban systems and industrial location supported this verdict. So we can infer that as far as the development of common cities, and not the rise of the globalizing cities, is concerned, it is not impossible for the industrial bases which lay equal stress on the secondary industry and the tertiary industry to be established. It is not necessary for these cities to establish the industrial bases dominated by service industry.

However, is this verdict suitable for the globalizing cities? In my opinion, we cannot apply it mechanically. Though there is a problem concerning industrial location and the division of labor in different industries, a globalizing city has to reflect the global advancement and global coordination, which is quite from the common cities. As a globalizing city, its fundamental functions are embodied in its more transregional ones, especially the globalizing functions, which are embodied by the transregional transportation hub, the gathering function of logistics and talent flow, the service function of professional business trade, the management function of the headquarters and international organizations, and the service function and innovation function is science and technology, education, finance, information, consultation, etc. The industrial bases of these transregional functions are the modern service sectors. The more developed modern service industry in a city means the more transregional functions. Therefore, if a globalizing city wants to reinforce its transregional functions, it has to rely on the high development of its modern service industry.

More important is that, as a globalizing city, its coordinative function based on the global connection has to reflect the basic features of advanced level of global economic development. For example, during the industrialization era, the globalizing cities were usually the centers of international manufacturing industries, which focused on the production of manufacturing industries and the coordinative functions in production and reflected the basic features of advanced level of global economic development. But in post-industrialization period, the high-level development of the global economy enriched the new connotation of a globalizing city and its epoch features: the globalizing city becomes the center of industrial business service and its industrial bases are regulated. On this precondition of regulating the industrial bases, the globalizing city has to face the problem concerning the specific industrial location and division of labor in different industries. Thus, we have to investigate the industrial bases of a globalizing city on the level of global economic development.

Starting from the 1980s, the global industrial structure tended to transfer from "industrial economy" to "service economy". During the years 1980 and 2001, the percentage of the added value in global service industry in GDP increased from 55% to 68%, and was as high as 71% in the major developed countries. The value of the service industry in the developed countries accounted for as much as two-thirds of the GDP, for example, that of the USA was the highest, reaching as high as 75% in 2002, whereas that of the medium-income countries accounted for as much as 57% in 2002, with the value proportion of service industry increasing at a rapid speed. The value of the service industry of low-income countries accounted for as much as 46% in 2002. At the same time, the employment proportion in service industry increased year after year in the western developed countries, reaching as high as 70%. In 1999, the employment proportion of the most developing countries was over 40%. The service industries contributing the most to the GDP and employment of developed countries include finance, insurance, real estate, and business services, which are the main new knowledge-intensive service industries aiming at the enterprises. The main power for the growth of service industry in developing countries is usually integrated in the traditional service industries such as commerce, hotels, transportation, and communications, and its contribution to employment mainly relies on the support from the commerce, society, and service aiming at the individuals.

With its rising position in economic activities, the service industry is increasing its contribution to the economic growth. The growth rate of the service industry exceeds that of the other sectors, and it accounts for an increasing percentage in the overall economic value. Moreover, it is reflected in the multiple effect of industrial relations. For example, the service industry in the UK is assuming an increasingly important role as an intermediate input in the production of other sectors, such as the manufacturing industry. The requirement growth in the service industry exerts an equal impact on the production of the overall economy (see Table 9.7).

Table 9.7. The Direct and Indirect Influence of Final Requirement Changes in the Commodities Supplied by the 100 Specific Sectors on its Economy.

Commodities	The Final Influence on Economy (Units)
Market-oriented service	174
Non-market-oriented service	126
Manufacturing industry	180
Primary sectors	197

Source: Deanne (1998).

The development of the world service industry resulted in the rapid growth of the world service trade. According to the statistics of the WTO, from 1980 to 2004, the international service trade increased by as much as 5.8 times. From 1990 to 2002, the yearly average growth rate of international service export was as high as 7%, which was higher than that of export at the same time, 6%. In view of industrial structure, the service trade focuses more on finance, insurance, telecommunications, information, and consultation. The traditional industries such as transportation and tourism accounted for a dwindling percentage. In the constitution of world service trade, the international transportation service trade decreased from 38.5% in 1970 to 25.7% in 2005, while international tourism accounted for as much as 28.2%, the other industries such as telecommunication service, finance service, insurance service, information service, and patent and franchise service increased from 30.8% to 46.1% (see Table 9.8). In detail, the service trade developed rapidly in the developed countries such as the USA and the EU countries, which has become the main source of trade surplus. In the third quarter of 2006, the trade surplus of the service trade in the USA was as much as US $18.294 billion while that of Eurozone was much as US $9.407 billion.

With the development and the production growth of service industry, the scale of service consumption is increasing, and the world service consumption is accounting for as much as half of overall consumption. Therefore, the present world economy is actually transforming to the

Table 9.8. The Changes of Constitution Proportion of the World Service Trade (%).

	1970	1987	1990	1994	1996	2000	2005
Transportation service	38.5	31.6	28.2	26.1	27.3	25.9	25.7
Tourism service	28.2	31.6	32.3	32.3	31.9	30.9	28.2
Other services	30.8	29.5	39.4	41.5	40.8	43.2	46.1

Note: The total of the three items does not equal to 100%.
Source: The Yearly Report of the GATT (1988–1989). The Yearly Report of the WTO (2005).

production and consumption of service commodities and entering into the era of "service economy". In this background, the presence of economic services has become an important binding condition for the enterprises to decide their policies in the regional choice. As we all know, urban economy is established on the spatial economy based on the comparative advantages, internal scale economy, and gathering economy, which is the result of regional choices aimed at profit maximization in enterprises. The development of the "transportation hub" for commerce trade enterprises, port cities, and crossing cities; the location as the raw-material-producing area for the resource-oriented enterprises; and the rising of the resource-type cities, the market location of the market-oriented enterprises, and the prosperity for the port cities, all these are not the regional gathering groups caused by the location policies for the different leading enterprises, which finally result in the shaping of the cities on different resources, at different economic scales and economic structures, with different functions (O'Sullivan, 1996). With the advancement of productive power and the development of division of production, the binding conditions for the enterprises' location decisions are changing, which causing urban industrial structural reorganization, with more enterprises entering or leaving cities and contributing to the cities' economy, finally, the urban economy and urban functions evolve in a senior direction. At present, the tendency of the economic service is forcing the original manufacturing enterprises to move outside, and more and more headquarters of the companies or service institutes gather in the central areas of the cities. Especially, globalizing cities are becoming highly intensified geographical spaces for the modern service sectors because of their specific regional advantages, environmental conditions, rich human resources, information resources, etc. The result is that the industrial structure dominated by the service economy is shaped, which supply large amount of modern service activities, especially in the production services.

Therefore, many cities, in particular the globalizing cities, underwent an important process of the transition of industrial bases, that is, the historic transition as the manufacturing centers. For example, the Ruhr Industrial Area in Germany used to be a famous industrial base of coal and steel. From the 1960s until 1996, the employment population in coal industry steadily declined to 70,000, and the steel industry lost its 40,000 jobs. The shipping industry employed only one-third of the original workforce. At present, among the labor force in Ruhr Industrial Area, only 8% is employed in coal and steel industries, while 63% is employed in the service sectors. Essen City attracts many company headquarters and has become a major management center for the enterprises; Durtmund City has become the base for insurance industry and technologies; Duisburg City has become a center for cargo gathering and microelectronics, and the whole Ruhr area has transformed from playing host to heavy industries to highly developed service industry.

Likewise, globalizing cities such as London, New York, Tokyo, and Paris had undertaken a transition process of industrial bases. From 1971 to 1989, the London manufacturing industry lost 700,000 jobs, the transportation industry lost 40,000 jobs, while the insurance industry and other commerce services gained 460,000 jobs. From 1984 to 1987, the percentage of the production service sectors in central London increased from 31% to 37%, which then rose to 40% in 1989. But the employment population in other industries decreased comparatively or absolutely. The percentage of employment in New York's manufacturing industry dropped from 29% in 1950 to 10.5% in 1987, while that in the production service industry increased from 25.8% to 46.1%. Among them, the law service, commerce service, and banking industry grew most rapidly. From 1977 to 1985, the employment population in law consultation increased by

62%, that in commerce service by 42%, and that of banking industry by 23%. This industrial transition began to slow down but is still continuing. From 1988 to 2002, the manufacturing industry in New York increased by negative 28.6%, while the education and health service increased by 9.6%, that of professional law service, professional business service, and professional science and technology service increased by 5.8%, 4.0%, and 3.8%, respectively (see Table 9.9). It is also the case in Tokyo, with rapid expansion of service sectors. From 1983 to 1988, offices and banks in Tokyo increased their occupied space from 1,129,000 sqm to 2,816,000 sqm, an increase of nearly 1.5 times (Yu, 1999). Paris carried out the policies of "distribution of industries" effectively, which limited the continuing gathering of the industries in central areas of Paris and forced many industrial enterprises to distribute to the surrounding areas. At the same time, Paris reinforced the gathering of senior service functions in city centers. Up to early 1980s, one quarter of the old enterprises opened in 1950s were closed down, and more than 3,000 projects were moved to

Table 9.9. The Changes in Employment Population in Some Industries in New York (Unit:1000).

Years	1998	1999	2000	2001	2002	The Changes from 1998 to 2002 (%)
Professional business service	525.2	552.9	586.5	581.9	546.2	4.0
Professional science and technology service	277.6	296.8	320.7	312.2	288.2	3.8
Professional law service	77.4	80.9	82.9	82.4	81.9	5.8
Advertisement and relative services	51.1	54.3	59.5	55.2	47.4	–7.2
Education and health service	588.7	605.7	620.1	627.1	645.4	9.6
Retail service	260.1	270.2	281.5	272.0	266.3	2.4
Manufacturing industry	195.9	186.8	176.8	155.5	139.8	–28.6

Source: Current Employment Survey, New York State Department of Labor.

other places. According to the data by Eurostat in 2000, from 1990 to 1998, the added value of the service industry in Paris area increased by 35% each year, while that of the industries (excluding architecture) increased by only 4%; at the same period, the average added value in architecture decreased by 15% each year (Zhu and Wang, 2004).

Due to the transition of industrial bases, the globalizing cities are now characterized by the companies dominated by modern service industry. For example, the percentages of service industry in New York, London, Tokyo, and Hong Kong are 86.7%, 85%, 72.7%, and 86%, respectively. And furthermore, there are more similarities in economy of these globalizing cities, especially in the industries which are driving urban economic development, such as finance, telecommunications, and media. The percentage of the employees in health, social security, and social welfare is 13.4% and that in professional technology service and finance and insurance is 7.8% and 6.5%, respectively. The data in 2001 about Greater London shows that service industries such as finance and business are not only the source of London's growth in economy, but also the sectors which employ more people, one third of the employees in Greater London are in finance and business service sectors (see Figure 9.2). In London, more than half of the jobs are from the sectors concerning finance and business service. About 70% of the employees are working in the sectors such as finance, business, hotel service, education, social work and health.

So we can see that, as the main nodes in the global network, the global cities are always the bellwether in the tendency of global service industry-oriented economy, and are undoubtedly the cities with highly service industry-oriented economy. In this sense, the industrial bases of the globalizing cities are not provided by the traditional heritage and the imaginary arbitrariness, but they are closely related to the development features of the global economy. As the globalizing cities, the industrial bases possess basic regulations. From this we can draw a conclusion: the globalizing cities have to transform to the industrial bases with highly economic service no matter what their original industrial bases are, otherwise, they cannot adapt to the requirements of the development of the global economy, which it is not easy for them to become the globalizing cities.

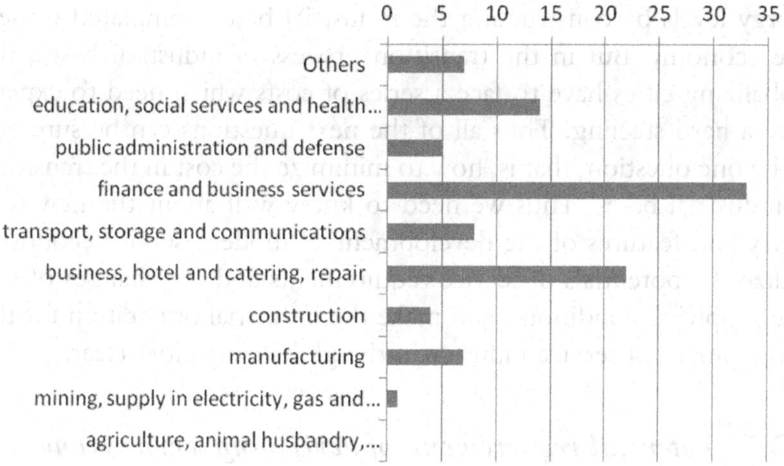

Figure 9.2. The Employment Constitution in Greater London (2001).
Source: Data released by ONS.

Though the transition of industrial bases in cities has to face bigger hurdles such as slow growth speed and worsening of structural unemployment, this is the cost the cities have to pay when their economy enters the new development stage. For these globalizing cities, this kind of cost is indispensible, in fact, it will bring corresponding benefits. As stated by Stanback and Noyelle (1982), the development of the service industry transformed the urban economy of the USA. The research conclusion drawn by Sheets *et al.* (1987) and the other researchers showed that the development of the service industry helped most American cities to weather the economic crisis which lasted until the 1970s. For the globalizing cities, their future benefits are embodied in the promotion of the city's energy level, which is the fundamental condition for the globalizing cities.

9.2. Orientation and Guideline of Industry Development in Globalizing Cities

The above analysis shows that the globalizing cities have to adapt to the requirements of the global economic service and improve their energy levels by constructing the industrial bases dominated by service economy. But in the transition process of industrial bases, the globalizing cities have to face a series of costs which need to experience a hard steeling. Thus all of the next questions can be summed up by one question, that is, how to minimize the cost in the transition of industrial bases. Thus we need to know well about the new tendency and features of the development of modern service economy, realize the potentials of service requirements and the changes of service supplying conditions, and make the industrial orientation for the development of service industry in the globalizing cities clear.

9.2.1. *Potential requirements of developing service economy*

Although it is necessary to form the industrial bases dominated by service economy for the globalizing cities, it is not driven by people's imagination regardless of objective conditions. If so, the frictions in the transition of industrial bases will be aggravated and unnecessary costs will be increased. Only by considering the situation for the right moment can we realize the minimization of transitional cost. Therefore, we should fully recognize the potential requirements to develop service economy in the globalizing cities and release the driving power of the potential requirements. At present, the globalizing cities in China have many favorable conditions and potential requirements to develop the service economy.

As we all know, compared to the manufacturing product, the service product, especially the new service products (including financial innovation, some social services, and personal welfare services), has a strong income elasticity, whose growth in requirements is most possibly the result of income growth of the residents and enterprises. Meanwhile, compared to the service industry, the prices of agriculture and manufacturing products decrease, which is another main reason. Because the price elasticity of agriculture and manufacturing products is smaller than that of service products and the increased expenditure on agriculture and manufacturing products is less than that of the service industry, there is a great increase in the requirements on service. Therefore, with the improvement in income level and life level, the increase in the leisure time and people's lifespan, the material marginal effects of the products begin to decline, and the people began to turn to the service consumption, thus there are direct and huge requirements on various kinds of service. The statistics show that, since the 1990s, the consumption cost of Shanghai's residents with respect to transportation, telecommunications, health, education, and culture increased by 15% to 30%. In 2003, this cost accounted for 23% of the overall consumption of the family. International practices tell us that, in the transitional stage in which the per capita GDP raises from US $5,000 to US $8,000, the expenditure on the above services consumption will increase by about 2% to 4%, and in 2010, this percentage will reach 26%–28%.

In addition, with the improvement of income level, the urban resident families will need more community services, which is increasing rapidly. The statistics in the developed countries show that the community service is a senior requirement with higher income elasticity. For example, in the OECD countries, in 20 years from 1971 to 1992, the percentage of the community and personal service in GDP increased from 6.8% to 9.5%, among which the proportion of service industry increased from 12.6% to 16.3%. More new service patterns spring up in this process, such as the household agent service industry, including convenience stores, household restaurants, door-to-door service of jardinière, baby hotels, and all-around service shops. Due to population aging and work pressures, more and more comprehensive health management service companies are established, which provide consultations and suggestions on health by professional doctors to the members; and service companies in which the parents are taught to play games with kids are established.

Apart from the growth in final service consumption requirements which are related to the per capita income, there is one important service requirement in the development of the service economy: i.e., the intermediate service input, which is related to the high development of industrialization, will be increased. International practice shows that the development of industrialization and the later transition to post-industrialization result in many requirements from the manufacturing industry on service. For example, in the rapid development stages during the 1970s and 1980s, Japan's intermediate requirement on service industry increased by 13.4% per year, which was higher than that from the manufacturing industry itself. If we analyzed the manufacturing industry in detail, we can see that the intermediate requirement from machinery and equipment industry on service industry is 20%; transportation machinery, 19.7%; electrical machinery, 14.9%; the primary products of the metal, 12.1%; and chemical products, 10.8%. At present, China's industrialization process is accelerating and entering the development stage of heavy chemical industry, which further complicates the relations between different industries. The industry chain will be further extended, and the trade scale between different industries will be expanded. With the increase of material products as the intermediate input between different industries, the intermediate input in service industry will be increased as well. In an intermediate service sector, the service aimed at the producers is closely related to the other economic sectors. The relation includes its close connections to manufacturing industry and the internal services. This relation produces two different effects. First, the growth of products automatically drives the requirement growth of the service to producers, which results in the further multilayer effects. According to a survey conducted by the USA in 1997, the service expenditure exceeding over US$80 million increased by 26%. In the overall expenditure of American companies, the information and technology service accounted for 30% of the overall expense; the human resource service, 16%; the market and selling service, 14%; and the financial service, 11%. All of these service expenditures accounted for 71% of the overall expenses. Second, the service to the producers is the medium in which the new added value is introduced to the process of the commodity production. This new added value can lower the production cost, promote the production improvement and the development of new products, and take more effective methods to deliver the commodity. Therefore, the more intermediate service input to meet the requirements on more commodities, in turn, is promoting and changing the mixture of the requirements on commodities.

At the same time, with the aggravation of market competition, the outlay of enterprise activities, especially the supporting services, will obviously increase if the enterprises want to keep their core competition and strengthen their core business. The investigations conducted by the Ministry of International Trade and Industry of Japan in 1970 showed that the main programs of external purchase were job training (0.1%), information system (19.7%), production methods (17.4%), accounting and taxation (14%), and R&D (13.7%). Meanwhile, there is a new tendency, servicization, in the development of modern manufacturing industry itself, and more and more added value is from the service sector and not the processing and manufacturing industry. Therefore, an increasing number of manufacturing industries will become intangible, which are custom-tailed by personal taste, and more and more services are supplied in distance and massively produced. This means that their business patterns are transferred to a certain service from the production of one product.

Combined with the above factors, there is another factor which exerts special impact on the development potential of service economy in the globalizing cities, that is, while the industrializing process is accelerating, China has to face the strategic opportunity when international manufacturing industries are transferred to China on a large scale. In particular, the Yangtze River Delta area and the Pearl River Delta area undertook many investment projects in the transferring of international manufacturing industries. They have become the bases of world manufacturing industries gradually, which is impacting the potentials of the development of service economy in the globalizing cites in the following two aspects:

First, the international transfer of manufacturing industries brings international transferring of service industries. Generally speaking, the developed countries or transnational companies realized the internalization of industrial production by trade or FDI, which requires the corresponding supporting services in the fields of trade, finance, accounting, laws, etc. Therefore, the industrial transnational companies established many relative service institutes from the very beginning. The services supplied by transnational companies are mainly the intermediate services, which showed that the service internationalization kept up with industrial internationalization. If we say that the international transfer of manufacturing and processing is mainly distributed in some areas, the corresponding supporting services tend to integrate in the main cities.

Second, the massive development and intensification of manufacturing industry in a certain area require the overflowing effects on services. The experimental analysis shows that the industrial development in the local areas in Shanghai is negative for the development of its service industry, which means that the industrial crossing coefficients in the same area are negative, which are –7.497, –0.978, and –4.607, respectively. The surrounding areas of Shanghai, that is, the industrial developments of Jiangsu Province and Zhejiang Province, exert the positive impact on the development of service industry in Shanghai. This means the industrial crossing coefficients in different areas are positive, being 2.447 for Zhejiang Province, 2.291 for Jiangsu Province, 1.181 for Zhejiang Province, and 5.582 for Jiangsu Province. In particular, the industrial development of Zhejiang Province exerts a positive impact on the development of the service industry in Shanghai (Cheng, 2005). Thus, the world manufacturing and processing bases established in the Yangtze River Delta area produce a great overflowing effective on the service requirement in Shanghai.

In addition, massive urbanization is another important factor which promotes the development of the service economy. For a long time, the process of urbanization was hysteretic in China. At present, in order to adapt to its industrial process, the urbanization process has accelerated. It is estimated that the urbanization rate in China will be 54.5% in 2020. In view of requirements, with more agricultural surplus labor flocking into the cities, rural people will become urban residents, who require more service consumption because of the promotion in their income levels and life levels. And moreover, the behavioral pattern of self-service will be completely changed, thereby promoting service externalization. The growth of this service consumption requirement possibly results in the development of the traditional service industry, which requires the traditional service sectors to increase the intermediate input and further promote the development of the modern service industry indirectly. In view of supplicant, urbanization brings the expansion of urban size, the improvement of urban facilities, the strengthening of urban functions, etc., which supply better physical space and material conditions for the development of the service economy. Thus they are helpful to the regional accumulation of service industry and the production of the accumulative effect. Moreover, the growth of the urban population will bring abundant and flexible labor supplicant to the service sectors. Because of the obvious dual employment structure of the modern service industry, besides senior professional talent, more common and flexible labor is necessary for auxiliary staff, support crews, and supporting service staff.

9.2.2. *The changes of supplying conditions for the development of service economy*

Under the condition that there is more potential in the development of the service economy, if the service supplying conditions remain unchanged, the development path of a service economy is only linear at most, and its development rates are different. But we note that the new tendency of the development of the service economy is the fundamental change in service supplying conditions. In particular, the improvement of information technology and information facilities supplies the powerful technology foundation for the service economy, which strengthens the supplying abilities of the service.

At present, the global information tide is at a comparatively matured stage, which forces the traditional industrial sectors to be transformed to a further degree. In this process, one prominent phenomenon is that the development of digital technology is making more and more products digitalized; information has become digitalized, and even the material products has become partly digitalized, which can transform into intelligence products after they are installed in the digitalized interfaces. Similarly, the products representing values can be digitalized too, for example, the digitalized currency, e-check, e-share, and e-bond. In fact, various kinds of services and processes can be installed for the expansion cores of e-business, where digitalized products can be exchanged on Internet. Except the byte flow, the production and exploitation of the digitalized products has no physical boundaries, which combine the production and consumption, the products, and the services closely. Obviously, this will exert a substantial impact on the development of the industrial economy. For example, the original entry barriers have become temporal and spatial obstacles in transmitting the service products. However, modern telecommunication and transmitting technology have reduced the importance of the concepts of time and space, which resulted in the changes in the non-storage of service and the traditional features of transportation. Thus, many services which originally needed synchronicity of production and consumption have separated these two processes, and they can be supplied from the final markets to remote places. At present, financial, entertainment, education, security monitoring, secretarial, accounting, and gaming services can be produced and sold in the places which are remote from the final markets. This is especially true in the case of long-distance medical care services. In addition, the information revolution not only improved the tradability of service but also overcame the original defects of personal services, which combined massive services with the personal services.

Therefore, the modern information technology and network are extensively applied in service industry sectors, which strengthen the service functions and expand the service scope in large scale. More and more non-intermediary services and virtualized services are appearing. For example, e-business makes trade more convenient and reduces the trade cost greatly. Compared to the previous year, the world trade volume of e-business in 2002 was increased by 73%. In addition, long-distance education expands the service scope rapidly and it covers more and more areas. In 1995, only 28% of American colleges or universities taught network courses, which increased to 60% in 1998. According to the statistics, more than 60% of enterprises supply training and further education to their staff by networks.

The application and networking of modern information technology changed some attributes of service activities and promoted the generalization and independence of service activities. In view of technology, especially, the rapid development of information and computer technology supplies the conditions to the technology application in the service sectors. The attributes of traditional services such as face-to-face, immovability, and non-storage can be changed to a great degree, which expands the scope and tradability of service supply. Thus, the extensive application and networking of modern information technology allows the modern service industry to demonstrate the new tendency of "manufacturing", that is, the scale economy and custom-made production, similar to the manufacturing industry. Thus, many new-type services (service categories or classifications) tend to appear, which endow the traditional services with new contents and improved service quality, and change traditional service patterns. Modern service industry is becoming the sectors of intelligence-intensive sectors, which are the high ends of value chains and radiate their high energy exceeding the boundaries of regions.

And moreover, with changes of technological bases, the value chain of production is gradually becoming the dominant producing pattern, and the organization structure of enterprises is being changed greatly. Due to the obvious advantages of networked services, the service enterprises are developing in chains, alliances, and integration, which are mostly in the network organizational structures, loose and flexible ones. For example, many service-oriented transnational companies are in such structures. Compared to the branch companies by direct investment, many of them tend to adopt the patterns of non-equity arrangement or partnership. The mother company and its subsidiaries are loosely connected by the network, each of them is more independent, and many of their business are conducted in the pattern of outer packing. This new organization structure makes their internal advantages less obvious, which will improve the supply abilities of modern services.

It is noted that, in this process, service innovation is on the rise. The modern service industry is not only the sectors in which the modern technologies are extensively applied but also those important sectors in which more innovations are carried out as well. Service innovation includes both technology innovations, such as service means, methods, and tools, and non-technology innovations, such as the function innovation in finance service. Different from the innovation in the manufacturing industry sectors, many of the service innovations are not technological or changes in process but functional developments. These functional innovations do not need much R&D input but require vast learning and knowledge accumulation, highly qualified talent, and a relevant institutional environment. With the extensive application of modern information technology and network, the technology innovations in service means, methods, and tools are thriving with increasing input on R&D. Since 1980, the R&D and investments in the service industries in most developed countries increased rapidly and occupied more and more shares. Between 1990 and 1998, the R&D expenditure in Canada's service industry increased by 17% annually, which was much higher than that of its manufacturing industry, which was at 10%. In France, it was 15%, much higher than that in its corresponding value in the manufacturing industry, 1%. Apart from Austria, where the expenditure on R&D in its service industry increased by 11%, lower than that of its manufacturing industry, 15%; the expenditure on R&D in the service industries in Japan, USA, and UK increased more than those in their manufacturing industries. Thus, the enterprises' expenditure on their R&D in the countries of OECD, the percentage of R&D in service industry increased from less than 5% to 15% in 1997 (OECD, 2001). Though the expenditure on R&D in Australia's service industry was decreased (its original proportion was higher), the expenditure proportion in other countries' service industries were increased by different percentages. Among them, the expenditure proportion on R&D of service industry was 30% in 1998; 28% in Australia; 20% in the USA; 16% in the UK; 7% in France; and 5% in Japan. In view of the service innovation in Canada, the industries with the highest innovation rate (the proportion of enterprise innovation) are finance (62%), telecommunication (45%), and technological enterprise service (43%); the important and extensive technology in innovation in service industry is information and communication technology (ICT). The R&D activities in service industry, which are most active, most productive, and growing fastest, are engineering and science services, computer and relative services, wholesale trade, finance, insurance, and real estate services (OECD, 1999).

For the globalizing cities in China, the changes of service supplying conditions have a special source and pattern, that is, the transferring of international service industry to the developing countries. Under the background of service economy era, the business operations of the world modern service industry are becoming more and more internationalized, networked, and integrated, and FDI has become an important form to explore the territory scope for services. In the early 1970s, the FDI in service industry accounted for only a quarter of world FDI. Since the 1980s, the FDI in service industry is thriving, reaching 42.8% in 1985 and exceeding that of manufacturing industry (38.7%). Since the 1990s, FDI in the service sector accounted for as much as 50%. With respect to FDI in the OECD countries, the total investment in service industry was obviously higher than that in manufacturing industry, and the services are retailing, finance, business service, hotels, restaurants, and telecommunication. The rapid growth of FDI in service industry is one part of internationalized economic activities in a wide range. According to the statistics on The Report of World Investment in 2003 by the UN, during the year 1999–2000, the world FDI rates are as follows: 3.3% in the primary industry; 22.6% in the secondary industry; 68.5% in the tertiary industry, among which, 24.9% in finance industry, and 11.5% in telecommunication services. At present, the transfer of the international service industry is speeding up and has extended to many fields such as information technology service, human resource management, finance, insurance, accounting services, logistics systems, and customer services. With the strategic adjustment of transnational companies and the rapid development of modern information technology, the service outlay combined by BPO and ITO has gradually become a new service trade pattern and is one of the most important patterns for a new-round industrial transferring in the world. The developed countries and areas in the world are the main places to export outsourcing, in the outsourcing of world service, the USA accounted for almost two-thirds, and the EU and Japan accounted for almost one third. While the developing countries are the main places to take over the outstanding, among which Asia takes over the most of outsourcing business, which accounted for almost 45% of the world service outsourcing business.

There are great complementary effects and transferring difference in China's service industry, especially, in high technology and the transferring of new service industries. In particular, many great cities have potential in attracting the FDI in service industry. With the end of the WTO's binding on China, the opening-up in the field of service will enter a new stage; the restrictions on the foreign-funded enterprises will decrease more in the fields of banking, insurance, education, medical care, health, transportation, telecommunication, etc.; and a new round of international industrial transferring in the fields of service is on the upgrade. The globalizing cities in China will take over much of international service industry transfer and attract more FDI in the service industry. All of these developments will bring a series of new service projects and service patterns to the globalizing cities, the original service fields will be expanded, and the development of service economy will be greatly promoted.

9.2.3. *The development of service economy based on the industrial merging*

From the above analysis, we can see that there are huge service requirement potentials in the transferring of industrial bases in the globalizing cities in China while facing the improvement of service supplying conditions. This means that there will be a possible choice space in promoting the development of service economy. In other words, the transfer of industrial bases in the globalizing cities will not follow traditional paths, that is, under the framework of industrial division, manufacturing will be transferred, allowed to perish, or replaced by service industry in order to promote the development of the service economy. In view of the practice in the globalizing cities in China, the simple industrial replacement lasts longer than expected, but the transferring cost will be huge. Therefore, the globalizing cities in China must be established on the present industrial bases to promote the development of the service economy. The industrial structure dominated by service economy must be constructed to support the flow economy in the metropolitans, a new path, that is, the industrial merging supported by informatization, may be followed.

The precondition of industrial merging is informatization, which is permeated and transformed in industrialization and servicization. In essence, informatization is not just one kind of technological form or technological mode, but an economic and social formation. If we say the industrialization is a round-about production pattern which is characterized by division of labor in different industries, scale economy, volume production, entity relevance and etc., then informatization is the direct production pattern which is characterized by industrial merging, network economy, flexible production, visual relevance, etc. Thus, the introduction of informatization to urban economy means the introduction of a new production pattern. In the production pattern of informatization, the expansion of production and consumption are not necessarily supported by high material consumption, they can be established on the basis of low cost. The socialized value mode with low cost is formed and established on the improvement of economic efficiency because of information transmission and the improvement in transfer. What is more important is that the production pattern of informatization is not lasting or an extension of the traditional industrialized path, and it is not the improvement of traditional industrial path under the new circumstances, either. It is a critical path transfer which is endowed by new contents. The core lies on the more and more obscure boundaries in service industry and some economic activities, especially in the manufacturing industry. The leading economic activities have transferred from manufacturing to services, which is embodied by the servicization in the sectors in manufacturing industry and is shown as the following:

(1) the products in the manufacturing sector are produced to supply some kind of service, for example, the products of telecommunication and home appliances;
(2) the knowledge and technology service sold along with the products; and
(3) the service will lead the manufacturing sectors to reform in technology and innovate their products. Therefore, informatization has promoted the industrial merging of service industry and manufacturing industry.

The industrial merging is developed on the bases of high industrial division of labor at the time of industrial economy, the premises are the increasing refining of industrial sectors, the complication of industrial relevance, the massive transaction between different sectors and huge transaction volumes, which is the result of adjusting on the solid boundaries between different industries. This adjustment breaks up the industrial boundaries, results in more mutual inflowing and merging, and gives rise to the concept of market region in which the buyer and the seller are closed related to the transfer to the concept of market space. Meanwhile, the competition in a certain scope in the minds of traditional manufactures will be replaced by an extensive and overlapping concept.

The coordination between the relative activities is competitive and cooperative either within the traditional market or outside the traditional market. The industrial merging is mainly embodied by the mutual crossing and overlapping of industrial boundaries and has become a new industry that is totally different from the past ones. The new industry is not just the simple combination and merging of the original industries, it is not the simple replacement of the original industries, either. It is the re-division of labor bases on the organic integration of original industries.

The development guidelines of industrial merging should be based on knowledge economy, cooperate by production value chain with the help of information, make the separate industries evolve into the industrial merging with overlapping, and realize the fundamental transferring in producing patterns. The proposed guideline in developing industry complies with the new tendency of industrial development in the new situation and contributes more to the innovation in patterns of industrial development. Of course, the development of industrial merging does not exclude the manufacturing of some product, and it should combine the product manufacturing and service supplying organically, that is, the product is a kind of service to be provided in the future, while the service is the actual product. Under the circumstance in which the customers are closely related to the product producers, only the supplying of both product and service can meet the consumption requests. At the same time, the development of industrial merging needs the tangible products to contain more and more knowledge and information, the value of the products is more and more intangible, such as designing and marketing. For example, some foreign traditional metal enterprises have transformed to service companies, with the value of their services surpassing the value of their products. Therefore, the developing guidelines of industrial merging needs mutual promotion and joint development of the secondary and tertiary industries, and it includes the basic ideas to develop the modern service industry in the first place.

What the development of industrial merging brings is the new changes, such as business overlapping between different sectors and market overlapping, which breaks the boundaries of division of labor and intervenes each other. The companies focus not on the vertical merging but on the horizontal merging between the companies with different functions. The relationship between enterprises is not only a competitive one, but a coordinative one as well. This is quite different from the past pattern in which only the self requirements are considered. Under the circumstance of industrial merging, besides the enterprises themselves, they should combine the functions in the operation procedure to realize the integration of business, such as CRM, SCM, and VBM, and moreover, they should consider the connection to the outside to realize the coordinative business with the help of the Internet. Thus, the development of industrial merging will produce a new-type competitive and coordinative relationship, based on the extensive application of information technology with industrial automation and intelligence, and there will a flexible tendency in industrial structure.

The industrial merging is not just a problem to meet the market requirements based on information, but it is a problem to exploit the information and knowledge and merge them to take part in more competition. The reason is that the industrial merging needs not only the exchange and merging of information from the different sectors but also the application of the information combined with the relative professional knowledge in order to get the service with much more information contents. In fact, this means the fundamental changes of information flow, that is, the flow of power and commodity trade is changed to the flow of knowledge. Thus, the key for an organization to own competition power which is different from the others is that it can merge new information with the existing professional knowledge. In this process, the core problems are knowledge creation and transmission process. Therefore the development guidelines of industrial merging highlight the functions of industrial innovation, which not only encourages the springing up of merged new products and services but also exerts impact on the improvement of original products and services.

Therefore, when the globalizing cites are constructing the industrial bases dominated by the service economy, the modern information technology should be applied to transform the traditional industries in order to promote the technological merging of industries. On the platform of information network, we should break the traditional industrial boundaries and their own development patterns and realize the business overlapping and production merging so that the new-type businesses can be explored and the new industrial sectors can be developed. Based on knowledge economy, with help of information means, we should organically integrate the production value chains in order to form a production service patterns in a connected sequence and realize the integrated development of advanced manufacturing industry and modern service industry. At the same time, we should transform the traditional industrial organizational structure and develop the network organizational structure in order to produce the adjusting mechanism of industrial activities, which is based on shared knowledge and with the overlapping of competition and cooperation.

9.3. Leading Development of Modern Service Industry

Modern service industry mainly refers to the sectors which supply services to the producers and are developed on high-tech ideas such as electronic information, modern management ideas, operation patterns, and organization patterns. It includes not only the new service industries that have emerged in modern economy, such as information service and e-business, but also modern service industries, which are developing at a rapid speed and account for proportion, such as finance and insurance, and professional commerce services. At the same time, it should include the traditional services which are transformed by information technology and have new core competition, such as the consulting business and modern logistics service industry.[1] These modern service sectors usually have the common features, namely, high human capital contents, high professionalism, and high added value. The dominant development of the modern service industry is one of the main symbols for the globalizing cities.

9.3.1. *The existing problems and obstacles for the development of modern service industry*

As analyzed above, the huge potential requirements for the development of the service economy and the improvement of service supplying conditions provide better opportunities and great possible spaces for the development of the modern service industry in the globalizing cities. In fact, metropolises usually have the spaces for modern service industry to cluster, which includes the entry of foreign service companies. Moreover, the international transferring of the service industry always follows the massive international transferring of the manufacturing industry. Taking the current situation into consideration, we find that most of the service trade is conducted between developed countries, and the path for international service industries to transfer to the developing countries is still slow. Connor and

[1]The concept of the modern service industry itself is more characterized by relative time, so its definition of meaning is prone to be ambiguous, there being a variety of different understanding. For example, Lai (2004) argues that the modern service industry refers to the modern producer services, production, which provides services for business activities and government administration rather than the final consumption. Zhu and Wang (2004) introduce connotation of the modern service industry by comparing it with the traditional service industry: high-tech, knowledge-intensive, and emerging. I seek a number of "standards" of modern industry (such as the new sectors having characteristics of modern industry in the time series, and high growth rates, important sectors being characterized by modern industry, and the traditional sectors being also capable of having modern industrial characteristics by injecting higher technology and knowledge content based on innovation) to outline the basic scope or boundary of the modern service industry. More broadly, more service industries can also be included, which meet modern consumer demand, accord with modern social and cultural philosophy, and adapt to modern life quality, such as community services, health services, education services, and so on.

Daniels once explained this experimental result. They thought that, before the service companies begin the negotiations on accessing the foreign markets, they need the professional service development at the lowest levels and the minimum expectation on systematic structure and rules. Many cities in the developed countries can meet these minimum conditions so that the enterprises are confident in seeking the cooperation partners and develop the marketing activities there (O'Connor and Daniels, 2001). It is true that there are many obstacles when the globalizing cities in China are attaching more importance to the development of the modern service industry; the reason being the bindings from all various kinds of systematic barriers.

As we all know, the continual improvement of the social specialization degree and the relative marketization degree makes more internalized services transfer to externalized ones, which brings independence of service activities. Therefore, the development of the modern service industry is decided by the driving of the market requirements, particularly, the drawing from the intermediate requirements of the industrial sectors and governmental sectors. However, the present division of labor in China's social specialization is still low, the non-service sectors (excluding the agricultural sectors and manufacturing sectors, including the government and household sectors) have their own externalized service activities, which means the self-service inside the sectors. Under this circumstance, the growth of intermediate service input will be limited and the sector service input rate will be lower, the rate here refers to the proportion of service intermediate input in the overall sector input. Take Shanghai as an example, according to the analysis on the sector service input rate in 2000, in terms of overall service input of three industries, the service input rate of service industry is the highest, 28.89%, which was followed by that of the primary industry, 18.62%, and that of the secondary industry, 14.85%. This shows that, on one hand, the development of service industry itself has a stronger self-reinforcing effect; on the other hand, the secondary industry realizes its service input by the producers and is less connected to the whole service industry. In view of the input into separate services, the input rates of three industries on cargo transportation and storage service are basically the same, from 2.45% to 2.83%. The finance and insurance service input rates in the service industry and the primary industry are the highest, which are 12.79% and 6.13%, respectively, which accounts for 44% and 33% of their overall service input. To our surprise, the finance and insurance services are not prominent in the service input of the secondary industry, only 3.18%, which accounts for 21% of its overall service input and ranks at the second place; it is lower than that of commercial service, 5.8%, which accounts for 39% of its overall service input (Cheng and Chen, 2005). This shows that the finance and insurance services in Shanghai are not rooted in the secondary industry and they did not gain sustainable development from the secondary industry. Due to the lower social specialization degree, the services of non-service sectors are more internalized, which means that the development of modern service industry neither connects closely to other industries and nor gains powerful supporting bases. It is more difficult for the development of modern service industry, even its proportion is enhancing, and it is easier for it to reverse again.

Superficially, the internalization of service activities of industrial sectors is caused by the low degree of division of labor of social specialization. In fact, it is caused by lower marketization. The externalization of service activities of industrial sectors is decided by the following two factors. First is the market competition pressure which the industrial sectors are facing. When the complexity of business is increasing and the marketing competition is becoming fiercer, the manufacturing enterprise will definitely adjust its business structure in order to maintain its core competition and will outlay the non-core business. Meanwhile the specialized division of labor and greater functions will help the service enterprises to integrate their own technology platform and service platform in order to further strengthen their own core business. Second is the translation cost. Like enterprise formation, the internalization of service activities can be considered as the result of saving transaction costs. If the transaction cost of outsourcing service is higher than that of self-service, the internalization of service activities will remain unchanged. Only when the transaction cost of outsourcing service is lower than that of self-service can the enterprises externalize some of their service activities. It is clear that the former formed a great motive power to promote the externalization of service activities while the latter provided a great attraction to promote the externalization of service. Only joint functioning by the two factors can promote the service activities from internalization to externalization. At the same time, if the modern service industry can adapt to the changes of market requirements and the decline of the information and communication costs on the market, the specialization of the modern service industry itself can be improved continually to meet the requirement of social diversity. Therefore, the growth of the modern service industry is synchronic with the emergence of professional companies which supply the more dispersed intermediate services. The experiences show that the modern service sectors in developed countries are characterized by their high heterogeneity.

At present, with the deepening of China's marketing reform and the forming of a basic pattern in which the supply of the products exceeds demand, there will be increasing market competition pressure on the physical products. Under the circumstance of constraint hardening, it promotes the non-core business outlay in this kind of enterprises. A recent sample surveys show that 95% of Wuxi's enterprises want to strip off the production of spare parts, 50% hope that the society handles their logistics, 90% hope to separate their partial logistics business, and 85% hope to strip off the logistics service. Certainly, under the circumstance of constraint softening of enterprise budget or the administrative protection, some of the enterprises' service activities are internalized. Comparatively speaking, the more serious problem is the increasing transaction costs of the outsourcing expense, which includes the following three factors:

(1) The incomplete service supplying results in the increasing transaction cost. In the 143 businesses of the service trade classified by WTO, some are blank in China, for example, commercialized taxation service, opinion pull service, security investigation service, and credit enquiry and analysis service. The service supplied by the existing service sectors is not complete, such as the

short-mechanism in finance service due to the lack of stock index futures. This lack of supply of outsourcing service in the enterprises is actually a reflection of the increasing transaction costs in a disguised form.

(2) The imperfect service system and lower service level result in the increasing transaction cost. On the premise of the customer's affordability, the current service supplying can be embodied by the following: (a) money can purchase the general services but it is difficult to buy advanced services and differentiating services, which reflects the simplification of service supplying; (b) money can purchase the common services but it is difficult to buy high-quality services, which reflects the lower level and extensive operation of service supplying; (c) money can purchase various kinds of single services but it is difficult to buy compound service, which reflects the segregation and lower added value of service supplying; (d) money can purchase some kind of static service at a certain time but it is difficult to buy consecutive dynamic service, which reflects the short-termism and short-sight of service supplying. The service supplying with bad comprehensiveness, lower service level, and lower service subdivision results in the increasing transaction cost.

(3) The increasing transaction cost caused by the bad market order, which can be represented by the following: the false information or fraud practicing in service supplying makes the consumers walk into traps, forcing them to exhibit psychological refusal and stay at a respectful distance from the services; the instability of service quality or the obfuscation of service standards make the consumers produce a psychological guard, making them cautious in choosing service consumption; and service reputation does not mean better service, and it makes the consumers complain more and more and reduce their positivity in service consumption. Moreover, because we are in the process of system transition, the expectation of a series of system transformations is not stable, for example, transformations in the fields of medical care and health, elderly nursing care, social security, and education, which restrains immediate service requirements.

The trade cost of the above outsourcing services is always increasing, in view of supply–demand, and it is a stiff problem of service supply and demand, which can result in the short supply of effective services and the increasing transaction cost in service trade. This scenario makes it difficult transfer the effective service requirements to the realistic effective service requirements. According to a survey on the households in Beijing, Shanghai, Guangzhou, chengdu, Xian, Shenyang and Qingdao, more than 70% of the surveyed need various kinds of services. Among them, nearly 2,400,000 households cannot get their electrical appliances repaired and about 1,270,000 households cannot get proper houses maintenance. This is caused by insufficient competition and is the representation of lowered level of marketing. For example, the reason why senior services and differentiating services cannot be bought is that the high arbitrary prices or non-market pricing, which cannot reflect the multilayer service requirements and cannot stimulate the corresponding supply growth. The reason why a high-quality service cannot be bought is the weak competition and monopoly, which make the supplicant of high-quality service lack internal motive power and the external pressure. The reason why the compound service cannot be bought is the market segmentation and industrial segmentation, which make it quite difficult to integrate all services according to the comprehensive requirements of the consumers. The reason why consecutive dynamic service cannot be bought is that the weak marketing consciousness and insufficient ability result in weak abilities in exploring the service innovation.

From the current situation, the marketization degree in the fields of modern service is not high, which is mainly caused by the systemic obstacles such as the administrative monopoly, traditional access, and pricing controlling. There are many discriminative limits in industrial admittance, which is less open to the non-public economy. For example, the added value from the non-public economy in Shanghai in 2002 accounted for 31.9% of its GDP, among them, the non-public economy accounted for 35.9% of the added value of the secondary industry, and 28.9% of the tertiary industry. The non-public economy accounts for 9.2% in storage, transportation and communication industries; 37.6% in wholesale, retail and catering industries; 23.1% in finance and insurance industries. The percentage rate is even lower in education, culture, health and entertainment industries. This administrative protection of one industry will result in less competition, reduced administrative monopoly profits, and higher service prices. All of these will influence the enhancement of professional services, and the effective services are in short supply. Therefore, the globalizing cities should develop the modern service industry in the first place in order to attract the service institutions from home and abroad to integrate in them. It is quite necessary to break through the systemic obstacles, improve the marketization degree, and give full play to the adjustment of market mechanism to the supply-demand relations in modern services.

9.3.2. *To seek for the breakthroughs for the development of modern service industry*

The practice in China tells the globalizing cities that, if they want to promote the rapid development of modern service industry, one of the most important aspects is to break through the inner-cycle development path for self-enhancement of the modern services. That is, on the foundation of enhancing the overall economic services, we should seek for the divergent development which is permeating in the whole economic system and find new growing points in the merging of the secondary industry and the tertiary industry. This requires the other industries, especially, the manufacturing industries, to outlay their business activities and increase the intermediate input of services, which promotes the servicization of the sectors in the manufacturing industry and allows their dominating economic activities to transition from manufacturing to services. Thus, the supporting services related to the manufacturing industry should be developed at a rapid speed, such as that of engineering equipment, industrial information, and other relevant public services in the fields of technology, modern logistics, industrial real estates, industrial consultation, and other industries.

At the same time, by the marketing deepening and specialization of market choice of modern services, the cost to promote the scale and trade of market growth begins to decline. In the specialized development of the modern service, we should attach equal importance to the external expansion in size and the internal improvement in quality, such as the changes in service patterns, and the aims are to strengthen humanization, convenience, and credit of the service industry. The scale expansion is mainly to open up new service categories and classifications, to increase new service types and business, and to improve the internal structure of the service industry. The quality improvement is to remold service industry in advanced ideas, to equip service industry with high-tech and information technologies, to improve the knowledge intensity and technology content of services, to strengthen the stability of services, to foster the new growing points of the services and to reinforce its radiation exceeding the boundaries of the regions.

For the globalizing cities, one special aspect in promoting the development of the modern service industry is to fully play the advantages of spatial integration of the modern service industry. The reason is that modern service industry tends to integrate in the central cities or the central areas of the cities. The external economic effects such as complementation and sharing brought by industrial integration are quite obvious and result in the development tendency of industrial clusters in certain regions, especially, the central business districts (CBDs) in the metropolises are occupied by many industrial clusters. Therefore, we should positively create a better industrial ecological environment to fully play the external advantages by close industrial relevance, shared resource factors, rich social capitals, and effective competition and cooperation mechanism. We should foster and promote the formation and development of service industry clusters and realize the scale economy and scope economy before a joint evolved mechanism of industries can be formed. In detail, CBDs, which are the carriers or platforms, have become the core cluster dominated by finance services, the derive cluster dominated by entertainment and high-end consumption, and the supporting cluster dominated by tourism and catering. Similarly, the high-tech parks have become the service industry cluster, which is characterized by R&D of products and technology innovation. By the regional integration of industries, the ecological foundation for the development of modern service can be optimized. On the integration foundations of modern service industries with diversity, multilayer and networking, the service radiation space can be expanded and the service value chain can be extended externally. In order to attract modern service industries to integrate in a certain region, the advanced modern telecommunication facilities, convenient transportation network, fine and harmonious living environment, office building at different ranks, and business integrated areas should be supplied. In addition, we should create more conditions to introduce advanced professional talents and train more and more service staff with specific talents.

Based on this foundation, we can grasp the opportunity of international industrial transferring, which should be undertaken by us actively in order to promote the leapfrog development of the modern service industry. When foreign investment is introduced to the service industry, the functions should be focused not just on the projects themselves or the size of investment. Therefore, the quality standards when introducing foreign investment in service industry are the following:

(1) the scarcity of the functions: the projects with scarcer functions should be introduced;
(2) the size of the function: the projects with more functions should be introduced;
(3) the integration of the function: the projects which can integrate the other services should be introduced.

It is necessary for us to explore the opportunities to improve the economic efficiency by promoting personal enthusiasm and competitive marketing. Therefore, we should relax the entry controls on the premise of clearing the industrial requirements and operation qualifications, enlarge the proportion of non-public economy, promote the growth of the number and size of service enterprises, and form competitive patterns in which the multieconomic entities are involved. On the premise of clearing the industrial standards and strengthening the industrial supervising, we should relax the operation controls, expand the operation scope of service enterprises, and carry out the market pricing patterns such as fixing prices according to the qualities and differentiating pricing. By the innovations in systems and mechanisms, the professional division of labor can be promoted with more service externalization, which can stimulate the internal driving force to develop the service industry in both sides of supply and demand.

After the important position of the globalizing cities in improving the productivity and international competition are located, the role of the governments in promoting the development of modern service industry is to supply the investment on infrastructures, maintain an open, competitive and transparent business environment, relax their control furthermore, and explore the opportunities to improve the economic efficiency by encouraging the individuals and the market competition. Therefore, with the industry requirements and operating qualifications identified, it is necessary to relax the market entry control, expand the non-public economy, increase quantity and scale of service companies and to create a complete competition structure with multiple economic entities' participation with standardized service and intensified supervision, it is necessary to relax operating controls, expand service business scope, and set the price based on service quality and market demand. Through institutional innovation, the service industry will be activated from both supply and demand.

9.3.3. *To promote the development of modern service industry*

To promote the development of the modern service industry in the globalizing cities, the key is to break the systematic obstacles, adjust the controlling policies, and introduce the competition mechanism. When China entered WTO, it promised to adjust the controlling framework of service industry in the process of China's opening-up in the field of service industry, clear up and abolish the outdated rules and regulations and the relative documents, formulate and implement new policies to relax the market access, eliminate the administrative monopoly in the service industry, lower the threshold for the entry of the service industry, and legislate when the conditions permit. Meanwhile, it is necessary for China to break up the various and unwritten roles, break the division between different sectors, decrease the unnecessary links, simplify the original examination and approval, and clear up unreasonable charges. The controlling policies should be adjusted, especially the ones concerning the pricing, in order to expand the operation of service marketization and promote the pricing of the service market.

In the process of orderly opening the private investment in the fields such as television, newspapers, distribution, and art shows, and expanding the industries' involvement in education, health, physical education, entertainment, tourism, information, finance, etc., to accelerate the restructuring of the original institutions, the original social service should be stripped out after distinguishing and designation of the services (both public welfare and non-public-welfare). We should explore the public bidding and auction ways of the rare service resources and collocate the social resources of service industry reasonably by the market principles. Meanwhile, the administrative management institutes related to social undertaking should transfer their functions from "undertaking the undertaking" to "managing the undertaking" and realize the management of all industries by means of economy, laws and administration. In the relative industries, the construction of the system of credit rating and the establishment of service standards should be accelerated, and moreover, the better reputation guarantee, service specifications, and service environment should be constructed. According to the principles of market economy and international practices, the functions of the governments, enterprises, and industry associations should be located clearly. The various associations in different service industries should be established and perfected in order to make it clear for the industries to be autonomous in management. These associations should fulfill their important roles in putting the regulations about market admittance in order, promoting the development of private economy, strengthening the self-discipline and management in the industries, working out the planning of these industries, and perfecting the statistics in service industry.

In the spatial layout of the modern service, the planning guidance should be strengthened, and the construction of the office buildings and related facilities should be accelerated in order to promote the integration of service industry. The modern service integration areas should be formed with high-end service, better commerce environment, and assorted facilities, which can be the core panel points in service industry with clear demonstration and strong radiation to promote the development of the relative service industries. The central urban districts should find their own "comparative advantages" in the construction of integration areas of modern service industry to form the layout of division of labor in service industry with their own features and malposition competition.

In addition, the input to the research capital should be increased, and the knowledge, technical contents, and development level of modern service sectors should be improved with the help of technical advancement. The informatization degrees of the service sectors should be promoted in order to facilitate the application of modern new industries and their organizational patterns. The system of professional qualification certificates should be advanced extensively and the standard system of service industry should be established. The path personnel training should be widened, and more overseas advanced talent should be attracted and employed in order to train the realistic service talents who can adapt to the requirements of international service industry and master the foreign languages. The training for positions and professions should be strengthened in order to improve the level of the personnel in service industry.

Chapter 10

Evolution of Spatial Structure of Globalizing Cities

Essentially, the evolution of the urban spatial structure is the reflection of human, social, and economic activities in space. Because of the significant changes in their economic activities, the globalizing cities must be evolved in the urban spatial structure. In its history, a normal, common, and acceptable form did not take shape because of the different research perspectives of every discipline, different cultural backgrounds, and different development levels. Due to the difference in the general structure of urban space and spatial structure of global cities, perhaps it is more appropriate to research from the perspective of economic globalization, information technology, network, and hierarchy of multinational corporations. In the same perspective, Friedman, Sassen, Thame Blake, Fanji Atlantis, Queensman, Wegenaer, those named here are just a few, explored its impact on city spatial structure in developed countries (Clark, 1982; Brotchie *et al.*, 1989). But to the globalizing cities in the developing countries, the evolution of their spatial structure is characterized by its base, condition, and environment. Therefore, in this chapter, based on the analysis of their tendencies of the evolution of the spatial structure of the globalizing cities, the author will focus on the relying paths and development models of the spatial structure of the globalizing cities.

10.1. Evolution Trend of Urban Spatial Structure: From Single Nucleus to Multicenter

Urban Spatial Structure is the layout model of combined urban elements. In essence, it is a comprehensive and complex reflection of the interaction between different factors such as human economy, society, cultural activities, and natural elements. It is the specific reflection spatially of the urban arrangement modes (Gallion, 1983). According to popular views in the Western world, the urban spatial structure is the combined relationship between the geographical location of urban functional areas and its distribution characteristics. It is the projection of urban functional organization on the spatial area. In the long run, the urban spatial structure is the process of dynamic evolution, and its speed of evolution is non-even. The globalizing cities are usually in the process of significant changes, and the rate of the evolution of urban spatial structure is usually accelerated. Thus, it is necessary for us to be familiar with the basic tendencies of the evolution in urban spatial structure and facilitate the significant changes in the process of globalization.

10.1.1. *The spatial structure of traditional city with single core*

Traditionally, urban planning and urban spatial structure will undertake multiple functions such as lifestyle, production, culture, education, and politics in a limited urban space. Therefore, an obvious urban functional center or a central city is formed. Moreover, the mono-center will spill over to the outside space, which is reflected in early theories of urban spatial structure. Among the theories, the most representative is the mode of concentric circle put forward by Burgess based on the analysis of using mode of Chicago urban lands. Burgess (1928) infers that urban space spreads in a divergent pattern. Burgess stated in his paper "The Residential Distribution of American Cities", published in 1928, that the center of the city is the central business district (CBD), outside the center, the first ring is industrial zone, next to it is the worker's residential zone and the high-quality residential zone, and the last is the so-called commuter zone. Hoyt, an American land economist, put forward the fan-shaped theory, in which he thought that the tendency of urban residential land extended to the suburbs along the main traffic lines with the least natural barriers. As a whole, the fan-shaped structural mode is based on the structure of a concentric circle, which maintains the spatial structure features of "mono-center" and "ring-layer structure". But he stressed the distinctiveness of the spatial distribution of the residential zone of the upper classes. Later, Mann (1965) combined the above two modes and put forward the theory of "concentric circle: fan-shaped". Similarly, Taaffe and the other researchers (1963) put forward the theory of urban spatial mode combined with the five parts, namely, CBD, central edge zone, central belt, outside belt, and suburbs. Russwurm (1975) put forward the territorial urban structural mode composed of the urban core zone, urban edge, urban influencing zone, and countryside backland.

In the practical development of cities, there appeared similar urban spatial structural modes described in the above theories. To sum up, they are two categories: the closed ring-shaped divergent structure and the open centripetal divergent structure. The former is a compact ring mode, which is the so-called mode of "pie-spreading", in which the population gathers in the urban center, the constructed zone spreads outward, and the urban shape extends outside in rings. Though limited by terrains and traffic lines, in essence, it is identical to the features of the fan-shaped structure put forward by Hoyt. The latter is a divergent non-ring mode, which can be divided into two kinds: one is the mode of axle strap, in which the city extends outside along a main traffic line or an express way, thus forming the linear corridor structure; and the other is the star-shaped divergent evolution mode, in which the city extends outside along several development axles, every business center extends from communication crossing to every main roads, and thus a star-shape structure is formed. The typical representative is the famous Copenhagen mode of "finger-shaped development mode": its characteristics are the divergent distribution of urban functions along the express traffic corridors and the wedge-shaped grassland between them. The city will extend outward along the different development axles.

In comparison, the two kinds of traditional urban spatial structure mode have their own advantages and disadvantages. In the closed ring-shaped divergent structure, the power of the economic center is usually strong, and the layout and extension of the city will have better compactness, and the rate of urban land usage is comparatively higher. Meanwhile, due to the fact that the new-extended zone spreads along the urban edge, it maintains a better cohesion with the former constructed zone. However, the mode of "pie-spreading" from the urban center to the outside will result in another ring beyond, which is not beneficial to the increasing energy spreading; thus the functional load undertaken by the urban central zone will be higher and higher, and the capacity of urban will be oversaturated and overloaded, especially in transportation and environment. And moreover, with the extension of the urban scope, the overall life cost of the residents will be increasing day by day.

Compared to the closed ring divergent structure, the open concentric divergent structure is urban spatial organic mode with the core of traffic axles. It enables the comparative gathering of urban extension and the complete exertion of the transportation infrastructure. In the meantime, it will be beneficial to the combination with the surrounding areas by the main traffic lines. Moreover, without the separation of definite ring-shaped roads and green belts, the increasing urban energy will spread easily with the help of public traffic main lines, thereby being helpful for the fast growth of cities. This mode is well identified by the urban state of Scandinavian countries. But this evolution mode will cause serious environmental pressure as well, especially in the mode of the axle belt. Though the rate of land usage is higher, the rational division of whole urban functions will be affected because of the limitation of the mono-axle. Though the star-shaped divergent evolution mode has more transportation divergent axles, and avoids the irregular spread of the urban constructed zone to surrounding areas and the appearance of a gathering urban zone like spreading a pie, the inappropriate planning and regulation will result in a "pie-spreading" process in a disguised form. Meanwhile, the whole life cost of the residents will be increasing with the extension of the cities. Irrespective of whether it is a closed ring-shaped divergent structure or an open concentric divergent structure, the common feature is the urban spatial structure with only one center.

For a long time, the mono-center mode was the main stream of urban spatial structural evolution. The typical representative is the famous Great-London planning mode put forward by Abercrombie in 1944, namely, the urban structure is made up of radiation ring roads, the closed green belts, and satellite cites. This was inherited by the latter Tokyo Capital Ring in Japan in 1959 and the Moscow Planning of the former Soviet Union. Influenced by the modes, the development of China's bigger cites inherited the urban spatial structural mode with monocenter. The urban spatial structure of the bigger cites such as Beijing and Shanghai is characterized by the typical features of this mode. Among them, Beijing has the typical concentric divergent rings, the main urban functions gather in the old city (mono-center), with ring roads and green belts surrounding the old city, and the urban population distributed in the suburban satellite cities. While Shanghai has the features of the typical star-shaped divergent structure, that is, with central city as the main body, the city extends explosively in low density along several development axles.

In the following, we will analyze the urban structural mode and the features of Shanghai City. Up to now, the urban spatial shape of Shanghai is from the constructed zone of the central city to the surrounding areas, which can be called a coexistence of "extension from axles" and "extension based on rings". The extension from axles (from south to north along the Huangpu River) refers to the extension mainly from Minhang District (Southwest) to Baoshan District (Northeast); the extension based on rings usually refers to the area including Pudong New District, Songjiang District, Qingpu District, Jiading District, and so on. At present, the extension along axles, including Minhang and Baoshan Districts, and the extension based on rings, including Pudong New District, are combined with the central city; in fact, they are the overflowing zone of the central city. Some sections of the extension based on rings, including Songjiang District, Qingpu District, and Jiading District, are combined with the central city. And moreover, the gap between Songjiang District and Minghang District as well as that between Jiading District and Baoshan District is becoming smaller and smaller, which can be said to be a whole area. Therefore, though the spatial structure of Shanghai extends in a star-shaped in low density, it is actually a pie-spreading extension based on central city. According to the graphs of aerial remote sensing, by 2005, the constructed areas of the central city and combined area extended to 898 sqkm, among which, the area beyond the outside ring increased from 74 sqkm in 1995 to 305 sqkm.

The overall planning of Shanghai in 1986 stated that we should change the situation of layers based on concentric circles and make use of every available space; take all the elements, including central city, satellite cities, small towns, and countryside towns into consideration; form a layout of open mode with multicenters and combined cities, with the central city as the main body; and finally combine the seven satellite cities, main small towns, and main cities in the surrounding provinces by expressways, first-class highways, and fast track transportation from a few main routes. As a consequence of this practice for a few years, the satellite cities did not come into being. In the late 1990s, Shanghai put forward a conception of "One City Nine Towns" and implemented it. In the actual practice, the construction of "One City Nine Towns" did not combine with the construction of track traffic transportation or new towns based track traffic transportation, and gathering population did not form at all. Instead, a few villa complexes and residential areas were constructed.

So, though the constructed zone outside the central city of Shanghai was spreading outward, the new cities did not develop independently, and the development zones, industrial zones, and construction of towns outside the new cities were constructed dispersedly. If we thought assume that the constructed zone includes the combined area over 1,500 persons per sqkm, factory area with low population density, bigger green land, and construction site for airports, its size was 447 sqkm in 1995, 616 sqkm in 2000, and 892 sqkm in 2005. It shows that constructed area beyond the central city accounts for one-third of the central city. However, the distribution of population is still in the mode of gathering in high density in central city and scattering in countryside and towns. In 2005, the density of Shanghai population was 2,804 persons per sqkm. According to the statistics of the Committee of Population and Family Planning, the permanent population density is 33,900 persons per sqkm within the inner ring, 17,500 persons between the inner ring and the medium ring, and 1,400 persons beyond the outside ring. The population density within the inner ring is 24 times as much as that beyond the outside ring. From above, this extension did not make city function transfer to the outside area, and the mode of population gathering in the central city did not change at all.

10.1.2. *The non-adaptive between the mode of mono-core and globalizing city*

Historically, the urban spatial structure with mono-core was a must in the process of the founding and development of a city. Many cities developed from a central point and then extended in the rings or along the axles in a static and regular state. For example, many medium and small cities in China were always in the mode of rings and axles in early time. That is why the mode of mono-core is a regular way of the development of common cities. Up to now, many cities are still in the mode of development. However, the increasing development of the cities, especially the further extension, requires us to change the original mode. The urban spatial structure is always in the process of evolution, and the ideal urban spatial structure is not the terminal one.

The evolution process of the urban spatial structure is always related to the change of the two basic vectors (scale and speed). To investigate the evolution of urban spatial structure should take the two vectors into account. Without them, it will be meaningless to discuss the ideal urban spatial structure or compare the advantages and disadvantages of development in different modes.

The evolution process of urban spatial form and structure is related to change of the scale and the speed. To a small-scale city, the mode of mono-core may be more appropriate. But when the city extends to some scale, this mode will not be adaptive. The reason is that development similar to spreading a pie will definitely result in serious disadvantages such as overpopulation, heavy traffic, and worsening environment conditions.

The evolution process of the urban spatial form and structure is related the vector of time. To a city developing in a regular speed, this mode may be more appropriate. But when the city developed in an irregular speed, this mode apparently is not appropriate. Thus, unlike the traditional planning theories which state that the evolution process of urban spatial form and structure is related to the vector of time, the choice of the development mode depends on the growth speed of the city, not on the degree of development. When the speed of the city development reaches a critical point, the rational development mode will be transferred. The irrational mode in the development stage in low speed will become more rational.

To a globalizing city, the two vectors are always obvious. A globalizing city usually has a bigger population and covers a huge area in the scale of development; some of them have become mega-cities. For instance, between 1982 and 2005, the number of permanent residents of Shanghai increased from 11.86 million to 17.78 million, which is a relatively large increase. A globalizing city is usually in the stage of irregular development with regard to development speed. Especially in China, in the process of accelerating development in cities, co-functioned by compensating effect and high-speed economy growth, the coastal cites are always developing in an irregular speed. For example, the constructed area of Guangzhou in 1978 was only 80 sqkm, but reached 279 sqkm in 1999. In the timespan of less than 25 years, "2.5 new Guangzhous" were constructed, with the annual growth rate being 5.9%. As a globalizing city, it is usually the destination place of population emigration and movement. Another example is Shanghai, in which the household population decreased in 12 successive years from 1993, while the permanent population increased rapidly as a result of floating population. The floating population in Shanghai was 2.37 million in 1997 and 5.81 million in 2005. In the net population growth, the floating population accounts for 91.24% of the whole population growth in Shanghai, which accounts for 25.51% of the floating population throughout the country. Though Beijing restricted the scale of population more strictly, it did not stop the increasing growth of urban population. When P. R. China was founded in 1949, the population of Beijing was 1.5 million, in the following 50 years, its population growth rate is 3.5%, that means that 1 million persons were added every 10 years.

With a huge scale and development in irregular speed, the development mode of urban spatial structure with mono-core seems to increase inappropriately. This kind of highly concentrated urban spatial structure without functional zones restricts the urban development in space and the complete exertion of urban functions. No matter the development in rings or the extension along axles, the huge energy resulting from urban gathering cannot be spread. The satellite cities beyond the central city cannot grow well inside and are consequently swallowed by the extending parent city. Though the ring roads like dams try to stop the spreading of the central city, the overflowing city function will rebound and exert more and more pressure on the central city, and consequently, a stronger overflow will come into being and pour over the dam and the people begin to construct new dams (Zhao, 2001). As a result, more and more rings will be constructed, and the pie will become bigger and bigger. The function of the central city cannot be spread effectively and full played. In the previous chapters, we state that the functions of a globalizing city should meet specific requirement and regulations, which is the strong and comprehensive coordinative functioning of a global strategy. In the urban spatial structure with mono-core, its comprehensive functions are difficult to be strengthened or reinforced in a limited space, or only single function can be reinforced. Obviously, this is incompatible with the requirements of a globalizing city.

Therefore, a globalizing city has to change the urban spatial structure with mono-core and determine new modes of city development. Otherwise, it will lose the development opportunities and stop the rising of a globalizing city. We have some expensive and profound lessons from international practices in this aspect. For example, Tokyo refused to change its spatial structure in a high-speed growth era and lost golden development opportunities. When the Second World War ended in 1945, the population of Tokyo was 2.78 million and the urban land usage was limited in an area with a radius of 10 km. With the economy reviving after the war, urban land exploitation, with the center as Tokyo, was spreading increasingly. By 1997, the core zone of Tokyo covered an area of 625 sqkm, and more than 32.58 million people lived in the metropolis area of 17,200 sqkm, which accounted for 25.9% of Japan's population. Due to the lack of urban function spreading effectively, the urban spatial structure with mono-core of Tokyo resulted in the highly gathering of urban functions in central city and caused land prices to rocket in the central city. But Japan hesitated to adjust Tokyo's urban spatial structure and distribute its functions. The urban development strategy of Tokyo in 1959 was the mono-pole mode of "Green belts + Satellite cities" at the beginning, which later changed to the mode of multicores and multicenters, but it was not so effective in practice. Later the conception of disperse land structure with multicenter, put forward by National Comprehensive Development Planning in 1987 was resisted by the local government of Tokyo, which was actually the beneficiary of the mono-core mode, and later the planning of extending the capital was put forward. As a result, the development of Tokyo was limited more by the concept of an urban spatial structure with mono-core.

Not surprisingly, Seoul is another example of a city following the model of urban spatial structure with mono-core. With the growth of urban scale, Seoul did not transfer its structural forms; the syndromes of Seoul are the same with those of Tokyo. Though Seoul was aware of these limitations earlier than Tokyo and finally put forward the planning of moving capital to another place, it lost the best opportunity because it has passed the climax of urban development. Seoul became a huge metropolitan city and it was impossible to construct a new capital like the old one (Fang, 2000).

Therefore, in the process of globalizing cities in China, it is necessary for us to realize that the long-term traditional urban spatial structure is inappropriate and we should adjust urban spatial structure and distribute urban functions and form a new spatial structural form which is more adaptive to the globalizing cities.

10.2. Remodeling the Spatial Structure of Globalizing Cities

In the context of globalization and interaction of information, modern cites and the spatial structure of the residential areas are characterized by the presence of multicenters. The main reason is the increasing variety of urban planning, fast transportation and communications, social and economical events, and the increasing extension of city scales. The international practices show that, in the modern metropolitan area, the mode of an urban spatial structure with a multicenter is more adaptive and more common; it is more adaptive to the globalizing cities, and thus it is a wise choice to reshape the urban spatial structure with multicenters.

10.2.1. *The transforming to urban spatial structure with multicenter*

In the development process of theories, after Burgess and the others put forward the theories of the urban spatial structure with monocenter, as early as in 1945, Harris and Ullman (1945) put forward the theories of urban spatial structure of multicore. To them, there are four factors influencing the distribution of urban events, namely, some events need a few areas located in the city center with proper facilities, some events needs the bordering areas, some events tends to have resistant or negative effects to other events, and some events have to locate in inappropriate places because they cannot afford to the expensive cost of the ideal ones. With the interaction of the four factors, the influence of history, or the features of some areas, the distribution of regional spaces formed their respective cores. But this theory attaches less importance to the functions between the multicores, especially to the analysis on the differences between the cores and the orientation of the overall development of the city. In 1981, Muller broadened the theory of multicores, and put forward a new mode of spatial structure of the metropolis, as an urban spatial structure composed of the central city, inner suburbs, outside suburbs, and city edges. Among them, outside suburbs form several small cities. Therefore, compared to the mode of multicores, this mode can be named the mode of multicenters.

In such a case, the population of the central city moves to the suburbs, including the main important industry sectors, and there is a tendency to gather in different centers of the suburbs. At the beginning, the sectors are mainly the manufacturing industry, followed by logistics, retailing, and service; facilities such as culture, education, sanitation, and entertainment. As more and more companies and financial institutions appeared in suburbs, the various kinds of economic events are distributed in different centers of the suburbs. So, the suburbs will have more complete functions and thus form the new city district closely related to the original central district of the city, and an urban spatial structure with multicenters is shaped. Of course, the emergence of urban multicenters is based on the connection of track transportation, which is distributed in the areas along the main lines of transportation. This fast track transportation network meets the needs of road traffic, information transmission, food, and entertainment of city life, and connects the different centers to an organic integrity.

As a globalizing city, it is urgent to adapt to the changes of this urban spatial structure. The reasons are obvious: one of them is that a globalizing city has to face and experience the new breakthroughs of science technologies, and the rising service sectors has replaced the traditional industries and become the mainstay industry, a global network system based on modern information technology has formed and changed, making it a core question to match the special functions of main nodal points to the urban spatial structure with multicenters.

In the process of a globalizing city, the high gathering of the energy is bound to transfer to a powerful extension, which will be divergent and influential to the surrounding areas or even to the whole country. The spatial distribution and structure make it necessary to break the limits of administrative urban districts and arrange it in a broader spatial scope. That is to say, we need to consider the spatial distribution and structure in a global urban scope. According to this requirement, a globalizing city needs to connect to the surrounding areas, including the other cities, but it is not the sole connection, which needs to cross the spatial separation of the suburbs (of course, this can be made up by the improvement of inter-city transportation), what is more important is to eliminate its impact on the divergent distribution.

Therefore, the functions of the central city are distributed to the suburbs, which form the connection of multiple points with the surrounding areas. That is, the outside direct connection is largely realized by the suburb central points, which results in the indirect connection with the central city. The functions of the central city need to be extended to the suburbs, but it is not sporadic extension, which is surface gathering in the broad scope of the suburbs, but a gathering of several panel points, which is a spatial gathering with emphasis. So, the relationship between the central city and suburbs is not a simple one, like "core-and-surrounding" any more, but a relationship of "core-and-sub-core", that is, a distribution structure of "divergent networks" between the central city and several new cities. This urban spatial structure with multicenters can meet the requirements of radiation and extension of a globalizing city in the stage of high-speed development. In this spatial structure, the radiation and extension of urban high-speed growth is not a successive overflowing wave any more, but a transition of independent quantum groups in a universal urban space (Zhao, 2001). In addition, the city is not driven by a simple engine, but by several parallel engines at the same time. This will be helpful for the effective release of all growth potentials and minimize the mutual friction between different functions.

The change of this urban spatial structure is actually the outward manifestation of interaction between the city and its outside environment and the interaction between different factors in the city system. Due to the gaps in the bases of urban development and binding prerequisites, this urban spatial structure is actually in a diversity mode, with different characteristics in reality. The following are two typical modes:

The mode of point axis forms several gathering region or points along the main traffic lines, with a series of green belts or agricultural lands between them. This mode avoids the disadvantages of the mode axle belt with mono-center and distributes its various functions effectively, and there is much more flexibility in urban development. With the green belts and agricultural system between the different gathering areas, it will be beneficial to the persistence of urban ecology, for it supplies an ideal place for people to have picnics and necessary vegetables and supplementary food to the city residents. This mode increases the cost of commutation and shopping, but if the efficiency of transportation is improved and a fast transportation system is constructed, it will result in a better development choice.

The mode of dispersed groups will limit the scale of the central city and distribute the new development in the surrounding areas, forming several sub-centers. The whole city is made up of several dispersed groups. The evolution mode of dispersed groups will be beneficial to distribute the overcrowded urban central area and form several subcenters in the medium scale. The spatial structure and function distribution will have a better flexibility, amassing and dispersing are interlaced in appropriate density. At the same time, urban and rural areas are interlaced too, which is beneficial to the ecological balance, and the residents can have picnics in their leisure time. This layout can boost the better-facilitated urban sections in a small scale in a better environment. Thus, this mode will be more prosperous to the development of bigger cities. With the increasing scale of urban construction, the cost of commutation and shopping will be increased as well, so a fast and convenient transportation system needs to established.

Irrespective of whether it is a mode of point axis or a mode of dispersed groups, their common points are the following. On one side, the city tries to limit the endless extension of the central area by increasing the central city density and the heights of the buildings. On the other side, several cities of different levels are formed surrounding the central city. These cities consist of a regional city, which can be a multilevel city or a city with multicenters. For example, Reyn, a city in France, is a typical representative of a city with multicenters. It has a real central city, and its density is increasing, surrounded by green belts. There are sub-cities around Reyn, with agricultural lands between the cities in different levels. All of them together consist of a single, whole regional city (Huet, 2005).

The urban spatial structure with multicenters changed the traditional and universal spatial distribution of cities, which embodied the new conception of urban development such as the coordination between the whole and the parts, and the union between division of labor and integration. Thus it extended the original space of the city and distributed the different and inter-relative group functions by its geographical features. With the support of modern transportation and communication technologies, the high concentrated urban functions are well distributed, with obvious features. At the same time, the division of different areas will not influence the sharing of the different urban functions. It realized the reintegration of urban functions in space and formed a modern city with integration of different functions in a bigger space scope.

Due to the fact that it is more flexible in adjusting urban spatial structure and more adaptive to the future cities, many cities, especially the globalizing cities, are adjusting the spatial structure and transforming to a city with more centers. For example, LA was confronted with many "city diseases" in 1960s and had to redraft its planning scheme. LA put forward the conception of 56 centers, 37 of them were in urban areas including community centers, sub-centers, and main centers. The regional guiding planning of Paris (The Strategic Planning of Paris Area in 1965 and The Guiding Essentials of National Territorial Development and Urban Planning in Paris Area between 1965 and 2000) put forward several strategic measures. First, it is necessary to consider the distribution of industries and population in a bigger scope, several city groups will be formed along the lower reaches of Seine in order to decrease the industry and population gathering in Paris area. Second, nine sub-centers will be constructed in the suburbs of Paris in order to alleviate the pressure of the central city of Paris. Third, five new cities will be constructed along both sides of Seine to contain 1.6 million persons, which can disperse the population of Great Paris Area and break with the tradition of intensive development in rings. Leon, Lille, and Marseilles followed the model of Paris and began to construct new cities around them. In order to effectively evacuate the population and industries in central areas, Tokyo formulated The Planning Scheme of Tokyo and The Law of Urban Rebuilding in 1956 and put forward the precise principles of rebuilding plan of Tokyo, namely, "One-center (Tokyo) to Multicenter (Shinjuku, Ikebukuro, and Shibuya)", "One-pole (Tokyo) to Two-pole (Tokyo, Tama New City)", constructing open urban spatial structure with multicenters by laws to change the current situation of function gathering in central city and promote the distribution of urban central functions. Singapore denied the divergent urban distribution in rings suggested in 1953 and reconfirmed the urban spatial structure like necklaces. On the basis of prosperity in old city areas, Singapore developed 8 new cities and 50 new towns round the islands on the South Coast and formed the space of green heart (the water sources and traveling and leisure resorts). The city centers are connected by fast and convenient track transportation and expressways. Some other cities which transformed into multicenter from mono-center are Cairo, Hiroshima, and Bombay.

10.2.2. *The dynamic mechanism of the evolution of urban spatial structure with multicenters*

The spatial structure of a globalizing city which is transiting from mono-center to multicenter has to face one problem — dynamism. The transmission of the urban spatial structure can be promoted only by grasping the inner dynamism and making the best use of the circumstances. Therefore, the shape and dynamism of the urban spatial structure is always the key problem in the study of urban areas. The Western theories explain it in different perspectives. Among them, the theories by analyzing economically can be the typical ones to explain the dynamic mechanism of the urban spatial structure.

The scholars have a common idea: the growth and extension of urban space depends on the evolution process of urban forms and spatial structure, and the social and economic mechanism is the contradictions between gathering and distribution throughout the urban development. The different combined forms in gathering and distribution result in the diversity of urban forms and spatial structure and the different features in different stages. Equally, the transmission of urban spatial structure of a globalizing city is the result of the combinations of gathering and distribution. By and large, the transmission from mono-center to multi-center can be illustrated by the transmission from gathering to distribution, and a relative gathering in distribution, which can be a special combined form of a relative gathering dominated by distribution.

Saarinen thinks that the dynamism of urban gathering is caused by social and economic reasons such as compulsory gathering, speculative gathering, and cultural gathering, and distribution usually includes the process and mechanism of differentiation, scattering, and isolation. The main elements influencing the separation of urban space are: insufficient development space in cities; development of the regional economy, which accelerates the interdependence in cities, with the result being the outside dragging co-functioned by the inner elements of the cities; the improvement of information means, making it possible for the cities to choose the industrial spaces; the pursuit of the residents for a better quality of life and environment; and the guidance of the government policies. Analyzing the above elements, we conclude that it is appropriate, in the transmission of urban spatial structure, for a globalizing city to transition from mono-center to multi-center.

In a globalizing city, under the context of the interaction of globalizing and informatization, especially a globalizing process that is involved passively, it is necessary to analyze the different elements influencing the transmission of spatial structure and analyze them globally. From this perspective, the traditional and classical economic theories, which discuss the influences on abstract land prices and deprive the realistic political elements, seem to be insufficient. In this matter, introducing the contents of political economy, the structural school of land economies will have more authority. In a new Marxism point, Harvey (1985) put forward that the change of urban spatial structure is the prerequisite for the capital flow and reproduction in the new productive forms in the relationship of the capitalism. This school explains internationally that the change of urban spatial structure is originated from the new territorial division of international labor. This means the developed countries have become the management and research centers in production. The chains of production are moved to the regions of developing countries, in which the cost of land and labor are less expensive. The result is that the manufacturing industry in developed countries is decaying, which cause the decaying of the traditional industrial cities. The new management center and researching center are usually located in the suburbs, which transform the city into suburbs. At the same time, the cities in the new rising countries have the advantages of land and labor and attract the manufacturing industry and processing industry; and the cities develop more and more and extend outside. From this, we can infer that the basic dynamism causing the urban spatial changes in developed and new rising countries is the flow of international capital.

To some degree, this theory reveals the impact of globalizing on urban spatial structure globally. As a whole, it can explain better the dynamism mechanism of the transmission of urban spatial structure of a globalizing city. But this explanation is not accurate, because it did not reveal the dynamism of the transmission of urban spatial structure in the perspective of industrial gathering. In the previous chapters, we point out that the territorial distribution of global production chains of transnational corporations has the tendency of relative gathering. With the extension of territorial gathering, the special productive service companies such as the regional headquarters and R&D centers of transnational corporations and financial institutions will move to the main cities of the region. In fact, to a globalizing city, both the transmission of manufacturing industry and processing industry in developed countries and the international transmission of service industry, which can be developed and extended, stimulate the transmission of a urban spatial structure.

In the above explanation, aiming at the relative gathering of universal production chains, we must introduce the theory of scale economic effects. This theory stresses that the scale economic effect with a similar functional land usage has a tendency of gathering, and finally, the gathering of urban land usage. The commerce, service, and industry need a certain scale of gathering, and result in different specific economic zones. Therefore, the CBDs in the central city become the center of commerce and finance, the original suburb industry areas, and newly built industrial development zones become the centralizing place of manufacturing and reshape the urban spatial structure. This theory explains why different development zones emerge in the process of international industrial transmission and become its main support, which is stronger persuasion. But this distribution of gathering is simplified, which means the service industry gathers in the main central city and the manufacturing industry gathers in the suburbs, which cannot explain well the reason of the new city's development based on the spatial structure with multicenters. These two problems will be discussed in the following chapters. Therefore, the introduction of this theory has to be amended.

Though the theories of global production chains and scale economics explain well about the dynamism in the transmission of a globalizing urban spatial structure, they cannot leave aside the basis of the theories about land distribution. The reason is that the changing land prices is the only result of international capital flow of global production chains and scale economy effect of product space gathering. In reverse, the changing land prices will influence the regional choice of capital flow and industry space gathering. That is, the difference of land prices inside the city will result in the redistribution of urban land and influence the urban spatial structure.

In market economy, the prices based on the relationship of supply and demand will decide the distribution of resources. In cities, the land prices decide the collocation of land resources, which is the current situation of urban spatial structure and directs future development. This basic idea enjoys very broad support and became the basic theory to analyze the urban spatial structure. In 1927, Haig suggested the regional conditions which relied on the value of urban lands and set the base of the economic model of urban spatial structure. In 1954, the American geographers, Harris and Ullman, also suggested that there were several separate centers inside the cities and the use of urban lands was growing around these separate centers, for example, commercial centers like CBDs and the other dominating centers of other special functions. These are the early bases of the analysis of the features of urban ecological space, and they are all the variables of economy, such as land, house rents, and statistic data. In the late 1960s and early 1970s, researchers such as Alonso (1964), Mills (1972), and Muth (1969) introduced Thunen's concept of regional rents in the balanced analysis of urban spatial structure. In particular, in neoclassical economy theories, Alonso (1964) analyzed the relationship between location, rent, and land usage. By analyzing the distribution of residential areas influenced by the land cost (land prices) and location cost (other expenses raised by location such as transportation cost), Alonso exported the functions of land rent biddings and found the regional structural balance points of individual manufactures. He pointed out that the different land prices result in different land usage, which were the most basic elements in shaping the urban spatial structure. Alonso explained more about the combined laws of land usages in finance, commerce, industry, residential areas, and suburban agriculture and systematized the economic theories of urban spatial structure which were developed and perfected by Brueckner (1986), Fujita and Ogawa (1982), Wheaton (1974), and the other researchers.

Many scholars in the West analyzed the theories by solid evidences and verified the dynamic explanation of changes in urban spatial structure in the theories of land collocation. Some scholars in China made some early efforts as well, for instance, Zheng (2004) analyzed the practical and digital land models of Jinan's urban land prices in different times and locations by applying Geographic Information System and concluded that the overall tendency of land prices changes was in accordance with the balanced theories of urban spatial structure, which was always changing successively in space. By applying the model of neuron network and data of housing release for commerce, Zhang (2003) studied the spatial changes of rents in different land usages in Luling County in Yunan Province; his results are the following: the net benefit (rent) from lands with the same function in the city center was usually the highest and will decrease with increasing distance from the city center; the equivalence line of the net benefit from lands with the same function was not the same as the concentric circles suggested by Alonso, limited by main roads, commercial center, distribution of public facilities, and rivers and geographical conditions, and the line was distributed in a complex polygon.

In the sense of micro and macro acts, or the rational decision from economic and active agents, it is necessary to consider the problem of "low input and high production". In choosing the sites for building factories or buying houses, the main basis is analyzing the land and transportation costs. When the transportation cost becomes lower, the suburbs will be extended. The overall input will be decreased with the low land prices in suburbs. Equally, when the effectiveness or cost of the suburbs (including the transportation cost, land cost, life cost, etc.) is bigger than that in central city, the suburbs will become new cities, because the input will be decreased for increasing the effectiveness of different units.

All in all, the theories of land collocation are more persuasive in analyzing the change of a common urban spatial structure. Therefore, explanation of the dynamic mechanism in the transmission of urban spatial structure from the perspectives of global production chains and scale economy requires the combination of these theories. Otherwise, the inner growth of the transmission of globalizing urban spatial structure cannot be well explained. However, the dynamic mechanism of globalizing urban spatial structure only in the theories of land collocation cannot reveal the features in the transmission of a common urban spatial structure. We think that the inner dynamic mechanism in the transmission of the spatial structure from mono-center to multi-center is based on the capital flow of global production chains, the industrial gathering of scale economy, the interaction of land collocation with land price as a core, and finally the process of location balance.

10.3. New Town Construction Based on the Spatial Structure of Multicenter City

In practice, the transmission of urban spatial structure from mono-center to multicenter is a combined process. That is to say, on the basis of old urban area with mono-center, with the successive extension of the cities, a new distribution form outside new cities and multi-centers result in the transmission of different modes of urban structures, which reflects the development and evolution of the different stages of the inside structure of urban spatial structure. Only the distance between the regulated areas and central areas, the relations between production and life and the new cities with relatively independence, and some scale can realize the transmission of urban spatial structure with multicenters. Therefore, in practice, we need to attach more importance to the construction and development of new cities in suburbs.

10.3.1. *The connotation and functions of new cities*

The development strategy of urban areas was carried out in some western metropolitan cities. One of the main points is to choose the right places surrounding the central city to construct the medium and small new cities with comprehensive functions. For example, the construction of new cities in large scale in the UK and other European countries after the Second World War was popularized. In the construction of new cities in 1960s in Holland, 15 new cities were planned, 13 of them were distributed in the famous Randstad. In fact, the construction of some new cities was successful while the others were not. For example, the construction of new cities in the UK and some other European countries was paused or even stopped by the disappearance of the dynamic power in constructing the new cities in high speed. The construction of new cities in Holland was a successful case. The poll showed the residents were unwilling to return to the original central city, and the employers, residents, and investors were satisfied with the new cities. But it resulted in the decaying of the central city, which was definitely a negative effect. The construction of new cities went on until the late 1970s, which resulted in the great cities in Holland such as Amsterdam, the Hague, and Rotterdam losing 500,000 residents and 100,000 jobs, as the vast old city and old industrial areas were abandoned (Du, 2000). From the lessons of success and failure, the problem to locate the function and the ones about reliance paths have to be solved in the construction and development of new cities.

First, we should state clearly that the concept of new cities is different from that of satellite cities. Though a satellite city has a respective scale, sufficient facilities of commerce and service (such as supermarkets and shopping centers), and complicated functions, it stays in close relations with the central city and continues to rely on it forever. However, the new city is an edge and relatively independent city with industries in high-density, multiurban functions, and is the new gathering center and growth pole of edge economy in the process of urban extension.

In addition, the concept of new cities differs from that of so-called new districts in some places in China. Beijing, Quanzhou, and other cities planned new districts in large scales, but they are actually closed to the central city, which are not brand new cities. In a great degree, the construction of new districts is the actual flow in large scales, which is the stronger backwave to the central city and does not change the spatial structure with mono-center basically.

As a new city in suburbs, it is characterized by the new gathering zone of new value of urban space, which is an important panel point between the central city and the suburbs, and even the surrounding areas. The aim of the construction and development of new cities is to contain the new urban functions, change the urban spatial structure from mono-center to multi-center, transfer the development mode from mono-core to multi-core, and realize the balanced space and coordinative development in metropolitan economy. Its obvious feature is to share the local urban functions, such as the moving of industrial areas and residential areas, and construct a stable, self-reliant, and complete social work system. The main functions of new cities are not the only extension and distribution of those in central city but the relatively independent urban functions based on the differences from the central city. Otherwise, it will become one satellite city of the mother city and cannot distribute the main functions of the city.

In the meanwhile, the new cities are not complete cities which are independent from the central city, but the organic compartments of the whole metropolitan city. Therefore, it is necessary to promote the construction and development of the new cities in accordance with the principles of integrity and order. In The Development Planning of Tokyo in Japan in 1956, it was stressed that the close relationship between the new cities and constructed areas was the compartment of regional urban space, whose aim was to promote the gathering development in semi-city areas, to strengthen the integrity of urban spaces, and to promote the coordinative and balanced development in urban areas. This was reflected in the construction of new cities in Paris, Tokyo, Singapore, and so on.

Thus, there is a problem of rational function distribution between the new cities and the central city. The central city gathers the key urban functions, industrial sectors, and their institutions. The new cities share the partial functions of the central city and gather some industrial sectors and their institutions, which are suitable to some urban functions. But the layout of their industrial space cannot be simplified by "service in central city, manufacturing in suburbs" principle, rather, it is the industrial space distribution based on the differences between central city and new cities. Besides the metropolitan industries, most manufacturing industries are gathering in the new cities and their surrounding areas. The service industries such as commerce, restaurants, hotels, entertainment, government, NGOs, international institutes, media, R&D, and universities are gathering in the central city, while the background service institutes such as technology, logistics, and data processing are gathering the new cities. As a whole, the spatial distribution of the urban industry is the following: the central city is dominated by service industry, and the new cities in suburbs are to simultaneously develop the manufacturing and service industries.

Due to the fact that the new cities shared the partial functions of the central city, they have different function locations and different characteristics and full play their own specific functions. For example, the planning of extending capital functions in the metropolitan rings of Tokyo clearly stated the exact leading function location in planning and constructing the new cities. The new city of Domo is located by the function of universities and commerce; Chiba, the gathering of international airport, ports and industries; and Ibaraki, the function of scientific city. In the eight new cities of Hong Kong, Tsuen Wan and Tuen Mun are dominated by container docks and storage transportation; Yuen Long and new city of Tai Po, the manufacturing industry; the new city of Tsueng Kwan O is developing in the direction of high-tech parks based on Hong Kong University of Science and Technology; Tung Chung north to Lantau Island and the new city of Ohori, the aero industries and ancillary service for the new airport (Liu and Liu, 2000). In the construction of new cities of globalizing cities in China, it is noticed that there is a problem of function location and the development of dominating functions and dominating industries. For example, Shanghai established the new city of Jiading District, which is dominated by automobile industry; the new city of Songjiang District, the industry of culture; and the new city of Lingang, the port industry.

It should be stressed that the leading or dominating function and features of the new cities are based on the fostering of their comprehensive functions. International practice shows that a new and relatively independent city needs to establish the polybasic systems of industrial structure and employment. Otherwise, it is not easy to supply the various and sufficient positions and to full-play the "anti-magnetism" in reality. If the residents in a certain scale cannot be attracted to live and work in the new cities, the so-called new cities will be empty cities. So in locating the leading functions of the new cities, it is necessary to combine the specialization and diversification organically, develop the distribution communities and pluralism actively, coordinate the industry gathering, supply more and more jobs, and meet the employment of the people from all walks of life.

10.3.2. *The relying paths of the evolution of new cities*

In the transmission of the urban spatial structure of China's globalizing cities to multicenter, we can borrow and apply the above theories and lessons about the function location of the new cities. But we may differ from the western developed countries in relying on the paths of construction and development of new cities.

With the extension of the suburbs, there are usually three stages in the relying path for the development of the new cities of metropolitan cites in western developed countries (Tao and Liu, 2003). The first stage is the stage of focusing the city, which means the new city is constructed in the near suburbs and dominated by the residential areas. It stays close to and adjourns the central city. The second stage is "semi-independent satellite city", which means, on the basis of the new cities dominated by residential areas, more commercial service facilities (such as supermarkets and shopping centers) are constructed with complicated functions; they have become the more important places for the middle classes to work and live, but they stay in a close relationship with the central city and rely on it as ever. The third stage is the edge new city stage, that is to say, with the rapid development of transportation, communication, and network technology, more senior residential areas and office building are being constructed in the suburbs, which promote the industry gathering and diversified urban functions. And eventually, the new cities will evolve into relatively independent edge cities.

But it is opposite in China, for the development of new cities of China's globalizing cities is usually closely related to the construction of the development zones. In the past 20 years, the obvious change in the suburbs of the bigger cities is the thriving of various development zones. It is interacted and pushed by different forces, among them is direct and foreign investment. As stated in the previous chapters, for a developing country involved in the globalizing and informatization as a developing country, foreign direct investment is the main outside strength in the process of globalizing China's cities. These companies invested by foreign companies, especially the transnational companies, combine their advantages of capital and technology with China's specific economic events. Many development zones are the first choice for the transnational companies in large scale, 30% to 40% of foreign direct investment is in the development zones in some cities. The rising of development zones in the suburbs of bigger cities in China is not only the outcome of manufacturing moving to the suburbs but it is also pushed by foreign direct investment and is the outside strength from the transnational companies. Apparently, there are some inner elements as well. For example, since the policy of paid use of land in China in 1987, the land price is the highest in CBD and is decreasing progressively, which promotes the gradual transmission to optimization and high effectiveness in urban land usage. The land in the central city is usually appropriate to the tertiary industry such as commerce, trade, finance, hotels, and office buildings, which has higher benefits and pushes the spatial reconstruction of original industrial events. Thus the lands of development zones in the suburbs become the main carrier of the spatial reconstruction. At the same time, the urbanization of the suburbs and agricultural modernization cause the transmission of land usage to non-agricultural use, which supply the land resources for the extension of urban land usage. In addition, the improvement in the agricultural productivity makes sufficient surplus labors freed from the countryside. The space gathering of township industries is another main strength in the booming of development zones.

While the suburbs in the foreign cities usually become the residential areas, these development zones in China will become the new industrial space, whose main function is the recombination of production elements such as capital, labor, technology, land, etc., in space. An industrial gathering will be shaped, including the vertical gathering, the horizontal gathering, and overlapping gathering. In essence, these development zones are the manufacturing gathering in the suburbs, which is currently a pattern and an important spatial panel point in the globalizing of economic events in China. Therefore, the construction and development of these development zones actually supplies new spaces for the disintegrating and distribution of functions of the central city, which plays an important part in the development of urban economy and the evolution of the urban spatial structure. These development zones have the similar functions of new cities in transferring the partial industries of the central city.

It is obvious that the construction of new cities of globalizing cities in China cannot set aside the development zones and find another new path. On the contrary, the construction of new cities based on the development zones can be more effective. As stated early, the stage of focusing the city of the construction of new cities in western developed countries is dominated by residence, later, it shapes the relevant industrial functions. However, as the new industrial space, the development zones have the relevant industrial function. The construction of new cities relying the development zones actually spans the stage of focusing the city and enters the stage of semi-independent satellite city. That is to say, the construction of new cities relying the development zones combines the functions of residence and industrial function and is helpful to the development of new cities.

In practice, it has to mend the inborn disadvantages in the construction of new cities which relies on the development zones. During the very early establishment of China's development zones, their simple function was envisioned as development, especially the land development for industrial production. In the planning of the development zones, the simple production layout lacks its relevant residence and service facilities. Apparently, it is totally different in the characters of the construction of new cities. Therefore, the construction of new cities, which relies on the development zones, should aim at the comprehensive development of the new cities with multifunctions. The further extension of the planning of development zones includes the land for industry, finance, trade, residence, culture and education, municipal administration, and green belts. It is a systematic project of reasonable planning and comprehensive development.

And moreover, the fatal disadvantage concerning China's development zones is the disorder of development and layout. In a very short time, the various development zones in different levels emerged like bamboo shoots after spring rain, characterized by their miniaturization and decentralization. After the later sorting and rectifying, some development zones were cancelled and merged. But this fundamental pattern was not changed. As we all know, as a relatively independent edge city, the new city needs to gather the relative space and a stronger industrial function support. This small and decentralized scattering of development zones cannot meet this requirement. These development zones cannot fit the regional choice at least in the planning. Therefore, the construction of new cities, which relies on the development zones, should be adjusted by the layout and distribution of the development zones. We should compare and choose the development zones with larger scales and stronger industrial function, or rely on the neighboring combined development zones.

Moreover, the construction of many development zones in China was planned as an industrial space to attract foreign investment. Though the convenience of transportation is considered, it is only the highway transportation based on cargo transportation. As a relative independent edge city, the new city is connected with the central city by convenient track transportation. That is to say, the new cities gather the industries and population that mainly rely on track transportation. Thus, the improvement of transportation connection and the establishment of the track transportation network are necessary in the construction of new cities relying on the development zones.

10.3.3. *The developing modes in constructing the new cities*

To the globalizing cities in China, the construction of new cities is to change the urban spatial structure with mono-center and extend the city capacity and radiation function in order to construct the main link between the main panel points in the global urban network. At present, some main cities enroll the construction of new cities into the key agendas. For example, in the 11th Five-year Planning Outlines of National Economy and Social Development, Shanghai stated clearly the construction of the nine new cities including Jiading, Songjiang, Lingang, Minhang, Baoshan, Qingpu, Jinshan, Nanqiao, and Chengqiao. Here we should say the construction of these new cities in the suburbs is not the traditional construction of towns but the construction of "a modern metropolitan city", considering Shanghai as a whole and abandoning the layout of doing different things in different districts or counties. Therefore, the construction of new cities should begin from the layer of Shanghai Metropolitan, the planning of Shanghai Metropolitan, and new cities should be scientific with a high starting point and be of high level and high quality. Different levels of spatial planning of new cities should be drafted and the functional location of each new city in Shanghai Metropolitan and even in the scope of Yangtze River Delta should be clear and definite.

International practice shows that the functional location of the new cities is very important, which influences both the establishment of development modes and the determination of the distance between them and the central city. For instance, the gathering development in the semi-urbanized areas in Paris is always the important compartment in the urban space, which attracts the increasing population in the overlapping zones of the city and the countryside and avoids the excessive population gathering in the central city of Paris. In the new cities near to Paris (30 km), there is convenient transportation connecting the central city in space. Taking the stable population in the central city as the presupposition, the new cities of London contains the moving population from the central city, avoids the connection with the central city, and keeps a considerable distance by green belts (usually 50–100 km). In the construction of new cities, Shanghai has to detail their functional location and shape the layout with definite functions, mutual complement, and cooperation with due division of labor and overlapping development. For Baoshan, Minhang, Songjiang, and Qingpu in the near suburbs, the construction of new cities should strengthen the inner development and avoid the connection with the central city. For Lingang, Jianshan, Nanqiao, and Chengqiao in the far suburbs, their connection with the adjourning cities should be strengthened in constructing the new cities.

Due to the above facts, it is necessary to make scientific planning on transportation development. To develop the group cities on the panel points along the axles is becoming the key mode of the development of both foreign cities and domestic cities. For example, it was stated clearly that the distance between the new cities and the mother city should be 20–40 km in the planning of new cities, according to the rule passed in 1970, and there is more convenient transportation modes between them. While developing the new city of Milton Keynes, great importance was attached to the transportation links between the new city with London and Birmingham. A fast transportation network is completed, which shortens the traffic time between the new cities and the bigger cities and increases the attraction of the new cities eventually. The overall planning of fast transportation network and information network between the new cities and the central city or between different new cities should be stressed in the whole scope of the metropolitan city, which will be the basis to fully play the role of distributing the industries and population in central city and thus promote the construction of the new cities in the suburbs relying on track transportation. The network structure in Shanghai central city and the divergent structure in the suburbs of Shanghai track transportation meet different requirement in different regions. The construction of track transportation in the suburbs should have two levels, that is, the main lines and the branch lines. The main lines are usually in a divergent structure and connect the central city and new cities in the suburbs; the branch lines should connect the new cities or the towns with the population of a certain scale.

The construction of new cities should be based on the clear planning and the development mode of dynamic balanced structure to maintain the sustainable development of the new cities. The development of the new cities is usually a dynamic process of evolution involving the interaction between the whole metropolitan system and its environment. In the process, the dynamic structural balance in developing the new cities will surely result in the unbalance of functional collocation and may be lost in the vicious circle of development trap. For example, the new cities attach too much importance to the function of industry fostering and residence and undertake too many industrial and real estate projects and pay less attention to the transportation facilities, social facilities (such as hospitals, schools, culture, etc.), and public service facilities. The lack of high-quality resource distribution will make it difficult to attract more people to work and live, and the abundant input does not translate into sufficient benefits, which makes it more difficult to input more and develop further. If lost in such a development trap, the new cities will become empty cities, and thus stagnate the construction of other new cities.

Thus the construction of new cities should be considered as an ecological system. It is necessary to grasp the pace of construction and development according to the changes in ecological niches. The connotation of ecological niches (Luo and Zhen, 2000) divides them into "condition" and "tendency". The former niche includes the energies, the resource possession, the levels of population and economy, the economic growth rate, and so on; the latter niche includes the exchanging rate of energies, the productivity, the population increasing rate, the economic growth rate, etc. The combination of the two niches is decided by the width and size of the ecological niches. Generally speaking, the condition is the basis of tendency, and tendency stimulates the transmission of the conditions. The change of the conditions is usually in the shape of "S" and is an accumulating process whose speed changes from slow to fast and then to slow again. The change of tendency is in the shape of a bell, which increases gradually at the beginning and then decreases gradually after reaching a certain summit.

The development and construction of the new cities are usually increasing rapidly in every aspect in the growing stage and have more developmental potentials. Meanwhile, it is characterized by unstable development and wide range of fluctuations. Therefore, it is necessary to deal with rational distribution in space and time and the coordinating development in the long run, improve their compound functions, and avoid the unbalance of dynamic structure. On one hand, the balance of urban functions in the whole new city such as residence, employment, shopping, offices, culture and entertainment, leisure, and public facilities should be emphasized. Its aim is to supply the residents of the new cities with diversified and comprehensive urban services, to meet the various requirements of the local people, and promote the gathering development of local social economy. On the other hand, the balance between the population scale and the employment capacity should be emphasized as well. One of the aims is to stop the aimless increase of population, which will cause great pressure of employment in the new cities. The other is to promote the coordination between different social and economic groups or classes by supplying the different employment and urban services. Coordination between the dispersed residence and the centralization of employment should be focused too, and we should combine residence with office spaces, especially the mixture of the residence and working sites in the micro-level. For instance, the fixed mode of functional distribution in the planning layout of the new city in Keynes, Hamilton in London was broken; the mode of a dispersed layout of industrial factories and other public institutions was adopted. The bigger factories were evenly distributed in the whole city and the smaller ones in the residential areas, the non-industrial employment centers such as clinic centers, colleges and universities, etc., will be distributed in the edge areas of the city. This enabled the possible even distribution of transportation load, and it will be easier for the residents to work nearby.

In addition, the ecological balance between the people and the nature should be stressed. The concept of the "countryside city" put forward by Howard was applied in the planning of new cities in foreign countries. Ecological corridors such as green parks, walking streets, avenues, and green belts were focused, and the countryside style between the buildings and natural landscape should be constructed for people and nature to coexist harmoniously, and new ecological communities should be created. In the construction of new cities, the local historical cultural resources should be cherished, the local traditional neighborhoods, ancient buildings, and villages in the construction of the new cities should be well preserved and exploited in order to enrich the historical culture heritages and connotation values and improve their specific attraction. All in all, the aim in the development mode of dynamic structural balance is to construct the relatively independent edge city with enriched functions, a complete structure and a good environment.

The international practice shows that the development and construction is in different modes. But the core involved in it is the problem of development bodies. The theories of urban political bodies created by Stone (1989) and Logan and Molotch (1987) suggest that, in the construction of cities, the relationship among the government (the so-called strength from the government), the groups of industry and commerce and finance (the so-called market strength), and the community (the social strength) is affecting the construction and change of urban spatial structure. To them, the changing of urban space is the material reflection of the change of political bodies (namely the alliances governing the power and wealth inside the cities). If the developers who invest in the commerce, retailing, or city center allied with the municipal government, the reforming of the city center will become a stress of the municipal government. If the overall investment is limited in a certain city, the changing of urban space will be following: the city center is newer while the common communities stay unchanged or even decayed. This will surely result in the outside moving of high incomes from the common communities and the decrease in land and housing. The low incomes will move in and replace the original residents with high income, and this will cause the reshaping of urban space. The real estate companies and huge construction companies, allying with the municipal government, will form new development zones, with selling points on the market becoming the stress of the municipal government. The government will invest more on the construction of infrastructure in new zones and thus attract more development investments, which transform the new zones into hotspots of outside extension. Thus, the membership and the leading position in the political body will cause the changes of urban space.

In reality, bound by the different conditions, the different combinations among the above three bodies will result in different modes in developing the new cities. Globally, there are three effective modes in the construction of new cities: the development mode with the government as the main body and the enterprises' operation, modeled by London; the development mode with governmental controlling and commercial management, modeled by Hong Kong; the development mode with the private developers as the main body; and preferential policies of the government, modeled by Tokyo. In a comprehensive perspective of China's present binding conditions, the development tends to take the model with the government as the main body and enterprises' operation. One of the prerequisites of the theories of urban political body is the private controlling of social resources in market economy. This prerequisite is not suitable in present China, for the local government in China controls considerable social resources, especially land and policy resources. And moreover, it needs the support from the government in the rapid distribution of urban scale and the mending of spatial structure, which cannot be undertaken by common market strengths. In addition, elements such as the relying paths pushed by traditional administration and the immaturity of market growth will urge the development mode of new cities dominated by the local governments.

In the development of the new cities, the main means applied by the governments is land resources. The input in infrastructure accounts for a high percentage in the growth in constructing the new cities, which cannot be supported by regular taxes. And moreover, the stable origin of taxes in new cities is not fixed and has to be resolved by transferring payment. In such a context, the benefits from the lands, especially form the primary land markets, become the key prerequisites. Thus, the well-organized benefits from land will decide the speed and quality of the development of new cities to a great degree.

Though the local governments in China control considerable social resources, they are limited in the large scale and fast development of the new cities. Thus the urban government will draw support from the markets and non-government capitals to accelerate the construction of the new cities and permit the various enterprises of different types to take part in it. To obtain investment from the industrial and commercial companies and the real estate companies, the urban government must meet their requirements and offer them the most favorable terms, such as the tax reduction or exemption, the improvement of infrastructure invested by government to attract the more investment. Therefore, an ally between the municipal governments and the enterprise groups with resources is shaped. The development mode dominated by the government needs the joint participation of market strengths, no matter whether it is operated by enterprise or commercial companies.

The practice shows the joint participation of the government strength and the market strength is the guarantee of accelerating the construction of new cities. But it is noticeable that the alliance between the government strength and the markets strength is usually greater than that of the society. China's social strength is being fostered and is apparently weak at present. On this occasion, their ally is usually at the cost of social benefits, and benefits from urban development are not shared by citizens. Thus, the supervision by the social forces should be strengthened, and the participation of social strength in decision should be fostered. In the process of developing the new cities, the governments should seek out the balance between the promotion in constructing the new cities by attracting investments and the benefits in constructing the new cities shared by the citizens.

In the end, no matter what mode it is, policy support from the government is necessary. International lessons illustrate that the relevant policies drafted by the government in land acquisition, financial taxes, housing construction, and attraction to the new cities will advance the smooth implementation of the planning in constructing the new cities. For example, the UK made the laws of land expropriation compulsory, which meant the local governments had the right to expropriate the land in towns or countryside for the development of action lands or force the land owner to sell the lands; France carried out the systems of "land bank reserve" and "preserved construction zones"; the US carried out the policies of "legal right to expropriate lands"; Japan carried out the flexible policies of "reserved zones" and "planned controlling zones" (Huang and Nin, 2003). In attracting the residents to the new cities and with the favorable policies, London developed the low-price simple housing at the beginning and provided free heating; France stated clearly the distance (20–40 km) between the new cities and mother city with large-scale public facilities. On one hand, Japan raised the land price in central city and limited the new factories and colleges or universities, on the other hand, it supplied complete life facilities in the new cities, and created the same or the better working and living conditions compared to that in the central city to attract urban population and industries. It is worthwhile for us to learn and borrow from the above lessons.

Chapter 11

Creative Cities and Cultural Creativity

The rise of global cities is actually the brand new process of a series of changes between the interior relationship and the exterior relationship. In this process, there are various problems and frictions, such as the adjustment of economic structure and the transmission of urban functions and development paths. In the meantime, there are a series of crises in the process, such as structural unemployment, unbalanced finance, social differentiation, unbalanced psychology, and disappearance of a sense of community belonging. International practices show that only creative cities can solve these problems and adapt to this brand new change. The creative city includes the development of all aspects in economy and the society and runs through the contents of different sectors in the urban development. However, the cultural strength is playing a leading role in the development of a modern city, and its combination with a creative city will result in the development of all aspects of the city.

11.1. Creative Cities: The Soul of Globalizing Cities

In the process of a globalizing city, outside strengths such as globalization and informatization are apparently necessary; otherwise, the prerequisites of globalizing will not come into being. The keys to react positively to the outside environmental conditions and grasp the development opportunities are the interior reflection ability and the adaptive adjustment. For a globalizing city in the context of globalization and informatization, the keys to promote the urban transformation are to stimulate the creation of individuals and institutions inside the city, to reform the systems, to improve the mechanisms, to foster the market functions, to develop the relative industries, and to allocate institutions and personnel. Therefore, innovation is the most important factor, and the soul, of a globalizing city.

11.1.1. *The basic assumptions of the organic body of the city*

As pointed earlier, the rise of a globalizing city does not rely on the regular capitals, the accumulation mode of essential factors, the simple extension of urban scales, or the growth of economic power, but on the rising of urban function levels and competition and cooperation in the global network based on the transmission of development modes, the updation of functions, the reshaping of industrial system, the adjustment of spatial structure, the reform of social organism, and the improvement of the ecological environment. If such a concept is established, the next problem will be "What strength can promote the rising of a globalizing city?" For some people, it will not be a problem at all. But in fact, this problem is not solved in the theoretical analysis.

The earlier leading views in the study of a globalizing city usually have an implied theoretical base and take the city as a machine in the assumptions such as world city, global city, or information city. That is to say, the city is a social and economic system with geographical and spatial densities and is being operated in the mechanism of urban physics. Thus, the change of social economy, in the views of the urbanologists, is only the transformation which is driving the machine, such as the promotion from national capitalism to global capitalism. To them, the transformation of the driving strength with the comprehensive function in the combination of local special factors "creates" the new and modern cities. In the sub-consciousness of the leading views, a global city is a mechanical device with the flowing and collocation of such key factors as global capitals. According to this assumption, the rise of a global city relies on the promotion of outside strengths and is the result transformed by the outside driving strength.

We do not deny the impact and function of the driving of outside strengths in the development of a city. It is illustrated that the transformation driven by the outside strengths such as globalization and informatization is the prerequisite for the rise of a globalizing city.

In this sense, globalization and informatization are the key strengths to push the globalizing city. But why is it that some cities can be transformed to globalizing cites while the others cannot, with the similar conditions and outside strengths in the same outside environments? Here a problem of the interior adjusting and adapting abilities arises, that is, the reactive abilities or reflective abilities in the changing outside environments and the transforming outside strengths. These abilities are key in a globalizing city's rise. Therefore, we tend to consider the city with these abilities as a dynamic organism which can replace the assumption of mechanical device in the leading views in the study of a globalizing city.

Michael (1997) put forward the opinion that the modern city is the center of economic reflexivity in a certain place or region and stated the interior initiative of the cities, which implied a theoretical basic point to consider the city as an organism. To him, as a complex with special, different and local social relations, the city functions the global capitalism. Its economic events such as manufacturing and service industries are interdependent and gather in the city. Interdependence is indirect or non-tradable which is not the direct connection of local trade in urban economy. The key factor in the differences between the bigger cities and medium-sized cities should be the conventions, customs and relations. Due to the transforming of modern capitalism, the importance of these factors in increasing and they construct the economic reflective abilities, namely, in the different layers of enterprises, markets, governments, households and other main bodies, the possibility of different factors to function in the process of economic transforming.

At present, with the quick permeation of the economic globalization and the development of the informatization network, the action patterns of various action bodies are diversified and react to the outside change more rapidly than before. The enterprises, governments, other institutes, and families have to adapt to the fast changes of other bodies and adjust their own actions. In this process, the result of assembling is that the reflex ability of the organizations and groups is strengthened. In economy, this reflex ability means to take part in competitive learning actively; in the society and consumption, the aim of the reflex ability is to gain "satisfaction" to deal with the corresponding conditions resulting from economic reflection, that is, the new risks that every enterprise, every family and individual, and every public institute have to face. The reflex ability of the city exists in the fields of production and consumption and depends on the relationship between the different bodies inside the city and the conventions and customs formed in the city, which result in the varied reflex abilities in different cities.

In the globalizing economy, the city is not only a component of a global machine, on the contrary, it has an obvious feature of local economic power. We can see clearly that the hosting of some global companies or institutes is actually to apply this local specialty. On one side, they hope to get the market path with local specialty and serve it and gain benefit from it; on the other side, they also hope to get the special reflex ability from the local specialty and take it as an input to global production and marketing system. All in all, as a comprehensive economic and social complex based on the geographical space, the city is an organ with reflex abilities. Its reflex abilities depend on the relationship between different main bodies and the conventions and customs formed inside the city. This means that organizations such as governments, enterprises, and citizens jointly participate and interact and are dynamic.

If we consider the city as an organ with reflex abilities and inside abilities, not as a device with mechanic structure, this organ will have to face the problems concerning how to react or reflex when facing the changes of outside environmental conditions or outside impetus. In general, there are two possibilities: the positive reaction and the negative reaction. The former is to promote the transformation and the development of the city adapting to the changes of outside environmental conditions, stimulate the inside vigor and creation, and absorb and merge the new outside impetus. In brief, it is a creative city. The latter has to adjust in the friction of the outside powers and inside factors, not adapting to the changes of outside environmental conditions. Therefore, in the implied assumption of a mechanic device in the leading ideas of global urban studies, we cannot deduce the inherent logic of a creative city. Only considering the city as an organ with reflex abilities and inside abilities can we extend the basic proposition of a creative city.

From the history of urban development, a creative city is a leading strength to promote urban development and realize urban transformation, and the creative consciousness is always playing an active role and exerting a positive impact, which fundamentally changes the urban spatial pattern, functional structure, and development orientation. Especially in the past 70 years, the countries and cities underwent a leap from manufacturing economy to information economy, and from information economy to cultural economy. This challenges the value system that targets the benefits and powers in traditional industrial society, creates new development opportunities for the space and thoughts in urban development, and paves way for the urban society to enter into a new era of innovation and development. From the development tendency of future cities, Hall (1998) once pointed out that three problems are the themes of the future cities: the transportation technologies and sustainable urbanism; the more unjust urban world; and the ever-changing economy, families, and citizen society. Apparently, these problems have to be solved in the means of a creative city. As Harris (2001) pointed, the city is always evolving, and the future cities have to update and remould themselves consecutively in economy, culture, society, etc. The development vigor of the future cities lies in their sufficient innovation abilities and flexibilities to exist and develop in an ever-changing environment.

For a globalizing city, its soul is the creative city. For a creative city updates and optimizes the urban industrial structure, promotes the shape of the industrial expansion and value chain, strengthens the urban value activities and value flow, and thus promotes the urban values. Meanwhile, a creative city is helpful in not only avoiding the urban diseases such as the unbalance in structure, the aggravation of social contradictions, the worsening urban environment, but also in helping to promote the urban development comprehensively, harmoniously, and sustainably, to shape the basic layout of modern urban economy, modern urban civilization, and modern urban life. In fact, a globalizing city differs from a common city in knowledge or the knowledge features and value orientation of the urban bodies, not the urban geography and natural resources. This creation consciousness reflects the degrees of the people's knowledge to update and decide the orientation and destiny of urban future development. Thus, a creative city is a positive response to the outside impetuses such as globalization and informatization, and it is an effective way and means to full-play the inside vigor and potential and promote the rise of a globalizing city.

11.1.2. *A creative city: its basic connotation and era features*

The basis concept of a creative city is to stimulate the innovation of the individuals and institutes inside the city, to excavate their potentials, and to create the values. Here we should guard against a misunderstanding in cognition, that is, a creative city covers not only the technological innovation, and we cannot discuss the problem of creation breaking away from the city itself. Therefore, we have to understand and know the basic connotation of a creative city.

As we all know, urbanization is initially an economic process in which technology plays an important role. That is the reason why the people tend to explain the process of its development and evolution in the concept of assembling economy based on technological progress. The saying "technology decides the possible territory of urban economy and spatial evolution" tells us the evolution of a metropolis relies more on the technological progress. Bairoch (1988) suggested that, in the past centuries, urban development was limited by transportation technology. Toynbee (1970) said that in the first 5,000 years of urban history, the geographical extension of the city was completely limited by the ability of communication on foot, he found the parallel relationship between the curve of urban expansion and that of technological progress. We believe the progress and breakthrough of the technology will bring new opportunities for a ready metropolis to face the sudden changes. The technological changes mainly influence the cost of transportation and communication and release the strength of economic assembling, which will result in the further development and updating of the metropolis.

In this perspective, we can see that the assembling economy can explain the evolution of the metropolis well. The reason is that it constructed the model of an assembling process based on the accumulating mechanism and can be used to explain the stability of the metropolis; meanwhile, it enlightened us about the index value of the technological reliance, such as the result of the changes of transportation and communication costs. But the explanation of the assembling economy to the evolution of the metropolis ignores the positive effects of the system, which implies the assumption that the system is limited by the outside world (Lise and Huriot, 2004). In fact, technology can only decide the possible boundary of the space form created in economic development. The system is the game rules in the society and its aim is to regulate the human behavior artificially; it encourages or hinders the communication of economic reform and various interactions. From the international practice, in a certain initial economic level, what decides the economic growth and development is the systematic factors but not the technological factors. The changes of the systems have their own logic and paths. The evolved system can result in a good economic effect and recession or stagnation as well. Therefore, the system arrangement regulates and limits a series of choice in the economy body to a great extent; it decides the forms of the economic organizations. The innovation of systems is based on the advanced civilization accumulated in human society and reflects the historical and cultural features of the country, thus it has an obvious comparative advantage.

We think that the system arrangement constructs a framework together with the technological conditions, in which the specific economic structure and spatial form are developed, and thus the functions and forms of a global city are shaped. In return, the features of the economy and space are influencing the evolution of the technology and the system. In the long run, this interaction makes the basic features of a global city both permanent and evolving. The evolution of specific functions of a global city is the result of combined actions in the changes of technology, system, and economy. Thus a creative city in the rising of a globalizing city covers the innovations in technology, system, economy, society, etc., and their interactions and combined functions as well.

Observing from the features of the city itself, it assembles a number of economic factors in high density; the factors are relative to each other, form a strong assembling effect, and have stronger economic distribution functions. In an open and competitive environment, the industrial and commercial industries inside the city are involved in the extensive international division of labor and exchange. Various new ideas, new concepts, and new technologies are widely and rapidly spread. In this case, a creative city has features such as innovation assembling, group gathering, and opening up. Accordingly, the abilities of a creative city include the common ones such as innovative concepts, innovative resource inputs, innovation encouragement and protection, etc. The more important ones are the assembling of urban energies, the increasing of energy levels, and the systematic innovation abilities to enlarge the economic flow.

Thus, a creative city usually has a stronger inclusiveness and integration, which covers the development of various aspects in economy and society and penetrates the contents of urban development. It includes:

The development model of a creative city — the transforming of the economic growth mode, the harmonious development of the society and economy, the overall development of the people, the sustainable development of the city, etc.

The basic functions of a creative city — the pivotal functions expressed by the flow of resource factors, the main panel point resulted from the effective collocation and added value of resources, the urban comprehensive service functions in order to serve the whole country and connect the whole globe, etc.

The industrial system of a creative city — merging the concerned industries and constructing the new industrial systems by new industrial paths, the priority development of modern service and advanced manufacturing, etc.

The spatial structure of a creative city — the spatial structure adjustment of function distribution and urban forms, the improvement of urban infrastructure system, the structure adjustment of population distribution in urban space, the relationship with its surrounding areas, etc.

The organization frame of a creative city — the transforming of urban functions and the adjustment of its organizations and institutes, the development of the social intermediary organs, the fostering of the community management and its organizations and institutes, the cooperation and authorization between different organizations and benefit groups.

The social organ of a creative city — the reforming of social population management and social resource management, the improvement of public facilities and public welfare, the citizens' participation in urban management, the social security and stability, etc.

The environmental atmosphere of a creative city — the vigorous industrial development environment, just and ordered market environment, good legal environment, suitable living environment, flexible and harmonious social environment, working environment which is beneficial for the gathered talents to full-play their talents.

The civilized life a creative city — construct the learning city, improve the education and health, promote the development of advanced culture, have a healthy public entertainment, develop the cause of physical culture and national fitness's etc.

All in all, the creation of a creative city includes not only the innovation of technology but also the innovation of various aspects such as economy, technology, society, and culture. Certainly, in the context of a creative city, what is more important and critical is the innovation of systems, which includes the formal systems and informal systems such as culture and customs, and moreover, the structural updating and efficiency improving based on the effective systems.

In addition, we must notice that a creative city is actually a dynamic process. Under the different backgrounds and the different stages of urban development, the contents and the stresses of a creative city are always changing and they are not the same as ever. Hall divided the history of western cities into three times in the perspective of innovation:

(1) the innovation time of technological-production, such as the industrial revolution in Manchester in the UK in the 1770s, the machine industry in Glasgow in the UK in the 1840s, and the industrial technological designing and innovation in Berlin, Germany, in the 1870s;

(2) the innovation time of cultural-intellectual, such as the emergence of Hollywood in Los Angeles, USA, the revolutionary impact by Elvis Presley in Memphis, Tennessee, USA;
(3) the innovation time of cultural-technological, the new cultural industries are becoming the new dynamic and innovation orientation of the urban development. According to the predictions by Hall, the new innovative city will include three categories: the old-line metropolis such as London, Paris, and New York; the sunlight-belt and easy-living metropolis, such as Vancouver and Sydney; and the reviving old cities such as Glasgow and Newcastle (Wu *et al.*, 2004).

For a globalizing city, the contents of stresses of a creative city should consider not only the realistic factors such as historical bases and the development stages but also the development tendency of a modern city and the obvious time features, that is, the combination of culture and art with modern technologies based on the internet technology and supported by the new service industries with added values. Under the background of globalization and informatization, the creative cities with cultural and technological innovation as their stresses are becoming the focuses of western urban study, which is the appearance of new economic spaces, for example, Scott's (2000a) study on urban cultural economy, and Florida's (2002) study on innovation classes, Pratt's (1997) study on the new media industries of the UK. Hutton's study on the economies of the western inner cities systematically describes the new economic activities based on the innovation, and knowledge of designing and advertisement is becoming the new orientation in London, Vancouver, and Seattle, in which a new social space is shaped (Thomas, 2004). It is noticeable that a creative city with the cultural and technological innovation as its core contents stresses more on the combination of culture and arts with information technology. In the information network revolution, the competition and cooperation between the cities will be extensive and further developed. In such an environment, factors such as the quality of living environment, the level of cultural service, and the acquisition of information or knowledge are becoming the important geographic issues.

In fact, besides the traditional geographical factors such as the land prices and the accessibility of spaces, the more specific and soft geographical factors are becoming more and more important. Meanwhile, the cities gain more opportunities to develop their own initiative and foster their fast reflection abilities, to improve their positions in the network by creating the attractive geographical factors. But in the past, the studies did not consider the combination of culture and information technology as the core contents of a creative city, but attached more importance to the geographical factors of IT manufacturing industries and the regions of hi-tech production assembling. The first result is that the cities focus simply on IT and its development, and enlist it as a new growth point of urban development; the second result is that the cities supply the relative policies to create the conditions for new technological production, for example, the construction of science gardens, technology city, and new industrial areas based on the flexible division of labors among different enterprises inside the cities. The concept of simply focusing on the production and industries of new technologies did not solve the problems arising from the urban development in the background of information network revolution. The scenario is the same as that in 19th century, when the cities attributed their basic economic development to the geographical advantages of the production of the steamers and ignored their application in the manufacturing process of various products and their impacts on the urban development.

Therefore, we must further our study on the impacts of information communication technology on the extensive urban economy and its operation, management, and distribution. We should recognize that what information revolution brings is not only the transformation of industries but also the changes in the living and producing patterns under the backgrounds of informatization, digitalization, and networking. The rapid development of modern information technology and the extensive spreading of social economies result in the changes of the whole production patterns and social living patterns. In the process of a creative city, the scope of its policy-making must extend from the simple researching of information technology to the various aspects such as production, collection, spreading, and application of extensive information in the social development. The strategic cores of a creative city must be the development of economy and society by applying the information technology to the greatest degree, and its global competition by the combination of the information technology with culture and arts.

11.1.3. *The paths and environmental conditions of a creative city*

As stated above, a creative city involves various fields and enriched contents, thus the patterns and paths of the realization of innovative targets will be diversified as well. Due to the dynamic development and its time features in the contents and the cores of a creative city, the patterns and paths of realization of innovative targets will have different stresses in different historical stages and have corresponding contents and stresses.

In a creative city with culture-technology as its key contents, the extensive application of modern information technology is not only the premise and base but also one of the main paths in realizing its innovation targets. That is to say, the residents, various organizations, and governmental institutes are applying information technology extensively to improve their own regions. Among them, the construction of modern long-distance communication and informatization facilities is to gain competitive advantages in order to attract the growing enterprises, which can create more knowledge and promote the urban development.

Some scholars named the alliance with the essential features of regional improvement by applying information technology as a "smart community" (Roger and Marco, 1999), its geographical scopes covers from a neighborhood to an alliance of multi-country regions. The smart community which is improving its region by the application of information technology has the following different features:

(1) the investment of high-tech and the acquisition of talents;
(2) the training of talents and profession;
(3) the competitive experience and the cooperative habit;

(4) the open and transparent finance;
(5) the abilities of transforming the debts to assets; and
(6) the formulation of the strategies to encourage the participation of the public. Every smart community has different resources and development targets in different patterns but has the same results in gaining the healthy development of economy and the common views of the public and their loyalty. The community must be smart in order to reach the aims of improving its region by applying modern information technology. Some scholars disassemble the word "smart" to the following: S stands for studying and strategizing, how to apply the long-distance communication and information technology in its own region; M stands for monitoring to information technology and economy, the tendency and changes of the residents' requests inside the city or the region; A stands for the arriving at how the bodies of the city and the region apply information technology to improve the regions; R stands for the reaching out of the cooperation between the city and its surrounding areas; and T stands for taking rapid actions: if it is lagged behind, it will mean that other cities gain the competitive advantages in the new economy (Kellar, 1998). The process of improving the regions by applying information technology is actually an adapting and adjusting process in which the city, as an organ, reflects to the outside factors. Particularly, it includes the contents of its combination with culture and arts.

The different value concepts and knowledgeable gaps are formed by different histories and cities, thus the main factors of the urban development at present are resulted from different value concepts, innovation consciousness and creative abilities. Thus the studying and creative abilities of the city and the innovation consciousness are very important in the process of a creative city. For this, some scholars put forward the concept of learning city or region. Though a universal definition of learning city or region is not determined, it is related to a system to promote innovations and is becoming the core strategy in the development of many cities (Larsen, 1999). The common point of a learning city or region is that all the participants focus on innovation and studying to foster their global competition, develop the industries and services of knowledge concentration, and establish their jobs on the basis of local studies and the abilities of innovation to face the changes. Therefore, studies (including individual studying and institute studying) are one of main paths of a creative city. Individual studies refer to the acquisition of knowledge and skills by formal or informal channels, which is usually a lifelong learning, not only the learning and training on campus. The institute (or system) studies refers to collective learning based on informatization and networking, which relies on the information exchange about production, procedures, and working organization. In the creative city with culture-technology as the core contents, the individual's life-learning is obviously important. Only by learning, an individual can gain higher salaries and better opportunities, while the society benefits from the labors who are more flexible and have more knowledge on advanced technologies. But this is only one part of the society, the more important is the combination of individual studies with the extensive surroundings under the background of globalization, which make the city or the regional system or institute recognize the importance of studying and innovation and enable itself to study. Therefore, a creative city requests all the participants and cooperators, no matter whether they are public authorities, private enterprises, or private organizations or individuals, to consider studying and knowledge spreading as the core chain in urban development.

Our experience shows that, in the process of studying and knowledge spreading, different main bodies will feel that they have a common target, recognition and trust, a common value orientation and the network relationship between the cities will be fostered, and thus a driving power of a creative city will be formed. It is noticeable that, for the enterprises and knowledge institutes assembling in the same region, culture and knowledge will be possibly shared and thus a process of interaction and mutual studying inside the city will be accelerated. At present, the large-scale global companies begin to seek for the merging their R&D activities with the local assembling in order to gain the highly localized researching and technological abilities and fully exploit and develop the network between the high-level enterprises, the local business support and institutional resources, and the globalization of the local markets.

The specific application and implementation of the main paths and means of a creative city cannot separate from the corresponding environmental conditions. What is more, the different innovation patterns and paths need some specific environmental conditions. A creative city with culture-technology as its core contents requests naturally the material bases such as urban economic bases and urban facilities but it also is limited by the soft factors such as the history of the city, its image, the value system or life patterns of the citizens, the citizen's sense of belonging to the city and so on. Rogers (1976) pointed out that a better social system environment which was beneficial to innovation was one of the main factors in innovation. The reason is that the transforming process from new ideas to new products, new values, and new wealth is not linear but has to undergo many ups and downs, in which the policies and human social environments to stimulate innovations are equally important. In 1978, Tornqvist, in the Geography Department in Lund University, developed the concept of creative milieu which was similar to the concept of innovative milieu put forward by the French geographer, Aydalot. The basic footing in constructing these concepts is that innovation exists in some intangible atmosphere. For them, the innovative environment is based on the culture of the communities inside the city; it is a coordinative functional mechanism which is beneficial to the innovative activities. The four core features of this innovative environment are the following.

(1) the information transmission from person to person;
(2) the knowledge included in reality or in artificial memorized storage;
(3) the abilities to develop some relative events though limited by the outside environment;
(4) the creative abilities, which means to create new things from the above three events, it is considered a type of coordinative function. Thus, the innovative environment refers to the trust and promise among the various activity bodies based on the culture

and systems, the sharing of the resources such as technology, information, and knowledge in the frequent interpersonal interactions; the basic order and atmosphere of highly coordinated and cooperative relationship between them. It is embedded deeply in the social structure and the interpersonal relationship network.

For a creative city, the crisis sense of the city may be the first and necessary factors in the innovative environment. If the government and the citizens of one city are quite satisfied with their current situation and development, the innovation will not be stimulated. If the city is quite successful at present, further increased innovation inside the city will become more difficult. The crisis sense in the current situation and the process of the urban development can make the city recognize its improper and unsatisfactory events, and the inspiration of innovation can be stimulated. If the city has such a crisis sense, a power can be emitted to face more and greater challenges, and the innovation can last forever.

Second, the innovative environment has an obvious and unbalanced feature. That is to say, the innovative environment is murky and unstable, like a river in the period of instability. This innovative environment is extensive in size and diversified in culture and has a better cultural exchange, both internally and externally. If a city is always developing in a stable situation and following the prescribed order, the opportunities of innovation will be lost, let alone the passion of innovation. As the mediocre cannot create, a highly conservative and very stable society which has no chaos is not the better place to produce creation. For example, an ambitious person likes to live in London but not Frankfurt because the life in Frankfurt is considered to be simple and boring. Therefore, attracting the high-ranking advertising talents in Germany to Frankfurt will be very difficult because there is no environment in Frankfurt to stimulate their inspiration (Beaverstock *et al.*, 2001). The unbalanced and diversified environment between the experimental requests and actual opportunities and the unstable conditions in operation can create more innovation opportunities, and thus a drive of innovation can be stimulated. According to the experience, we know that a highly creative city is usually a city in which the old orders are challenged or the old orders are toppled while the new orders are not shaped, that is, the city where the economy and society are being transformed. These transforming cities are in the rising tide period in the development of economy and society, in the throes of the transforming in social relationship and values and world views, and in the tense state of struggling between the conservative strength and the radical strength. And thus a vacuum space in the society and the gaps in the social orders will emerge. The vacuum and the gaps supply the possible space for the new innovative activities and the emergence of innovative abilities, which is quite important for a creative city with culture-technology as its core contents.

In addition, joint participation which is beneficial to innovative activities and the environmental environment of effective organizations are equally important. The internal dynamics of a creative city is from the innovative thoughts and the self-consciousness sense and reliance that are encouraged and stimulated in the city, which means everyone in the city should have the sense of participation and responsibility. This participation is not just a slogan, but entails innovative ideas to be stimulated and the ways to be taken in exploiting the various resources. This common participation enables the gathering main bodies to focus the sharing of resources, to interchange the knowledge of implied experience, to produce studying and knowledge overflowing, and to promote the flowing of information and knowledge and the creation of new ideas. At the same time, every layer, from the individuals to the institutes, needs to train its abilities to comprehensively integrate and practice and to put the innovative ideas into practices. It means that the element of innovation should be penetrated in each process of urban decision making, no matter whether they are public or private institutes, the economic field, or the social and cultural fields. These mechanisms and abilities of effective organizations are critical to keep the vitality and vigor of the city and the basic ability requests of a creative city.

All in all, the sense of crisis spurs the creative city on the exchanges of information and culture, the assembling of knowledge, the coordinative function of the variability and diversity of the activities, the common participation, and the mechanism of effective organizations create important environmental conditions for a creative city. This innovative environment is beneficial to promote the virtuous cycling in self-renewal and self-improvement of innovative activities, which maintains the sustainability of a creative city.

11.2. Cultural Strength and Creative Industry During the Rise of Global Cities

In the current urban development, a creative city with culture-technology as its core contents transforms the new cultural industries into the new dynamic and innovation orientation of the urban development. In the globalizing cities in China, besides the creative cities, we should attach more importance to the cultural innovation representing the urban soft strength and foundation of cultural and innovative industries as new economies.

11.2.1. *The orientation of cultural strength in the urban development*

Pushed by globalization and informatization, the city is not only the center of economy and politics but also the center of modern cultural innovation and spreading. Combined with the development tide of the time, the high-quality residents are updating the innovation of advanced and modern culture continually and spreading it globally and making themselves one of the main components in the global mass culture. More important is that a new strength, that is, the strength of urban culture, is replacing the simple material production and technological progress and becoming the mainstream in the urban economic development.

The urban culture is expressed by the history of the city, its social structure, its visual image, and so on, which is reflected in the various aspects such as social and cultural activities, the physical environment, etc., and further functioned in urban residents. The public combine the perception of the culture with their memories and thus a cultural image of the city is formed. In a broad sense, the urban culture includes the following three aspects:

(1) the difference and merging between the life patterns in the city, in the countryside, and their junctions;
(2) the urban culture constructed in the diversity of the patterns sought by the urban residents;
(3) the image demonstration of the new pleasant residential areas in the city and the sites of urban entertainment, which is important to improve the city's attraction and its economic development. In the long run, these contents are always the themes of urban researching (Bittner, 2001; Roost, 2000; Kirchberg and Göschel, 1998; Zukin, 1995; Kearnes and Philo, 1993; Kirchberg, 1992; Wynne, 1992; Crane, 1992).

The charm of the urban culture lies in that it can change people in their consciousness, concepts, and modes of thinking and thus create the image, standing, and reputation of the city for the potential consumers in the city. And moreover, the culture itself becomes the dynamic of income and economic growth and creates more new industries unknown to the public. In addition, in the present world, the social trust and competition constructed by urban culture will become the main factors to decide economic competition. Thus the Republic of Korea thinks that the 21st century is the era of urban culture, and to strengthen the construction of urban culture will become the most important chain in maintaining urban vitality and competition in the 21st century.

Why is the cultural strength increasingly dominating in urban development? Professor Florida once suggested a hypothesis: With the enrichment of material life in the after-industrial society, people would be concerned less about the economic conditions such as wages, but they would request more of humanity and environment such as music, arts, climate, humidity, afforesting of the city, and various convenience facilities in urban life. It is quite similar to the value of "after-materialism" that Inglehart (1990) proposed earlier. He once pointed out that, in the developed countries, people's concern about economic growth was replaced by lifestyles and the realization of self-value. Gobbi proposed a similar point of view in the perspective of leisure and stressed that the position of leisure will be further strengthened and the people would be concerned more about the relationship between leisure and health. It is expected that people will devote more time, energy, and money to various fields such as the relaxation of mind and body, free recreation, artistic culture, health tour, and so on. Thus, the cultural environment and atmosphere of the city will be more attractive to people, particularly, the workers who have received higher education, and the enterprises which need them will assemble in these cities following such labor force.

In a broad angle of view, the culture has a vital force, which is innately connected to innovation. The reason is that the culture is guiding the value system and development targets of the city, the innovation space and innovation orientation of the city can be found after observing the various functions of the city in the perspective of culture. Therefore, the cultural features and qualities of every city supply rich soil and abundant resources for it to develop innovatively and stand out in competition and cooperation. A great variety of geographical modes related to cultural economy and media industries were formed in 1980s, a concept that proposes the cultural producing will lead the local gathering of specialized companies and form the representative globalizing cities such as Los Angles and London, which are the experimental examples to support this opinion (Scott, 1997). More and more people realize that the international impact and controlling power of a globalizing city reflect in not only the economy but also its political impact and cultural permeating power as well. For a globalizing city, material capital and material wealth are the media, its powerful economy and modern industries are the basic support to become the main markets in the world and the hub of economic contact, and the culture is the base of an urban spirit. The culture is considered as the prime motivation of economic development and the main path of shaping the international image of these cities.

Furthermore, the culture is the core resource for a globalizing city to maintain its distinctiveness and competitive advantages in the world. Under the background of globalization and informatization, the globalizing cities tend to be the same in urban patterns, systems and regulations, and the activities of citizens, so the differences between cultures are becoming more important and valuable. For example, as a famous world cultural city with a history of more than 2,000 years, the government of Paris in Great Planning of Paris in 1994 proposed the development targets of Paris is to be a city with historic sites, artistic buildings, and cultural heritages and a city full of energy, creation, and vitality at the same time. As a result, the core competition of urban development in Paris was formed with its specific cultural resources and the traditions of a historic cultural ancient capital along with the charms as an international city. New York is not only the center of American finance but also the center of its science, culture, and information. The specialty of London lies in its global businesses and finance services; its world-class historic heritages, arts, culture, recreation, and media; the high-quality communication facilities; and its outstanding education and medical treatment. These advantages of London lead it to be a leading city in world businesses. Therefore, these globalizing cities have profound cultural establishment, high cultural storage, and advanced cultural facilities, which form well-operated urban cultural industries in the system of market economy and develop the relative industries such as tourism. These cities are loaded with local traditional cultures, they are good at attracting and merging the cultural elements from the other districts, and they gain the greatest benefits from the urban cultural resources when they become the gathering centers of the world cultures.

However, the globalizing cities in China at present tend to focus on the accumulation of material capital and material wealth and neglect the construction of the soft strengths such as history and culture. In the construction and development of some cities, the manufacturing or the simple aim of business is always developed in the first place, the others, even the housing construction, are usually secondary. The patterns and policies of urban construction and development are designed to carry on the flowing of transnational capitals. The development patterns of some economic special zones are typical among them. These pattern modes of international metropolises are usually functional, which are more obviously stiff and severe in the aspects of atmosphere, space, and spirit.

In fact, it is more and more important for the urban culture to attract the flow of transnational capitals, especially the flowing of relative talents. In the condition of modern technologies, these are irrelative for the market to be in City A, City B, or City C. But it is a fact that a person has to live in some place. The life consciousness of the special technological talents in the companies is becoming stronger, even some important decision makers of a certain company have their individual motivation (the same to companies), they know well about the places to work and live. For example, some management consulting companies in London think that it is unnecessarily important to establish an office in London in view of serving the clients. But in view of a consulting team, the emotions, and the social factors, they hope to move into London (Beaverstock *et al.*, 2001). Apparently, the place where the special technological talents and the decision makers in the companies choose to live will be the important labor market and the office site. This reinforces the importance of a city to be a consuming site and shows the charms of urban culture.

Therefore, more and more countries begin to stress on the cultural construction in urban development in order to improve their attraction to the flowing of capitals, especially the flowing of relative talents. For example, the Singapore Government publicized The Report of Reviving the City by Culture and Arts in 2000, which sketched the prospects of cultural development in Singapore in the new century and proposed the target of transforming Singapore to be the center of world culture, and put forward the corresponding six strategies as the following:

(1) to foster the enormous groups appreciating and participating culture and arts and strength the art education to the teenagers;
(2) to develop the flagship art companies, to increase the government investment and foster the talents of relative technologies and management;

(3) to affirm and foster the talents of arts;
(4) to supply good cultural facilities such as libraries, museums, and theaters;
(5) to advance on international stages, to strengthen the cultural connections between different countries, and to encourage the international co-operations;
(6) to develop the reviving economy of culture and arts, to create more vigorous activities of arts and culture, to strengthen art marketing and cultural tourism, to encourage the sponsoring to the arts, etc. In February, 2003, the mayor of London publicized the city: the Strategic Drafts of Cultural Capital and the Mayor Culture, which proposed the four targets of cultural development in London: (1) to strengthen its position as a first class cultural city in the world; (2) to consider the creative abilities as the cores to push London to be more successful; (3) to ensure all London citizens to participate the urban culture; (4) to ensure its greatest benefits from London's cultural resources.

At present, some central cities in China have began to focus on their cultural orientation in urban construction and fully exploit their own cultural details and civilization in order to shape their urban features and form innovative enterprise culture and urban spirits, thus to strengthen their reputation in the world. For example, Guangzhou, Guangdong Province, proposed to build the city into a modern cultural central city. Wuhan, Hubei Province, proposed that the innovation of urban environment should be showcased to the world, and the city should display its characters, highlight its cultural details, create the new bright spots, and transform into "Cultural Wuhan". Hangzhou, Zhejiang Province, proposed the cultural concept of urban development, namely, Learning in Hangzhou, Living in Hangzhou, Business in Hangzhou. Ningbo, Zhejiang Province, proposed the construction of cultural facilities such as Culture Corridor along the Three Rivers, which shows its cultural connotation and modern atmosphere. We should say that it is a kind of progress if the cities have this consciousness and establish this concept. But it is still too far from a globalizing city.

The globalizing cities in China should combine the vigor and the innovation ability of the city with the cultural creative ability with an emphasis on urban innovation activities. The city policy-makers should know well about the development orientation of the culture, make and consider the policies in the prospect of culture, and establish an interactive and cooperative relationship between the cultural resources and the public policies. The public policies here involve economic development, housing, health, education, social service, tourism, urban planning, building designing, urban appearance designing, and cultural policies themselves. In the implementing process of policies, we should focus on the different key points in urban development and choose the different methods, among which the cultural resources is the center of innovation. The various urban resources should be integrated to promote the harmonious development inside the city and the cultural progress in urban culture, which are reflected and merged and appear in various aspects of the city such as urban landscape, industrial traditions, social network, and individual skills. Therefore, the globalizing cities in China should fully play the dominative role of cultural strength, penetrate the cultural elements in the activities of innovative cities, and consider the cultural construction as a breakthrough in promoting the comprehensive development of the cities.

11.2.2. *The innovative culture and the creative industry*

The core of the culture-technology innovation of a modern city is the organic combination of cultural factors and modern technologies, that is, with culture and originality as the core, production of new values by applying knowledge and technologies and inspiration of originality express in certain materialization. In the layer of industrial development, it is represented by the rising and development of creative industry. The most typical examples are the film industry in Hollywood, the musical industry in Memphis, the fashion industries in Paris and Milan, the multi-media industry in Toronto in 1990s, the musical plays in Austin, the new rock industry in Manchester, and the recreation and news media in Hamburger.

At present, we have no universal definition to the creative industry. Caves (2000) defined the creative industry as the following: The creative industry supply us with the products and services extensively related to the values of culture, arts, or recreation, including the publishing of books and periodicals; visual arts (such as paintings and sculptures); performing arts (such as dramas, operas, concerts, and dances); recordings, movies, and televisions; even fashion, toys, and games. In his book, *The Creative Economy* Howkins defined the creative industry as the economic sector whose products were protected in the scope of intellectual property law. Intellectual property has four categories: the patent, the copyright, the trademark, and the design. Each category has its own legal entities and management institutes and is produced in the hope of protecting the various kinds of creative products. Howkins (2001) thinks that each form of the intellectual property law has its corresponding massive industries, and the combination of these four industries results in the creative industry and the creative economy. According to the official definition of Britain, the creative industry is the events based on individual creativity, skills, and talents to create wealth and employment by developing and exploiting the intellectual property, which includes advertisement, architecture, art and antique, crafts, designing, fashion designing, movies, interactive recreation software, music, performing arts, publishing, software, and TV and broadcasting (Drake, 2003). Hong Kong defined the creative industry as the following: It is a set of economic events which can develop creative abilities and skills and distribute the property of the intellectuals in order to create cultural connotations (a producing system by which to create potential wealth and employment) or distribute the concerning products and services, which includes advertisement, architecture, artwork, antique and handiwork, designing, the movie and TV sectors, digital recreation, music, performing arts, publishing, software and electronic computers and broadcasting.

Although there is some difference in the definition of the creative industry, it is clear and common for us that the creative industry is the product of the amalgamation of technology, economy, and culture, especially the mingling and subliming of the digital technology with culture and arts. The creative product is the materialization of new ideas and new technologies. This organic mingling of culture with modern information technology is characterized by its intelligence, features, personality, and artistry, whose values are not limited to the ones of the products themselves, but lie in the added values derived from the products. Therefore, though the creative industries have great variety and diversity, all of them have many common features, in addition, the creative industry is not always in the tide of making money, motivated by some smart businessmen.

The origin of creativity is the personal experience of the jobholders, which is from the individual inspiration and insight, thus the factor of the individual is decisive in the creative events. In the view of the creative progress, the inspiration relies on the interaction between persons, which is closely related to the social network. The American professor Csikszentmihalyi (2001) thinks that the creativity is the result of the interaction of the interior factors in a system. The system is composed of three parts:

(1) the profession, composed by a set of suitable regulations and programs;
(2) the professional, which includes the authorities and foregoers in this field;
(3) the individual, the specific individual who produces the new idea, the new discovery, and the new invention and is recognized by the insiders of the field.

The idea that the value base of a creative industry is the human capital based on the social network stresses the inner reliance between one and another, and due to their close geographical locations, it has obvious features of the industry cluster. The forming of the cluster of creative industries results from factors such as the outside scale economy and scope economy. In addition, the other factors such as the promotion of inner competition and the push to creation and the saving of trade cost play an important role. As the center of information assembling and knowledge production, the cluster effect of the city not only supplies the development space for the generation, distribution, and commercialization of creative activities but also the best suitable places for the cluster of creative industries. The features of the cluster of creative industries are more obvious in the globalizing cities. For example, in 2000, the average per capita in creative industries in London is £2,500, which doubles that in the national creative industries which is £1,300. Over one-third of the 1,600 companies in performance and arts are located in London. Nationally, over 90% of musical business events; 70% of recording rooms; 75% of the total income in the industries of movies, TV, and broadcasting; 33% of the agents in arts and antique; 46% of the employees of advertising; and 80–85% of the fashion designers are clustered in London. About 1,850 publishing enterprises and 7,000 academic periodical offices are located in London, and more, *Times*, *Financial Times*, *The Daily Telegraph*, *The Observer*, *BBC*, and *Reuters* are located in London as well.

Different from the other commodities, the products of creative industry has extensiveness and overlap in application. One creative idea can be applied in many different sectors in the creative industry. For example, a good creative viewpoint can be applied extensively in the industries such as movies, TV, TV plays, and Game software. Similarly, a well-preformed creative idea in the creative industry can be applied or further improved in the sectors of other industries. For instance, the special designing of many products and types for enterprises result in their own teams of software development and customizing, advertising, and public relations.

Anyhow the creative industry is not a self-sufficient productive system, which is closely linked to other sectors. The creative industry relies more on creativity, distribution, and the abilities of network technology and behavior skills, which needs matching support from the other sectors; at the same time, the creative industry creates values for the other service sectors and the society, which are interdependent and interactive. For example, the leisure art causes a series of basic education and practice in the field of arts. The arts here include ceramics, painting, calligraphy, musical instruments, and performance arts, which serve the different markets (education and leisure) and audiences (the young people, the parents or guardian of children, and the amateurs). Another example is that the restoration, controlling, and perseverance of the cultural heritage resources with the help of creative designing and the technology of multi-media can become the main measures to promote the tourism; in return, the cultural tourism can supply the capital to the creative industry and thus turn the cultural heritage to the attractions of tourism. But the more important thing is that the economic activities rely more and more on the creation of knowledge and culture, and the creative industry is becoming closer to the events of other sectors; the boundary between the creative industry and other sectors is fuzzier. For example, at present, the industries of jewelry, toys, garments, furniture, and manufacturing of electric appliances are closely combined with the process of cultural creation.

Due to the feature of network, multiplicity, and multi-sector in the creative industry, we have to revaluate the culture and creative abilities at an advanced level of modern technology in order to evaluate its effects on economic society and urban development. We should further understand the real connotation of creativity, knowledge, culture, and economy and their interrelationships. We cannot consider the creative industry as a kind of label or slogan; otherwise, we will have a presentational recognition of the relationship between the creative industry and urban space and vigor. For example, the superficial phenomenon of British Tate Gallery of Modern Art is that it is located in a deserted power plant, which will deprive us of its indivisible part in urban development (the remolding of the landmass in the south bank of central London).

In a creative city, as the result of organic combination of cultural thoughts and knowledgeable skills, the rise and development of the creative industry not only embodies the enriched urban cultural connotations and cultural spirits but also creates and outputs more artistic fashions, consumption consciousness, and lifestyles, which will create immense potentiality for more wealth creation for the city and create more and more values sustainably. The creative industry relying highly on creative abilities, irrespective of whether it is the economic motion of self-development or the creative input as another form of economic events, will inspire the interior energy of the city, play an increasingly important role in urban development, and produce a blue print in which the creative input will bring in extensive tangible and intangible values for the society and the whole economic system. Thus the cities in Europe form the following idea, that is, the culture or the creative industry will possibly become the base of a new economy, a method to create new urban image. Thus the cities will be more attractive to the flowing capitals and jobholders (Hall, 1998). For example, in recent years, the cultural creative industry in London has become the main economic pillar in the city, the wealth created by it ranks only second to that created by the finance services, which has become the fastest growing industry and the third biggest employment sectors. Since 1977, the average growth rate of the value produced by the creative industries in the UK is 9%, which is higher than the 2% in the traditional industries; it is 2 times more than that in other industries, and its contribution rate to economy is 4%. The estimated annual production value of cultural creative industries in London is £25–29 billion, and the number of the employees in these industries is 525,000. Another example is that the new media industries (the digital media industries combines the traditional media and internet technologies) in New York has become the most vigorous and fastest growing new industries. Between the years 1997 and 1999, the number of employees in the new media industries in Great New York is increasing at the rate of 40%, which amounts to 250,000 in all, among which the employees in the new media industries inside New York is more than 100,000. The annual growth rate is much higher in such industries as printing, advertisement, manufacturing of movies, and TV and broadcasting, and the annual income growth rate in the new media industry is as high as 53%, which amounted to US $17 billion in 1999.

Advocated by the cities such as London and New York, an increasing number of cities put forward the development strategies in the creative industries. Hong Kong clearly put forward that the creative industry was the key chain in the system of knowledge and economy. In order to push the development of the creative industry, in May 2004, the Special Administrative Region of HK started the foundation of HK $250 million to promote the "Designsmart

Initiative" and established the "Creativity & Designing Center". In 2002, Singapore published The Development Strategies of Creative Industries. In 2002, the annual added value created by the creative industries in Singapore accounted for 2.8–3.2% of its GDP, which is higher than amplitude of its GDP. The number of the companies involved in creative industries in Singapore is more than 8,000, and the number of employees is 72,000. The target of Singapore is to rise the percentage contribution of creative industries to GDP to 6%. Taiwan in China put forward the development planning of cultural creative industries in The Critical Development Plans Facing the Challenges in 2008, which considered the cultural creative industries as its core industry, which has become the second fully supported industry after the high-tech industry. A total of 50 creative life industry projects were planned in the five years afterward, and it was hoped that 300 billion Taiwan dollars and 100,000 jobs were created and 2.25 billion new Taiwan dollars were invested.

In view of experience and proof, if a country or city had a stronger creative culture, it would have the revival of creative industries. However, the promotion of the creative culture is not only a problem of education but also an extensive social problem, in which the protection of intellectual property is the basis of fostering the creative culture. Therefore, the promotion of creative industries needs comprehensive policy support. For example, the pushing policies in the creative industries in the UK include the following six policies: the wide-spreading of creative exports, the education and skill training, the assistance in financing of enterprises, the supervision of taxes and regulations, the protection of intellectual property and local rights of autonomy. The main measures taken are included in institute management, talent training, and capital support and production operation. The supporting policies include the ones in the chains such as the R&D, manufacturing, sales, and exporting of cultural products. USA encourages all the states, the enterprise groups, and the whole society to support cultural arts by various laws, regulations, and policies and create a better environment for the development of the creative industry in laws, policies, capital, talent, and market operation. The measures supporting the development of the creative industries in Hong Kong include education, training, exporting promotion, financial support, and digitalization promotion.

11.3. Strengthening City's Cultural Creativity and Creative Force

Generally speaking, the cities own the comparatively advanced culture, but it does not mean that all or the most cities has the creation and creativity in culture. Florida (2002, p. 31) explains "creativity" as "the abilities to process the original data, perception and matters and produce new and useful things". This strong cultural creativity is the necessary and essential condition in the rise of the globalizing cities. Therefore, an emergent task in the rise of globalizing cities in China is to strengthen the cultural creation and promote the cultural creativity.

11.3.1 *The fusion of global culture and local culture*

In the rise of the globalizing cities in China, the strengthening of cultural construction and innovation and the promotion of cultural creation and creativity have to be blended into the creative activities. One of the critical problems is how to deal with the relationship between the global culture in city centers and the regional or national special culture.

We see that the transnational activities and producer service classes resulting from economic globalization begin to produce new cultural structure and process and spread rapidly throughout the world by regular activities and organizations (Knox, 2002). The most obvious is that the famous brand products, services, and videos enter into the global markets and form the global culture by international advertising agency, animation, and TV series. The omnipresent transnational architecture patterns, retail chains, fast-food chains, costume styles, and music, together with the omnipresent trans-state emigrants, business visitors, and tourists, will transmit the fusion limited by no regions.

In a more abstract sense, the globalization and informatization is the compression of space and time, which is closely related to the production and development in a faster pace and the development of the politics. When the relationship between the traditional families, neighbors, regions, and nations is subverted by the high-tech and high-speed network, one certain quantitative change is carrying on and thus result in the more decisions, choices, flexibilities, interaction, aims, and images, which evolve into the fundamental change of a new lifestyle and world point of view. Briefly speaking, the globalizing of the world cities promotes the new process, which includes a consistent form of composition and new connotation and the shifting of new materialism (Oncu and Weyland, 1997).

In the spreading and development of the globalizing culture, the globalizing cities are playing an important role. In reverse, the spreading and development of the globalizing culture are embodied in the globalizing cities. That is to say, the color of the globalizing culture in globalizing cities is most dense and enriched. The reason is that, as the main panel point in the urban network, the globalizing cities are the centers of transnational exchange and the assembling places of global culture. The transnational exchange of people contributes directly to the development of the globalizing culture in the globalizing cities. In The Cultural Role of the Globalizing Cities, Hannerz (1996) stresses that there are four kinds of people playing a more important role in transnational cultural exchange, namely, the international business elites, the foreign immigrants in the first-class world cities, the practitioners in cultural industries, and the tourists. Among them, the international business elites belong to the critical group. They are engaged in transnational jobs and consume transnational products and services. They assemble in the globalizing cities and make global decisions and handle global investment and information, design, and market the international products and shuttle between the different places globally for work and leisure. Their living places are in a cross-culture environment, which is a mixed and blended place (Iyer, 2000). For them, the globalizing cities are not just the places to work; the cities reflect their lifestyles in the features of matter and world, their life stories with many experiences, and transnational feelings. In return, their new feelings will influence the local residents and will be accepted by them. By observing the life of these international business elites, more and more people see their own life that they should lead and begin to copy them rapidly. Therefore, the globalizing cities are usually in the color of globalizing culture. The globalizing cities in China have to face the problem of accepting the globalizing culture.

Certainly, the globalizing process is not a simple convergence. Meanwhile the globalizing promotes the similarities in material culture, systems, and lifestyles; the globalizing process is usually in different patterns and is combined with the local practices, which means the differences. The reason is that there will be a running-in process when the global flowing is in the local different politics, economies, and social systems. In this process, it is accepted, refused, subverted, or exploited in different patterns. Therefore, the global flowing will not blot out the localization, but fuse and reform the localization. Though the globalization has the tendency of universalizing in many social and life fields, it will cause the differences and specialty in social structure functioned by the different opposite strengths in the society, which will become a kind of individualism. Thus the new cultural structure and process produced by these transnational activities is flexible and opposite but not convergent or consistent. It includes not only the homogeneity and simultaneity of the culture but also the distribution and split of the culture. Meanwhile, it includes the universal individual principles (such as the relativism consisting of the specialty of redefinition, differences, and individuality) and individual universal principles (such as the transnational activities of different classes, different ethnical groups of people, and different residents in different regions) (Robertson, 1992).

Therefore, the globalizing culture clustering in the globalizing cities is complicated, dynamic, and extensive. Equally, the globalizing cities are the places of special cultural categories, where the new cultural patterns and schools are constructed and the new theories and new ideas are originated. In the globalizing cities, these groups can establish the new network and apply the new cultural connotations to describe the daily life in the new living spaces, which includes the transforming and adapting of the traditional communities and the social cultural space in the regions of the ethnic groups of people.

This contributes more to the cosmopolitanism of the globalizing cities, promotes the potential development of various cultures and create the multicultural space (only in some cities such as London, New York, San Francisco, Los Angles, and Sydney) (Knox, 2002).

In addition, it is noticeable that the pluralism of the globalizing culture clustering highly in the globalizing cities aggravates the cultural gaps between the different social groups, and lead to even breakage of the culture. The reason is that globalization not only brings the functional composition of labor markets, consumer markets, political institutes, and economic organizations, but also breaks the traditional political boundaries and unites the people. In the meanwhile, it causes new splits. For example, the labor force is split to various parts due to different races, skin colors, gender, age, and regions. This aggravates the cultural differences between different social groups in some degree, even the cultural breakage. Thus the elite class in the society represent various cultures (the traditional culture and different cultures in the world), while the other social groups maybe represent only local or narrow mono-culture. In a sense, the origin of the clashes inside the future cities is that between different cultures (Huet, 2005), which may bring about great risks to the urban development.

Therefore, in the process of cultural innovation in the globalizing cities in China, two tendencies have to be avoided: a full embrace of the global culture and a partial stress on the local and national culture. When accepting the global culture, a problem of discovering the regional and national characters in urban culture arises. At present, in the practice of constructing urban culture in China, most cities attach more importance to their own historical culture and their specific cultural details. For example, Guangzhou refines its urban historical culture to the birthplace of China's ancient Silk Road, the cultural center of the regions in south of Five Ridges and the front of reforming and opening-up. Many cities are declaring the previous heritage archives in China, the national park of China, national cultural protection sites, historical blocks, world cultural heritages, etc., relative photo albums and books are published, major historical stories and folk dances are performed, and historical heritage songs are composed. It is doubtless that the national and regional characters have to be stressed in urban cultural construction and development. In particular, many cities in China have long histories, some of them are the ancient capitals of six dynasties; some, the historical famous towns; and some, the assembling places of talents and cultures. All of them have profound historical and cultural details, which should be carried forward. Both the developments of the economy and the society have to maintain their local cultural characters. The urban development has the integrated and vivid effects only by coordinating with the local culture. In this sense, the thorough excavating of the local culture and the merging with the various cultures of different nationalities by exchanging with the outside world can serve as the bases of a global urban mansion.

11.3.2. *The social bases and human resources of urban cultural innovation*

As we know, culture itself and its development rely on the matters, which need the relative hardware construction and reflect them by a series of activities in specific patterns. For the creativity of urban culture, the most important material bases are the development of economy and the social wealth, which is the essential prerequisite. In history, most of the creative cities in culture are the highly developed and the richest ones at that time, with several exceptions (Athens is an example in case). The important role which the social bases are playing is revealed in the construction of Florence Baptistery, London Royal Theatre, Louvre, Vienna Town Hill, or Berlin Theater. Particularly, the comparatively advanced cities in culture require comparatively improved cultural and artistic facilities and enriched and colorful cultural and artistic activities. In this sense, the cultural and artistic facilities and activities are becoming the key factors in the reorientation and image recreation of the cities. For a globalizing city, strengthening cultural creation and improving cultural creativity need the relative material input and fully equipped cultural and artistic facilities, such as grand theaters, artistic centers, museums, and entertainment sites in order to reshape the urban landscape; for example, landmark buildings, urban sculptures, cultural landscapes, etc. Equally, the various cultural and artistic activities have to be launched positively, especially, the hosting of the major and influential events, such as international movie festivals, TV festivals, book fairs, folk-custom cultural festivals, large-scale cultural and artistic performances, and various cultural forums.

The above is the necessary prerequisite for the urban cultural creativity. But the only prerequisite cannot create a city with stronger cultural creativity. The extreme example is that some highly developed cities in economy are actually cultural deserts. For the urban culture, it is easier to build the hardware facilities, the image landscape, and the fashion's popularity while it is more difficult to foster urban spirit, to refine urban quality, and to improve the urban realm. As an intangible strength, the details of the urban culture are always exerting impacts on the urban soul. It needs to be self-examined, self-treasured, and gradually accumulated. The gaining of the cultural and spiritual values has to be through a cultural evolution process which is gradual, unconscious, and natural, and moreover, it is a process of accumulation of quantitative changes. In this sense, the culture is never made up and imposed, and the cultural spirit cannot be replaced by some image or understated. Therefore, the cultural standards of a globalizing city cannot be judged by the urban hardware facilities, the landscape symbols, and the diversity of culture and entertainment events. Strengthening cultural creation and improving cultural creativity should focus on the fostering of cultural and spiritual values and the construction of cultural software and contents.

Furthermore, we presume that strengthening the cultural creation and improving the cultural creativity need the relative cultural and artistic facilities. If they are not ample, it is quite necessary to construct and increase these facilities. Even so, it is not necessary to construct the new ones. Some important facilities have to be reconstructed while some of them can be remolded. At present, many cities in China usually adopt the way of "Reconstruct before Refresh", and seek the so-called "modern" architectural styles and the luxurious appearance. In this process, the cost of residents' removal, the investment on the infrastructure, and the cost of the routine maintenance become higher and higher. What important is that this practice discards even cut the urban history, and thus obliterates the important role of the history in reinforcing cultural creation and improving cultural creativity. In fact, a successful city usually can cope with the crises with the help of traditions and consider the history as the origin of innovation. The urban images created in history such as the historical buildings, the street views, and the educational and cultural facilities can be the bases of more innovations. History is usually an important promoter in the cultural innovation. Therefore, in constructing the cultural and artistic facilities, it is necessary and possible to reuse the older facilities which include the original industrial facilities, for example, an old industrial warehouse can be transformed to a media center, deserted trolley bus garages can be reconstructed to the new exhibition centers, or old ordnance factories can become the artistic centers. The historical features of these building make them more attractive, and it is their profound historical backgrounds that stimulate their inspiration of cultural innovation. Thus, to reconstruct and reform the original facilities to the cultural and artistic facilities can decrease input and save the cost; more important is that we can strengthen the cultural creation and improve cultural creativity with the stimulator of history.

The urban cultural innovation activities need some material bases, at the same time, they need more creative talents. Hall thinks that the geniuses may be more important than the wealth itself. The creative cities are usually the universal ones which attract exceptional talent from remote areas. Hall lists the massive emigrants in ancient Athens including the foreign residents living in ancient Greece and the freed slaves; the artists to Florence from the remote countryside; the musicians to Vienna from the other provinces and the artists to Paris; and the Jews to Vienna in the late 1800s. If there was no such a lasting renewing of the creative blood, possibly, the cities may not have thriving creative industries.

Therefore in the rising process of the globalizing cities in China, one of the most important things in strengthening the cultural creation and improving the cultural creativity is to attract a large sum of cultural creative talents to assemble and create the special environmental conditions for the emergence of creative talents. However, the growth and assembling of these creative talents need the common environmental conditions such as economic development and cultural flourishing, and the more important ones are some special environmental conditions as the following.

The first one is the environmental condition of economic and social reforms (Hospers, 2003). When one city is in an unstable state such as in the process of social reforms and cultural changes, new benefit differentiations will become more obvious, and thus cause the emergence of new social classes and economic and racial groups. These new social benefit groups will establish their position in the process of reforming and their social status will be higher. At the same time, the cities are usually the centers in which the different thoughts and cultures clash with one another; different trends of thoughts, different concepts and multiculture begin to result in conflict or even collide in the society. The emergence of a series of new changes, new problems, and new crashes in reality is sure to shock people's thoughts and concepts, which means more chances and thus the inner driving power in the process of cultural innovation. Therefore, in the environment of great changes in economic society, people are easier to accept new thoughts and ideas, which is helpful for the emergence of talent in solving practical problems and thus attract a large sum of talents to assemble in the cities to study and explore the new problems.

The second one is the loose environment in a multipolar social structure. Florida (2005) defines "tolerance" as one of the key factors for a creative city, the other two being technology and talents, and he thinks tolerance is the concept to measure the openness, inclusiveness, and diversity of one city. The charming cities are not necessarily the metropolises, but they must have the urbanity of tolerance and diversity. This diversity means not only the different races, but also the different knowledge backgrounds, working skills, and behavioral patterns of the people. It can be extended to the different images and architectures of the city. The diversity of the people usually brings cultural diversity. In such an environment, people can find subcultural societies with the same interests, and they are inspired and stimulated in communicating with them. The co-existence of multiple cultures means the mutual interpenetration, interaction, and competition, and thus cultural creativity can be generated in communication or collision. The multipolar social structure itself means the spiritual splitting and cultural diversity in the mainstream society, which supplies a loose environment for the cultural innovation. This will be helpful for the emergence of innovation activities and creative talents and thus will attract more talent and promote the cultural exchanges. For example, creative groups from the various places, especially for the younger generation, usually have the experience and pressure of elbowing out from the local mainstream society. If a city has no such multipolar social structure, once elbowed out by the mainstream society, these people will find it difficult to find a location in the cities. On the contrary, in a city with a multipolar social structure, even elbowed out by the local mainstream society, these people will possibly find the other asylum-seekers, who will supply the necessary aid and support for their innovation. Even though they cannot rule out the possibilities of being elbowed out, they will not lose their creativity, will even be even welcomed warmly, and soon present the new creation and originality on the basis of their inspiration from the real world and produce new spiritual products with the current features.

The third one is the activity stage with extensive influence. To see if it can produce a great social influence is an important factor in promoting the assembling of creative talents and activating cultural innovation. If the cultural innovation of one city can produce more extensive social influence, it means more attraction to the creative talents. It is true that the quality of the creative products is the basis of producing great social influence. In this sense, the high-quality and high-level works can produce extensive social influence. But the importance of spreading power in promoting the social influence cannot be denied. In the time of information explosion, the spreading power is playing a critical role in catching the world's eye. The creative spiritual product with a stronger spreading power will definitely produce the more extensive social influence or vice versa. This powerful spreading is based on the timely discovery, the deep exploitation, and the overall planning of the creative spiritual products. This will be realized by the publicizing and reports on TV and broadcasting, newspapers, periodicals, the major websites, even combined with the commercial speculation. That is to say, the stronger spreading power has to be combined well with the professional institutes, planning companies, and the various media, which will construct an influential activity stage for urban cultural innovation. Obviously, if the city is easier to become famous, it will mean the more attraction to creative talents. The scale effect, complementary effect and overflowing effect of the assembling of the creative talents will in return increase the social influence of the city. Therefore, the spreading power based on the mighty media is one important environmental condition in promoting the urban cultural innovation.

Though the creative talents are playing an important role in strengthening cultural creation and promoting cultural creativity, we cannot neglect and underestimate the importance of the masses in cultural innovation. In a degree, the masses culture is helpful in promoting the understanding and exchanging between different groups and cultures, it will be easier to promote the emergence of cultural innovation than the consumption of elegant arts. In particular, with the development of modern technology and economy, the motivation of people's getting around is becoming varied, and people's flowing is reinforced, which includes not only the flowing inside the country, but the flowing between different countries as well. For example, the annual number of the tourists to Paris is 70 million, which exceeds the population (62 million) of the country (Huet, 2005). With the strengthening of flow-ability, the mixture of the people, mainly the mixture of different cultures, is increasing as well. This will exert a long and immeasurable impact on strengthening the cultural creation and promoting the cultural creativity.

As a globalizing city, it is usually the assembling place of large-scale flow of different people with obvious variety of population. For example, the rate emigrating population in New York, London, and Tokyo is over 8.71%, which means one-tenth of population in the state of flow, and these cities have a stronger flow-ability. In addition, all the cities, except Tokyo, have a relatively low rate (4.55%) of international residents; the rate in New York and London is 24.2% and 27%, respectively (see Table 11.1), while the permanent resident

Table 11.1. The Population Rate of Emigrant and International Population to New York, London, Tokyo and Shanghai (Percentage).

	New York (2000)	London (2000)	Tokyo (2004)	Shanghai (2004)
The immigrant population over the total population	9	8.71	9.87	1.43
The international population over the total population	24.2	27	4.55	0.70

Source: Zuo and Wang (2006); National Health Service Central Register; International Passenger Survey, Office for National Statistics, UK; US Census 2000; The Statistics Bureau of Internal Affairs Ministry of Japan; *Shanghai Statistical Yearbook of 2005*.

population in these two cities accounts for 15% of the local population with the stronger population variety. Therefore, the cities such as New York and London are typical emigrant ones. The American census in 2000 shows the residents born in the other countries account for 35.9% of the population of 8 million. Between the year 2000 and the year 2001, London welcomed more than 190,000 immigrants. One-third of Londoners belong to the ethnical groups. By the year of 2016, more than 700,000 persons will enter London.

It is sure for the population flow-ability and population variety to bring the diversity of cultures and languages. For example, the number of languages used by the citizens of New York is over 120, and more than 300 languages are used by the population of 7.5 million in London. It is important for them to be involved in the local markets, which is the power reflection for a globalizing city. One of the bases supporting New York and London to become globalizing cities is their cosmopolitan nature. There the companies can find the employees from different countries and regions and in different languages, which is easier to make the business go smoothly. For instance, in the offices of London investment banks, most of them are international employees from different countries and regions. The diversity of population structure and multicultural life result in important cultural features of a globalizing city. It is the coexistence of multirace, multicultural, and multiclass structures that foster the creativity in an open, positive, tolerant, and flexible mind, which will become the lasting drive in cultural mixture and cultural innovation. As stated by many demographers and economists, immigrants can bring new ideas and supply a stable creative stream for us, and are an important strength in keeping the growth of the population in cities. Therefore, to maintain a higher rate of immigrant flow is the critical task for the sustainable development of the globalizing cities.

No doubt, in population flowability and diversity, high-quality labor has to be stressed, for they are play an important in strengthening cultural creation and promoting cultural creativity. Generally speaking, the globalizing cities are the highly assembling places of experienced and high-quality labors. Observing the educational level of the labors at the age of 25 or more, which is an international standard index, we can see that the practitioners in the globalizing cites such as New York, London, and Tokyo usually have a higher quality. In 2000, the rate of population with bachelor or higher degrees at the age of 25 or more is 28.3%; 27.1% in Tokyo; and 31% in London. The labors with high quality and senior skills can bring the added value of the wealth and attract more people with high quality to assemble in the metropolitans, which bring the flow of ideas, and in return, reinforce the attraction of the assembling places. This high assembly of human capital can make the cities have more abilities to face the harmful impact easily in the development process, realize the self-rebuilding in the process of structure transforming, promote the cultural creation and cultural creativity greatly, and enhance the urban soft power of the cities rapidly. New York Federal Bank investigated the challenges that New York faced in its creative development, which stated clearly that, if the city must strengthen continually its attraction, perseverance and fostering to the labors with high quality in order to be successful like the past. The competition of a metropolitan usually relies on its connotation, not its expansion in spatial territory.

In this aspect, we have a long way to go. Though the quality of Shanghai population is improving, the percentage of the population with bachelor or higher degrees at the age of 25 or more is as low as 5.1% in 2005, which is much lower than that in the metropolitans in 2000. The education level of the population is low, the worse is that we lack the labors with high quality, thus the assembling degree of the talents is still low. According to the fifth census, the population with bachelor degrees at the age of 25 or more accounts for 5.8% nationally; while it is 9.7% in New York; and 16%, in Tokyo. In the rising process of China's globalizing cities, one critical task is to increase the flow of migrating population, especially the assembling of labors with high quality and senior skills, and form the basic layout of the population structural diversity and the pluralism of cultural life. This is not only the requirement of economic development, which will be helpful in enterprise's expansion and in forming an attractive regional environment, but also results in a better social base for strengthening cultural creation and improving cultural creativity.

Chapter 12

Systemic Framework of City's Governing Structure

In the globalizing process, the city and its government play an important role. Varsanyi (2000) pointed out that, in the globalization era, we must understand how the various social strengths inside the city create the transnational flow. The study of the local development dynamic is a process based on some places, which studies the process of local society, politics, culture, and economy and its means to combine the global strengths. Therefore, in the rise of a globalizing city, especially in its transforming process, one more important problem is how to shape an urban governing structure which benefits the transnational flowing of various social strengths. The perfection of the system framework in this urban governing structure is one of the critical stages in a globalizing city.

12.1. City Governing During the Rise of Global Cities

The urban governance involves various factors such as the development targets, prime power, and means, which is directly related to the development and destiny of urban development. The effectiveness of urban governance is directly related to both the cost and the course of a globalizing city.

12.1.1. *The urban governance and its modes*

Urban development is realized by a certain functional system. This development system is directly related to the shape and process of urban development, which is of public concern. In the development of modern cities, urban governance is increasingly replacing the traditional urban management or control, thus becoming a new concept and mode. In fact, governance is not a completely new concept; it was put forward in the early study of politics. But there are different opinions on the understanding of "governance", and a widely recognized and accepted concept has not yet been shaped. Simply, governance is a process of restraining, coordinating, and controlling (Rhodes, 1996). Differing from the traditional government management or control, most scholars think that governance refers to the relationship between the citizen society and the political power, the restrainers and the restrainees, the government and the citizens (McCarney *et al.*, 1995). Urban governance is the relationship between the urban body and the urban benefitees or the operating system between different urban bodies.

Logan and Molotch (1987) put forward a "development machine" model in their book *Urban Wealth: The Spatial Plutonomy.* In this model, they put forward that the development of the American cities is a process of interaction between important benefit bodies. Similar to the government sectors, the real estate developers, the financial institutes, the public institutes, the politicians, the other organizations, and even sportsmen comprise the dynamic group, which promotes the development machine to realize the exchanging value of urban assets, gain maximized benefit or wealth of the assets, and consider them as the main methods to resolve the various problems resulting from the urban development (Lin, 2002). Stone (1989) put forward an urban political model to analyze the development process of American cities in a more extensive sense. In this model, the urban powers are distributed in local governments and private sectors in the market economy, and the urban political system is a cooperative system arrangement. By this arrangement, the local governments and the private sectors share the powers of urban governance. The local governments and economic elites have the resources of urban governance: the local governments have the power of legislation and are policy-makers, while the economic elites have the capital to create employment and increase finance and taxation. Stone (1993) analyzed the model further in the perspective of plutonomy and pointed out that the city's government could have the absolute power to draft and implement policies; similarly, the private sectors could not promote the urban development by independent actions. Therefore, the urban political system model is the medium of the two sides to construct the cause and effect between the policy effects and the outside surroundings like an organ. Though the urban political system model reflects the reaction of various benefit bodies to the outside pressure, the most important is to concern the inner and dynamic changes in the alliance construction, or the informal cooperation which surpasses the government and private sectors. Stone understood the inner and dynamic changes of the urban political body by the social production model of the power. He thinks the political power expressed by urban political body should be the power or ability to promote the urban development, rather than the privilege or social controlling power overtopping the others. This ability or cooperation is not stable, it should be innovated or maintained. By the selective incentives such as contracts or agreements, employment or the special service to the special communities, the urban political system can solve the social problems and maintain the participation of certain benefit bodies in the development alliance. Of course, the benefits gained from the development alliance by the benefit bodies are not only material but also nonmaterial. Later, based on the above basis, Mossberger and Stocker (2001) summed up the features of urban political system as follows.

(1) The political system is a non-formal but comparatively stable resource which controls and functions the urban development policies. It is realized by a form system arrangement or non-formal cooperation.
(2) The political system aims to ensure the communication between the government, which controls the public resources, and the private sectors, which control the economic resources. Besides, it includes the participation of other communities such as middle class African-Americans.
(3) The cooperation is not inborn, we should strive for it, and the urban political systems do not exist in all the cities.
(4) The political system is a comparatively stable system arrangement, it is not necessary to change with the replacement of the administrators.

(5) The property of the political system is decided by the resources controlled by the participants and the relationship between them.
(6) The political system can arrive at an agreement by the selective incentives.
(7) The political system does not show the complete accordance in values and beliefs, but they tend to be in accordance with each other in the cooperation process.

These explanations to the operation system of urban development process stress that the urban governance is a kind of system arrangement of urban development and decide the benefit sharing between urban benefit groups and their abilities to participate the urban decision-making. Thus, the urban governance focuses on the process, which is the process for the benefit groups to realize their collective aims coordinated by local authorities, which is an interactive process between the government and citizen society, the public sectors, and the private sectors. It is shaped jointly by the systems of politics, economy, and social values. From this sense, the urban governance supplies a new way to solve the problems of urban development, which allows the researchers and decision-makers to emphasize the relationship between the government and the non-government sectors and attaches more importance to the strengths from the citizen society.

But it is noticeable that the urban governance is not abstract and has a neutral-value. In the different urban development contexts, its construction and orientation reflect the corresponding norms, values, beliefs, and conventions, and thus a general and universal urban governance mode does not exist at all. We can investigate and distinguish the various urban governance models from the role of the local governments, the collocation modes, and the relationship between the local government and the citizen society, etc.

Peters (2001) classified governance into four models after investigating the process of reforming and practicing of urban governance and function transforming in the western developed countries.

(1) The marketing government — focusing on efficiency and introducing the competition system to the complete process of urban governance and governmental operation.
(2) The participating government — merging social benefits into urban governance and constructing an ideal communicating community between the government and public.
(3) The flexible government — focusing on drafting corresponding policies, adjusting work stresses, the stage targets and organs in a proper time, never facing new challenges with fixed models.
(4) The moderating government — advocating to eliminate limitations on unnecessary and overelaborate formalities inside the government, release energies stored in the public sectors, and increase innovation and efficiency of the government.

Pierre (1999) categorized the various governance modes in the western countries into four common models in four dimensionalities: the participants, the targets, the means, and the effects. Namely, they are the managerial model, the corporatist model, the pro-growth model, and the welfare model. Each reveals the concrete governance types about its participants, targets, means, and effects (see Table 12.1).

(1) The managerial model considers the producers and consumers of the urban public services as the participants according the market principles; its aims are to strengthen the production and collocation efficiency of public services and make the consumers choose the products and their producers. One of its main features is to introduce professional managerial ideas of the private sectors which are based on the markets to the public sectors, which will allow the managerial modes to have stronger market adaption and reaction. In the mean time, its first assessing criterion is the consumer's satisfaction, thus it helps to enhance the productivity of the public services.
(2) The corporatist model is to ensure the benefits shared among the group members and the democracy enjoyed by everyone by the direct participation of high officers in the benefit groups and

Table 12.1. The Comparison Between the Four Urban Governance Models.

	Managerial Model	Corporatist Model	Pro-Growth Model	Welfare Model
The participants	Managerial and consumers	Public and benefit groups	Business elites and high-ranked officers	Officers and bureaucracies
The targets	To increase the efficiency, to meet requests of consumption	To distribute, to ensure the benefit of each member	To promote economic growth	To redistribute, to ensure inflow of national capital
The means	Extensive managerial means based on the markets	Participation of the public and negotiation talks	Extensive means to promote the economy and attract investments	Network between the governments in different levels
The effects	Enhanced efficiency	Unbalanced finance	Economic growth	Unsustainability

the indirect participation of the public and the co-ordinations and negotiations between the redistribution sectors. One of its main features is to introduce the benefit groups and the public to the process of the urban politics, form the extensive participation of the public, ensure the benefits of group members and shape the urban services and policies.

(3) Based on the partnership between the systematic public sectors and the private institutes, the pro-growth model is to promote economic growth and the decision-making power by extensive means, especially the public–private partnership, to promote the economic development and attract foreign investments. One of its main features is to promote the interaction between the public sectors and the private sectors and the local economic growth by constructing the common public–private events.

(4) The welfare model is to solve the urban economic problems by the network relationship between the local and the higher-rank governments, in which the local government remedies the local financial shortage by winning over the national allowances.

If value judgment is applied, we can find that these different governance models have their own advantages and disadvantages. The main problem of the managerial model is that it cannot coordinate the innate managerial ways between the public sectors and the private institutes and mediate their contradictions because it focuses on the various managerial means based on the markets and the authorities rely more on the professionals from the private institutes. To most cities, this model is not flexible and the choice of the consumers is not a definite factor for the local governments. The main problem of the corporatist model is that it can result in the finance problems because what various benefit groups are concerned about is public expenditure but not taxation growth. If finance problems arise, the local expenditure will be decreased and the motivation of the group's involvement will be weakened, which will make the city rely more on the participants, and the local governments will be in a weak position in the negotiations with the benefit groups. The main problem of the pro-growth model is that it will decrease the participation and sharing of the public for the urban politics and rely more on private capital as the taxation base, which will result in more competition in attracting private investments. The main problem of the welfare model is that the motivation to develop the local taxation base will be weakened for the local governments, which will rely more on the transferring payment of the central governments. Thus it is not easy to attract foreign investment, and even the motivation for inner investment will be lost.

The above classification of urban governance models is only a kind of theoretical abstract which supplies a reference frame in our empirical research. The practical governance model is more abundant and complicated; it never falls simply into the above classification. At the same time, as a type of system arrangement, urban governance is evolving and innovating with the urban development, and thus these governance models can be shifted from one to another.

12.1.2. *The basic features of China's present urban governance*

Referring to Pierre's classification of urban governance models and the practice of China's present cities, which are adopting a series of measures to become more globalized, we cannot simply sum up the governance model of one city. In the process of economic transfer, China's urban governance model has its obvious historical alterations and specialties; it shows the intersecting, blending, and coexisting multimodels of the different governance models.

Savitch (1990) once pointed out that the local governments are not a phenomenon of mono-element, but multi-element, and that the different elements follow different agendas, face different problems, respond to different pressures, and reflect different supporters. In the process of China's economic transfer, the elements of local governments include the diversification of the development targets, such as the economy, society, and politics; diversification of economic and political concentration; and social democracy and sharing. This diversification will result in the intersection and mixing between the different governance models. Due to the fact that every model of urban governance has its own political targets, organizing strategies, and main participants, the different organizing logics and participants will result in different models of urban governance, different connection of government sectors, and co-existence of different governance models. Apparently, this intersection, mixing, and coexisting of different governance models make it difficult for us to judge its attributes in a simple way, and thus a specific and careful analysis is necessary.

By investigating China's present urban governance, we can find that the composition and colors in favor of the pro-growth model are becoming more obvious. The most common phenomenon is that the local governments are very particular about the connection between their location on the international stage and their development targets; they tend to promote economic development by a series of means such as urban planning, resource (especially the land) development, favorable policies, and an optimized urban environment. In this process, close cooperation between the local government and the public sectors and private institutes (such as foreign enterprises and private enterprises) is formed, and the effects of economic growth are shared by the local governments and the business elites. At the same time, the local governments win over the national finance support and the investment to the infrastructure and promote the urban economic revival and development by making the best of the governmental network relationship. It is similar to the welfare model in this point. What is different from the typical welfare model is that the model does not request to the timely finance support from a higher government to make up for the local finance shortage and revive the city, but require policy support, such as special policies and examination and approval of large-scale projects from the early establishment of economic special zones to the later economic development zones, high-tech parks, bonded zones, and even the present comprehensive experimental zones, in order to promote the large-scale expansion of urban economy.

In the present stage of China's urban governance, the pro-growth model and the welfare model are intersected and mixed, in which the pro-growth model is the leading one. The bases and the common points of these two models are the urban economic growth led by the governments, which is dominated by a strong pro-growth alliance; the main bodies of the alliance include the central government, the local governments, and the personalized global capital (including the capital from the private sectors). In reality, we can see that the strategy to promote economic growth is advocated by the urban governments, which is more practical and widely adopted in many China's cities. Therefore, in the present stage of China's urban governance, the pro-growth model and the welfare model are mixed based on certain historical backgrounds, oriented by the economic growth, and led by the local governments.

In this type of urban governance, the local governments play an important role in promoting urban economic growth. However, in the process of system transferring and the reforming of power separation between the central governments and the local governments, the urban governments control more powers and resources, especially land resource, and have more decision-making abilities in the urban development problems, which allow the urban governments to involve in local economic development to some extent. The change of positions of the local governments occurs not from the change of the relationship between the central government and the local governments, but from pressures such as employment and social stability which the local governments are facing, which enlarges the scope of decision-making and positive participation. Meanwhile, oriented by the world markets in a direct and positive way, the local governments have to attract investments from home and abroad in order to increase the economic growth. The local governments usually can motivate the local political powers in economic policies and labor policies than the other social policies, and they cooperate well with the private institutes in the public services. These enable the local government attract certain obvious commercial features, including risk taking, creation, publicizing, benefit drives, etc.

However, in a closer investigation, we can find that different benefit groups are shaped by economic development. These groups demand to enter the decision-making process of the urban policies to maintain their own benefits, with an increasing strength. At the same time, guided by the thoughts of constructing a harmonious society, with the promotion of social and political democracy, they demand to enter the decision-making process of urban policies to a great extent. These new changes and new demands urge the appearance of the managerial model and the corporatist model in urban governance. Apparently, this is an urban governance model which stresses on the interaction between the governments and the society.

At present, the citizens' participation and interaction between the governments and the society in the urban governance are in the initial stages, dominated by a weak urban residential alliance. Its main important point is that the non-government organizations are not well developed. Due to the strict controlling in registering government-sponsored non-governmental organizations (GONGOs have to be supervised by an administration institutes in a higher rank), the GONGOs have to change their titles such as a registered enterprise or a subsidiary institute of a certain enterprise, an informal club or salon, or a dispersedly registered company. The registered formal organizations such as communities or societies are closely related to the governments or the ones with governmental backgrounds. In addition, some governmental institutes found some GONGOs organized by the governments. Its partial aim is to transfer the budget pressure to the markets or hope to attract the outside investments (Ho, 2001). Therefore, the comprehensive governance system between the governments and the society is an alliance composed by the governments and the non-governmental institutes and prospective governmental communities to realize economic development, environmental protection, and comprehensive balance of social justice. But the problem is to determine how much autonomic power should be enjoyed by the GONGOs organized by the governments and spell out their functions, the reason being the governments' impact on their capital, personnel, and decision-making.

Certainly, with the separation and the localization of China's governance process, more favorable conditions are offered to the fostering and development of the GONGOs, though the central government has macro-control over the local governments. Comparatively speaking, with the premise of maintaining political stability, the local governments are willing to relax the concerned policies and controlling, which allows the events of the GONGOs to be favorable to the local development (Howell, 2003). Thus, more independent GONGOs spring up, especially in the level of local governments. They are semi-governmental or semi-private organizations, or public–private organizations. But they do not completely depend on the capital supplied by the governments, and thus have more decision-making powers. These social organizations draft new plans, encourage extensive participation of the citizens, facilitate every sector's benefit, supply various professional and social services, and practice democratic procedures (Ma, 2002). Generally speaking, participation and decision-making of these formal social organizations are usually in political form, including drafting and revising concerned laws and regulations. For example, the appearance of China's Environmental non-government organizations ENGOs means a brand new interaction between the government and the society in the public field. Apparently, the governmental sectors and the main positive elements in the citizen society, for example, the interaction between GONGOs, creates a dynamic motivation for the existence of a globalizing and sustainable city.

Therefore, as pointed by McCann (2004), China's present urban governance has an obvious feature of "Dual City". In the fast development process of the economy and the society, on one side, the mixture of the pro-growth model and the welfare model based on the governmental power is more common and dominant. On the other side, the mixture of the managerial model and the corporatist model based on the social power begin to appear, which make up the urban governance.

12.1.3. *The impact of China's present urban governance on the rising of a globalizing city*

As stated above, China's present urban governance has an obvious feature of "Dual City", in which the mixture of the pro-growth model and the welfare model is dominant. But what impacts do this kind of urban governance, oriented by growth and led by governments, exert on the rise of a globalizing city? Maybe the answer is not a simple yes or no, but required judgment or conclusion after a specific and multilayer analysis.

It is not new for us that the urban governance is oriented by growth and led by governments. The widely accepted so-called "urban management" is actually the realistic reproduction of this kind of urban governance. As we all know, the concept of urban management was explored by two researchers by studying many businesses of brokers (McGill, 1998), which is a specific form of the businesses of a broker and is actually to reach the aim of distributing the resources by controlling the concerned powers. In its practical application, business logistics are involved in the means of urban politics and urban administration to manage the city as a selling product (Jessop and Peck, 1998). Therefore, oriented by benefit maximization, the city is managed as an enterprise, and the urban operation efficiency is increased by the government's enterprise management. In the perspective of urban governance, its essence is oriented by growth and led by the government.

An understanding of China's present urban management tells us that, in the perspective of the government, this management means to integrate and operate the urban natural resources, infrastructure resources, and human resources on the markets by economic means. The theoretical basis of urban management is that the city is a valuable entity. By managing the city, the values are maintained and increased (Zhu, 2002). Or as a means of urban competition, urban management shapes or improves the urban image, highlights the city's advantages, reinforces the city's attraction, and improves the city's competition and the residents' welfare. Or it can be stated as the following: using market means to gather, recombine, and operate, according to the market principle, the natural-generated capital (such as land, water resource, sunlight, and air) and human-functioned capital (such as municipal administration and public facilities), and related extended capital (such as the naming right of the roads, bridges and etc.), which construct urban space and urban function medium. The final aim is to supply capital to the urban development. In actual practice, the target orientation of urban management focuses more on the economic growth and local fiscal revenue. Its main means is to use the massive land capital controlled by the urban governments; national capital, operated by the local governments; and policy resources, to operate them on the markets (such as land lease, financing on capital market, and secured loans), improve investment environment, amplify inside capital operation ability, attract outside investment, promote urban growth, and amplify financial sources. In return, the strengthening of economic power and the amplification of financial sources solidify the resource collocation ability of the urban governments and further strengthen the autonomic power of the local governments.

This urban management mode has comparatively obvious effects in the short run, especially at the initial stage of a globalizing city. As stated above, economic globalization causes the global flow of the resource factors and forms a global network, thus improving the urban position, and becomes the main panel points of the organized and coordinated production and reproduction. In this case, the negotiation skills of the local governments on the transnational capital and their abilities to create the concerned conditions to adapt to the economic globalization become the key factors for them to reshape the urban image and their location in the global urban network (Mayer, 1995, pp. 231–249). In China, the urban governments usually control the land, state-owned enterprises, and local financial capacity; have a stronger mobilization in economy and politics; and thus promote foreign investment attraction, capital financing, development and opening-up, urban construction, etc. (Harvey, 1989; Hall and Hubbard, 1996). It is also true in practice. The implementation of economic growth strategies oriented by urban government will result in fast growth of urban economy and large-scale urban construction. In a very short time, the urban image is changed, especially the urban infrastructure and urban appearance, and the investment environment is optimized, at least the hardware environment. The policy supports gained by the local governments from higher-level governments and the favorable terms created by the local governments based on their own conditions undoubtedly attract outside investment. A stronger gathering effect is created after the regional or national headquarters of transnational companies, the international financial institutes, investment companies, and R&D centers of the transnational companies relocate to a region. Apparently, this is helpful to develop the connections in the global network, strength the flow, enlarge the economic flow, and improve the position of the panel points in the urban network. Therefore, this is a positive promotion in the construction of infrastructure of a globalizing city in China.

But the problem is that the city is usually different from a common enterprise: the city must have a diversified target functions to realize the maximization of the whole urban benefits by integrating, collocating, and optimizing the various urban recourses, not by seeking the simple maximization of economic benefits. It is very easy for the urban governance managerial model oriented by growth to ignore the various target in ecology, environment, culture, social welfare, etc., let alone the realization of the complete and harmonious development. But to the rising of a globalizing city, the problem is not to develop the economy simply or to construct a simple economic center, but to foster comprehensively, the global strategic coordination function for a harmonious development in the whole economy and society. Meanwhile, this urban governance model is not beneficial to the sustainable development of the city, for the input in improving urban image will be increased while the expenditure to the public welfare will be decreased, which will result in intense contradiction and a dualistic image of the city. Thus, the vulnerable groups in the city will not be focused but excluded from the urban progressing path, and the painstakingly created urban myth will be lost in the end. And thus, from the whole process of the rise of a globalizing city, this urban governance model cannot consecutively promote its healthy development and even be negative in its further development.

The urban governance model oriented by the government will easily result in over-intervention of the economy by the government. The urban governments function as the supervisors and arbitrators in the market operating and are involved in direct investments, and they more or less distort the market mechanism. For example, foreign direct investments are granted special favorable terms. In addition, some stimulating means are carried out by the management institutes of different levels inside the city. These management institutes are considered as the connection bridges between the local powers and global benefits. Comparatively speaking, the market adaptability of these management institutes is weak and it is difficult to cope with the emergencies. If there is an unclear division of labor and responsibility, the operational efficiency will be lower. This will supply the space and possibility for the concerned sectors to seek for benefits, for what the sectors are concerned with are only the benefits. If the sectors can gain special rights, extensive benefits, or fees from some project, they will spring out in order to have the final say; if some troubles or responsibilities arise from the project, these sectors will shuffle mutually and delay them. These contradictions and clashes always take place in the sectors which need to connect closely and collocate with each other.

The urban management pattern is oriented by growth and always stresses on the close interaction between the government and the private sectors, which promotes the growth of the urban economy and urban development. Thus the main participants of urban management are the government officials and commercial elites; who form an alliance, in which they control the urban government and control the resources on the markets, respectively. In this frame of alliance, the urban planning and policy-making of the government stress more on serving the strategy of economic development, investors and the urban expansion, and benefits to the society, and the citizens are easily neglected. For example, the government requires some communities to move in order to supply the lands that are wanted by the property developers. And moreover, in order to attract the investment, the urban government may weaken the managerial function of urban planning, including simplification of planning approval processes, transformation of decision-making power of the urban planning, modification of the urban planning on the requests of the developers, etc. The urban government does not hope to clash with the developers because of the benefits of all the citizens, especially the common ones.

Therefore, the main defect of this urban management pattern is its lack of consciousness of public participation. A good system of public participation is not formed, and the positive effects of various non-official societies and leagues are not exploited and fully played. In the four management patterns stated by Pierre, this pattern is the one with least public participation. The society participation is not independent in essence, and thus the cooperation between the government and the society is actually the product of inability, which relies totally on the administrative sectors, totally disregarding efficiency. Even the non-official organizations play a certain role in the horizontal network but lack actual abilities and autonomous rights, and the main body of the management is still the administrative management sectors. Due to less public participation, the supervision on the rights is mainly self-correction, self-examination, and self-supervision inside the administrative systems, which includes the supervision of the higher authorities over the subordinate sectors and the self-supervision of the concerned sectors (the link between supervision and the self-supervision is complete), and the public supervision from the society is neglected. Therefore, in the examination and approval of the key policies of the urban development, there exist some disadvantages, such as will of the leading officials, replacement of law by power, and black case work.

All in all, this urban management pattern is more attractive to foreign investments in the short run and thus promotes urban economic development and urban development. However, the rise of a globalizing city is a long-lasting process of attracting the foreign factors or institutes, which relies more on the environmental conditions for the normal operation of the market system. In the long run, this urban management pattern will not always be beneficial to the optimization of investment environment or increase the attraction to the foreign factors and institutes. On the contrary, it will influence and restrict the normal operation of the market system, which is worsening the investment environment, and thus the lasting attraction to the foreign factors and institutes will not be maintained.

12.2. Essential Requirement of Mode Innovation for City Governing

Impacted by the economic tide and economic globalization, the traditional management pattern is becoming increasingly unsuitable for implementation. Especially, with the consecutive and stable growth of China's economy and the advancement of the political democratization, some benefit groups dissociating the political structure begin to involve in the urban politics by the original masses society and the newly founded societies because their economic power is increasing day after day. Therefore, in the rising of China's globalizing cities, urban management patterns have to be innovated. As a problem that the city has to face at present, this will promote the process of urban democratization. Among them, the improvement of the management patterns and the league patterns is the main development orientation in China's urban management patterns.

12.2.1. *The public participation oriented by people*

The innovation of the urban management pattern has to solve the problems of the orientation. This involves the orientation of the innovation of the urban management patterns. The main bases of this orientation are the objectives of the urban management patterns in order to comply with the global urban development.

As we stated in the previous analysis, with the increasing deepening of globalization and informatization, the global cities are usually the main panel points in the global economic network. These cities are the centers of the regional economy, culture, and politics and they have become the representative of the development vigor in the country. By contrast, the concept of the country is becoming increasingly ambiguous, and the cities will control the whole world in practice. A new change will emerge: a fundamental change in political power and public power of the globalizing cities, that is, it is the cities, but not their countries, which exercise public power and supply public benefits. These globalizing cities are creating more and more public benefits, and they establish the development strategies of public benefits and exercise them in the daily routines in honor of the public.

Furthermore, the globalizing cities will form a network with the other cities in the world, and thus a brand new local society will be constructed. The local society exists not only as a geographical territory but also as a network. In the present urban society, the traditional models of time, space, and field are smashed because of diversity, which brings a variety of the human attributes. In the future urban organizations, the various events of the people will cover different regions, not just a single place as before. Accordingly, the social classes to which the individual belongs will be various, and pluralism of individual attributes will be formed (Huet, 2005). Therefore, in the development process of future metropolises, the entire local society tends to undergo a series of constructions and recombinations and develop in the orientation of a citizen city.

Thus, in order to adapt to the requirements of the global urban development, public participation is obviously important and has become a leading factor in the urban management. In the theoretical studies of urban management, the importance of public participation is increasingly being stressed. The earlier urban management concept, which distributed resources by controlling the concerned power, was revised and enriched in the development process of the following 20 years. As pointed by Churchill (1985), the implication of urban management is becoming increasingly abundant. Urban management does not refer to only systematic control but a series of behavior relationships. In urban management, various activities of the city residents and the various management behaviors are influenced mutually. And moreover, Cheema (1993) stated clearly that urban expansion is unavoidable and the final settlement of the urban problems is the effective management of the city. The urban management should be a whole concept, whose aims are to strengthen the decision-making powers of the urban government and non-governmental organizations and their abilities to gain the best effects in executing these decision-making abilities.

At present, many cities in the world, especially the globalizing cities, consider the development rights of every citizen as the basic concept in the process of making development strategies and stress cooperation, environment, safety, life quality, and individual development and participation in the urban development planning. For example, Paris attaches more importance to the citizen's participation and cooperation and weakens the centralized management. For Paris, with the emergence of more globalizing cities and increasing international cooperation between the non-central governments, the importance of every individual should be highlighted in the political dialogues. The Paris government focuses more on the effectiveness and proximity effect in this aspect and maintains a close relationship with Parisians in order to improve solidarity, safety, environment, and life quality. Therefore, the Paris government stresses more on the improvement of citizens' life quality, which is the preferential policy. In its neighboring poverty-stricken regions, the Paris government is trying to perfect its administrative management scope; the measures include the confirmation of the most beneficial regional development in a certain region with the effective participation of the residents. In addition, the ideal of Singapore in the 21st century is that every citizen is a member of urban construction and everyone can share the fruits of urban development. Thus, individual development and public participation are the focal points of the government policies. The first task of the government is to produce more changes and create more development spaces, which allows every citizen to full play his or her potential. Meanwhile, the government also takes efforts to stimulate the full participation of the public, profit from the wisdom and efforts of all inhabitants for the urban construction and development, and improve the international competition of Singapore.

In the practice of present China, NGOs, such as enterprises, leagues, scientific and research institutes, and universities and colleges will play an increasingly important role in the market economy. With the accelerating pace of the reforms in political systems, this tendency will become increasing clear. In order to adapt to this tendency, the local governments should integrate all the participants and arrange the necessary systems and make it a complementary and positive cycle (McGill, 1988). In effect, public participation in urban management is beneficial to strengthening the supervision from the society, which transforms public supervision to an important factor in ensuring urban management according to laws. And moreover, public participation can be beneficial to draw upon the wisdom of the masses, increase the linkage between the policy designing and the implementation of management, decrease the conflicts and contradictions in carrying out the policies, and prevent the emergence of more problems in management. Therefore, public participation will become the key principle in urban management, which is an essential measure in adapting to the transforming of the socialist market economy in China's urban construction.

To establish and improve the system of public participation in the urban management structure requires the coverage of the main benefit groups in urban politics. The system requires joint participation of the enterprises, government, and main benefit groups. The perfect urban management system is based on the management structure of urban development decision-making, operation, supervision, and assessment. NGOs should play a positive role in urban management. The science and democracy of urban management should be strengthened in the principle of justice, equity, and effect in order to improve the urban comprehensive management. In this new pattern, urban management is not the government management in which the local governments make the decisions and then let the public institutes carry them out and thus change the society and economic life, but a complicated process of multiinstitute coordination by consistent negotiation and alliance and the cooperation between the public sectors and the private ones. It has the following three features:

(1) The pluralism of management body: the main body of urban management is not just the public governmental sectors. Various sectors in the society, including the private sectors, semi-public sectors, and volunteer organization can participate in the process of urban management.
(2) The cooperation of management patterns: the urban management is not the process in which the governmental institutes make the decisions independently and practice them in. It requires coordination and cooperation between the different main bodies (the benefit-related bodies), in which cooperation between the public and private sectors is emphasized.
(3) The uncontrollable management results: the coordination and interaction between the public sectors and the private sectors in management process is a natural developing process, and the results are not controlled completely by the individuals and the institutes, which may be different from the original estimation.

In the practice of China's urban management, public participation is at the initial stage, and various forms such as public summons, seeking public feedback, hearings, and bills by the deputies to the people's congress emerge, which exert an impact in the governmental decision-making. But this needs to be further improved, such as regulation of the forms and procedures of public participation and legal affirmation of the position and extent of public participation. In particular, critical construction projects need a legal process of public participation, and the forms and time of public participation should be clearly stated. This process involves mach systematic construction and it needs a process. As a temporary measure, in the key links of the process of decision-making — argumentation — designing — examination and approval — implementation — feedback, public participation can be introduced. Aiming at the different stages and content, specific corresponding forms should be determined, such as the public announcement on the news media, or counseling sessions by group representatives. With the accumulating lessons, the public summoning system, the consulting system, the feedback system, and complaining system involving public participation should be deepened and improved. In the organizations involving the public participation system, leagues, societies, and committees composed by the experts at different levels should be established in order to coordinate the benefits between different sectors and groups, settle the disputes, and facilitate judgment, arbitration, and interpretation in the concerned appeal. In addition, the supervision function of the NGOs including enterprise, leagues, scientific and research institutes, and universities or colleges should be fully played. At present, organized and guided by the government, many cities in China have established the model and standing urban planning committees under the government office open system, while the other cities initiated the e-information query system of the government affairs. All these create the conditions for the public supervision in China and will be helpful to establish an improved and well-equipped system of public participation.

The improvement of the strategic framework of urban management depends on the adjustment of power structure to a large degree. For example, the final aims of the transmission of the governmental functions by reforming the political system are to construct the limited, responsible, and service-oriented governments. But the confirmation of power scope and its implementation should be perfected by the legal systems. Furthermore, in a deeper view, it needs the powerful support of informal system arrangements, such as the corresponding social cultures. For the innovation of urban management structure, the wrong concepts and behavior patterns have to be changed, and the origin of the changes is the culture itself. Here, culture does not mean fine arts only but refer to a complete life pattern. This is why the cultural factors such as concepts, consciousnesses, morality, and customs composed secret, lasting, and stable social bases for supporting and restricting the urban management system.

12.2.2. *The transforming of the governmental functions: the stressed public service*

The innovative urban management pattern based on public participation does not mean weakening of the functions of the local government. The reason is that the urban management is an interactive process between the government and the citizen society and the public sectors and the private ones. The local government dominates the urban management in practice, therefore, to understand the organization ability of the local government is the key to understand urban management. An honest and effective urban government is an indispensable factor in urban management. But the problem lies in the type of the functions the urban government is playing in order to match the urban management pattern based on public participation.

As we know, the previous economic and social life had a clear territory in which the most people lived, worked, shopped, and paid taxes inside the same city or region. But the scenario is totally different now. The enterprises choose the places of manufacturing and marketing worldwide by comparing the advantages and disadvantages, the labors can serve by computer at home or at any corner of the world, people can do shopping at home and at any time, and moreover, they can choose their residence by comparing the advantages and disadvantages of the local government services. In the view of urban development, especially for the rise of a globalizing city, the choice of location for an enterprise or an individual cannot be ignored. Under this circumstance, if a city wants to attract residents and investors in the world competition, the local government must have stronger competition and be good at cooperation. That is to say, the urban government must reflect positively to technological progress, informatization, transnational companies, and modern economic activities based on the services. The government should try to supply high-quality service at low cost and use advanced technologies to help the citizens by increasing the provision of services and information and their say in decision-making. Therefore, with the increasing opening-up of the modern economy, globalization, and rising position of the city in modern economy, the functions of the urban government are not weakened, rather, it is required to play a more important role in providing public service.

This will involve the reasonable location of the local urban government. Generally speaking, the duties of the local urban government are to ensure the supply and maintenance of infrastructure and public service in institutes and finance, and its main tasks are to do well in urban planning, construction, and management. The management of the urban government includes the following: management of policies and regulations, population, lands, architecture, planned markets, designing markets, environment, resources, traffic, etc. Among them, public service is the main tool and means for the government to implement public policies. Thus the urban government has to transform its functions, intensify the functions of public service in the social and economic development, and, as an aim, draw up and plan the urban development strategies in the long run.

The governmental public service is a dynamic concept, whose connotations are increasingly deepened with the development of urban economy and development. And moreover, for the different urban developments, such as the common cities and the globalizing cities, their governmental public services are usually different in requirements and key points. Under the context of globalization and informatization, in order to promote the scientific, coordinated, and sustainable development of a globalizing city, the government public service will embody the following three aspects:

(1) The learning-oriented society should be advocated to improve the overall quality of the citizens. A globalizing city has to face the challenges brought by the globalization and knowledge power in the attitude of innovation. Therefore, the government public service should focus on the construction of a learning-oriented society, promoting the development and exploitation of human resources and improving the overall quality of the citizens. For example, the government should supply learning opportunities for all the children in spite of their family, economic, and social backgrounds; the curriculum should revised in order to encourage individual innovation; different education methods should

be adopted to meet the different requirement of different students; the definition of "success" and "talent" should be redefined; students' interests in arts and physical education should be encouraged; and a stimulating learning environment should be created with the help of information technology. At the same time, the key points in the education system should be adjusted to encourage the citizens to learn throughout their lives. People at different ages should be offered the chance for learning and acquiring skills, and moreover, employees should be offered the chances for necessary education and training, and thus they could have new development opportunities by life-long learning. If enough financial resources are present, the funding of life-long education should be made for each individual on his or her own account in order to promote him or her to learn and gain the necessary skills and knowledge for the later re-employment.

(2) A better environment should be constructed in order to attract outside talent. A globalizing city should maintain abundant vigor and strong competition for its social and economic development and transform itself into a global center for the gathering of talent, ideas, and capital in order to create more innovation and offer more and new opportunities. Thus, the government should create a better environment by supplying excellent and effective public services to attract outside talent, allow them to integrate into the local society, and create more opportunities and flourish for their living places.

(3) Self-identity should be strengthened in order to strengthen the social cohesive force. Besides hardware constructions such as the urban infrastructure, buildings, and afforestation, and the software constructions, such as market order and a positive investment environment, a globalizing city should strengthen the "heartware" construction when facing the accelerating globalizing tendency and the development of knowledge economy. The heartware here includes social intangible resources such as social cohesion, political stability, collective willingness and common values which have particular systematic features. For example, Singapore thinks it needs to strengthen the construction of

heartware in order to be glorious in the 21st century. The public service of the government lies its strengthening of the heartware. Therefore, the government should coordinate the relationship between the different groups, including the spirit of mutual respect between the different countries or regions and between the different ethnic groups of people. The government should maintain a harmonious relationship between the young and the old. A kind and gentle relationship between the successful and unsuccessful people should be constructed in order to strengthen the people's integration and feelings of belonging to the same community step by step. The government should build and complete the social security systems and let all the citizens share the fruits of urban development. An effectively operated community network can be constructed by carrying out network management inside the city.

The concepts of professional management based on the market should be introduced to the governmental institutes in order to strengthen the functions of public service of the government. The government is actually the producer of public service at all levels, which are assessed by the cost, efficiency, requirement, and professional management. It plays a positive role in rationalizing the relationship between the different sectors, defining the powers and responsibilities of the different sides, and improving the market adaptability and the abilities of coping with the emergencies. Therefore, the reforms to the governmental management should be accelerated, such as simplifying the governmental organs and improving the efficiency, legalizing the office procedures, regulating activities and behaviors, decreasing the administrative examination, approving and strengthening the integration of the sectors, strengthening the flexibility of the planning and perfecting the mechanism of information feedback, and fostering the better service environment in order to promote the service at high efficiency and low cost. At the same time, the practitioners of the public service sectors should be stimulated to foster a better service attitude to meet the requirements of the public for high quality and high grade. All of these factors are involved in the transformation of thoughts and concepts and the creation of different management cultures and doctrines.

But we have to point out that while the strengthening of the governmental function of public service means that the public service supplied by the government must be sufficient, it does not mean the provision of public service must be taken on only by the government or that any public service should be non-commercialized. At present, it is quite common in China's cities that the government is both the supplier and the producer of the public service. In addition, public service by the government is never run based on the commercial principles. This will result the rapid expansion of the governmental institutes and personnel and the high cost and low efficiency of the public service because of monopolization and non-commercialization. In fact, the supply of the public service is never equal to its production, because they can be separated to a great degree. The main responsibility of the government is to supply public service, which is not necessarily produced by the government. The production of some public services can be made by NGOs while the government is responsible for the purchase of the service and then supplies it to the society. Even though the public service is produced by the government itself, it should follow the principles of commercialization, reduce its cost, and improve its efficiency. Therefore, in the construction of infrastructure and supply of the public service, the commercialization in the service supplied by the government and the corporatization of the public-run service should be advocated. Meanwhile, a beneficial marketing environment should be constructed in order to attract the private-owned enterprises to invest in the construction of urban infrastructure.

In this respect, we can learn from some successful cases. For example, from 1993, Hong Kong (HK) began to operate some governmental sectors in the postal service and the telecommunications by the means of operation funds. These sectors are operated in the principles of semi-commercialization or commercialization, the initial funds are allocated by the government, and then these sectors assume sole responsibilities for their profits and losses. These sectors are operated by the collected charge, and the government will not allocate the funds. But while the concerned personnel are still civil servants, the planning and resource allocation becomes more flexible. Even though the charging and operation planning are conducted in the principle of commercialization, this transformation helped the sectors in the operation funds and transaction funds to participate in the market competition. The sectors which originally supplied the service to the governmental sectors expand their service to the non-public sectors and the public; while receiving the service, the other governmental sectors can turn to the private market for the necessary service. In addition, the government established some limited companies or legal public institutes which are independent from the government and are owned wholly by the government, such as the Housing Committee, The Bureau of Medical Management, The Bureau of Airport Management, The Bureau of Trade Development, etc; and the public enterprises such as the Subway Corporation, Kowloon Canton Railway Corporation, the Land Development Corporation, the Mortgage Corporation Limited etc., which supply public services originally provided by the government. After these institutes are operated on their own, though they are allocated funds from the state treasury fully or partially, they are operated in a flexible mechanism of corporatization in business principles and means, are responsible for their own profit and loss, and adjust the service charges accordingly. This way has the following advantages:

(1) With the governmental finance and the fundamental operation capital, the institute can have the status of independent legal entity, borrow or lend money from the outside which is operated in a flexible capital structure and business operation means, and thus can undertake the retribution ability of the project itself using the most rapid and suitable financial planning.
(2) The users are self-paid and recover the cost in order to lessen financial aid from the government and improve management and efficiency at the same time.
(3) It can be helpful in benefit cushion. Once an extensive benefit conflict appears, the government will be ready to coordinate.

In this process, it is certain that the government keeps the economy in operation via publicized, clear, and effect laws, and if possible, involves itself in reduced business operation. It is necessary to operate on the principles of prudent business, "cost-recovering", and "paid-by-users" even in the case of public service which is supplied by the government. Its aim is to decrease the subsidies and thus make the public sectors and the private sectors reach a comparatively fair and common ground even if there exists competition between them. Doing so is beneficial to promote their efficiencies and service levels.

12.3. Systemic Framework of Governing Structure

The innovation of urban management patterns lies in the improved public involvement and the realization of governmental function transformation; one of its aims is to increase the efficiency of governmental operation. The governmental operation is from the governmental systems. These governmental systems are embodied in the governmental influence on economy; the making of concerned laws, regulations and systems; the implementation of the policy of economic regulation and controlling; the maintenance of social and political stability; and the adaptability of political systems. The key factors are the institutional arrangement of the management hierarchical structure, establishment of a consultative government, and functions of the NGOs. If so, the government's levels of decision-making and public service will be improved, the covering square of information service and operation will be expanded, an effective governmental service environment with high quality will be created, and all this will supply the effective institutional arrangement for the globalizing cities.

12.3.1. *The institutional arrangement of management hierarchical structure*

In the design of urban governmental systems, there is always a contradiction between the unity of the public service and the government's adjoining with the citizens. The former requires a unified management institution inside the metropolitan area in order to avoid the multipoint and distributive management; the latter requires the management hierarchy inside the metropolitan area to be simplified, which can supply high-quality public service to the citizens directly. Some scholars think that there is always a conflict between the overall, coordinative, and effective planning and management aspirations and the balancing of the powerful and various local benefits (Gowling, 1997). Thus, in the practical operation, the method of dealing with the relationship between the unity of public service and adjoining service to the citizens directly is involved in the efficiency of the government, which is related to the institutional arrangement of government's management hierarchical structure.

In the existing systems in China, the administrative regions at all levels are considered the basic units for the institution setting and service supply. Generally speaking, a city has a dual-level government, at the city level and at the district or county level. The classification and the number are equal between the governments at the district level and the municipal government. In the process of reforming, some cities such as Shanghai implemented a dual-level treasury in order to motivate the positivity of the districts or the counties. To a great degree, this promotes the development of the local economies and makes the public services and public management more accessible to the citizens. Meanwhile, this results in isolation and cutthroat competition of the governments at different levels, especially in attracting investments and industrial development, and moreover, the whole benefits of the city will be swallowed and divided due to the bounds of administrative regions and the unity of urban development will be challenged.

This is the result from the features of China's system of government, which reflects a common problem globally, that is, the result from the institutional arrangement and counterbalancing system of the dual-level government, the city government and the district government. There are always arguments and disagreements in this problem. The public choice theorists argue that the metropolitan is a huge public market where the citizen can choose the public commodities which compete against the others (Park and Oakerson, 1989; Teaford, 1979). The competition in public service between the governments can decline the cost and thus make the government management more effective (Schneider, 1986); more powers are delegated to lower governments and the merging of the governments are not advocated. The consolidators thinks that the number of the government should be decreased, and the management coverage should be consolidated. According to the requests of scale economy, the management of the metropolitan can supply more effective services, decrease the financial deficit, and promote the economical development (Rusk, 1993; Frisken, 1991). In the practice of an international metropolis, the lack of collective power and unified management will result in the layout of confused and scattered management, which is not beneficial to the rise of government efficiency and urban development. For instance, between 1965 and 1986, London maintained a dual-level governmental management mode, namely, the Parliament of Great London and that of Autonomous cities. But in 1986, the Thatcher government carried out reforms in public administration and revoked the Parliament of Great London, which resulted in a confused and scattered management in London. Therefore in May 1998, after referendum, the government of Great London was founded and the mode of the dual-level government management was reinstated.

In the management of the dual-level government management, the key is to foster a complete and effective balancing system. Though it is necessary to delegate certain powers to the lower governments, the city government still has the final say in decision-making, which maintain the unified control and management power of the city. Compared to the city government, the power of the governments at the level of districts is obviously weakening. For example, though USA is a federal country, the local governments usually have stronger consciousness of autonomy, and the management mode of a city-district is characterized by "powerful city and weakening districts", which is embodied the institutional setting of New York government institutions, the allocation of personnel, the division of functions, and so on. Compared to the city government, the governments at the district levels have less power and function, and their role is to act as a medium between the representative of the local benefits and the city government or the communities at a primary level. Even if they have some power of examination and approval, they are counterbalanced between the governments at a high level and the communities at a primary level. The institutional arrangement of the management hierarchical structure of powerful city and weakening districts does not mean the wide and excessive involvement of the city government but implies the unified management of the metropolis, which limits the respective function and power and concentrates them in the governmental sectors at the city level in the premise that the governmental functions are limited. Therefore, the powerful city and weakening districts are comparatively powerful and weakening; accordingly, as a whole, the coverage of urban governmental function is still limited.

However, what is more important is not the limitation on the power or the concentration of the power. The practice shows that the high concentration of power is not beneficial for the district governments to give full play to their positivity in supplying public services and meeting the requests of the public in gaining public services. The key lies in the reasonable adjustment and arrangement of the function and power in the governments at both the city level and the district level. For example, Tokyo is implementing the management mode of the integrated management of the metropolis and the comparative division of the power in the district governments. On May 8, 1998, Japan passed and issued The Partial Reforming Law in Local Governments. By strengthening the financial autonomous rights of the 23 districts inside the metropolis, their independence and autonomy are improved. This law established the position of the districts as local public entities. At the same time, the function and power of the governments at the metropolitan level and district levels are adjusted. The service functions and their respective finance powers such as water supply, drainage, and fire protection, undertaken by the district governments, were handed over to the metropolitan government, and jurisdictions such as sewage treatment, which are closely related to the citizens, were transferred to the district governments. Similar to the districts, the city, county, or village is limited in affairs which are closely related to a citizen's life, such as the setting and management of the primary and secondary schools, the setting of the running water and sewers, fire protection, national health insurance, tax collection from the residents, etc.

In addition, in the process of adjustment of urban management hierarchical structure, there is a development tendency, that is, a new hierarchical structure is formed that it is very different from the traditional dual-level government system. For example, in 1998, London resumed the dual-level government management mode. But London did innovate in the management mode which was consistent in the city level and the district level; the governments at district levels were not subordinated to the metropolitan government or administrated by the metropolitan government. However, they are cooperative, like partners. The difference between the metropolitan government and the district governments lies in their responsibilities and duties. Though the metropolitan government and the district governments face the citizens, are close to the citizens, and supply public services to them, as a whole, the government of Great London represents the whole London, while each autonomous city government represents its own regions. The government of Great London undertakes the heavy responsibility to make Great London thrive consistently; its strategies and planning stress on its promotion in position in the world. More concretely, the mayor is in charge of the compilation of the strategic planning in air quality, biodiversity, culture and tourism, economic development, transportation, waste treatment, etc. In addition, the mayor is responsible for the development planning of space strategy to ensure the fundamental framework to construct land usage on the whole. Thus an institution elected by people, the London city council, is necessary to provide advice and conduct supervision to the city government. So, in the government at city level, the government of Great London separates three powers: decision-making, implementation, and supervision. Namely, the mayor exercises the administrative power, and the parliament controls the examination power. The autonomous government serve the citizens in more direct ways, which include education, social service (such as children's protection, daycare, and household service), housing construction, highway maintenance, regional planning, street cleaning and refuse disposal, and culture and leisure industries (such as libraries). The governments pay more attention to the effectiveness and high quality of the public service, so those at the district level are in the prescription system, namely, the representative rights and administrative rights, which are exercised by the parliaments of the autonomous cities. From this, we can see that management mode is inconsistent in the governments in higher level and lower level. Meanwhile, on one side, this management mode can ensure the realization of local autonomy; on the other side, it can promote the consistency and unity of the management of local public affairs.

To borrow dual-level management modes from the metropolises in other countries is surely important, but it does not mean to choose one of them and copy it simply. The key is to see the accurate location of governmental functions and learn their scientific lessons. Though the functional divisions of the dual-level governments of the metropolises in other countries are obviously different, its basic tendency in the reforms of present governments is to keep the limitation of governmental functions. The earlier mentioned examples, New York, Tokyo, and London, show limited management functions in the dual-level governments. The urban government controls the fields directly such as the maintenance of social order, the promotion of public service level, the development of culture and education and public welfare establishments, and the other administrative affairs and has less involvement in economic activities. The government supplies and adjusts urban public articles, and does not act as the leader of the social economy.

The limitation of the governmental functions in foreign metropolises is what we should learn and borrow. Superficially, the problems that have arisen from the hierarchical structure of China's urban governmental management are the results of an unclear definition of the functions of dual-level governments and improper handling of the relationship between concentration of power and division of power. Their roots are the incomplete transformation of governmental functions, wherein the service is forcefully nested, adhered to, and overlapped with that of the administration, which strengthens the main benefit position of district governments and results in the distortion and expansion of governmental activities. In effect, the irrational endowment and exertion of the governmental functions result in the existence and upgrading of the clashes between different district governments and the sectors of higher authorities.

Hence, the core problem is to transform the functions of the governments, locate accurately the functions of the government, and construct the governments of limited power and functions. On the premise and foundation, the division of functions of the city and district governments can be clearly defined. Generally speaking, the city government is operated as a strategic government, which can be the platform for the integration of policies and the coordination of multicenter management system. The city government should focus on the lasting and sustainable development of the city and the promotion of its position in the world. The district government is the one for daily operation, whose key is to supply the regular public service (see Table 12.2). On the basis of the guarantee of the unity of urban development, the local governments should given as many autonomous powers as possible, and the vitality of district governments should be stimulated in order to realize the integrated management of the city and the local autonomy.

Table 12.2. Strategic Government and Daily-Operated Government.

Items Compared	Strategic Government	Daily-Operated Government
Targets	Lasting and sustainable development	To meet the citizen's requirements of the public products and service
Responsibilities	Decision-making and planning, the promotion of its positioning the world	Supply the specific public products and public service
Inner Organization	The discrete sectors of decision-making, execution and supervision	The sectors of execution and supervision
Orientation	The changing environment	The public affairs
Authority	Influential force	The executive force

Source: Yan (2005).

12.3.2. *The extensive involvement of NGOs*

Under the management structure of public involvement, the city government is managed in the idea of the government of limited functions, which is a refining and flexible organic structure. This means more NGOs should be established, which are involved in the decision-making of the government and implementation of the relative policies made by the government. These NGOs are actually playing the roles of the government to lead and promote the development of economy and society which becomes an effective mechanism to adjust the various contradictions. Therefore, the extensive involvement of the NGOs and the management of limited government are the two aspects of organic integration of the management structure arrangement with public involvement, that is, the management of the limited government needs the extensive involvement of the NGOs and vice versa.

From the international practice, we can see that the management of the limited government usually adopts the policies of positive non-interventionism. On one side, we should reduce the intervention if we want to ensure sufficient and extensive freedom; on the other side, when the whole economic operation encounters great problems with negative influence, the active measures should be taken to intervene and solve them. As a whole, the management of the limited government is implementing its economic policies with many laws and regulations. For example, the government controls the benefits of the public services and facilities with franchises; pollution prevention; and the protection of the consumers and the individual. Special and temporary controlling is undertaken according to the relative laws and regulations, for example, rent control is implemented because of the insufficient supply of buildings. Some laws and regulations are considered as the norms of government control, while the others have contents such as the establishments of certain organization to carry out the partial supervision of the government, or popularize the intention and the development planning of the government on behalf of the government.

Generally speaking, the management tendency of a limited government is self-regulated or self-controlled by the public market figures which guard the first barrier according to the market self-discipline. What the government guards is the second or the third barrier, which embodies the decision of certain implementation and controls the concerned market involvers. In practice, except the economies of scale and the public utilities, which are influencing the economies of scale, the other professions are regulated by the government in the form of market self-discipline. Obviously, this will supply extensive development space for the thriving of the NGOs which will play a more and more important role. On the contrary, when the government takes all the responsibilities and duties, the development of the NGOs will surely be excluded, and thus the functions of the NGOs will accordingly be restrained. The result is that the NGOs cannot develop well, and the existing number of NGOs will be reduced.

Therefore, in China's urban management, when NGOs are fostered and their involvement is encouraged, the principal problem is to transform the partial functions of the government in economy control and implement the intention and relative policies of the government with the help of the NGOs. In particular, the distribution of partial functions of the government should be realized in the governmental institutions, and some functional sectors of the government should be transformed to non-government institutions which can take certain government management in a way or another. Borrowed the lessons from HK, we can see that certain government function sectors can be surely transformed to semi-official intermediaries, for example, the Bureau of Trade Development of HK, the Bureau of Export Trust Insurance, the Bureau of Productivity Promotion, the Association of Banks, and the Bureau of Vocational Training. The semi-official features of these intermediaries lies in the following. First, they are characterized by their official shades and are the legal institutions according to relative regulations, and some committee members are officials of the government. Second, they are different from the governmental institutions in that they are more independent, and most committee members are experts in different fields and noted public figures who are not paid by the government. Even though some committee members are from the government, they have no privileges and have one vote, like the other committee members. Even though these intermediaries supply paid service, they are different from the other enterprises because their aims are not to gain benefits, they do not advertise, and what they focus on is the justice and reputation. Meanwhile, they can give full play to their special advantages of being semi-official, for example, their advantages in organizing and coordination and the supplying of overall services. They can remedy the disadvantages of insufficient financial resources of the enterprises, the purchasing difficulties, and the inconsiderate overall planning, and thus the scale operation of the enterprises is promoted. All in all, if some functional sectors of the government can be transformed into semi-official intermediaries, the governmental institutions can be simplified with new vitalities. These intermediaries can help the government to regulate the economic and social affairs, and the mode of managing the great society by the minimal government is realized.

What is noticeable is that the fact that the management of the limited government spares the room for the development of the NGOs does not mean the unlimited development of the NGOs. On the contrary, the government should foster, support, and supervise the NGOs to help and supply the necessary safeguard for their healthy development and their full play of the functions. The operation mechanism is stated as the following:

(1) the government promotes the relative industries to establish the industry associations or reshape the self-disciplined organizations to supervise the service level, operation and professional integrity of the industries, and so on. For example, the government can form concerned examination systems, registering system, and system of identifying the operation qualifications. The self-disciplined organizations inside the industries have their own system to approve the specific operation qualifications and have the power to withdraw the relative qualifications. By the membership, the self-discipline organizations formulate the operation of relative business unless the market involvers become the members of the organizations.
(2) The government determines the power, functions, and constitution of the self-discipline organizations according to the legal procedures.

(3) The independent individuals appointed by the government should be included in the council of the self-disciplined organizations in order to strengthen the supervision and counterbalance.
(4) By the laws and the concerned measures, the transparency and social accountability of the industries should be supervised and more importance should be attached to social and consensus supervision.
(5) By reorganization, the supervision of the governmental sectors and public institutions on the concerned industries should be strengthened.
(6) The government should strengthen the direct or indirect supervision on the industrial sectors which have earlier encountered serious problems.

The premise of realizing the extensive involvement of NGOs is to establish various institutes with different functions. Only by this can it become the main important composition in the urban management with extensive involvement in different fields and in every aspect. In this effect, lessons from HK can be learned. The NGOs of HK are characterized by their large numbers, scale, variety, and different functions. The different types of NGOs in HK can be roughly divided into the following:

(1) Statutory official organizations: The chairmen and their members of these organizations are usually made up of non-official figures who have administrative rights. These organizations either employ full-time workers to promote their work, such as the Bureau of Trade Development, the Association of Tourism, and the Bureau of Productivity Promotion, or appoint one governmental sector to carry out their functions, for example, the Housing Department of HK (a government sector) is the implementing institute of the Housing Committee (the statutory official organization).
(2) Statutory supervision organizations, such as the joint exchange of securities, exchange of future exchanges, federation of the insurance industries, and association of tourism industries.

(3) Statutory professional and functional institutes: The professional institutes in HK are usually recognized, regulated, and controlled by the concerned laws. Their members should have professional qualifications acknowledged by the HK government, which are registered and confirmed by other procedures. Examples include the Association of Engineers in HK, Association of Planners, and Association of Accountants. Though some self-disciplined organizations are not regulated in operation qualifications statutorily, there are some groups regulating the membership of the members, the integrity of moral behavior, the intellectual abilities of operation such as the Association of Urban Affairs, Association of Banks, Association of Computers, etc.

(4) Organizations of agents: Their behavior and operation are based on the statutes and cases, and their main business brokerage. Examples include securities brokers, merchant banks, private banks, insurance brokers, and real estate brokers, who are involved in the market trade on behalf of the parties and paid commission, and thus the parties' interests are safeguarded.

(5) Folk organizations: They are composed of non-governmental or non-profit organizations and are registered and established by the regulations on the societies or associations, including charity groups and social service groups. And the others themselves are professional groups, such as the Federation of Social Workers. These folk organizations play the role of maintaining people's benefits and advocating social reforms, such as the Greenpeace and human rights organizations.

(6) Interest groups: They are the representatives of the professional interests and play a coordinative role in governmental policies and collect and exchange opinions inside the industries, such as chamber of commerce and trade unions present in all industries.

These NGOs embody not only the partial management functions of the government but also the service function in their coordination and balancing the interests of the enterprises, and they supply all kinds of service for the society, enterprises, and government, which forms a huge service system. At the same time, the NGOs strengthen the supervision on enterprises and rectify the violations and the concerned operations in time, which ensures a normal track of the economic activities and solves all kinds of economic disputes and greatly reduces the verdict pressure of the judicial systems. It is worth mentioning that the above numerous non-governmental organizations are almost made up of young and professional figures who are often active in the community and have a friendly image among the people. These sectors are fundamentally open in handling the businesses, and the people can enter and leave the offices and meet the staff there. There is clear division of labor and responsibilities inside these organizations. The businesses are handled in a simple, convenient, and clear pattern and procedure in order to promote the efficiency. Because the NGOs overcome the bureaucratic style of work to the greatest degree, with the professional knowledge, the service objects are easier to gain the more scientific and advanced bases and results conveniently in low cost. The independence of these NGOs and their pursuit for the better professional images can represent the justice in some degree.

12.3.3. *The management mode of consultative government*

In the urban management mode with public involvement, though the operation framework of the government is dominated by the administration, the rights of decision-making are in the hands of the governmental sectors. The management mode of consultative government needs to establish the multilevel consultative framework in the operation mechanism of various fields in economy and society, which is the main important systematic arrangement. As a globalizing city, its focus should be on the lasting and sustainable development of the city and its promotion in world position, which needs the powerful support of the decision-making consultation.

With the help of the consultation system, the government can learn about the people and listen to the ideas and professional opinions from the business circles, the benefit groups, and the folk groups, which can make the formulating of the policies or development plans more scientific and professional and reduce the social reaction when these plans are put forward and there are clashes in their implementation. Therefore, many countries and cities formulated the comparatively perfect system of decision-making consultation. For example, the council system in Japan is composed of the figures from the government, the academy, and the business. These figures compose the committee with the scholars as the center, which collects the ideas from the maximum range, integrate the views of all walks of life, adjust the relationship of stake and interest between the governmental institutes, and coordinate the relationship between the different provinces and different ministries. In addition, there are four researching and consultation institutes such as the Federation of Economic Groups, the Conference Group of Industry and Commerce, the Federation of the Groups of Operators, and the Association of Economics in Japan. And moreover, there are the professional research institutes of decision-making such as the Comprehensive Research Institutes of Normura and Mistubishi, which conduct professional research by authority and put forward the influential research reports aiming at the great problems in the national development. The consultation research on decision-making in the USA has strong independence and creativity. Each consultation institute puts forward its different opinions and suggestions on certain important problems and supplies the multiside and multidimensional reference to the decision-making of the government. For example, the comprehensive, professional, and independent research institutes, such as Rand Corporation, are authorized by the government to research thoroughly and comprehensively on the main economic and social problems at home and abroad. Other examples are that the researching consultative committees such as the Council of Foreign Affairs and the Heritage Foundation focus on one or two important and significant subjects. The government attaches more importance to these consultative institutes and their researching results and are positive in purchasing their services.

At present, in China's urban management, the local governments are emphasizing on the consultation of decision-making in order to make the decisions more scientific and democratic. Thus a great variety of consulting councils are established for the extensive professional opinions in the level of the local governments, which is considered the necessary procedures in decision-making and is developing in the professional orientation of decision-making. But no mater the scale or the functions, the functions and impact of consulting committees do not reach the stage to change the governmental management mode, and the management mode of "the Consultative Government" is not shaped at all. As a whole, in the formulation of policies and development planning, the governments are dominated by the signature and the final say of the leading cadres in the governments. The governments figure out the solutions themselves and then make the governments at a lower level to implement them or impose their willingness on the public. In this process, though the governments lean over to the others and listen to the opinions and suggestions from the experts and the professionals, in most cases, it is frequently temporary and arbitrary, and the consultation of decision-making is not organic and systematic. Even though some consultation institutes are established, they are disordered and incomplete, and the complete organic system is not shaped. Moreover, all these consultative institutes are neither statutory nor have legal rights. What they have is only mono-function of consulting, and their influence is decided by the degree of openness of the administrative officers. In most cases, these consultative institutes exist in name only and are usually luxurious furnished; the development of certain consulting activities is on the so-called necessary process.

The essence of implementing the management mode of "Consultative Government" is the transformation of governmental management mode. Beside the vertical management mode in the traditional governments, the horizontal management should be realized in order to cope with the complicated problems that the city is facing, such as problems in environment, family policies, and social exclusions. The trnsformation of this governmental management mode is not to seek opinions and suggestions from experts and professionals temporarily, but to institutionalize decision-making and enable the consulting organizations play an important role.

Therefore, to realize the management mode of a "Consultative Government" requires the establishment of all kinds of consulting committees at the first place, to shape a complete consulting organic system form the institutes with supreme powers for each functional sectors of the government. For example, the consulting framework of HK in highest rank is the Bureau of Administration, where besides the administrative official, there are three official members of the Parliament in the Government Secretariat, the Financial Secretariat, and the Justice Secretariat; and the other members are the non-official members appointed by the administrative official as consultants. In addition, the consulting committees with different functions and contents in different levels and policy categories are established in different government sectors. Many consulting committees invite non-official figures to become members, and most of them are professionals and leading figures in industry and commerce.

On the original basis of the government consulting organizations, the consulting organizations should be established in different levels and their scale should be expanded. The most important thing is to increase the functions of the consulting organizations with the respective powers, whose aim is to play an increasingly important role in governmental management. For example, in the current system of the consulting organizations, as the consulting institute in the highest level, the Bureau of Administration is not just the simple advisory and discussion institute, for it has the final say in legal decision-making. Of course, the initiative rights of decision-making are in the hands of the authorities of the government.

Due to different functions and categories of the consulting committees in the different governmental sectors, we should make a difference between them. Some committees are the statutory organizations with the powers endowed by the laws. All the statutory official consulting committees have different functions and powers. Some statutory consulting organizations have the decision-making powers in the affairs endowed by the scope of their responsibilities and rights, and they even undertake the rights and responsibilities of accepting the complaints and implementation. For instance, the Council of Urban Planning and the Committee of Consumers in HK are the cases in point. Some other consulting organizations are not statutory ones from the beginning, but the tradition of accumulating of the past operations allows them to have certain rights in decision-making: one of the examples is the Consulting Committee of Transportation in HK.

All in all, what these consulting organization have is not the simple function of consulting. Quite a few consulting organizations, especially the statutory official organizations, are endowed with the rights of decision-making, the acceptance of complaints, and the rights and responsibilities of implementation, which play an important role in governmental management. For some key problems of decision-making, the government and some consulting committees authorized by the government can publish the consulting documents and the drafted documents of the concerned policies, such as the Green Books and the White Books. Some of the consulting organizations appointed by the government are involved in the first stage of policy-making and put forward their suggestions, while the others are involved in the later stages; both are decided by the established functions such as the legal regulations of the concerned consulting committees.

In the systematic arrangement, its whole process is shown as the following: the government puts forward its suggestion, conducts the research, and then begins the consulting process. After collecting ideas after consultations, the government judges and adopts the useful ones and then rectifies them; or after the repeated discussion inside the government and the consulting in different levels, the administrative authority makes the final decision (the drafting of some policies is decided by the consulting committees with decision-making rights and they are then examined and checked by the Bureau of Administration), which is followed by the legislative procedure and then the financial allocation for their implementation.

To sum up, the system of the consulting committees can attract the social elites outside the government, including local experts and leaders in business, and borrow their expertise, insights, views, experience, personal experiences, and the social relationship network. Meanwhile, the professionals working for the government, such as the experts in environmental protection, finance, and economy, are involved in the policy-making to some degree. Moreover, when researching how to formulate new policies or key development plans, international consulting companies can be invited for consulting research, and foreign experience and professional knowledge of overseas experts can be borrowed and consulted. Thus, the professional analysis in different angles can be helpful to the decision-makers of the government, which will make the government more professional with regard to decision-making on economy and making the concerned policies. By this channel, the process of policy-making can draw on the wisdom of the people, non-official figures, and market involvers and can take this opportunity to exert their impact on the decision-making of the government, which helps the government to keep informed of the public pulse. All these measures guarantee the professional, scientific, and democratic decision-making of the government.

Bibliography

English version of the Chinese Bibliography

Bai, Z. "New York Renmin University Press, 2001es", *Urban Problems*, No. 5 (1996).

Bauer, C. "Make the City Move, the U.S.," *Newsweek*, September 23 (2002).

Cai, J. and Xue, F. "Define the Formation of the World's Cities — The Case of Shanghai", *Foreign Urban Planning*, No. 5 (2002).

Cai, L., Zhang G. and Wang, Z. *The Rise of the International Economic Center* (Shanghai People's Publishing House, 1955).

Chen, J. "The Industry with the Structure and Position of the Yangtze River Delta Region", *China Industrial Economy*, No. 2 (2004).

Chen, Z. and Hu, Y. "Western Urban Governance: Concepts and Models", *City Planning*, No. 9 (2000).

Chen, Z. and Song, P. "Add to WTO and the Era of Globalization, China's Urban Development", *Foreign Urban Planning*, No. 5 (2002).

Cheng, D. "Shanghai Service Industry Supply and Demand of Non-equilibrium and Jiangsu, Zhejiang and Services Industry Association — Based on the Non-equilibrium Model and Jump Regression Analysis", *Academic Monthly*, No. 7 (2005).

Chen, D. and Chen, X. "Enhance the Interactive Development of Producer Services and Consumer Services", In *Modern Service Industry Research*, Zhou, Z. (Ed.) (Shanghai Academy of Social Sciences Press, 2005).

China Association of Mayors (Ed.) *China Urban Development Report* (2001–2002)," (Xiyuan Press, Beijing, 2003).

Csikszentmihalyi, M. *Creativity: Flow and the Psychology of Discovery and Invention* (Chinese version) (Shanghai Translation Publishing House, 2001).

Du, N. "An Analysis of the Dutch City of Spatial Organization and Planning Practices", *Urban Planning Overseas*, No. 2 (2000).

Fang, K. *Beijing Old City Update: Investigation, Study, Exploring* (China Architectural Press, 2000).

Gobbi, J. *Recreation In Your Life* (Chinese version) (Yunnan Publishing House, 2000).

Gowling, D. "London's Urban Planning and Management: Recent Changes", *Urban Planning Overseas*, No. 4 (1997).

Gu, C., Zhang, Q. and Cai, J. *Economic Globalization and China's Urban Development — The Cross-Century Urban Development Strategy* (The Commercial Press, 1999).

Gu, G. and Chen, H. *Opportunities and Challenges — On the Construction of Shanghai International Centre For the City* (Shanghai Jiaotong University Press, 2000).

Guang, P. L. "Hong Kong China Commercial City", *China's Urban Economy*, No. 10 (2005).

Guo, Y. "Industrial Production and Its Historical Evolution in the Theoretical Analysis of the Impact of International Urban Form", *Urban Planning*, No. 4 (2000).

Guo, J. "Building a Modern International Metropolis Research", *Financial and Economic Issues*, No. 9 (1995).

Huet, A. "Looking to the Future of Urban Society", *Urban Management*, No. 4 (2005).

Hao, S. "International Competitiveness, Improve the City and Urban Governance", *Open Herald*, No. 9 (2002).

He, J. and Sun, Y. "Reflection of FDI on the Impact of China's Regional Economic Development", *World Economic Research*, No. 11 (2005).

Hong, Y. and Chen, W. "Urbanization Patterns, New Development", *Economic Research*, No. 12 (2000).

Hu, G. "The International Division of Labor in the Manufacturing of Sustainable Development in the Yangtze River Delta: Bottleneck Analysis", *Economic and Management Research*, No. 7 (2005).

Hu, H. "Vigorously Develop the Productive Services, Comprehensively Enhance Industrial Competitiveness", *Shanghai Comprehensive Economic*, No. 4 (2004).

Huang, Y. "Read *Creative Cities with Economic Development* by Pete Hall", *Foreign Urban Planning*, No. 4 (2001).

Huang, S. and Ning, Y. M. "The New Town and Revelation", *Modern City*, No. 4 (2003).

Institute of Contemporary Shanghai, *Yangtze River Delta Development Report 2005* (Shanghai People's Publishing House, 2005).

Jiang, J., Zhang, X. and Wang, Y. *City Competitiveness* (Shandong People's Publishing House, 2003).

Krugman, P. *Development, Geography and Economic Theory* (Chinese version) (Peking University Press, China People's University Press, 2000).

Li, L. "City of Internationalization and International Cities", *Urban Problems*, No. 4 (1994).

Li, L. and Xu, X. "The Preliminary Thinking of Building an International City of Guangzhou", *Economic Geography*, No. 2 (1994).

Li, G. *et al.* "The Comparative Study of Urban Development of Beijing and the World City", *Urban Issues,* No. 2 (1996).

Lian, Y. "Urban Transformation and Urban Competitiveness", *Audit,* No. 2 (2003).

Liu, B. T., Lu, M. and Li, T. "Tokyo Institute of Structure Evolution Model and Its Driving Force", *World Geography,* No. 1 (2003).

Liu, C. "To Enhance the Thinking of the Nanjing City's Comprehensive Competitiveness", *Social Science,* Suppl. (2002).

Liu, J. D. and Ma, Z. Q. "Foreign Cities Center City Administrative Area Functions", *City Planning,* No. 3 (2003).

Liu, Y. and Liu, G. "With Reference to Hong Kong: Shanghai Suburbs, the Construction of Targets and Countermeasures", *Urban Development,* No. 10 (2000).

Luo, X. and Chen, F. "Niche Theory in Urban and Rural Areas Combined with the Preliminary Study of the Ministry of Applications — Case Study of Nanjing", *Economic Geography,* No. 5 (2000).

Ni, P. (Ed.) *China Urban Competitiveness Report* (Social Sciences Documentation Publishing House, 2003).

Ning, Y. "The Rise of Cities in the World and the Development of Shanghai", *Urban Problems,* No. 6 (1994).

Ning, Y. "A New International Division of Labor: The Development of World Cities and Central Cities of our Country", *Urban Problems,* No. 3 (1991).

Peters, G. *The Future of Governing* (Chinese version) (China Renmin University Press, 2001).

Saarinen, E. *The City, Its Growth, Its Decay, Its Future* (Chinese version) (China Architectural Industry Press, 1986).

Shen, J. and Zhou, Y. "Cities in the World the Meaning of Revelation and Urban Development in China", *Urban Problems,* No. 2 (2003).

Shen, J. "The Formation and Development of the Tokyo the World's Cities and Its Inspiration", *Economic Geography,* No. 4 (2003).

Shen, K. Y. (Ed.) *Focus metropolis — Shanghai City's Comprehensive Competitiveness of the International Comparison* (Shanghai Social Sciences Press, 2001).

Shi, Y. and Zhang, R. "From the Multi-center City to City Economic Circle — The Yangtze River Delta region to Coordinate the Development of Spatial Organization Model", *Urban Planning,* No. 4 (2001).

Sun, S. "Construction of Modern International Metropolis of Planning Implementation Mechanism", *Urban Planning Forum,* No. 3 (1998).

Tan, Z. "The Formation of the Tokyo Metropolitan Problems and Countermeasures of the Enlightenment of Beijing", *Urban Planning Overseas,* No. 2 (2000).

Tang, M. "Developing Countries Giant City Status Causes Challenges and Countermeasures", *Urban Planning Forum,* No. 1 (2003).

Tang, Z. "The Basic Characteristics of the International City and Forming Conditions", *Urban Problem*, No. 6 (1993).

Tao, X. and Liu, J. "Foreign Suburbanization Experience Lessons and Their Inspiration to China", *Urban Problem*, No. 4 (2003).

Wang, S. "China's International Metropolis of Construction", *Journal of Zhongnan University of Economics and Law*, No. 3 (1999).

Wang, X. "Beijing — Building a Modern International Metropolis of Basic Connotation", *Urban Development*, No. 2 (2002).

Wang, Z. "Multinational Companies to a Global Company to China's Economic Transformation and the Opportunities", *Study Times*, March 8 (2007).

Werner, H. *Urban Economics* (Chinese version) (Chinese Society Science Press, 1990).

World Bank. "East Asia's Urban Transformation", *Business Weekly*, August 1 (2003) (Chinese version, translated by Li Yuan).

Wu, F., Li, Z. and He, S. "Build Cities of the Golden Age — City Hall Peter World", *Urban Planning Overseas*, No. 4 (2004).

Xia, Y. and Lu, X. "Yangtze River Delta Regional Economic Growth and Industrial Isomorphism Regional Economic Integration", *Nantong University (Social Sciences Journal)*, No. 1 (2006).

Xiong, X. "Fast Orbit Transportation Construction and Big Cities Structure Upgrade and Economic Growth", *Management World*, No. 2 (2000).

Xu, K. *Civilization and Prosperity — Chinese and Foreign Urban Economic Development Environment is Studied* (Southeast University Press, 2002).

Yan, R. "Greater London Government: Management of World City Innovation", *City Management*, No. 3 (2005).

Yang, B., Zhu, D. and Jing, Z. "Urbanization Stage Characteristics of China Urbanization and the Choice", *Shanghai Economic Review*, No. 2 (2006).

Yang, X. "Shanghai and International Metropolis the Comparative Study of the Economic and Social Environment", *Shanghai Environmental Sciences*, No. 8 (1996).

Yao, S. "International City Established Background and Opportunities", *Urban Planning*, No. 3 (1995).

Yao, W. *The Economic Causes Global City* (Shanghai People's Publishing House, 2003).

Yu, T., Gu, C. and Tu, Y. "The New Period of the City and the Competitive Ability of the City", *Urban Planning Forum*, No. 4 (2001).

Yu, D. and Wei, Y. "International City, International City Area and Internationalized City Research", *Urban Planning Overseas*, No. 1 (2003).

Yu, W. "After the War New York London and Tokyo of Social and Economic Structure Evolution and Its Reason", *Urban Problem*, No. 2 (1999).

Yuan, R. and Ning, Y. "Globalization and Development of National City Research", *Urban Planning Forum*, No. 5 (1999).

Zhang, H. "Western Countries Urban Land Use Pattern and Its Small Cities in Our Country Land Quality Classification of Application", *The Journal of Quantitative and Technical Economics*, No. 2 (2003).

Zhang, J. "Talk About an International Metropolis", *Urban Problem*, No. 5 (1996).

Zhang, Y. "Since the Reform and Opening up of the Development of the Third Industry Shanghai Analysis", *Shanghai Economic Review*, No. 2 (2004).

Zhang, Y. and Huang, R. *2007 China International Status Report* (People Publishing House, 2007).

Zhao, Y. "High Speed Development Condition of Urban Growth Mode", *Urban Planning Overseas*, No. 1 (2001).

Zhen, M. "On the Analysis of the Shanghai International Metropolis", *Urban and Regional Economics*, No. 9 (2001).

Zheng, K. "From the Comparison of the Hong Kong and See Shanghai Industrial Structure Development", *Shanghai Economic Forum*, Nos. 1–2 (2004).

Zheng, X. "Digital Land Price Model to the Analysis of Urban Land Price in Time and Space Application", *Resources Science*, No. 1 (2004).

China Association of Mayors and the Editorial Committee of China Urban Development Report, *China Urban Development Report* (2001–2002) (Xiyuan Publishing House, 2003).

Zhou, Y. "The New Century: The Prospects of the China International City", *Management World*, No. 3 (2000).

Zhou, Z. *Information and Industrial Integration* (Shanghai Joint Publishing, Shanghai People's Publishing House, 2003).

Zhou, Z., Chen, X. and Huang, J. *The World City — International Experience and the Development of Shanghai* (Shanghai Academy of Social Science Press, 2004).

Zhou, Z. *The Modern Service Industry Research* (Shanghai Academy of Social Science Press, 2005).

Zhu, Q., Mo, J. and Mai, F. *World City Social Index Comparison* (China City Press, 1997).

Zhu, T. "City Management: Improve the Competitive Ability of the City's New Idea", *Jianghai Journal*, No. 2 (2002).

Zhu, T. "Industrial Isomorphism of Yangtze River Delta with I", *Jiangnan BBS*, No. 2 (2003).

Zhu, X. and Wang, H. "Paris Industrial Structure Evolution and Characteristics", *Urban Planning Overseas*, No. 5 (2004).

Zhuo, Y. "After Long Time To Long Triangle Development Trend And Main Characteristic Analysis", *Urban and Regional Economics*, No. 10 (2005).

Zong, J. and Gu, P. "The City Public Management Research — The New Field of City Management Research and Development", *Journal of Tianjin University (Social Sciences)*, No. 4 (2003).

English Bibliography

Abu-Lughod, J. *New York, Chicago, Los Angeles: America's Global Cities* (University of Minnesota Press, Minnesota, 1999).

Alderson, A. S. and Beckfield, J. "Power and Position in the World City System", *American Journal of Sociology*, 109: 811–851 (2004).

Allen, J., Massey, D. and Pryke, M. (Eds.)*Unsettling Cities* (Routledge, London, 1999).

Alonso, W. (1964) *Location and Land Use* (Harvard University Press, Cambridge, 1964).

Amin, A., Massey, D. and Thrift, N. *Cities for the Many Not the Few* (The Policy Press, Bristol, 2000).

Appadurai, A. *Modernity at Large. Cultural Dimensions of Globalization* (University of Minnesota Press, Minneapolis, 1997).

Armstrong, W. and McGee, T. G. *Theatres of Accumulation: Studies in Asian and Latin American Urbanization* (Methuen, London, 1985).

Arrighi, G. and Drangel, J. "The Stratification of the World-Economy: An Exploration of the Semiperipheral Zone", *Review (Fernand Braudel Center), 10(1): 9–74*(1986).

Bairoch P. *Cities and Economic Development: From the Dawn of History to the Present* (The University of Chicago Press, Chicago, 1988).

Baras, R. *Economic Change and Urban Real Estate Markets* (PMA, London, 1988).

Batten, D. F. "Network Cities Versus Central Place Cities: Building a Cosmocreative Constellation". In *The Cosmocreative Society*, Anderson, A. E. (Eds.) (Springer, Heidelberg, 1993) pp. 137–150.

Batten, D. F. "Network Cities: Creative Urban Agglomerations for the 21st Century", *Urban Studies*, 32(2): 313–327 (1995).

Bauman, Z. *Globalization: The Human Consequences* (Columbia University Press, New York, 1998).

Baumol, W. J. "Macroeconomics of Unbalanced Growth: The Anatomy of Urban Crisis", *American Economic Review*, 57(June): 415–426 (1967).

Beaverstock, J. V., Doel, M. A., Hubbard, P. J. and Taylor, P. J. "Attending to the World: Competition/Co-operation and Co-efficiency in the World City Network", *Global Networks*, 2(2): (2002).

Beaverstock, J. V., Hoyler, M., Pain, K. and Taylor, P. J. "Comparing London and Frankfurt as World Cities: A Relational Study of Contemporary Urban Change", Anglo-German Foundation for the Study of Industrial Society, August (2001).

Beaverstock, J. V., Smith, R. G. and Taylor, P. J. "A Roster of World Cities", *Cities*, 16(6): 445–458 (1999).

Beaverstock, J. V., Smith, R. G., Taylor, P. J., Walker, D. R. F. and Lorimer, H. "Globalization and World Cities: Some Measurement Methodologies", *Applied Geography*, 20(1): 43–63 (2000).

Beaverstock, J. V., Taylor, P. J. and Smith, R. G. "Geographies of Globalization: US Law Firms in World Cities", *Urban Geography*, 21(2): 95–120 (2000).

Begg, I. "Cities and Competitiveness", *Urban Studies*, 36(5–6): (1999).

Bell, D. *The Coming of Postindustry Society* (Basic Books, New York, 1973).

Benenson, I. "Multi-agent Simulation of Residential Dynamics in the City", *Computer, Environment and Urban Systems*, 22: 25–42 (1998).

Berg, L. and Braun, E. "Urban Competitiveness, Marketing and the Need for Organizing Capacity", *Urban Studies*, 36: 5–6 (1999).

Bertuglia, C., Bianchi, G. and Mela, A. (Eds.) *The City and its Sciences* (Physica-Verlag, Heidelberg).

Bittner, R. (Ed.) *Urbane Paradiese. Zur Kulturgeschichte des Modernen Vergnügens* (Campus, Frankfurt-M./New York, 2001).

Bourdeau-Lepage, L. and Huriot, J.-M. The Metropolis in Retrospect: Permanence and Change (2004). See http://www.lboro.ac.uk/gawc/rb/.

Braudel, F. *The Perspective of the World* (Harper Collins Publishers, London, 1984).

Brenner, N. "Global Cities, Global States: Global City Formation and State Territorial Restructuring in Contemporary Europe", *Review of International Political Economy*, 5(1): (1998).

Brenner, N., Jessop, B., Jones, M. and MacLeod, G. (Eds.) *State/Space: A Reader* (Blackwell, Oxford, 2003).

Brian, J. G. "Restructuring and Decentralization in a World City," *Geographical Review* **85**(4): 436–457 (1995).

Brotchie, J. *et al.* The Future of Urban Form (Groom Helm, London, 1989).

Brown, E., Catalano, G. and Taylor P. J. "Beyond World Cities. Central America in a Space of Flows", *Area*, 34: (2002).

Brueckner, J. K. "A Model Analysis of the Effect of Site Value Taxation", *National Tax Journal*, 39: 49–58 (1986).

Bura, S. *et al.* "Multi-agent Systems and the Dynamics of a Settlement System. *Geographical Analysis*, 28(2): 77–87 (1996).

Burgess, E. "Residential Segregation in American Cities", *Annals*, CXXXX: 105–115 (1928).

Cairncross, F. *The Death of Distance: How the Communications Revolution Will Change Our Lives* (Harvard Business School, MA, 1997).

Camagni, R. "Beyond Complexity in Urban Development Studies." In *The City and Its Sciences* (Physica-Verlag, HD, 1998), pp. 363–385.

Camagni, R. P. "From City Hierarchy to City Network: Reflections about an Emerging Paradigm." In *Structure and Change in the Space Economy*, Lakshmanan, T.R. and Nijkamp, P. (Eds.) (Springer-Verlag, Berlin, 1993), pp. 66–87.

Carrier, J. G. and Miller, D. (Eds.) *Virtualism: A New Political Economy* (Berg, Oxford, 1998).

Castells, M. *The Rise of the Network Society: The Information Age: Economy, Society, and Culture,* Volume I (Blackwell, Oxford, 1996).

Caves, R. E. *Creative Industries: Contracts between Art and Commerce* (Harvard University Press, London, 2000).

Chase-Dunn, C. "The System of World Cities, A.D. 800–1975." In *Urbanization and the World-Economy*, Timberlake, M. (Ed.) (Academic Press, New York, 1985).

Chase-Dunn, C. The System of World Cities, A.D. 800–1975. In *Urbanization and the World Economy*, Timberlake, M. (Eds.) (Academic Press, New York 1985).

Cheema, S. G. (Ed.) *Urban Management: Policies and Innovations in Developing Countries*, (Greenwood Praeger Press, Westport, 1993).

Chen, X. *As Borders Bend: Transnational Spaces on the Pacific Rim* (Rowman & Littlefield Publishers, UK, 2005).

Christaller, W. *Central Places in Southern Germany*. Transl. C.W. Baskin (Prentice-Hall, Englewood Cliffs, New Jersey, 1966).

Clark, D. "City Development in Advanced Industrial Societies". In *Cities in the 21st Century*, Gappert, G. and Knight, R. V. (Eds.) (Sage Publications, London, 1982), pp. 60–83.

Clark, D. *Urban World/Global City* (Routledge, London, New York, 1996).

Coe, N., Hess, M., Yeung, H. W., Dicken, P. and Henderson, J. "Globalizing' Regional Development: A Global Production Networks Perspective", GPN Working Paper No. 4. (2003). Available at: http://www.art.man.ac.uk/Geog/gpn.

Cohen, R. "The New International Division of Labour, Multinational Corporations and Urban Hierarchy." In *Urbanization and Urban Planning in Capitalist Society*, Dear, M. and Scott, A. (Eds.) (Methuen, London, 1981), pp. 287–315.

Cox, K. R. (Ed.) *Spaces of Globalization* (Guilford, New York, 1997).

Cox, K. R. and Mair, A. "Community and Locality in the Politics of Local Economic Development", *Annals of Association of American Geographers*, 78(2): 307–325 (1988).

Crane, D. *The Production of Culture. Media and the Urban Arts* (Sage, London, 1992).

Crane, D. *The Production of Culture. Media and the Urban Arts* (Sage, London, 1992).

Damette, F. *La France en villes* (DATAR-La Documentation Française, Paris, 1994).

Deanne, J. "Inflation and Growth in a Service Economy", *Bank of England Quarterly Bulletin*, November 1998.

Deas, I. and Giordano, B. "Conceptualizing and Measuring Urban Competitiveness in Major English Cities: An Exploratory Approach", *Environment and Planning A*, 33: (2001).

Derudder, B., Taylor, P. J., Witlox, F. and Catalano, G. "Hierarchical Tendencies and Regional Patterns in the World City Network: A Global Urban Analysis of 234 Cities", *Regional Studies*, 37(9): (2003).

Dijk, H. V. (Ed.) *The European Metropolis 1920–2000* (Erasmus Universiteit Rotterdam, 2003).

Douglass, M. "Globalization and the Pacific Asia Crisis Conditionpace-economy of Globalization: Comment oes", *Asian Geographer*, 19(1–2): 119–137.

Douglass, M. "The Rise and Fall of World Cities in the Changing Space-economy of Globalization: Comment on Peter J. Taylor's 'World Cities and Territorial States Under Conditions of Contemporary Globalization'", *Political Geography*, 19(1): 43–49 (2000a).

Douglass, M. "World City Formation on the Asia Pacific Rim: Poverty, "Everyday" Forms of Civil Society and Environment". In *Cities for Citizens*, Douglass, M. and Friedmann, J. (Eds.) (John Wiley & Sons, Chichester, 1998), pp. 107–138.

Douglass, M. and Friedmann, J. (Eds.) *Cities for Citizens* (John Wiley & Sons, Chichester, 1998).

Drake, G. "This Place Gives Me Space: Place and Creativity in the Creative Industries", *Geoforum*, 34: 511–524 (2003).

Drennan, M.P. The Dominance of International Finance by London, New York and Tokyo. In *The Global Economy in Transition*, Daniels, P.W. and Lever, W.F. (Eds.) (Addison Wesley Longman, Harlow). 352–371.

Dunning, J. H. (Ed.) *Regions, Globalisation and the Knowledge Based Economy* (Oxford University Press, Oxford, London, 2000).

Dunning, J. H. "Explaining the international direct investment position of countries: Towards a dynamic of development approach", *Weltwirtschaftliches Archiv* (1981).

Dunning, J. H. "Location and the Multinational Enterprise: A Neglected Factor?," *Journal of International Business Studies*, 29(1): 45–66 (1998).

Dunning, J. H. "Location and the Multinational Enterprises: A Neglected Factor?" *Journal of International Business Studies*, 29(1) (1998).

Felsenstein, D., Schamp, E. W. and Shachar, A. *Emerging Nodes in the Global Economy: Frankfurt and Tel Avir Compared* (Springer, Netherlands, 2007).

Fischer, C. S. "Toward a subcultural theory of urbanism", *American Journal of Sociology*, 80: 1319–1341 (2002).

Florida, R. and Gates, G. "Technology and Tolerance: The Importance of Diversity to High Technology Growth", Survey Series (The Brookings Institution Center on Urban and Metropolitan Policy, Washington, DC, 2001).

Florida, R. *Cities and the Creative Class* (Rouledge, New York, 2005).

Florida, R. *The Rise of the Creative Class: How its Transforming Work, Leisure, Community, and Everyday Life* (Basic Books, New York, 2002).

Friedman, J. *World City Futures: The Role of Urban and Regional Policies in the Asia-Pacific Region* (Hong Kong Institute of Asia-Pacific Studies, The Chinese University of Hong Kong, Hong Kong, 1997).

Friedmann, J. "Where We Stand: A Decade of World City Research". In *World Cities in a World-System*, Knox, P. L. and Taylor, P. J. (Eds.) (Cambridge University Press, Cambridge, 1995).

Friedmann, J. "World City Hypothesis", *Development and Change*, 17(1): 69–83 (1986).

Friedmann, J. and G. Wolff. "World city formation: An agenda for research and action", *International Journal of Urban and Regional Research*, 6(3): 309–344 (1982).

Friedmann, J. and Wolff, G. *Notes on the Future of the World City* (School of Architecture and Urban Planning, University of California, Los Angeles, 1981).

Frisken, F. "The Contributions of Metropolitan Government to the Success of Toronto's Public Transit System: An Empirical Dissent from the Public Choice Paradigm", *Urban Affairs Quarterly*, 27: 268–292 (1991).

Frobel, F., Heinrichs, J. and Kreye, O. *The New International Division of Labour* (Cambridge University Press, Cambridge, 1980).

Fujita, M. and H. Ogawa, "Multiple Equlibria and Structural Transition of non-Monocentric Urban Configurations", *Regional Science and Urban Economics*, 18: 161–196 (1982).

G. B. Government Office for London, "Four World Cities: A Comparatives Study of London, Paris, New York and Tokyo", (Llewelyn Davies Planning, London, 1996).

Gallion, A. B. *The Urban Pattern* (Van Nostrand Reinhold Company — Van Nostrand, 1983).

Gaschet, F. and Lacour, C. "Métropolisation, Centre et Centralité," *Revue d'Économie Régionale & Urbaine*, No. 1: 49–72 (2002).

Gereffi, G. and Kaplinsky R. (Eds.) "The Value of Value Chains: Spreading the Gains from Globalization", *IDS Bulletin*, 32: 3 (2001).

Gereffi, G. and Korzeniewicz, M. (Eds.) *Commodity Chains and Global Capitalism* (Praeger, Westport, 1994).

Ginsburg, N., Koppel, B. and McGee, T. G. (Eds.) *The Extended Metropolis* (University of Hawaii Press, Honolulu, 1991).

Godfrey, B. J. and Zhou, Y. "Ranking World Cities: Multinational Corporations and the Global Urban Hierarchy", *Urban Geography*, 20(3): 268–281 (1999).

Gordon, P. and Richardson, H. W. "Employment Decentralization in US Metropolitan Areas: Is Los Angeles the Outlier or the Norm?" *Environment and Planning A*, 28: 1727–1744 (1996).

Gorman, S. P. "Where are the Web Factories: The Urban Bias of E-business Location", *Tidschrift Voor Economische en Sociale Geografie*, 93: 522–536 (2002).

Graham, S. "Global Grids of Glass: on Global Cities, Telecommunications and Planetary Urban Networks", *Urban Studies*, 36: 929–949 (1999).

Grant, R. "The Gateway City: Foreign Companies and Accra, Ghana." In Paper delivered to the Third World Studies Association Meeting, San Jose, Costa Rica (1999), p. 21.

Grant, R. and Nijman, J. "Comparative Urbanism in the Lesser Developed World: A Model for the Global Era." In *Sixth Asian Urbanization Conference* (2000), pp. 5–9.

Gravesteijn, S. G. E., Griensven, S. and Smidt, M. (Eds.) *Timing Global Cities* (Netherlands Geographical Studies, Utrecht, 1998), p. 241.

Guillain, R. and Huriot, J.-M. "The Local Dimension of Information Spillovers. A Critical Review of Empirical Evidence in the Case of Innovation", *Canadian Journal of Regional Science, 24(2): 311–340* (2001).

Hall, P. "Modelling the Post-industrial City". *Futures*, 29(4): 311–322 (1997).

Hall, P. "The Future of Cities", *Computers, Environment and Urban Systems*, 23(3): 173–185 (1999).

Hall, P. "The Global City", *International Social Science Journal*, 48(147): 15–23 (1996).

Hall, P. *Cities in Civilization: Culture, Technology and Urban Order* (Weidenfeld and Nicolson, London, 1998).

Hall, P. *Cities in Civilization*: *Culture, Technology and Urban Order* (Weidenfeld and Nicolson, London, 1998), p. 998.

Hall, P. *The World Cities* (Heinemann, London, 1966).

Hall, T. and Hubbard, P. (Eds.) *The Entrepreneurial City: Geographies of Politics, Regime and Representation* (John Wiley, Chichester, 1998).

Hall, T. and Hubbard, P. "The Entrepreneurial City: New Urban Politics, New Urban Geographies?" *Progress in Human Geography,* 20(2): 153–174 (1996).

Hamnett, C. "Social Polarisation in Global Cities", *Urban Studies*, 31(3): 401–424 (1994).

Hamnett, C. "Social Polarisation in Global Cities", *Urban Studies*, 31(3): 401–424 (1994).

Hamnett, C. "Why Sassen is Wrong, a Response to Burgers," *Urban Studies*, **33**(1): 107–110 (1996).

Hang Seng Bank "Hong Kong: The Road to Becoming a World City", *Hang Seng Bank Economic Monthly*, November/December (1999).

Hanneman, R. A. and Riddle, M. *Introduction to Social Network Methods* (University of California, Riverside, CA, 2005). Available at http://faculty.ucr.edu/~hanneman/nettext/ [accessed on October 8, 2008].

Hannerz, U. *Transnational Connections* (Routledge, London, 1996).

Hannerz, U. *Transnational Connections* (Routledge, London, 1996).

Harris, C. D. and Ullman, E. L. "The Nature of Cities," *Annals of the American Academy of Political and Social Science*, **242**: 7–17 (1945).

Harris, N. (2001). City Development Strategies and The Unknown City. See sm:\cds\erika\resourcesdocs\19.doc.

Harvey, D. "From Managerialism to Entrepreneurialism — The Transformation in Urban Governance in Late Capitalism", *Geografiska Annaler Series B rnance in Late Ca*, 71(1): (1989).

Harvey, D. *Urbanization of Capital* (Blackwell, Basil, 1985).

Healey, P. *et al.* (Eds.) *Managing Cities: The New Urban Context* (John Wiley & Sons, London).

Hepworth, M. "Planning for the Information City: the Challenge and Response", *Urban Studies*, 27(4): 537–558 (1990).

Hill, C. R. and Kim, J. W. "Global Cities and Development States: New York, Tokyo and Seoul", *Urban Studies*, 37(12): 2167–2195 (2000).

Hillier, H. "Mega-events, Urban Boosterism and Growth Strategies: An Analysis of the Objectives and Legitimations of the Cape Town 2004 Olympic Bid", *International Journal of Urban and Regional Research*, 24(2): 449–458 (2000).

Ho, P. "Greening without Conflict? Environmentalism, NGOs and Civil Society in China", *Development and Change*, 32: 904 (2001).

Hodos, J. "Globalisation, Regionalism and Urban Restructuring: The Case of Philadelphia", *Urban Affairs Review*, 37(3): 358–379 (2002).

Hohenberg, P. M. and Lees, L. H. *The Making of Urban Europe, 1000–1994* (Harvard University Press, Cambridge, 1995).

Hohenberg, P. M. and Lees, L. H. *The Making of Urban Europe*, 1000–1994 (Harvard University Press, Cambridge, 1995).

Hopkins, T. K. and Wallerstein, I. "Commodity Chains in the World-Economy Prior to 1800", *Review*, 10(1): 157–170 (1986).

Hospers, G. J. "Creative Cities: Breeding Places in the Knowledge Economy, Knowledge", *Technology & Policy*, 16(3): 143–162 (2003).

Howell, J. "New Directions in Civil Society: Organizing around Marginalized Interests". In *Governance in China*, Howell, J. (Ed.) (Rowman & Littlefield, Lanham, MD, 2003).

Howkins, J. *The Creative Economy: How People Make Money From Ideas* (Allen Lane, London, 2001).

Hoyt, H. *The Structure and Growth of Residential Neighborhoods in American Cities* (Federal Housing Administration, Washington, DC, 1939).

Hunmin, K. "How Worldly are World Cities? From Concept to Measurement". Paper presented at the *Second World Forum on China Studies* (Shanghai, September 2006).

Hymer, S. "The Multinational Corporation and the Law of Uneven Development." In *Economics and World Order from the 1970s to the 1990s*, Bhagwati, J. (Ed.) (Macmillan, New York, 1972), pp. 113–140.

Inglehart, R. *Cultural Shift in Advanced Industrial Society* (Princeton University Press, Princeton, 1990).

Iyer, P. *The Global Soul: Jet Lag, Shopping Malls, and the Search for Home* (Knopf, New York, 2000).

Jacobs, J. *The Nature of Economies* (Vintage, New York, 2000).

Jameson, F. "Postmodernism, or the Cultural Logic of Late Capitalism", *New Left Review*, 146(July–August): 59–92 (1984).

Jessop, B. and Peck, J. "Fast Policy/Local Discipline: The Politics of Time and Scale in the Neoliberal Workfare Offensive". Paper available from the first author at: Department of Sociology, Lancaster University, Lancaster, UK (1998).

Johnston, R. J., Taylor, P. J. and Watts, M. J. (Eds.) *Geographies of Global Change* (2nd edn.) (Blackwell, Oxford, 2002).

Kasarda, J. D. and Parnell, A. M. *Third World Cities.* (Sage, London, 1993).

Kearns, G. and Philo, C. (Eds.) *Selling Places: The City as Cultural Capital, Past and Present* (Pergamon Press, Oxford, 1993).

Keil, R. "Globalization Makes States: Perspectives of Local Governance in the Age of the World Cities", *Review of International Political Economy*, 5(4): 616–646 (1998).

King, A. D. Global Cities: Post-Imperialism and the Internationalism of London (Routledge, London, 1990).

Kirchberg, V. and Göschel, A. (Eds.) *Kultur in der Stadt. Stadtsoziologische Analysen zur Kultur* (Leske & Budrich, Opladen, 1998).

Kirchberg, V. *Kultur und Stadtgesellschaft* (Deutscher Universitätsverlag, Wiesbaden, 1992).

Knox, P. and Taylor, P. (Eds.) *World Cities in a World System* (Cambridge University Press, Cambridge, 1995).

Knox, P. L. "Globalization and Urban Change", *Urban Geography*, 17 (1): 115–117: (1996).

Knox, P. L. "World Cities and the Organization of Global Space". In *Geographies of Global Change*, 2nd edn., Johnston, R. J., Taylor, P. J. and Watts, M. J. (Eds.) (Blackwell, Oxford, 2002), pp. 328–338.

Korff, R. "The World City Hypothesis — A Critique", *Development and Change*, 18(3): 483–493 (1987).

Krätke, S. and Taylor, P. J. "A World Geography of Global Media Cities", *European Planning Studies*, 12(4): 459–477 (2004).

Kresl, P. K. "The Determinants of Urban Competitiveness: A Survey." In *North American Cities and the Global Economy*, Kresl, P. K. and Gaert, G. (Eds.) (Sage, London, 1995), pp. 45–68.

Kresl, P. K. and Gappert, G. (Eds.) *North American Cities and the Global Economy* (Sage, Thousand Oaks, CA, 1995).

Krugman, P. R. "Competitiveness: A Dangerous Obsession", *Foreign Affairs*, 73(2): (1994).

Krugman, P. *The Self-Organizing Economy* (Blackwell, Oxford, New York, 1996).

Lakshmanan, T. R. and Nijkamp, P. (Eds.) *Structure and Change in the Space Economy* (Springer-Verlag, Berlin, 1993).

Lanvin, B. *Trading in a New World Order: The Impact of Telecommunications and Data Services on International Trade in Services* (Westview Press, Boulder, 1993).

Larsen, K. "Learning Cities: The New Recipe in Regional Development", *The OECD Observer*, Paris, Summer (1999).

Lea, J. and Courtney, J. (Eds.) *Cities in Conflict: Planning and Management of Asian Cities* (World Bank, Washington DC, 1985).

Leamer, E. and Storper, M. "The Economic Geography of the Internet Age", *Journal of International Business Studies*, 32: 641–665 (2001).

Lefevre, H. *The Production of Space* (Blackwell, Oxford, 1991).

Leslie, D. A. "Global Scan: The Globalisation of Advertising Agencies", *Economic Geography*, 71: 402–426 (1995).

Leslie, D. and Reimer, S. "Spatializing Commodity Chains", *Progress in Human Geography*, 23(3): 401–420 (1999).

Lever, W. F. and Turok, I. "Competitive Cities: Introduction to the Review", *Urban Studies*, 36: (1999).

Lever, W. F. Correlating the Knowledge-base of Cities with Economic Growth", *Urban Studies*, 39(5–6): 859–870 (2002).

Lin, C. S. G. "The Growth and Structural Change of Chinese Cities: A Contextual and Geographic Analysis", *Cities*, 5: 299–316 (2002).

Lise, B. L. and Huriot, J. M. "The Metropolis in Retrospect: Permanence and Change", *GaWC Research Bulletin*, 140(A). (2004). See http://www.lboro.ac.uk/gawc/rb/rb140.html.

Lo, F. C. and Yeung, Y. M. (Eds.) *Emerging World Cities in Pacific Asia* (United Nations University Press, Tokyo, 1996).

Lo, F.-C. and Yeung, Y. M. *Globalization and the World of Large Cities* (United Nations University Press, Tokyo, 1998).

Loftman, P. and Nevin, B. "Going for Growth: Prestige Projects in Three British Cities", *Urban Studies*, 33(6): (1998).

Logan, J. and Molotch, H. *Urban Fortunes: The Political Economy of Place* (University of California Press, California 1987).

Logan, J. R. and Molotch, H. L. *Urban Fortunes: The Political Economy of Place* (University of California Press, Berkeley, California, 1987).

Lösch, A. *The Economics of Location* (Yale University Press, New Haven, CT, 1954).

Lukermann, F. "Empirical expressions of nodality and hierarchy in a circulation manifold", *East Lakes Geographer*, 2: 17–44 (1966).

Ma, Q. "Defining Chinese Nongovernmental Organizations", *Voluntas: International Journal of Voluntary and Nonprofit Organizations*, 13(2): 113–130 (2002).

Malecki, E. J. "The Economic Geography of the Internetuntary and Nonpro", *Economic Geography*, 78(4): 399–424 (2002).

Mann, P. H. *An Approach to Urban Sociology* (Routledge Press, London, 1965).

Marcuse, P. and van Kempen, R. *Globalizing Cities* (Blackwell, Oxford, 2000).

Markusen, A. "Fuzzy Concepts, Scanty Evidence, Policy Distance: The Case for Rigor and Policy Relevance in Critical Regional Studies", *Regional Studies*, 33(9): (1999).

Markusen, A., Lee, Y.-S. and DiGiovanna, S. (Eds.) *Second Tier Cities. Rapid Growth Beyond the Metropolis* (University of Minnesota Press, Minneapolis, 1999).

Martin, R. (Ed.) *Money and the Space Economy* (Wiley, Chichester).

Massey, D. "Understanding Cities: An Interview with Doreen Massey", *City*, 4(1): 135–144 (2000).

Massey, D., Allen, J. and Pile, S. (Eds.) *City Worlds* (Routledge, London, 1999).

Mattingly, M. "Meaning of Urban Management", *Cities*, No. 11 (1994).

McCann, E. "Urban Political Economy Beyond the Global City", *Urban Studies*, 41(10): 2315–2333 (2004).

McCarney, P., Halfani, M. and Rodriguez, A. (Eds.) "Towards an Understanding of Governance: The Emergence of an Idea and its Implications for Urban Research in Developing Countries". In *Urban Research in the Developing World. Vol. 4: Perspectives on the City*. Stren, R. and Kjellberg, J. (Eds.) (University of Toronto Press, Toronto, 1995), pp. 93–141.

McGee, T. G. "The Emergence of Desakota Regions in Asia: Expanding a Hypothesis." In *The Extended Metropolis: Settlement Transition in Asia*, Norton Sydney Ginsburg, Koppel, B. and McGee, T.G. (Eds.) (University of Hawaii Press, Hawaii, 1991), pp. 3–25.

McGill, R. (1998) "Viewpoint Urban Management in Developing Countries", *Cities*, 15(6): 463–471 (1998).

Meyer, B. and Geschiere, P. (eds.) *Globalization and Identity: Dialectics of Flow and Closure* (Blackwell, Oxford, 1999).

Meyer, D. *Hong Kong as a Global Metropolis* (Cambridge University Press, Cambridge, 2000).

Meyer, Laurence H. "The Present and Future Roles of Banks in Small Business Finance", *Journal of Banking & Finance*, No. 22, 1109–1116.

Michael, S. "The City: Center of Economic Reflexivity", *The Service Industries Journal, London*, 17(1): 1–27 (1997).

Mills, E. S. *Urban Economics* (ScottForesman, Belnview, IL, USA, 1972).

Mollenkopf, J. E. *Urban Nodes in the Global System* (Social Science Research Council, New York, 1993).

Moss, M. L. "Telecommunications, World Cities and Urban Policy", *Urban Studies*, 24(6): 534–546 (1987).

Moss, M. L. and Townsend, A. M. "Spatial Analysis of the Internet in US Cities and States". Prepared for Technological Futures — Urban Futures Conference at Durham, England, April 23–25 (1998).

Mossberger, K. and Stoker, G. "The Evolution of Urban Regime Theory: The Challenge of Conceptualization", *Urban Affaires Review*, 36(6): 810–835 (2001).

Moulaert, F. and Djellal, F. "Information Technology Consultancy Firms: Economies of Agglomeration from a Wide-area Perspective", *Urban Studies*, 32(1): 105–122: (1995).

Muth, R. F. *Cities and Housing* (University of Chicago Press, Chicago, 1969).

O'Connor, K. and Daniels, P. "The Geography of International Trade in Services: Australia and the APEC region", *Environment and Planning A,* 33: (2001).

O'Neill, H. and Moss, M. L. "Reinventing New York. Competing in the Next Century's Global Economy", Urban Research Center, Robert Wagner Graduate School of Public Service, New York University (1991).

O'Sullivan, A. *Urban Economics* Irwin Publishing Company, Toronto, 1996).

OECD. *Background Paper: Service Industries in Canada.* (OECD, Paris, 1999)

OECD. *Economic Outlook.* (OECD, Paris, 1999).

OECD. *Innovation and Productivity in Services* (OECD, Paris, 2001).

Olds, K. "Globalization and the Projection of New Urban Spaces: Pacific Rim Mega-projects in the Late 20th Century", *Environment and Planning A*, 27: 1713–1743 (1995).

Olds, K. and Yeung, H. W. C. "Pathways to Global City Formation: A View from the Developmental City-State of Singapore", *Review of International Political Economy*, 11(3): 489–521 (2004).

Oncu, A. and Weyland, P. *Space, Culture, and Power. New Iidentities in Globalizing Cities* (Zed Books, Atlantic Heights, NJ, 1997).

Ong, A. *Flexible Citizenship: The Cultural Logics of Transnationality* (Duke University Press, London, 1999).

Orr, J. and Topa, G. "Challenges Facing the New York Metropolitan Area Economy". Federal Reserve Bank Of New York, 12(1): (2006).

Parks, R. B. and Oakerson, R. J. "Metropolitan Organization and Governance — A Local Public Economy Approach", *Urban Affairs Quarterly*, 25(1): 18–29 (1989).

Parnreiter, C. "Global City Formation in Latin America: Socioeconomic and Spatial Transformations in Mexico City and Santiago de Chile". Paper presented at the *99th Annual Meeting of the Association of American Geographers*, New Orleans, 4–8 March. GaWC (2003).

Parnreiter, C., Fischer, K. and Imhof, K. "The Missing Link between Global Commodity Chains and Global Cities: The Financial Service Sector in Mexico City and Santiago de Chile," *GaWC Research Bulletin*, 156.

Peck, J. and Yeung, H. W. C. (Eds.) *Remaking the Global Economy: Economic-Geographical Perspectives* (Sage, London, 2003).

Pelton, J. *Eutnes View: Communications, Technology and Society in the 21st Century* (Johnson Press, New York, 1992), pp. 58–65.

Pelupessy, W. "Industrialization in Global Commodity Chains Emanating from Latin America". UNISA Latin American Report, 17(2): (2001).

Pierre, J. "Models of Urban Governance: The Institutional Dimension of Urban Politics", *Urban Affairs Review*, 34(3): 372–396 (1999).

Porteous, D. "The Development of Financial Centres: Location, Information Externalities and Path Dependence," *Money and the Space Economy*, 95–114 (1999).

Powell, W. W. "Neither Market nor Hierarchy: Network Forms of Organization", *Research in Organizational Behavior*, 12: (1990).

Pratt, A. "The Cultural Industries Production System: A Case Study of Employment Change in Britain, 1984–1991", *Environment and Planning A*, 29(11): 1953–1974 (1997).

Pred, A. R. *City-systems in Advanced Economies. Past Growth, Present Processes and Future Development Options* (Hutchison, London, 1977).

Rabach, E. and Kim, E. M. "Where is the Chain in Commodity Chains? The Service Sector Nexus." In *Commodity Chains and Global Capitalism*, Gereffi, G. and Korzeniewicz, M. (Eds.) (Greenwood Press, Westport, CT, 1994).

Reed, H. C. "Financial Centers Hegemony, Interest Rates, and the Global Political Economy". In *International Banking and Financial Centers*, Park, Y. S. and Eassayyad, M. (eds.) (Kluwer Academic Publishers, Boston, 1989), pp. 247–268.

Reed, H. C. *The Pre-eminence of International Financial Centers* (Praeger, New York, 1981).

Rhodes, R. A. W. "The New Governance: Governing without Government", *Political Studies*, 44: 652–667 (1996).

Riddle, D. *Service-led Growth: The Role of the Service Sector in the World Development* (Praeger Publishers, New York, 1986).

Robertson, R. *Globalization: Social Theory and Global Culture* (Sage, London, 1992).

Robinson, J. "Global and World Cities: A View from off the Map", *International Journal of Urban and Regional Research*, 26(3): 531–554 (2002).

Roger, W. C. and Marco, G. W. "Adopting Innovations in Information Technology — The California Municipal Experience," California Institute for Smart Communities, San Diego State University, San Diego, **16** (1): 3–12 (1999).

Rogers, E. M. "New Product Adoption and Diffusion", *Journal of Consumer Research*, 2(March): 290–301 (1976).

Roost, F. "Fragmentierte Stadtregionen." In *Die Disneyfizierung der Städte*, Roost, F. (Ed.) (VS Verlag für Sozialwissenschaften, 2000), pp. 121–129.

Rossi, E. C. and Taylor, P. J. Banking Networks Across Brazilian Cities: Interlocking Cities Within and Beyond Brazil 22(5): 381–393 (2005).

Rubalcaba-Bermejo, L. and Cuadrado-Roura, J. "Urban Hierarchies and Territorial Competition in Europe: Exploring the Role of Fairs and Exhibitions", *Urban Studies*, 32(2): 379–400 (1995).

Rusk, D. *Cities Without Suburbs* (Woodrow Wilson Center Press, Washington, D.C., 1993).

Russwurm, L.H. "Urban Fringe and Urban Shadow." In *Urban Problems*, Bryforgle, R.C. and Krueger, R.R. (Eds.), Rev. Edn. (Holt, Rinehart and Winston, Toronto, 1975), pp. 148–164.

Sabolo, Y. *The Service Industries* (International Labor Office, Geneva, 1975).

Saseen, S. *Cities in a World Economy*, 2nd Edn. (Pine Forge Press, Thousand Oaks, 2000), pp. 55–56.

Sassen, S. *Cities in a World Economy* (Pine Forge, Thousand Oaks, CA, 1994).

Sassen, S. *Losing Control? Sovereignty in an Age of Globalization* (Wiley, Chichester, 1997).

Sassen, S. On Concentration and Centrality in the Global City. In *World Cities in a World-System*, Knox, P.L. and Taylor, P.J. (Eds.) (Cambridge University Press, Cambridge, 1995), 63–78.

Sassen, S. *The Global City: New York, London, Tokyo* (Princeton University Press, Princeton, 1991, 2001).
Savitch, H. V. "Post Industrialism with a Difference: Global Capitalism and World-class Cities". In *Beyond the City Limits,* Logan, J. R. and Swanstrom, T. (Eds.) (Temple University Press Philadelphia, PA, USA, 1990), 150–174.
Savitch, H. V. and Kantor, P. "City Business: An International Perspective on Marketplace Politics", *International Review of Urban and Regional Research,* 19(4): 495–512 (1995).
Schmitz, H. "Global Competition and Local Cooperation: Success and Failure in the Sinos Valley, Brazil", *World Development,* 27(9): 1627–1650 (2000).
Schneider, M. "Fragmentation and the Growth of Local Government", *Public Choice,* 48: 255–263 (1986).
Scott, A. J. (Ed.) *Global City-Regions: Trends, Theory, Policy* (Oxford University Press, Oxford, 2001).
Scott, A. J. "Global City-Regions and the New World System", In *Local Dynamics in an Era of Globalization: 21st Century Catalysts for Development,* Yusuf, S., Wu, W. and Everett, S. (Eds.) (Oxford University Press, New York, 2000), pp. 84–91.
Scott, A. J. "The Cultural Economy of Cities", *International Journal of Urban and Regional Research,* 21: 323–339 (1997).
Scott, A. J. and Storper, M. "Regions, Globalization, Development", *Regional Studies,* 41(S1): S191–S205 (2007).
Scott, A. J. *Regions and the World Economy: The Coming Shape of Global Production, Competition, and Political Order* (Oxford University Press, Oxford, 1998).
Scott, A. J. *The Cultural Economy of Cities* (Sage, London, 2000).
Scott, A.J. (Ed.) *Global City-Regions: Trends, Theory, Policy* (Oxford University Press, Oxford, 2001).
Scott, A.J., Agnew, J., Soja, E.W. and Storper, M. "Global City-regions," Paper presented at the Global City-Regions Conference, UCLA, October 21–23 (1999). Available at http://www.sppsr.ucla.edu/globalcityregions/abstracts/abstracts.html [accessed on 16 September 1999].
Senbenberger, W. "Local Development and International Economic Competition", *International Labour Review,* 132(3): (1993).
Sheets, R., Nord, S. and Phelps, J. *The Impact of Service Industries on Underemployment in Metropolitan Economies* (D.C. Heath and Company, 1987).
Shin, K-H. and Timberlake, M. "World Cities in Asia: Cliques, Centrality and Connectedness", *Urban Studies,* 37(12): 2257—2285 (2000).
Short, J. R., Breitbach, C., Buckman, S. and Essex, J. "From World Cities to Gateway Cities", *City,* 4(3): 317–340 (2000).
Short, J., Kim, Y., Kuus, M. and Wells, H. "The Dirty Little Secret of World Cities Research — Data Problems in Comparative Analysis", *International Journal of Urban and Regional Research,* 20(4): (1996).

Short, J.and Kim, Y. (1999) *Globalization and the City* (Longman, Harlow, 1999).

Simon, D. "The World City Hypothesis: Reflections from the Periphery." In *World Cities in a World System*, Paul, L., Knox, P. J. and Taylor, P. J. (Eds.) (Cambridge University Press, Cambridge, 1995), pp. 132–155.

Simon, D. World City Hypothesis: Reflections from the Periphery. In *World Cities in a World System*, Knox, P. and Taylor, P. (Eds.) (Cambridge University Press. Cambridge, 1995). 132–155.

Singlemann, J. *From Agriculture to Services: The Transformation of Industrial Employment* (Sage Publications, Beverly Hills, CA, USA, 1978).

Smith, D. A. and Timberlake, M. (1995) "Conceptualising and Mapping the Structure of the World Systems City System", *Urban Studies*, 32: (1995).

Smith, M. P. *Transnational Urbanism* (Blackwell, Oxford, 2001).

Soja, E. *Thirdspace: Journeys to Los Angeles and Other Real and Imagined Space* (Blackwell, Oxford, 1996).

Soja, E. W. and Scott, A. J. "Los Angeles: Capital of the Late Twentieth Century," *Environment and Planning D: Society and Space*, **4**(3): 249–254 (1986).

Sotarauta, M. and Linnamaa, R. "Urban Competitiveness and Management of Urban Policy Networks: Some Reflections from Tampere and Oulu," *Technology, Society and Environment*, **2**: (1998).

Stanback, T. and Noyelle, T. *Cities in Transition* (Rowman and Allanheld, Totowa, NJ, USA, 1982).

Stone, C. "Urban Regimes and the Capacity to Govern: A Political Economy Approach", *Journal of Urban Affairs*, 15(1): 1–28 (1993).

Stone, C. *Regime Politics: Governing Atlanta, 1946–1988* (University Press of Kansas, Lawrence, 1989).

Storper, M. "Globalisation and Knowledge Flows: An Industrial Geographers Perspective." In *Regions, Globalisation and the Knowledge Based Economy*, Dunning, J. (Ed.) (Oxford University Press, USA, 2000), pp. 42–62.

Storper, M. "Territories, Flows and Hierarchies in the Global Economy." In *Spaces of Globalization*, Cox, K. R. (Ed.) (Guilford, New York, 1997), pp. 23–51.

Stren, R. E. "Urban Management in Development Assistance: an Elusive Concept", *Cities*, 10(2): 125–138 (1993).

Sýkora, L. "Metropolises in Transition, Metropolises in Competition: Globalization of Central European Cities and Their Integration into European Urban Network," Paper given at European Conference Urban Utopias: New Tools for the Renaissance of the City in Europe, Berlin, pp. 595–619 (1995).

Taaffe, E. J., Morrill, R. L. and Gould, P. R. "Transport Expansion in Underdeveloped Countries: A Comparative Analysis," *Geographical Review*, **53**(4): 503–529 (1963).

Tapscott, D., Lowy, A. and Ticoll, D. *Blueprint to the Digital Economy: Creating Wealth in the Era of E-Business* (McGraw-Hill Book Co., New York, 1999).

Taylor, P. J. "Hierarchical Tendencies Amongst World Cities: A Global Research Proposal", *Cities*, 14(6): 323–332 (1997).

Taylor, P. J. "So-called "World Cities": The Evidential Structure within a Literature", *Environment and Planning A*, 31(11): (1999).

Taylor, P. J. "Specification of the World City Network", *Geographical Analysis*, 33(2): 181–194 (2001).

Taylor, P. J. "World Cities and Territorial States: The Rise And Fall Of Their Mutuality", In *World Cities in a World System*, Knox, P. L. and Taylor, P. J. (Eds.) (Cambridge: Cambridge University Press, 1995).

Taylor, P. J. and Hoyler, M. "The Spatial Order of European Cities under Conditions of Contemporary Globalization", *Tijdschrift voor Economische en Sociale Geografie*, 91(2): 176–189 (2000).

Taylor, P. J. and Walker, D. R. F. "World Cities: A First Multivariate Analysis of their Service Complexes", *Urban Studies*, 38(1): 23–47 (2001).

Taylor, P. J. and Walker, D. R. F. World Cities: A First Multivariate Analysis of their Service Complexes", *Urban Studies*, 38(1): (2001).

Taylor, P. J., Catalano, G., Walker, D. R. F. and Hoyler, M. "Diversity and Power in the World City Network", *Cities*, 19: 19(4): 231–241 (2002).

Taylor, P. J., Docl M. A., Hoyler, M., Walker, D. R. F. and Beaverstock, J. V. "World Cities in The Pacific Rim: A New Global Test of Regional Coherence", *Singapore Journal of Tropical Geography*, 21(3): (2000).

Teaford, J. C. City and Suburb: The Political Fragmentation of Metropolitan America, 1850–1970 (Johns Hopkins University Press, Baltimore, 1979).

The London Planning Advisory Committee. London: World City (1991).

Thomas, A. H. "The New Economy of the Inner City", *Cities*, 2(2): (2004).

Thrift, N. "Distance is not a safety Zone But a Field of Tension: Mobile Geographies and World Cities", In *Timing Global Cities*, Gravesteijn, S. G. E., Griensven, S. and Smidt, M. (Eds.) (Netherlands Geographical Studies, Utrecht, 1998), pp. 54–66.

Thrift, N. J. "Cities Without Modernity, Cities With Magic", *Scottish Geographical Magazine*, 113(2): (1997).

Thrift, N. J. *The Geography of International Economic Disorder* (Blackwell, Oxford, 1989).

Timberlake, M. and Xiulian, M. "The Emergence of China's 'World City': Shanghai's Shifting Position in National and Global Networks of Cities". Paper submitted to World Forum on China Studies sponsored by the Shanghai Academy of Social Sciences (2006).

Timberlake, M. *Urbanization and the World-Economy* (Academic Press, New York, 1985).

Townsend, A. "Networked Cities and the Global Structure of the Internet", American Behavioral Scientist, 44(10): 1698–1717 (2001b).

Townsend, A. "The Internet and the Rise of the New Network Cities, 1969–1999", *Environment and Planning B: Planning and Design*, 28: (2001a).

Toynbee, A. "Preface." In *A Study of History*, Somerville, D.C. (Ed.) (Oxford University Press, London, 1970).

U.S. Department of Commerce. Service Industries and Economic Performance, p. 13 (1996).

UNCTAD. *World Investment Report 1997: Transnational Corporations, Market Structure and Competition Policy* (UN, New York, Geneva, 1997).

UNCTAD. *World Investment Report 2000: Cross-border Mergers and Acquisitions and Development* (UN, New York, Geneva, 2001).

UNCTAD. *World Investment Report 2005: Transnational Corporations and Internationalization of R&D* (UN, New York, Geneva, 2005).

UNCTAD. *World Investment Report. Transnational Corporations and Competitiveness* (UN, New York, Geneva, 1995).

UNCTAD. *World Investment Report. Transnational Corporations and Export Competitiveness* (UN, New York, Geneva, 2002).

United States Department of Commerce. *Survey of Current Business*, 80(1): (2000) Washington DC.

United States Department of Commerce. *Survey of Current Business*, 80(1): (2004) Washington DC.

Urban Utopias: New Tools for the Renaissance of the City in Europe. *European Conference Proceedings*, CD-ROM (TVVF, Berlin).

Varsanyi, M. W. "Global Cities From the Ground Up", *Political Geography*, November: 19 (2000).

Virilio, P. *Polar Inertia* (Sage, London, 1999).

Warf, B. "Telecommunications and the Changing Geographies of Knowledge Transmission in the late 20th Century", *Urban Studies*, 32(2): 361–378 (1995).

Warf, B. "Telecommunications and the Globalization of Financial Services", *Professional Geographer*, 41(3): 257–271 (1989).

Webster, D. and Muller, L. "Urban Competitiveness Assessment in Developing Country Urban Regions: The Road Forward". Paper prepared for Urban Group. INFUD. The World Bank. Washington, DC, 2000.

Weiss, L. *The Myth of the Powerless State* (Cornell University Press, Ithaca, New York, 1998), pp. 70–80.

Werna, E. "The Management of Urban Development, or the Development of Urban Management? Problems and Premises of an Elusive Concept", *Cities*, No. 5 (1995).

Wheaton, W. "A Comparative Static Analysis of Urban Spatial Structure", *Journal of Economic Theory* 9(2): 223–237 (1974).

World Bank. Cities in Transition: A Strategic View of Urban and Local Government Issues (2000).

Wynne, D. (Ed.) *The Culture Industry* (Avebury, Aldershot, 1992).

Yeung, H. "State Intervention and neo-liberalism in the Globalizing World Economy: Lessons from Singapore's Regionalisation Program", *The Pacific Review*, 13(1): 133–162 (2000).

Yeung, H. W. and Olds, K. "From the Global City to Globalising Cities: Views from a Developmental City-state in Pacific Asia". Paper presented at the *IRFD World Forum on Habitat-International Conference on Urbanizing World and UN Human Habitat*. Columbia University, New York City, USA, 4–6, June, 2001.

Yeung, Y. "An Asian Perspective on the Global City", *International Social Science Journal*, 147: 25–31 (1996).

Yeung, Y. "Geography in the Age of Mega-cities", *International Social Science Journal*, 151: 91–104 (1997).

Yulong, S. and Hamnett, C. "The Potential and Prospect for Global Cities in China: in the Context of the World System", *Geoforum*, 22: 121–135 (2002).

Zook, M. A. "Old Hierarchies or New Networks of Centrality: The Global Geography of the Internet Content Market", *American Behavioral Scientist*, 44(10): 1679–1696 (2001).

Zukin, S. *The Cultures of Cities* (Blackwell, Oxford, 1995).

Postscript

This book is the result of five years of hard work. I would like to first thank those people who have guided me on my way to research. That I am now part of the academic frontier is mainly because, in support of the Propaganda Department, the year 2002 saw Shanghai Academy of Social Sciences identify political economics as one of the key disciplines and listing an international metropolis as one of the main research directions. As the academic leader, I presided over the research project. Reviewing the spiritual path to the study, the initial germination of the idea stemmed from the integration of the two logic main lines in today's world. One is the interaction of globalization and informatization — the transition of multinationals to global companies — and the rise of the global city that acts as the primary node in the world economy. Another is the shift in the focus of the world economy to the rise of great powers in developing countries — the integration of major cities of the developing countries into the global network of cities. The intersection of these two logic main lines has put forward questions about the rise of global cities in developing countries, which is a very real practical problem, as well as the present global city theory hypothesis. From the beginning, this research project has obtained strong support from leaders of the Propaganda Department: Prof. Wang Ronghua who is the Vice Chairman of the Municipal CPPCC and President of Shanghai Academy of Social Sciences; Zuo Xuejin, Executive Vice President of Shanghai Academy of Social Sciences; and Prof. Yin Jizuo, Former President of the Academy of Shanghai Social Sciences, which has led to the establishment of a good foundation for the research work.

In the development process of this project, there are two important scholars who have played a fueling role in my research. One is Prof. Sassen, founder of the well-known global city theory, who agreed to travel to Shanghai to take part in a symposium, thereby giving us a chance to take part in academic discussions with her. She presented us with the new edition of her book *Global Cities — New York, London and Tokyo*, which was translated into Chinese under my supervision and published. Another is Prof. Chen Xiangming from the University of Illinois, who was often involved in-depth discussions and collaborative research with us and also acted as my go-between contact with international experts and scholars studying global cities. I have edited books along with them, such as *World Cities — International Experiences and Development of Shanghai* and *The Rise of Shanghai* (English edition). Many of their views have a significant impact on my research.

I would also like to acknowledge the academic team involved in this research project. Researchers Chen Wei and Han Hanjun of the Institute of Economic Research, Shanghai Academy of Social Sciences, were involved in this project and also worked with me earlier to edit the *Blue Book of Shanghai's Economic Development.* Associate researchers Huang Jianfu and Jin Caihong and Dr. Wang Qi participated in the organization of several international seminars and international academic exchange programs, and in the translation and proofreading work of foreign classic scholarly works and literature. Some PhD candidates, including Qu Jianbo, Yu Jianguo, Li Guojun, Shen Guilong, Sun Xiaofeng, Li Zhengtu, Zhu Pingfang, Wang Zuqiang, and Yang Pingdeng were involved in the translation of the book *Global Cities — New York, London and Tokyo.*

In May 2002, we organized an international seminar called "Shanghai's Economic Development and the Comparison of International Metropolis", in which more than 50 experts and scholars from the USA, Japan, Singapore, South Korea, Taiwan, Hong Kong, and other domestic major cities participated, facilitating extensive and in-depth academic exchanges on the global city theory practice, which has further deepened my understanding on this issue. In 2004, I had the privilege to succeed in my application for the

National Social Science Fund Project, Development Model of Modern International Metropolis and the Path (04BJL038). This research expanded the more comprehensive in-depth study on the globalizing cities in the framework of the global city theory and on the basis of China's actual conditions, concluding in August 2006. Some results of this research appeared in many publications. This book is based on the results of the study, with further modifications and improvements.

In April 2006, I transferred to Development Research Center of Shanghai Municipal People's Government to engage in decision-making and consulting, which, in the meantime, provided me with an opportunity to come into contact with the actual situation of the metropolitan management and development and have an increased perceptual knowledge. It prompting me to think deeply about the series of major issues in the rise of a global city, for example, how to deepen connotation of Shanghai's building "Four Centers" and a modern international metropolis strategic objectives in the context of the interaction of globalization and informatization; what type of kind of basic framework the urban transformation based on the construction of a modern international metropolis needs; what kind of the relationship exists between global cities and the global city region; what mode and route choice need to be taken in Shanghai's ascendancy into a modern international metropolis under the existing constraints; and how to conduct urban innovation and governance. The Development Research Center organized interrelated researches on these issues, producing a series of research reports. In this process, Prof. Wang Zhan, the former Director of the Centre and the present Deputy Secretary-General of the Municipal Committee, and other colleagues made a number of insights, which have given me great inspiration. In the usual discussion, Director Zhou Wei of the Municipal Government Research Department; Deputy Director Zhang Daogen of the Municipal Committee Research Department; Zhu Jinhai, Researcher, Institute of Economic Research of Development and Reform Commission; Deputy Director Cao Jinxi, General Office of the Municipal Government; Prof. Shi Liangping, College of Business Administration, East China University of Science and Technology; and Prof. Chen Xian of Shanghai University have provided so many wonderful insights. As a result, I now have a further deepened and sensible understanding of globalizing cities, which are reflected in the modifications and improvements in the book, making its questions and assumptions more realistic and interpretation of many phenomena full of more unique perspectives and rationality.

In addition, I would like to express my deep gratitude to Mr. Chen Xin and Mr. He Yuanlong of the Shanghai Century Publishing Group, who have supported and helped me in my research work for a long time.

The book's publication is only a summary of the initial results of my recent study on globalizing cities. It should be said that this is just a basic assumption of the problem that requires study, with many contents need further expansion and refinement. To this end, I sincerely hope that readers put forward criticism, and I welcome more fans with the same interests to participate in the discussions and study of this issue.

Zhou Zhenhua
August 2007

Index

Printed in the United States
By Bookmasters

Printed in the United States
By Bookmasters